Seven Maids

Through the Looking Glass

By Inge Borg

New Generation **Publishing**

Seven Maids

Through the looking glass

The Walrus and the Carpenter,
were walking close at hand.
They wept like anything to see
Such quantities of sand......
*If **seven maids** with seven mops*
Swept it for half a year,
Do you suppose the Walrus said
That they could get it clear?
I doubt it said the carpenter, and shed a bitter tear.
(Lewis Carroll.)

Ingeborg-Evelyn 1935
Erika 1907   Gabrielle 1959
Cölestine 1882   Polly 1983
Josephine 1847   Leela 2002

My thanks to Elspeth Jack and Anne Hyatt, also to Liesl Hearst and Peter Huhne, but above all to Gabi for her wonderful contribution and the painstaking corrections of Tony Summers. Throughout, during the years of soul and memory searching, there was the calming and perceptive influence of my partner Alan.

Contents

Josephine's Story

'An explosion, a gunshot, dear God, what was _that_ …' thundering, rumbling, grumbling close by, eerie echoes from one craggy mountain top to the other have woken Josephine. Her heart was pounding so fast she could hardly breathe…all she took in was morning light, just visible through a gap in the curtains. Cautiously she slid her hand across the other side of the bed but smooth cool linen reminded her she was alone. 'Of course, poor Karl is not back, still somewhere in Serbia, many hours' journey away…

..and now, a crazed dog! Could it be ours?' Frowning, she listened more carefully.

'Hard to tell with dogs… ours may already have wandered off, tail wagging, tongue hanging out, with Karl's brother and that wife of his; the three of them together… _'to strengthen the heart'_, that's what our dear relatives say each time they come to stay, and _'how we love it, just being here, in this magical setting.'_

Distracted from the shock thoughts raced through her mind:

'Our relatives seem to have moved in, not that…Oh no, _another_ shot! Hunters, perhaps, out early, after those dangerous brown bears?'

Her heart had begun racing again. Flat on her back, brows knitted, she listened to the ominous silence.She lay quite still, as she re-lived the extraordinary disturbance at bedtime, only last night: an event which had got her and everyone else out of bed because _'it was up and running'_, as her brother-in-law kept shouting down the stairway: his fabulous invention, his _'Perpetuum Mobile'_.

Time and time again he'd been told there could be no such thing…even eminent professors had confirmed this. But no, 'I will never give up'… Joseph remained persistently determined to prove them wrong.

'Not quite right in the head, with his wretched notions and his artistic temperament… a law unto himself, this Joseph Hofbauer, so unlike my no-nonsense Karl. Hard to believe they are brothers…

…however, last night, in all fairness, we _really did see_ this machine, _and_ it seemed to be working. What am I to think about all this? How I wish Karl was home, it would be good to talk to someone sensible.'

'Strange, no birds this morning, not even one. Frightened away of course…'Frowning she sighed morosely, then pulled over to the edge of the bed to wriggle her toes on the soothing bearskin rug. Arms up, stretching, she shook her head of long dark hair…only some, or should one say, very few silver strands so far. And then, drawing back the curtain, she peered into the early morning fog. This was her waking-up ritual for as long as she could remember; a statuesque woman, impressive, past her best but still someone to be reckoned with.

'I could do with a little longer in bed,' she thought, 'still, now the curtains are open…' shivering a little, suddenly almost frail, she pulled a cashmere shawl around her shoulders. 'Autumn is on its way…might as well go down to see if Grethe has lit the stove, perhaps *she* knows what is going on. No sounds from the children yet…how could they sleep through that thundering noise.' Clinging to the banister she walked downstairs slowly, listening for signs of life. The kitchen door stood half open. Someone had gone out into the vegetable garden in a hurry.

'Ah, I see. Grethe, yes, she's probably gone to fetch more logs…however, the oven does seem lit?' Josephine sat down by the large scrubbed pine table. Only when the maid returned this day could begin in the proper order of things. Discontented, still half asleep her thoughts drifted back to earlier days when she, just a small girl, had heard gossip about Joseph, or 'Sepp', then an un-biddable boy with tendencies to drift off, usually to be found quite alone in the woods, or just playing by the river…

….someone had given him that zither…. he seemed to know everything about the instrument before he even got near a teacher. From whom had he inherited this mysterious talent? Within a few months he was packed off to Trieste for music lessons. Later, to his family's surprise, little Sepp became quite well-known, soon making a respectable income from his performances.

'A virtuoso,' the family marvelled, and proudly wished him well.

And now, just last night, his huge moment, his new mad dream which had finally come true, at last, his *'Perpetuum Mobile',* whatever that was. With eyes shut Josephine sat waiting for signs of life. She reconsidered her brother-in-law's invention. Might it still be working?

'There, not again, that barking beast! *Our* dog then, after all….'

Footsteps, noise, people approach and arrive at the backdoor. 'Yes, here he is, *our* dog'…Josephine rose, frowning when she heard a man's voice, no, two voices, repeating soothing injunctions, hysterical sobbing. 'Can this be *our* Grethe's wailing? Du lieber Gott! What has the foolish girl been up to?'

Still in her nightgown, certainly not dressed for company, Josephine hesitated by the door as the hysterical maid was pushed, led in, supported by…'oh no, the village priest and with him the ancient beadle, far too advanced in years to be on duty at this hour…*and* with a gun, and our dog ! So it *was* him after all, making all that tumult earlier on….'

'Gnädige Frau,' the priest intoned, 'God forgive us: we bring truly terrible news, alas…' breathing hard he just managed to guide the girl to a chair before she slumped forward. Fearing an ominous disaster, Josephine supported the young woman's head, rubbed her temples and then her hands, imagining unspeakable things which may have overcome her. The elderly men were wringing their hands. Shaking his head from side to side, the beadle covered his eyes with one wrinkled hand and placed the other on his chest: 'Your husband, Gnädige Frau, is he not with you? Our news concerns him even more than you…'

…'my husband, gentlemen, why, he is away, in Serbia, on business… he may be home in a day or so. His younger brother is staying with us for a few days, but I have complete authority to deal with all emergencies. I *do* run the business in his absence'…she added primly, 'so please, what in God's name is going on?' Still stroking the whimpering maid Josephine noted the ashen-faced girl was getting back some colour…

'Well, *do* compose yourself, Frau Hofbauer, if you are quite certain.'

Grey-haired heads still shaking, eyes wide open in horror, the beadle and the priest steeled themselves. Slowly, cautiously, the old priest leaned forward and looking straight at Josephine he said:

'With profound regret, Gnädige Frau, we must inform you… what we have witnessed, without any doubt. Pausing, he weighed his words, 'it concerns the very man you mention, your husband's brother Joseph.'

'Dear God,' ….Josephine frowned and drew a deep sigh.

Stressing each word, the priest announced: 'Joseph lies dead in the wood. It appears he has shot, first his wife…then himself…not far from here.' Staring at the gun and at his own muddy boots, the priest crossed himself. And then, in a solemn, even deeper and more resonant voice he added: 'may their souls rest in peace.'

The men looked at Josephine, her mouth had dropped open. She seemed to have stopped breathing.

Drained and faint, eyes now closed, one hand clutching her shawl, the other over her mouth, she tried to take this in…then, gasping for help from some unknown source, *never reveal private emotions to strangers…you must remain dignified, even now… this is how I've*

9

been taught to behave by my Mama... she managed to remind herself. Drawing herself up to her full height, apparently in control but trembling all over she tried to speak:

'Gentlemen, this is appalling'...attempting, but unable to order her troubled mind...'the bodies, where are the bodies... can the bodies be brought to the house?' Eyelids shut she imagined the injuries, the mess, the blood, the unspeakable reality. 'Please assist me,' she whispered, '...the funeral *must* be here, in our home, very quietly...with your help, of course...' Her voice had begun to shake, she fought the tears, then, turning to the priest ...'and you, Father, you have known him most of his life, taught him at school...whatever *can* be done *must* be done...please ensure that everyone else here in Neumarktl and St. Anna fully understand this tragedy. I beg you to decide, only *you* can decide... whether my brother-in-law has committed a mortal sin.'

Her face was ashen; Josephine heard herself speak in an unknown voice, her lips were trembling. On yet another level of thought she told herself: 'Pull yourself together: dear Sepp was clearly out of his mind.'

Turning back to the priest she muttered: 'My poor husband, the tutor, the children, the people of St. Anna and Neumarktl, what will everyone think?' She staggered unsteadily across the large kitchen, supporting herself along the way to the ancient oak cabinet to find, with trembling hands, four small glasses and a bottle of Slivovitz.

'May the Lord forgive us, but what we need now is strength.' She looked at the maid who was sitting up, eyes tightly shut. 'Even you, Grethe, I expect you to pull yourself together and help with the children's breakfast; we will explain about this unspeakable event as simply as we can, without frightening them...there has been *an accident*....do you understand, Gretchen...look at me: this is a calamity... we have no choice!' The pale, shivering maid looked obediently at her mistress:

'Jawohl, Frau Hofbauer,' she managed, sniffling and nodding.

Fortified by Plum spirits the elderly worthies shuffled off, shaking their heads, to discuss emergency arrangements for a double funeral, as soon as possible. Coffins must be brought, a service must be arranged. Josephine was now showing commendable calm and control. Only after the officials were well out of ear-shot she sat by the kitchen table, still in her nightgown, her head on crossed arms, sobbing helplessly.

'Our Mama is weeping'. Three small daughters, in long white nightgowns have come down to see what is going on, stand silently, afraid to touch her. Such a thing has never happened before. Terrified, the two younger ones begin to sob as well. They were to be taken to neighbouring Neumarktl for some days, to spend time with relatives.

The tutor was dismissed. It was September 1897.

*****

Two closed coffins in the drawing room; a private ceremony, candles flicker, everyone in black. The strong silent 'head' of the family, Karl Hofbauer, had returned just in time from his business trip to Serbia. He stood by Josephine, both their faces ashen, they have dark shadows around the eyes.

Old women in black whispered prayers and crossed themselves.

'How could he do this terrible thing', pondered Josephine, 'such a gifted, man; what a waste, he must surely have known how much we loved them both.'

Josephine's husband consoled her... it *was* a Catholic funeral, and no-one even spoke of that dreaded *mortal sin*...the village priest had received permission to give a special dispensation in this case. Sepp's former teacher, the priest, remembered all too well events in the past and the youngster's unstable and sensitive nature.

Mourning relatives and villagers were still filing into the silent house and now stood waiting for words of consolation and prayers from the 'shepherd of the flock'.

After the funeral older residents of Neumarktl gossiped about the causes of Sepp's instability: had it arisen due to the unusual circumstances of the tiny boy's baptism? During a freezing winter's afternoon this new-born babe had apparently been carried in a padded cushion on a sleigh-ride to Neumarktl's church. Fortified with mulled wine for the return to St. Anna, midwife and godparents found *no* new-born in the cushion when they reached home.

In total shock they'd turned back, eventually found the infant headfirst in the snow...already turned a threatening shade of blue.

In days long past, when Josephine first heard about this, she had occasionally wondered whether there'd been some rearrangement in that small skull.

Now the same priest, the man who had first baptised and later instructed young Sepp, intoned prayers over the coffins and consoled the sorrowing family. During a brief ceremony he stressed, nodding his head with each word:

'No, no, Joseph Hofbauer was not an evil murderer; yes, God sees the hearts, God has lifted him up. I am quite certain, Gnädige Frau, Herr Hofbauer.' He nodded encouragingly, spoke soothingly and with great authority: 'your younger brother and his beloved wife...they are both safe with God.'

'Deo gratias…'

*****

Needless to say there was much talk in both St. Anna and Neumarktl. Almost everyone had memories of Sepp or was connected with the family in some way.

Josephine, the business woman, always so proud of Hofbauer successes at work continued to remain perplexed by her brother-in-law, who, with his immense talent for music and for science had shown neither skill for business, nor for living.

Each new day she was haunted by a feeling of guilt. 'Why did I lecture him about all those business ventures in our family…it must have made him feel lacking in manly courage and enterprise.' Try as she might, the return to normal life, to office work and settling her the three little girls after this tragedy… these were tasks she could barely handle.

The house felt forlorn, dark, cursed and empty.

Her pain fed on itself, remained alive and grew. She made a desperate attempt to clarify her endlessly disturbing thoughts.

With a scratchy worn nib she penned an account of her life…………*.....up until this troubled time*…my 'life was so simple,' she wrote, seated at her desk, gazing across fields to the mountain. I, Josephine Hofbauer…daughter of Josepha and Andreas Klander, saw the light of day in February 1847, was christened on that very day in my home, house no.134, in the mountain town of Neumarktl, in Lower Austria. I was the seventh child in a prosperous Austrian family, whose men had, since 1600, married women with Slovenian, Italian and also German names. We speak at least two languages here, often three.

After a few years in the care of nuns in a nearby convent I stayed at home and soon helped to run my family's hotel. There is little to say. I always was, I still am, a hardworking, practical, plain-speaking woman.

Following what seemed a lifetime of 'waiting', in 1881, on the 22nd of June, I, a thirty-four year old spinster, finally committed myself to a man. My handsome husband, Karl Hofbauer, a successful man in 'wood', had inherited a prosperous business from his father. How does Karl see me?

I am no beauty. My tiny waist has vanished. I see flecks of grey in my dark hair. He tells me he approves of my solid, good sense; that I 'get on' with things; I hope he thinks of me as honest, self-reliant, strong. Our first child, our dangerously weak Cölestine, was born on the 6th of April, 1882. Fearing for her little life the midwife instantly

12

baptised the new-born…a 'Nottaufe', (emergency baptism), to spare the infant from spending eternity in Limbo, according to the belief of our Catholic faith.

Three years later we moved to this newly built mansion in St. Anna, a small village near Neumarktl, with its reputation for industry: the Illyrian Quicksilver Company, a brewery, timber works, and our own sawmills. Karl Hofbauer's,(it still feels strange to say 'my husband's) highly respected family had come, two generations ago, from a small village near Vienna.

I so enjoy working in the office. Our business has expanded rapidly. There have been difficulties, even bankruptcy, but with some borrowing of money (from my sister) and good sense, I personally helped to keep it all going. My need to be free is overwhelming; in earlier days my own dear Mama had come to live with us to care for little Cölestine. Now we have three daughters, and all remain robust and in good health. We were fortunate to have my Mama with us; when she passed away Cölestine was already twelve years old. From this time our eldest began, without realising, to slip into the role of substitute 'carer' for her small sisters. This was surely very good for her…

Of course I always remained in control. Now our family villa is also a haven to a steady stream of visitors, mainly family. My sister, Ludowika, until recently married to a Knight of the Realm, comes for regular visits with her children. When the Knight died she settled in to stay for an undetermined length of time. I had managed to pay off my debt by then. We became quite close during those months… having overcome our 'sisterly' differences. A tutor was engaged for all seven children.

During those contented days, there were, under one roof: myself and my dearest Karl, my widowed sister, all the children, my bearded, beloved brother-in-law Joseph ('Sepp,' derived from Joseph, very common in these parts) also his wife, a shy lady from Trieste, apparently fabulously rich… not to forget the tutor and the maids. Karl regularly travelled far and wide through Austria, Croatia, Serbia and Hungary to find and purchase the best timber. In *his* field he is an artist too. The wood he buys is turned into veneer in our factory, still situated on the banks of a small mountain stream at the base of our valley.

Brother-in-law Sepp, God rest his soul, did so love to entertain us all with dazzling performances on his zither. Everyone clamoured for lessons. I was the first to show any talent, he said. Greatly flattered I engaged a photographer, all the way from Laibach, to take a photograph of one of these happy lessons. We were all outside in the garden, on a warm summer's day.

I so remember that tight high-necked black dress I was wearing, and how I had to lean over the table to inspect my brother-in-laws' hand on the zither: 'What fingering was that, Sepp? Show me again!'

The camera had captured Cölestine looking truly bored. How shocked I was when she told me just the other day that she had felt left out, because I and Sepp were always so happy doing things together (well, *someone* had to supervise the Slovene workers), and that, when Sepp would go to talk to his wife or do new experiments with his scientific inventions, Cölestine felt, well, 'abandoned'…to look after the younger ones…as mentioned before….

We did *so* like to sit outside, enjoy the sunset, the cool mountain air. Together we'd stare at the spectacular colour change of the rocks, that warm pink glow, and no-one knew why it happened. 'Sepp, *you* are the scientist, do please explain why the rocks go pink', we all pleaded.

'I can teach you to play the zither, but alas, I have no idea about the colour,' was his reply. 'Teaching music is not as much fun as it used to be. Now I'd rather read books about physics and photography. And lithographic stones, how I love those! My dear wife is paying for all my new interests, but is endlessly complaining… her funds are dwindling.'

'Aha, mein Lieber,' I tried to make light of it, 'we've heard about your extravagances! And what about us, do you enjoy teaching *us*?'

He smiled, one of his mysterious, evasive smiles…and I reminded him again: 'you *surely* know how much Karl and I would like you to work with us in the sawmill, the office so needs another man and you could earn more than enough to buy all you need for your intriguing scientific studies….' Sepp had twice been offered a job at the factory, made *some* attempts, but, well, *inexplicably,* he could not, would not take the bait.

My dear husband, a businessman with vision, had already offered him a post in Vienna where the family firm opened an outlet of the wood veneer industry, a potential goldmine…but no, Sepp could not come to grips with this either. When he returned to Neumarktl to make another attempt at 'working' in the office, it was, in truth, mainly to renew his obsession with that annoying Perpetuum Mobile of his! Only occasionally he spoke of returning to Trieste, and to his musical life.

I understand, according to the Laws of Thermodynamics, a 'Perpetuum Mobile' is an impossibility: like eternal life, like raising the dead, but then, musicians are accustomed to overcoming 'impossibilities'. They think they can *will* them to give way, to remove barriers…

I, Josephine Hofbauer, like most women, have learned to be a patient observer: I noticed Sepp's extravagant purchases, all at the expense of his wife's inheritance. So I thought to use a subtle strategy: crumbling old papers, found rolled up among my own Mama's possessions,' these might open Sepp's mind to the dedication *some* men in our family have shown.'

I hoped he might learn from them!

It was *my* decision to surprise my brother-in-law with this crumbling document: it now has value as a reminder that mothers have a great need to leave behind information for the family. *There is a strange urge to remain part of the still living, when one senses time is running out.*

These were Josepha Klander's efforts, they must have taken her an immense time. Written by my own beloved Mama a life-time ago, I read this true history to my brother-in-law, a laborious effort, for both of us.

It may not be of interest to everyone.

The great 'Fire', 1811.

This truly terrible event in Neumarktl started <u>accidentally</u> in the foundry of the Klander family. The fire was fanned by a strong wind and the flames passed down the entire village and destroyed most of the houses. 100 workshops burnt down. At least 70 people were killed. My father-in-law Mathias swears it was not his fault, but I'm not so sure. He did penance anyway, by providing free iron shutters for every new house that was built.

I, Josepha, married to Andreas Klander, <u>do not feel guilty.</u> My parents did not know about this fire. They might not have arranged this marriage for me, had they known. Or perhaps they knew, but thought it was a good thing since Napoleon gave Neumarktl 80.000 Fr. to rebuild itself.

Napoleon stayed in our family hotel, when it was called 'Pri Klandru', for three whole days in 1809, during his advance through Europe'.

'Andreas Klander, born 1807, son of the slightly hunchbacked Mathias and Magdalena; He married me in 1837, he was just a boy really…..medium height, clean-shaven and could not pronounce 'V' because he had polyps on his lips. His own family and even his children say he was 'serious, strict, a despot, a tyrant.' Although not lacking in entrepreneurial spirit his <u>many ventures</u> failed one after the other…Here they are:

<u>Postmaster of Neumarktl</u> His brother Alois, employed assistant, helped himself to some money…so Andreas had to pay the costs and was relieved of his post.

In <u>Transport</u>….he took a wagon-load of sugar over the Loibl Pass, was caught by a snowstorm and had to over-winter, inadequately covered…lost the entire load. 7000 florins in the red.

Roadworks to Pristava...mudslide, continuous rain. Discontinued.

Vienna, 1848: Revolution. Andreas , owner of a saw-mill and of a grain-mill in St. Anna took several wagon-loads of freshly sawn veneers to Vienna ...where they were requisitioned by revolutionaries to build barricades in street-fighting. There was no recompense, the saw-mill had to be sold.

'Poor,poor man! Enough, there surely can't be more?' Sepp, interrupted the reading at this point, he was plainly feeling uncomfortable.

I gritted my teeth and continued, relentlessly:

Gasthaus zur Post, or 'Pri Klandru,' (later re-named 'Hotel zum Grafen Radetzky' because the famous Fieldmarshal stayed for a few weeks.) I will have to sell this place. It is so in debt there will be hardly any profit. I don't quite know what to do with Napoleon's bed, somebody in the family should keep it. (A very nice man and friendly with Andreas' mother Magdalena.) Evil tongues had much to say about Magdalena's son Johann Nepomuk who was born about the correct number of months after Napoleon's departure.'

'Aber geh!', Sepp pretended to be shocked, 'you never told me before, sister-in-law. Too proud then, are we, to spread this appalling story about? One day y*our* children will read all about *their* grandfather from a reliable source... this *is* important ...you must keep these papers safe, and of course I know it was *your family's* sawmill bought by my father, *and that I should now by rights be involved with it...'*

'For sure', I nodded, 'you know how we need you, Sepp. Believe me, even I had no idea father was such a 'loser'...perhaps this was the reason my parents quarrelled so much. Villagers 'talk' because I, a woman, sit in the office most days. It does not trouble me: Karl and I make a good team, *we* never disagree and I enjoy the contact with our workers...besides, it stops me eating all the time........'

After this account Sepp looked trapped, even guilty. Had my strictures touched a raw spot? He replied: 'I'm not like you, I truly cannot bear spending so much time with those Slovenes, dirty, stupid and noisy....*I don't trust them...'* Giving me a searching look he knew at once his remark had angered me.

If his own brother was pleased with Slovenian workers, thought them loyal and strong, why was Sepp so contrary, I wondered. Was it his 'artistic temperament'?

Suddenly I felt hot and uncomfortable in his presence. I rotated my shoulders, loosened my tightly encased stoutness.

And making sure Sepp was really listening, I said:

There are always people like you. You never even tried to learn Slovenian... shame on you, it is really so un-helpful !

I can only suppose he felt my anger: a few days later his 'invention' failed and after that he killed himself....and also his poor wife.

This is where Josephine's unreliable tortured nib produced another large **blot** and her account ended.

<<<<<<<<<>>>>>>>>>

Josephine and Cölestine are already sharing their history.   Now we observe their interlocking lives through ...

Cölestine's Story

My first memory is being with my Grandmama. She and I looked after my small sisters. Later, when I was old enough to go to school, my Mama and my Papa, who went to work every day, deemed the half-hour walk from St Anna to Neumarktl too exhausting for my small person and so I was sent to live with my father's sisters. They lived near the school.

After two years I was moved to the house of three cousins of my mother's, all spinsters. They ran a grocery store. The youngest was an uncontrolled person who threw cups and plates against the wall when things did not suit. I was afraid. After a while my parents sent me to Miss Pirz, an elderly daughter of our extremely old doctor. Only on Sundays I went home to my family. After my grandmother died I became a boarder at the convent. (From a letter written years later.)

1897. Now no longer a boarder Cölestine inhabited her own room back in St. Anna. Lessons with the tutor made her tired, she crept away to rest, her back ached and she often wondered why her right shoulder looked a bit higher than her left,…peering into the spotty old mirror…

'Am I a hunch- back? How awful…' Instead of brooding on this unhappy fact she decided to write a letter to her favourite nun at the convent:

…..I have a new tutor. I must read from a fat History book. For tomorrow I memorise a poem by Goethe. My cousins are all here. The girls paint and make a great mess with their colours and brushes, the boys argue and fight. I scold them, saying their paintings are too big …and so is this mess…so they painted a very small picture as a joke…no more than five centimetres squared. I love it: it is 'my' mountain, the one I see from our garden and the rickety old fence. I will ask the woodcarver to make a special frame for it. No-one has ever given me a painting before and I like it because I can take it with me wherever I go….

Months passed, tutors come and go. In the summer there was a notable visit from two further cousins. Another letter informed:

We have had a busy time with visitors from Trieste…two gentlemen. I did not know them before: yet both are cousins. I'm ashamed to tell you I cannot stand the younger one, only a 'second' cousin, called Manfred, haughty and always mocking me, just because he thinks he is so clever. He claims to be a scientist, rather like Uncle Sepp was.

Cölestine was haunted by the memory of Uncle Sepp's shouting, as he ran, in the dark night, from one room to the next: 'for all eternity…for ever, it moves, just like I *knew* it would!' Awake enough to pad along and admire the machine buzzing and whirring she heard him shout: 'you see, you see: *I told you*!' …'but I was tired and wished to return to my bed. When we woke the following morning' Cölestine tells us, 'something terrible happened: Mama was sobbing in the kitchen as we came down for breakfast. She explained later how Uncle Sepp had wandered off early with his wife and Papa's gun and how he probably said: 'go ahead, dear, the path is a little too narrow here', and then he must have shot her, and himself a few moments later, and all this happened because his *invention* had come to a halt during the night.'

Her uncle's tragic action caused the young girl to carry a great burden of 'shame.' Again and again she imagined the wife stepping in front of him, walking on, oblivious and trusting, while he took aim to kill her. Cölestine carried this image with her all her life. Wild, frightened thoughts would pass through her mind: 'how everyone loved him, and he loved my Mama so much, and then the two deaths; perhaps he simply could not bear to disappoint us all? Oh, poor Uncle Sepp, what was wrong with you?'

'Now I am always home, to keep Mama company. Papa is, as usual, away on his business trips, and because I am fourteen I can go to the office when Mama wishes. I am learning many new things. In the office we speak Slovenian.

All Uncle Sepp's belongings have been given to the church, for the poor, apart from his zither, which now belongs to me. Also his wife's clothes, all given away, but for the exceptional heavenly blue silk gown. Mama feels I could be cheered up with a new grown-up garment suitable for some as yet unspecified happy event, difficult to imagine…the dressmaker from Neumarktl has come to take measurements. She knows how to conceal my slightly uneven back, so no-one would ever notice.' Cölestine thinks of the dead lady: 'I'll always remember her now'.

****

'It goes without saying that the suicide of Uncle Sepp affected our lives very deeply. When Christmas drew near we simply couldn't bear the thought of staying in the house still so full of dark memories. It was decided that we would all spend Christmas with Mama's sister in Graz. My father hoped that Mama

might come out of her deep depression if she spent some time away from St. Anna.... that she might begin to forget the pain of the terrible mishap.

Papa travelled back home to St. Anna on St. Stephen's Day and promised to come back on St. Sylvesters' Day. We received a letter from him in the morning: there had been a breakdown of the machinery in the factory and he could not return to us until it was all running again, until any defect had been put right. He also said he might arrive on a late train, but if he had not arrived by 10pm we should not expect him.

On the last day of that terrible year we waited from one train to the next for my father's appearance. In the evening we all sat in the drawing room, there were eight of us, and we passed the time playing parlour games. We heard the clock strike ten times. My Mama said sadly:' I don't suppose he'll come now...'

At that moment we heard Papa's characteristic footsteps passing through the entrance hall, through a second room and then we saw the doorknob turn. We leaped up and shouted 'Papa' or 'Uncle', hurrying towards the door. There was no-one at all! All the other doors were securely shut and we experienced a terrible feeling of emptiness. We discussed it at length. We could not understand it.

The next day a request came from St. Anna: that Mama should come, that he was very ill, and that he had not wanted to spoil our fun over New Year.'

Exactly fourteen days later my Papa died from Typhoid fever, caught on his latest business trip.

Thus ended my childhood; from then on I shared all my mother's cares, and believe me she had more than her share. I was fifteen years old. All these deaths, in such a short time, were too hard to bear and soon she became ill. The doctor feared she could only live another fortnight.

'Praise be to God,' **writes Cölestine**, *'the doctor was in error, because my Mama eventually reached the age of ninety-seven. But at the time all this was very trying, when I was still so young with two younger sisters and no male relatives apart from my eighty-four year old guardian. After a spell of about two years my Mama recovered.*

She even spent time in Laibach, (Ljubljana) for a health-cure. By then she had actually decided to sell all the business and property.

Widowed, but with my assistance, my brave Mama ran the business for three more years before the venture and the land, as well as our home were sold to cotton-spinning merchants Gassner and Glanzman. The deal was completed in the summer and in October 1900 we left St. Anna and Neumarktl and moved across the mountains to Graz. '

The new owners eventually brought huge benefits to Neumarktl because they decided to use the waterpower of the river to run their factory and also to create electric power for the entire area.

(The account of aforesaid mysterious event was written by Cölestine many years later, when she was already a mother of her own grown-up children.)

*****

After the long loneliness of life in the valley they tried to enjoy town-life to the full...theatre, concerts and ball after ball in the winter months. Cölestine did still sometimes think about her haughty and mocking cousin Dr. Manfred Ragg, now also known as Fredy.

'Clearly, none of us longed to return to St. Anna, even though we could never forget it. Graz had a great deal to offer and as time passed we, the Hofbauer girls, were much in demand... I was thought to be a most desirable dancing partner.'

Now well-off, Josephine spent money on her children. Artistic photographers immortalized Cölestine and her sisters in wondrous gowns, looking both desirable and marriageable.

'How quickly it all passes', wondered the now middle-aged former business woman. Observing and guiding her daughters' lives she created a circle of friends and in her newly furnished home she saw to it the young ladies met as many young persons of both sexes as possible to secure whatever futures might be on the horizon. She also enjoyed playing cards. It is not known if she was 'happy.'

'Fräulein' Cölestine Hofbauer claimed, in her own account, to be 'popular' in the ballrooms of Graz. There were also more homely occasions: a photograph exists, showing an unpromising array of young gentlemen, nearly all mustachio-ed and, sadly, rather stupid-looking. This *may* be explained by earlier photography, because in those days people had to hold still counting up to twenty (at least), to ensure sufficient exposure. However, it must be said: the girls don't look *nearly* as stupid.

Formalised mating games then, carefully but discreetly supervised by mothers and aunts, anxious to place their daughters into lives of their own...surely always a hotbed of intrigue and hopes.

'In the back of my mind there is always the ghost of cousin 'Fredy', noted Cölestine in a letter. Despite the attentions from other suitors she held herself in check, more like an amused bystander. And yet, when they finally met again, along with other relatives, the dashing Dr. Manfred Ragg took little notice of her, if anything, he repulsed her, while being *utterly* charming to everyone else. How does one interpret such behaviour? Why...true love, of course!

21

'A visit to Vienna where we met once again, proved that all had changed and before we knew … we had become engaged, secretly of course, and for a long time, as Fredy didn't have anywhere to accommodate a bride', Cölestine revealed in another letter. One summer later the two had a terrible outburst because Cölestine had danced all too eagerly with someone else, which caused her secret 'betrothed' much displeasure. For two whole years they lost interest in each other.

Cölestine's sisters played a quiet role in the background: Valerie, two years younger, always thought to be a 'wild' child preferred rough games, mostly with boys, the dirtiest children about. Also sent to convent schools, Valerie's promising voice was eventually trained to a high level of proficiency. The youngest sister, Margarethe, very beautiful and not too bright, was remembered mainly for an unhappy love-affair. There will be more about these young ladies…..

One cannot help feeling sorry for 'Cenzi', (Cölestine's new nickname): she had become an adult at the age of twelve.

Josephine and her three daughters spoke German with a heavy Slovenian accent for the rest of their lives.

In 1905 cousin 'Fredy', or, more importantly, Dr. Manfred Ragg, the chemical engineer, was offered a job in London.

This triggered a conciliatory mood and without too much fuss he and 'Cenzi' became engaged officially. Any remaining doubts were dispelled. Finance was a factor of course. In the old days young gentlemen had to come up with complex proof of their abilities to keep cherished daughters from 'good' families.

As there was no father to ask awkward questions about such things Fredy got round his prospective mother-in-law Josephine with charm and wit. Cenzi, more than ready for a new life in England, tried to learn to cook, and even attempted English grammar…while Josephine joined in the new challenge, when the twice weekly English teacher appeared, with her 'hau doo joo doo' and 'pliezt too miet joo'.

In April 1906 Fredy arrived to gather up his bride. Josephine broke down while embracing her first-born, fearing for the young couple's future in such a distant foreign place as London. She sobbed.

Travelling with them was Fredy's step-mother Hermine, a large, fearsome-looking lady. And, having heard much about the peculiarities of English food, they also imported a lady cook.

Woodford Green, North London: a splendid three-story Edwardian villa called 'Upwey' was their new home. One can't imagine why they would want such a big place. Did they know Cenzi was already pregnant? The first-born-to-be was already more than just a twinkle in her father's eye. Allegedly quite homesick, the young bride absorbed a creditable amount of English in those early years.

Judging from photos there was a steady stream of visiting relatives, to fill life with chatter and antics in the garden, such as a bizarre custom of putting on ridiculous garments and clowning about, looking silly. Was this something one did in the 'olden days'? The young Raggs were sharp and funny, but definitely not ridiculous. There is a photo of Fredy sitting on the top rung of a tall ladder, wearing a hat and carrying an open parasol, supported right and left by his still slender young wife and his corpulent stepmother. Seated on the lower rungs is a young woman in a white apron, hands demurely on her lap. Is she the cook? And Fredy, the great scientist, is he the instigator of all this nonsense?

It is not easy to be a young person uprooted into a new country and having to cope with developing a different persona. Cölestine was engrossed with a new husband, a mother-in-law *and* being pregnant. There must have been other help in such a big house, and learning to communicate with all those strange English people was surely cause for concern. Cenzi seemed strong enough to cope. In those days it was swim…or sink. (The English say it differently.) She swam, happily.

****

Her dearest Mama, Josephine, who by then began to *look* formidably old, came just once. Did she also try a few words of English? And Cölestine's sisters appeared for a while. She was hardly ever alone. It would be fair to speculate she was leading a pleasant life, doing things surrounded by helpers and family. She spoke some English by now, for sure, and she never had to cook, unless she really wanted to.

On the 10th of January 1907 Cölestine's first daughter was born: 'Erika Hermine Josephine' was well-named: Ericaceae are the hardiest and least demanding of plants.

****

Poor Fredy trudged off early each morning to work in a bleak laboratory in Silvertown belonging to the firm of Suter, Hartmann & Rahtjen. This was an area near the docks in London. Fading photographs give little clue as to his activities: there is a horse with its nose in a nosebag, standing near mountains of barrels, in the distance a depressing building with a 30ft chimney. His tasks were something to do with the invention of a rustproof paint for use on ships and trains.

23

Small wonder he needed to let off steam when he was at home with his family and guests...

Cölestine's first-born had a nanny, Nurse Mary Parker: there exists a photo of nanny pushing an elaborate metal push-chair containing her charge directly into what looks like a dense thicket. No doubt Erika's later talents in English conversation stem from this early age. One needs to learn languages as young as possible otherwise you never 'get' the accent...well, Erika Ragg learned English in the cradle.

Four years later a second daughter was born, and then yet another. By this time the eldest had already begun her schooling in Woodford Green. The three small girls surely reminded Cölestine of her own childhood in Neumarktl, although little Erika was fortunate enough to return home each day during *her* schooldays; no farming out to peculiar relatives, as in Cölestine's youth.

The young mother will have pored over Erika's first Term Report from 'The Convent', Woodford Green, Essex. It showed that her child was in Infants Division, and the tiny tot's General Progress was 'Very Good.' There was 99/100 for conduct and the same for politeness, however only 90 for punctuality and, even worse, 85 for order. The adult Erika, later to be known as 'Eka' was already fully encapsulated by the Rev. Mother de Sales in 1912 at the tender age of five and a half. Could it be true that all our traits are firmly in place by that age?

Cölestine carefully filed away six reports, from Sept.1912 to Sept 1914. The final report was blank but for a date, Sept.9th 1914, with a signature by the Rev. Mother.

Scrawled across the page were the words; *not examined*.

Here then was a moment of history: testimony of the first real dramatic event in tiny Erika's life and, by extension, in the life of her resilient mother: the First World War had begun. Family Ragg were now labelled 'aliens' in a country which had been their home for nearly eight years.

It was like wild-fire: the assassination of an archduke, Franz Ferdinand at the hands of a young Serbian nationalist, set in train a mindlessly mechanical series of events that started the first global war... a classic case of one thing leading to another...

Three small daughters had gone down with whooping cough during the summer months, while 'Papi' absconded to Austria to get a quick break from the misery at home, now found himself trapped and separated from his family when war broke out in August.

Telegrams flew between 'Mami' and 'Papi:'

Dr.Ragg was in real trouble: no money in the bank for five tickets to return his family to Austria, even worse: he had been summoned by the military. Worse still: he was running the kitchen of an army hospital.

In later years this was seen to be very funny indeed. Papi had not set foot in *any* kitchen in his entire life. Those sick and wounded men he had to keep nourished were in greater danger than they realized.

His family in Woodford were also in difficulties: no money, three retching whooping cough victims, now suddenly labelled the 'enemy'.

Cool and practical Cölestine swallowed all pride as she passed the hat round in her husband's firm pleading for necessary funds to return to Austria. This was urgent: the family had been informed they will be interned in a camp with other aliens currently being rounded up in England.

'Mami, *please* can I come with you, I promise I will not cough, not even once.' Little Erika was beside herself with misery.

Cölestine had to pick up Erika's report from the school alone, it was more or less blank.

Although loyal Nurse Parker was caring for the small girls right up to departure day Cölestine must have been presented with difficult choices: leaving behind the family's belongings was one of them. Who knows how she dealt with so many problems.

By the time they arrive in Den Haag by boat, the second daughter, Dagmar, had pneumonia so they stayed in Holland until she recovered. Cölestine will have had a testing time. No doubt Erika played a responsible role in all this, she was seven after all.

All this acquired 'Englishness'…how much of it would stick?

Cölestine and Erika had a fair dose of it.

****

Less than one year later Cölestine was proud to see her firstborn had a splendid report from the new school in Hollabrunn, dated 28.5.1915. She saw the mark of 1 for every single subject, the highest you can achieve in the Austrian system. Erika, assigned to the 2nd year class was living proof that English education was seriously good. Well done, little 'Eka!' Well done, British schooling! Was it conceivable she never missed England at all?

Hollabrunn was probably not *quite* up to the standards of the English education system. A very tiny town, in wine lands north of Vienna, close to the Czech border, no doubt a scenic place, it was, above all, the new home of 'Grossi', (Grossmutter = grandmother) the famous Josephine, business-woman of the Klander clan, who used to play the zither, could speak Slovenian and had become a gaunt old lady, thin as a matchstick, wearing tiny glasses on the end of her nose. No-one knows why she had chosen to live in Hollabrunn. Cölestine, so very relieved to be with her Mama and to speak her mother-tongue again, felt great relief: she remembered only too well those daily struggles in Woodford Green. Now they all lived in a small house with a tiny walled garden full of potted plants and had little to worry about, other than having to water the plants and go out to purchase daily provisions. Josephine's son-in-law was an officer about to be sent to the Italian front, but his family were safe: there was sufficient food; the War was far away, somewhere in France, somewhere in the Ukraine......

And Cölestine? What was really going on in *her* head:

'My poor little Mama, so patient with our invasion! She seems to have lost weight ...and such terrible eyesight! How can one bear being here, Hollabrunn is almost as dull as Neumarktl, and she knows no-one, just the doctor and that notary... one thing is certain, this small house really can't hold us all...I simply must find a place to rent, if Fredy's army pay allows it. School fees are higher than those in Woodford, but we're saving money: we have no Nurse Parker. How I miss her, that 'nice' English girl. Erika is forgetting all her English. We'll all feel better when we have a house of our own....and soon my sisters are coming for a weekend. They just don't seem to find themselves the 'right' men... I can't think why they are so hard to please...

Sister Valerie, two years younger than Cölestine, that 'wild' child, in the Neumarktl days, the one who preferred to play rough games, mostly with boys, had been sent to a convent school, where her promising voice was being trained to a high level of proficiency. Her voice was suitable for opera. She already had engagements in larger towns such as Klagenfurt, Teschen and Innsbruck. She'd had good reviews but somehow seemed to lack the temperament to be able to establish her career in the jealous world of performers. Valerie's life remained a continuing worry for Josephine.

The younger sister, Margarethe, beautiful, but not too bright, was experiencing an unhappy love-affair with a Jewish gentleman, who could not bring himself to leave his wife. She had travelled with both of them in Syria, Egypt and Palestine and ended up broken-hearted, in Vienna where she eventually learnt to run an office for a lottery organization.

The Great War seemed unreal in such a backwater as Hollabrunn. 'Home' for Cölestine was normal, despite cramped conditions with her ageing Mama, who gladly devoted herself to small grand-daughters, just as *her* own mother had done, in Neumarktl, almost twenty years earlier. But now there was poverty: clothes must be handed down and turned, shoes carefully repaired, passed on; like most people in Europe they were *obliged* to become inventive.

The once so busy Josephine, now a busy 'Grossi', often marvelled at her own past courage, when she, a fine lady in the late 1800's had supervised undoubtedly rough Slovenian woodcutters each day. How she missed them now.

'And yet, here I am. Useful again!' My only dream: to buy a home in Bad Ischl, the Kaiser's family summer residence, has come to nothing with the outbreak of the war. Just look at me: a wizened old lady, faced with three small grand-daughters. Cölestine has absolutely no intention of going out to work, not that I really want her to...but,...'Josephine had become conscious of the never-ending cycle of mothers and daughters, like a huge wheel, turning over and over.

Just two women in the house then, small as it was, cooking, cleaning and coping with the needs, messes and flare-ups of three little girls. Thank God there was a sound, strong, sensible bond between them.

The terrible war, begun in September 1914, dragged on. They read about ghastly events in the newspapers, but tucked away in the heart of Europe they were mostly absorbed by the daily round of keeping the children happy. If only 'Papi', the scientist, would reappear from wherever he might be...first at the Italian front, later deemed more suitable to work as an industrial chemist for the War effort, he was now posted to an island, Arbe, off the Dalmatian coast, with full responsibility for the running of a Bauxite mine. This meant he only had annual leave. However, his modest salary kept the entire family going.

On Sundays, at Mass, Josephine, Cölestine, and the children prayed the War would soon be over. Food shortages were beginning to bite, people learned to 'make do', becoming skinny and under-nourished. Nevertheless, in 1917, Fredy, alias Papi, was able to visit, he even left behind the prospect of yet another addition to the family. A son was born in September 1918.

The Austrian Monarchy collapsed. Having been granted leave to be with his family at this time Papi was spared from unthinkable disasters: newly appointed as Commander of the island... the Croats had put a price on his head.

Just in time, in November drizzle, an Armistice....the war was over! Now there was already a tiny *new* Manfred, soon known as 'Pucki'.

Was this what Cölestine wanted? She must have been extremely worried: *four* children, a soldier-husband totally without an income, no home of their own….what prospects could there possibly be now?

After months of searching Dr Manfred Ragg followed up an advertisement in a specialist newspaper offering employment in a paint factory in Norway. And he succeeded: the family would live in a small whale-ing town, Sandefjord, near Oslo, and his brief will be to continue his research from the pre-war days. Everyone breathed a sigh of relief.

Another upheaval for the children, but a blessing, although mixed, for Cölestine: still not much money, rented accommodation, (only *two* rooms) and all that cooking, scrubbing, shopping and learning to cope… in Norwegian. Bravely she got on with things.

One can only *try* to imagine how Gross-mama Josephine feels, alone again, in her tiny house in Austria. She learned that her old home, Neumarktl was now called 'Tržič' which is Slovenian for 'New Market'…and that the entire area had become a joined state of Slav peoples: Slovenians, Croats and Serbs: the new Yugoslavia.

The family observed these events with interest from distant Norway. 'Grossi' had found new friends, the notary and the house doctor: they came regularly to her house to play cards.

***

Cölestine, with Erika and her siblings, mostly up to their ears in ice and snow if the photographs are to be believed, had the happiest of times, despite domestic constraints. Norwegians were friendly, and Papi's salary had become, at last, very acceptable.

Until, one day, Papi hit the proverbial jackpot.

His invention, a rustproof paint called Arcanol, reached world-wide status in a very short time and soon after they were posted to Hamburg, where, (despite the misery of recession after WW1) the Raggs no longer had financial problems at all, they acquired a villa of some elegance in Reinbeck, a suburb of Hamburg. They named it 'Jotun' in gratitude to a mythical Norse giant, plainly a bringer of incredible good fortune, and also the name of the firm in Norway.

In the early 1920's when the Arcanol business expanded across the world, Papi grew richer and richer, while Germany, completely crushed from the Treaty after WW1, became an uneasy place to live.

Amongst the signatories to the Treaty of Versailles, a peace settlement involving hundreds of delegates, there were many who wanted Germany to be crushed completely. Europe had been devastated and the Germans were held responsible for the war and its consequences. Some leaders, like Lloyd George, representing Britain, and particularly the youthful economist Maynard Keynes, were more cautious: there should be less revenge and more reconciliation; President Wilson proposed the League of Nations.

Nevertheless, the eventual results of the Treaty were extremely harsh: large tracts of land all around Germany were given back to neighbouring countries, army and navy were reduced to laughable numbers, no air-force was allowed, no submarines. There was the complete loss of vital industrial territory, loss of coal from the Saar and Upper Silesia ...a severe blow to any attempts to rebuild the economy. These huge financial penalties linked to reparations showed Germans that the Allies wanted nothing but to bankrupt Germany: the country was ordered to pay some astronomical sum like £6,600 million. Raging through Europe at this time was a further devastation: the Spanish Flu epidemic, killing another 25 million people.

In the midst of so much misery Cölestine and her family felt uncomfortable. Political movements in Germany were radicalising young men into rival factions, who looked to communism and fascism to bring Germany back on its feet.

'We don't really belong here,' they knew all along, toying with the idea of returning to Austria, back to Carinthia, close enough to be where they both came from. Papi smiled: 'I shall buy you a castle, dear Mamilein, to make up for all the bad years. I promise: We will end our lives in style.' Did Cölestine think her husband was joking? Practical and sensible, not given to romantic notions, she always believed her first duty was to her children, to send them out into the world competently trained and strong. The second was to look after her man...

For the moment the first thing was to employ a cook and a maid, just like in the 'good old days' in St Anna and in London. They could afford it, even now, when the most basic foodstuffs fluctuated in value from just a few marks to hundreds, even thousands of marks.

****

The Raggs were fun to be with. They were great hosts, lively and cultured, Papi even owned a pianola on which he explored Mozart, Beethoven and Schubert symphonies, while the entire family read books from Papi's wide-ranging library. Each family member had a sarcastic, caustic streak, and with it came razor sharp wit, zany humour...

Because of Papi's business they entertained 'personages', in a 'stylish' manner. In the 1920's, for example, Papi had frequent business dealings with a dashing young man from West Africa, someone to do with shipping. He called on the Raggs every time he came to Hamburg on leave, he more or less adopted them, and they made him feel part of the family. His own family lived in Pomerania...their lives also devoted to shipping; even a grandfather who had risen to the rank of admiral...

Cölestine, by now an astute mother, took a guilty peek at her shy fourteen-year old's diary: 'how can my parents be so nice to that guest: 'der olle Ihlenfeldt' (that old Ihlenfeldt), is coming again; Mami has sent me to buy champagne and tulips. What a ridiculous amount of money to spend just because they like him so much...let's hope he's soon sent back to his black people,' Erika had recorded.

Excerpts from Erika's diary between 1923 and 1926 allowed Cölestine various insights into her child's budding psyche. Having shown classmates some photographs of a family gathering including 'Reinhold Ihlenfeldt and co., Erika reported: 'gales of laughter from everyone. Ellen (my friend) was quite beside herself. How is it possible all the girls think he is so smashing? I'm quite well informed about him now.'

On the 9th Erika she wrote: 'Tomorrow the boys are coming. How I hate these creatures!' The next entry: 'Sunday: homework, housework. I loathe that Ihlenfeldt. Such arrogance and disregard! Even the others noticed it. I did not say a word to 'Mr. I'. If only he didn't come. Mami *forces* me to be downstairs with *them*.' This was in June, 1923. Erika was 16 years old. Only eighteen months on: '...and now Ihlenfeldt: I was terribly anxious when he came. Well, we all rushed to the door at the same time, so details were lost. He has become, oh miracles, quiet and modest and a bit fatter. I had the best intentions to be nice and talkative, but it seems to be impossible with this person. Thank God I only blushed once, when he said, you're just as quiet as you used to be'...but I'd had too much champagne and, with a headache, showed myself from my worst side: I said nothing at all. He is staying in Hamburg, but I hope they soon send him back to his black Mammy. I don't know why he makes such a strange impression on me. I secretly compared him to Willy, and I have to admit that my poor little friend lags behind somewhat'. (Willy Hacker, a current boyfriend.)

Cölestine has settled into an armchair in Papi's study and Papi lights the stub of an unfinished cigar... it is late, the last of the guests have left. She needs to put her feet up. Papi's eyes are shut: 'entertaining after work is really just like 'more work' these days' he pondered, but would not like to upset his wife who had just put on such a splendid show, for his benefit....'and have you ever seen such an exquisite bouquet as the one young Ihlenfeldt brought today? He must be doing rather well for himself...isn't it strange how much he seems to enjoy being with us here in Reinbeck,...why, no sooner his ship docks in Hamburg he wants to come out to see us...flattering really. He's almost like a son now. Too bad he is a Lutheran; do you suppose he fancies Erika? I must say, she does seem to have a soft spot for him!'

Papi, nose still glowing from an evening's wine and brandy, considered the fine young Reinhold who had so attached himself to his house and home: 'we must keep an open mind with all our daughters... we'll need to find men with prospects... I dare say, this Reinhold does make a very good impression, how long has he been coming here now...nearly five years,'...Papi stared up at the ceiling, then at his large china eagle on the bookshelf. 'I feel sleepy now, my dear, let's go upstairs, get a good night's rest.'

To imagine anyone's life in Germany a bed of roses in those troubled times after the World War would be ridiculously ignorant. There was inflation, deprivation, hardship and political trouble wherever one looked. It seemed the Raggs were cushioned from the worst. And yet: 'not immediately, perhaps when the children have left school we should get out of here,' was what Cölestine thought and her man totally agreed. It was during these threatening years that Josephine Hofbauer, alias 'Grossi' became ancient, and, in the years of inflation, even quite hard-up. Cölestine, by now a quadri-lingual mother of four had matured and become stout. 'We must go home. Back to the south of Europe', she muttered, often enough. It had become her mantra.

'Though, where *is* home', she wondered: 'Neumarktl, Woodford, Hollabrunn, Sandefjord? She did keep forgetting that her beloved Neumarktl was now a Slovenian town, with an unpronounceable new name.

Erika's Story

'I am so proud of having started my life in Woodford Green: it makes me different from the other girls at school: I'm miles ahead in English, know it from the 'inside' so to speak…well, I quite like this feeling of being special…especially here, in Hamburg.'

Now in the final years of ferociously serious German High school she toys with the idea of becoming a student of archaeology. After years of being the oldest child, which, needless to say, can be extremely wearying, the escape from home and school seem a tantalising prospect. Would she admit, even to herself, that all she really wanted was to be wooed and carried off by a man, any wonderful man, (someone like that Reinhold Ihlenfeldt for example,) and never have to do a stroke of work of any kind? 'We've been writing to each other for quite some time, discussing religion, philosophy, even politics and Reinhold regularly sends photographs of his adventures on the Gold Coast to Papi and to all the family…not just one or two, but many.'

Well, whole albums, even.

A photo of Erika coyly dancing on the lawn of her parents' immaculate Hamburg garden, but nevertheless in the arms of some other young man, perhaps a school friend had just been pasted into the family album. There was indeed some romance with such a person, but intended or not, the entire Ragg family had captured the heart of that affectionate young Ihlenfeldt who re-appeared each time he was sent back from Africa on business, bearing flowers and making himself part of the family. In *his* diaries there were remarks about the delightful Ragg children and how pretty the girls were, *especially* young Erika, who had turned that corner from teenager with long pigtails to shy enchantress.

Soon, with her parents' blessing, she began an earnest correspondence with that poor lonely fellow slaving away in Africa, well, not only earnest, but regular…. and such very serious topics they chose to impress one another!

They had discussed the undesirability of 'mixed-faith' marriages (Reinhold's brother had just had a bad experience) or, more generally, about Faith and God. They exchanged endless gentle hints about the importance of keeping in touch, and impressed each other with fragments of poetry and other people's clever philosophical thoughts.

Erika had a particular axe to grind: the necessity of young women to be 'independent', and wanting to learn something that would allow her to stand alone, to *keep* herself. Reinhold firmly argued against this need, upholding the idea of a pure, unsullied woman who lived only for the man she would marry...'well, he's just one of those old-fashioned men...'she thought,.. 'a shame, really'.

Reinhold, a mere shipping agent, must have read shelves full of books in those two years to keep up the intellectual level. Could this be one of the better ways to get to know another person: by correspondence? In 1928, shortly after he returned to Hamburg for a month to recover from his seven year stint in the tropics Erika and her romantic suitor got engaged.

He knocked on the door to Papi's study, trembling from head to foot, to ask for Erika's hand in marriage. Papi had known all along this was 'a good thing' although he felt obliged to explain he was in no position to offer a 'large' dowry as he had another three children to bring up. Fully aware of Reinhold's respectable place in the world of shipping Papi had every reason to believe his daughter would be well cared for and wished her suitor all conceivable happiness.

When Reini emerged from the study he found the entire smiling clan gathered outside the door to witness an official engagement kiss.

***

So here it loomed: the dreaded 'mixed marriage,'... in this instance, between a Catholic from Austria and a Lutheran from Pomerania. A beautiful, innocent virgin has given up all aspirations to university studies, claiming the right to disappear from her Catholic family into darkest Africa with a Protestant, to live amongst foreigners. In the jungle!

Well, to be precise, in a British Colony. In those days Britain still clung to its excellent reputation for nation-building in distant places.

And Erika Ihlenfeldt, twenty-two years old and head over heels in love experienced a change in life style that bordered on the fantastical: she travelled by ocean liner, first class, to the Gold Coast, lounging about on deck-chairs with a glamorous husband who knew everyone, all these smart people, and adored her, only her. She understood her English had just the tiniest German twang, nothing *like* as terrible as Reinhold's...and that it would soon improve.'

***

Accra, a fast developing town with an indigenous population of 60,000 and about 900 whites from various countries, had electricity, telephone, water supplies, roads were paved, cinemas and bars added to the lively social scene. After work, at 5pm, everything ground to a halt so people could rush off to tennis, golf, riding, swimming. Then followed the 'sun-downer'… and evenings were mostly enjoyed with some sort of party. Here there was less racial discrimination than in some parts of Africa, everyone mingled naturally, based of course on education, interests, and social stratification.

The love-birds settled into their tropical home (with an old slave cellar) in the native town right on the seafront of down-town Accra. From a raised veranda Erika and Reinhold gazed across the sea to watch ships being unloaded in the distance. There was no harbour then; in those days whatever arrived by boat had to be transferred into narrow long-boats rowed by athletic black almost naked men, glistening in the spray.

A shipping agent's life consisted of one dramatic event after the other: the bay of Accra became littered with goods that had dropped into the ocean, never to be retrieved. Someone had to bear the cost.

Soon Erika realized there was nothing else to do but 'take an interest', or shrug, look pretty, and entertain numbers of multinational guests.

The cook tolerated her presence, nodded politely at all her requests, and produced great meals in spite of her attempts to meddle.

She was blissfully happy. During this time the couple became known as 'Eka and Reini'.

For Germans living in the country the most difficult aspect was British social distancing, still in place in 1927, nearly 10 years after WW1. By the time Erika came to Africa such hard feelings were dying down; the young couple was soon seen in the 'best circles' of Accra, at garden parties of the Governor, also on smaller occasions at Government house and at the Accra Club. Erika spoke passable English with only the slightest trace of an accent; this too was a great help. The Club, housed in an 'old' building dated 1895, offered a library and billiard room, a bridge-room and of course a bar and restaurant. Members could sit out on the veranda and were entertained, on Sunday evenings, by the Accra Police band. After the constraints of life in Hamburg with all the family, Erika, in fashionable new clothes and with her handsome, popular husband, was, more or less, in heaven. He found time to drive her inland to visit African villages and lush landscapes and took her on business trips to adjacent African countries; hot, new, strange, entrancingly romantic and exotic adventures. With an embarrassingly large number of servants, who cleaned, cooked, served and laundered, who shopped and planted and carried and drove, all milling about in immaculate uniforms, the 'Madam' soon picked up the required 'pidgin English'. This was a linguistic experience all of its own.

Reini's passion always had been photography. In his own meticulous way he made a record of all he saw (over ten years) and created album after album, sending pictures to both sets of parents. But then Reini had been doing this all along, for as long as he'd known the Raggs…for the past seven years, meaning to impress them, of course.

'I am the luckiest woman alive' thought Erika.

In later years she would look back on that decade in Accra as the best time of her life…only the tiniest bit homesick of course, just as Mami had probably been during her years in England, and just as Grossi must have felt: forlorn, widowed, friend-less at first in Graz and later in Hollabrunn, but imagine the compensations: all that social 'high life,' and never having to lift a finger…

Most of us only realize the good times when they are long over. As Josephine, Cölestine and Erika moved through their early married lives they all had their share of adjusting to do, learning to fit in, learning to change, communicate with strangers. It is called 'broadening the mind.' There was much of that.

Beloved Mami, dearest Papi,   *Accra, Jan. 3rd. 1930*

Imagine this: after breakfast Reini took me down into the court yard and there it was: a new car, just for me.!!!It is a Chevrolet Roadster (no roof) He simply said, 'happy birthday' even though it isn't my birthday until next week,..can you imagine how thrilled I am? He has been showing me how to drive in his own car for some weeks now, and tonight we are planning a careful drive ,in mine , along the beach road, where there is not a great deal I can bump into. He is worried I might feel bored sitting about all day long but he is wrong: I have several books from the Club library, plan my wardrobe for our busy social life (the ladies here like to look glamorous) and of course I have to tell cook what to do! Reini trusts him, he has worked for him for many years. Cook doesn't really like me to make suggestions because I obviously don't know yet what is available here.

Reini always has his hair cut by the chauffeur.(Can you imagine!) Should I let him cut mine? I'm quite concerned about this. We are looking for a picture of the 'Bubi' hair-cut, for him to copy. Can you cut out something from a newspaper and send it?

We go to the Club often and drink gin and tonic.

How are my 'ugly' sisters and my 'horrible' brother. When does he start at his new boarding school with the monks in Lavanttal? I do miss you all and wish you could come and see how happy we are. Reini is adorable. We have two kittens, both stripy and so funny. Before I forget: sometimes African traders come to the house, selling strange carvings and metal objects. Shall I buy something bizarre for House Jotun? I can just see such things on the veranda in Reinbeck. Please let me know. All love, Erika......

Liebes Ekalein,

we think of you so much, all of us! Your 'ugly sisters 'are at school and green with envy when you write about your new life. A car, just for you! Is it really necessary? We always managed without one. Anyway, I don't think I could drive because of my bad eye.

Do be careful you sleep properly tucked -in under those mosquito nets, I can imagine how sweet your blood must taste to hungry mosquitoes, but I'm told they don't care for tonic water. ..to say nothing of those cockroaches...Yes, Pucki has been accepted as a boarder, and I'm sure it will do him good when he starts there in September.

I don't know what to say about African things. They sound interesting. Please remember to take Quinine every day. And do drive with care. Be embraced by your loving Mami

Erika sometimes forgot to take her preventative medicines and had several bad bouts in Accra hospital with Malaria and Blackwater fever... Being the wife of a shipping agent had one very great advantage: *free* boat journeys home. After Erika's illnesses she invariably returned to Hamburg to recuperate.

By 1933 radical political changes were taking place in Germany. The Nazis left Papi alone; fortunately he was protected by his Italian passport, having been born in Trieste.

Some of these trends were felt even in the depths of Africa, but the repercussions and results were not remotely understood by expatriates working abroad. Reinhold had never shown interest in politics. Having been in Africa since he was twenty-one years old it appeared both he and Erika lived very much on the edge of these happenings, even though they were closely linked with their 'Heimat' through work, literature, music and family ties.....

An unexpected event took place in the early months of 1934 when Mami and Papi in Hamburg opened a telegram from their son-in-law in Accra: he had been appointed German Consul for the Gold Coast and Togo-land. He posted a cutting to them from the Gold Coast Gazette.

THE GOLD COAST GAZETTE, 7thApril, 1934.

It is hereby notified for general information that the King's Exequatur, empowering Herr Reinhold Ihlenfeldt to act as Honorary German Consul at Accra received His Majesty's signature on the 12th February, 1934.

Needless to say Erika and Reini's social life escalated with this appointment. Not that they weren't sufficiently in demand already; by now both of them spoke passable English, they were good-looking, hospitable and the British community, as well as other diplomats were friendly. The desirable young couple got a taste of a more than enviable social life, from visits to the race course, to garden parties and elegant soirees and even dinners for visiting royalty from other nations.

*****

Infant mortality amongst Europeans was very high. Over and over again the couple's decision was: 'no family-building... not until we are posted to some place with a better climate, or until we return to Europe.'

*To have or not to have, a child...*this was endlessly discussed, corresponded about, weighed up...mulled over.

After four years of married life Erika had found a solution: 'I *must* get pregnant here, travel back before it is time to give birth and leave it in Hamburg with Mami and a trained nurse; with any luck there will soon be a posting to a better climate and *then* we can enjoy being a proper family. Wiser and older persons: the family doctor, the parish priest had warned them against this plan. But the urge to procreate was so very strong... it just seemed it was now or never.

Splendid! This was such a generous offer from Mami and Papi. To have another baby in the house, even with a trained nurse, might be a challenge: Mami was already fifty...

'One can still be a 'mother' aged fifty' said Cölestine bravely, game for another round of maternal duties. The house in Reinbeck was large and so, when all was said and done, there was little in the way of this grand design.

On evening walks, in a cool ocean breeze, the would-be parents in Accra strolled to the lighthouse and back, discussing, more than once, a name for the as yet un-conceived offspring. If it were a boy he could be 'Wolfgang' and if a girl, Reinhold had a weakness for 'Ingeborg' or for 'Eva'. Erika had no strong feelings. A close friend of theirs, Evelyn Dade, offered to be godmother and so a combination of Ingeborg-Evelyn was discussed at great length. 'Evelyn,' might be the first step to being the tiniest bit British…along with being conceived in a British Crown Colony…

A baby was transported in utero to Hamburg three months before the birth. Judging from Erika's dimensions it would surely prove to be *a very large Wolfgang.*

****

ETA was the end of December, 1934: everyone was standing by, the father-to-be in steamy hot Accra, Eka in freezing, snowy Hamburg, a nurse, Sister Erna, in her starched uniform and the saintly Cölestine, living up to her 'heavenly' name, all on a cloud of readiness, more than to supervise the new arrival,…it shouldn't be too bad.

Expanding in a bloated sort of way, Erika lolled about shapelessly. Christmas came, and went. Then the New Year celebrations…

'I go for careful walks in the snow, but still nothing happens', she writes to Reini, 'the doctor suggests there's been some mistake in the calculations made in Accra; not even my birthday celebrations on the 10th of January brought on the slightest birth tremor. The resident in my stomach is very, very lazy and comfortable. I despair.'

At last, on the 23rd of January, an 8-pound Venus made a belated appearance, only a month late but, according to the Vereins-Hospital staff, a remarkable specimen, by any standards. Photographs were taken of the shattered mother with her dumbfounded new-born.

Examining this offspring from head to toe Erika's unflattering assessment was: 'a *Pomeranian peasant-child…hm,* with slitty blue eyes.' She was face to face with the daunting task of being a 'mother'.

In those days *new mothers* rested in bed for at least a week.

By February the youngest resident of Haus Jotun was well established with an entourage of doting uncles, aunts, grandparents, a noticeably slimmed-down mother and a trained nurse in uniform. The picture-book cradle with much gossamer white muslin, a cot, a white pram, and instant potty-training, (indeed, it was thought the thing to do: holding a potty under a baby would achieve results)…all this was carefully photographed to allow the absent father in Africa to take part at a safe distance.

After seven weeks Sister Erna, the mother-substitute, went into action with baby gymnastics. Photos of a writhing naked infant suspended by her ankles were posted to Accra. Could it be *all* Third Reich babies were treated like that in the first months of their lives...or was this simply a highly trained nurse, showing off before the photographer?

Until March Erika hardly appeared in the photos; she was obviously weaning herself from mother-dom, leaving her offspring in more experienced hands. Or was she preparing herself for the martyr-dom of abandoning her baby?

But first there was Christen-dom with all the family gathering and celebration deemed necessary for such an event. Ingeborg-Evelyn was duly received, at last, at least, into the bosom of the Church.

After that Erika returned to Accra, possibly with mixed feelings. As time passed at least ten photographs of Ingeborg's developing activities were taken *monthly* and posted to the baby's distant progenitors.

Did these parents cling to each other with great love and affection, while enduring the bittersweet pangs of guilt of both having - and not having a child?

The infant's blue eyes had, regrettably, changed to hazel.

Twelve months later the parents return to Hamburg. The baby met her father for the first time. This momentous event took place in the nursery, with only Erika (and the nurse, in case of emergency) in discreet attendance; the rest of the family hid in a dark corridor peering through a gap of the door...

Reini admitted later that his heart rate was up, that he was very moved, but also terrified of doing anything that might arouse the displeasure of the 'princess.' One attempt at lifting her into his arms ended with screams and tears... small arms reaching imploringly to Nurse Erna. Erika and Reini had not expected miracles, but the famous 'call of the blood', well, it was not in evidence.

It took a while. The next clever ruse was for Erika to dress in a starched uniform just like the nurse and to attempt feeding and bathing ceremonies. After four weeks of patient effort Ingeborg-Evelyn began to accept her mother. Dad was rejected time after time. This non-acceptance lasted until a week before the planned parental return to Africa, when 'her highness' fell for her father's cigarette lighter, which she wanted to blow out. Blowing out candles on the first ever Christmas tree was her greatest thrill. She continued blowing out imaginary candles in the corner where the tree had stood for many months. Father and daughter began to be friends of a kind… for all of one week.

Photography continued: a chastening memento of that difficult first encounter between father and daughter (blank disbelief on a one-year old face quite sad to see), the magical German Christmas tree with real candles, sparkly lametta, and gingerbread rings, tentative, wary parents…until Eka and Reini rented a car to enjoy a two month trip around Europe. First: a call of duty (as consul), to attend a party given by von Ribbentrop in Berlin, at that time acting ambassador to Britain. After that the couple needed to get about in Germany because they had seen so little of it in their younger days: they were now obliged to talk knowledgeably about their 'Vaterland', a place they barely knew while still at school.

Did they have any idea what was really going on in Germany?

Spending all one's home-leave with a one year-old, who would then get too used to you and therefore make the next parting too painful all round, was something the young parents had discussed at great length. They had a distressing row in Linz, as described in one of Reini's numerous diaries, almost as if it was their first misunderstanding since they were married. Going on long car-journeys can bring out the worst in people.

Poor Mami had already coped with three changes of nurses by then.

More pleasingly there was an inspired intervention by Erika's young brother, home for his holidays from boarding school: his favourite cartoon clown 'Knups' in a newspaper, had led him to observe an uncanny resemblance   between the clown and Ingeborg, who was henceforth called 'Knups', an amusing blend of clumsy plumpness and affection. The name caught on at once.

Now: a good shrink may remonstrate: giving a young female a *male* name may have deleterious effects on her development, warp her mission in life, change her hormones, appearance and so forth. But for the moment 'Knups' was a well-proportioned, adorable package of cute smiles, golden eyes and shiny blonde ringlets, in every way a model girl baby.

******

Life was about to change dramatically: 'Dearest Mami, you will be free again: we, the 'Africans,' have news of a posting from Accra to Cape Town, probably in 1938, at last, a chance to become a proper family!'

Erika's parents could now plan their long-hoped for escape to Austria, where Papi had, in a mad moment, acquired a 13th century castle, Magaregg, with four towers (no draw-bridge). Papi might have liked a drawbridge: to get away from Hamburg in 1938 seemed just the thing, an escape to a quiet backwater near the border of Yugoslavia. The Nazis continued to ignore him, with his Italian passport.

Besides, this sixty-five year old wanted nothing more than to play symphonies on his pianola and to enlarge his stamp-collection. No more science, no more business, no more babies and nurses, just peace and quiet.

Wishes of a sixty-five year old gentleman must be respected.

In 1938, shortly before Mami and Papi's 'apotheosis' in their wondrous castle, Erika bundled up her child, travelled by train to Vienna and Hollabrunn to meet with *and* say goodbye to Josephine before the sea-journey to CapeTown. Knups was ecstatic about sleeping in a 'room on wheels'...seemingly unperturbed by leaving her first home or indeed her dearest Mami in Hamburg. She was introduced to Mami's mother! This was an impressive array of mothers and daughters to take in.

One imagines three generations in such proximity: Josephine, Erika and Ingeborg...for one brief moment, touching, chatting, smiling together. Mami might have been there as well, but she was already packing to leave Hamburg. There was no photograph of this moment. It would almost be worth trying 'regression' just to re-live such an event.

Later, during a quick flight to Genoa to board an ocean liner, Knups befriended the entire crew and passengers on the flight: Erika had fainted (altitude sickness?) and the small traveller blithely entertained, and was cared for, by everyone. Erika reported to Reini that 'your daughter seemed to prefer male passengers and flirted with most of them.'

Not bad going then...for a three and a half year old.

*****

September: Mami rolled up her sleeves and 'got on', which was what she always did. After all those early uncertainties, here she was in her new incarnation: the *'queen' of her castle*. How often did she go down to her *own* chapel in the base of the front right-hand tower, to thank God for her good fortune? Now life was all about curtains and rugs, unpacking and feathering the nest, if one could call such a huge place a nest. The most pleasing thought: having all the family here, enjoying the countryside and being together, from time to time...that is what really kept her going. And to be only a few miles from Neumarktl, her old 'dream' home! There was nothing much new for Grossi, still very much alive, nearing ninety, and peering through little spectacles on the end of her pointy nose: she was known to beat her elderly gentlemen friends into submission by winning at most of their regular card-games.

'How incredible', thought Erika on her way to Cape Town: 'my Mami, in a castle, and now so near to her roots: just a quick drive and there it will be, her so beloved Neumarktl.'

****

Papi, soon settled in his study, along with the wise china eagle one sees on all his photos, *began to study the past.* His castle, only one treacherous mountain pass (the Loibl Pass) away from Yugoslavia, allowed him to access old church registers, village priests, distant relatives, finding both alarming and delightful tales about earliest ancestors, the Klanders and others.

By now Cölestine had all she'd ever hoped for: a fairly grumpy but loving and successful husband, four children - eventually dotted all over the globe, financial stability, a huge kitchen in which to bake unbelievable Strudel with dough so thin you could read the newspaper through it, and above all, good health. If there was anything missing she never let on. Compared to her spinster sisters Cölestine lived a picture-book life, fulfilled and successful beyond all dreams.

After the difficult settling–in period Erika had visions of her Mami seated in a castle, wearing elegant gowns and being waited on by bowing servants…just like a Strauss Opera.

****

Not so! Cölestine worked from dawn to dusk: the place was vast: distances from room to room took it out of her! The kitchen could be reached only after a stately descent past knights in coats of armour (well, *just* the coats of armour) to an ancient grey stony kitchen two floors down, dark and below the ground, when one looked out from the sunken windows. Thank God for a pulley (in a tunnel) on which plates and glasses and food could be transported up and down between the lower ground floor and the dining room, but people had to march up and down themselves. If they needed a rest they could step into the chapel just by the staircase. Out of breath by the time they got to the top they would find handsome rooms with high tiled stoves for heating, wooden parquet floors covered with Persian rugs and rather uncomfortable 'Louis Quinze' chairs. Hidden near one of the many high windows was Papi's famous pianola. While he sat listening to the sounds of symphonies on his piano-rolls he'd gaze out across fields and parklands all the way to the Karawanken, those towering mountains separating Austria from Yugoslavia. It was a picture book scenario.

The family, needless to say, was agog.

A visit to the Schloss was undoubtedly an ennobling adventure. It dated back to the fourteenth (or was it thirteenth?) century, had been built by Italians. Each visitor felt 'different', a little grander, more privileged, or just simply romantic, wandering about inside and outside, in such lovely surroundings. When passing by the ancient Roman urn, under the vast tree to the left of the building, everyone imagined all the others who had seen it ...or who had once lived and died in this magical setting.

But now there were clouds beginning to form on the horizon, ominous rumblings, for all to hear and fear. Where-ever they were, the Josephines,   Cölestines,   Erikas   and   Ingeborg-Evelyn-Knupses, something was about to happen to them all that none could escape – let alone understand.

****

Meanwhile, in the castle:

'How do you feel about a special dinner party to celebrate our return to Carinthia, my dearest...I mean, we need to build up a circle of friends and acquaintances here,' white-haired Papi rambled on at bedtime, after another long evening re-assessing his stamp collection...

He decided to say no more for now; the exhausted Mami had enough on her plate: besides, he was trying to digest the news he'd gleaned from the wireless earlier, about Hitler and Chamberlain who had come to some 'agreement' in the matter of the Sudeten problem....'A relief, but not a real solution', he assured her 'for the moment a war has been averted. But how pleasing it would be to have *some* friends, new or old, to talk about these troublesome politics...even better, to be able to forget all about it.'

Europe breathed a huge sigh of relief. Things continued as before.

By now the Ihlenfeldts had journeyed via the Mediterranean through the Suez Canal, where Reini proudly remembered his Admiral Grandfather accompanying German royalty...('whenever *that* was, in 18 hundred and something'),.. and then on, right around Africa. His new post in Cape Town required being acquainted with harbour facilities and staff along the entire East Coast of Africa.

There were calls to be made in Port Said, Port Sudan, Aden, Mombasa, Dar Es Salaam, Porto Amelia, and finally Beira and

Lourenco Marques, East London and Durban. The journey took over six weeks, temperatures were unbearable. In those days there were only fans.... no air-conditioning. Erika, the new mother was suffering: not used to such heat her child was becoming difficult to handle. The practical father, Reini, took matters into his own hands, carried his daughter to the ship's hairdresser and had her shoulder-length locks cut off...without consulting Erika. A serious row took place. Knups smiled sweetly and did feel much cooler.

Fortunately for the 'new' parents the 'Tanganyika' had a well-organized nursery. There was also a young lady missionary, who loved looking after children. This was a bonus. Erika (and her man), still finding their way as parents, believed Knups was testing their so-called skills: she had announced to other passengers that her *real* parents were in Hamburg. There were surprised questions.

To top it all Erika was endlessly 'unwell'. In Beira, an Indian medic diagnosed mercury poisoning caused by a combination of camomel and orange juice. Meanwhile her three year old had become stubborn, resentful and intractable. The endless journey was a trial for all.

A full six weeks later 'home' became a reality:

Table Mountain, that unforgettable sight! It was the 9th of October, 1938.

The best way to arrive in **Cape Town** is definitely by ocean-liner.

Spread along the horizon rests Table Mountain, flanked on the left by Devil's Peak, on the right, Lions Head... once you've seen this sight you never forget it. The closer you get, the more personal it becomes, a great majestic enveloping power. Some sort of God. You gaze at it and want it to hold you, protect you, perhaps even to devour you.

Erika and Reini settled in speedily. Most of their savings were immediately spent on their first 'own' house, nestling on the ribs of the Lion...just before his tail-end magically turns into Signal Hill. A boring little bungalow it was, built at the top of a sloping garden with at least 30 steps to climb before you reach a miniscule veranda, but the views were magical day and night, the bay and of course, the harbour. Sitting on the veranda one heard distant calls of the muezzin in the Muslim quarters, a few streets down.

Subconsciously, Erika and Reini must have been trying to reproduce the rather more substantial residence in Accra; they even called their new home 'Accra'.

During those early months of acclimatizing, meeting new friends and colleagues, there were daily rumblings of political turmoil. Erika remained in close touch by post with all her relatives and soon got the hang of 'coping' with *only* one maid, one part-time gardener, and 'Wilmot', who drove the office car.

Mother and daughter slowly became fonder of one another, perhaps because the infant knew how to pretend to be more stupid than she really was. She knew this would gain her increased affection. When the new regime didn't suit she' say: 'I'm going back to Reinbeck', or just simply: 'Mami never said *that*'!

One day Erika discovered her daughter packing a suitcase, clothes and toys. 'I'm ready to go home now,' the child announced solemnly.

There was endless wrangling about food. Eating meat was one obstacle: that loathed lump of chewed matter carried from one cheek to the other and then secretly spat out, always, without fail, discovered by Erika; or downright rebellion when locked in the nursery for something or other, such as jumping out of the window...

Reini gave his not yet four-year old daughter her first-ever spanking.

At this time the nightmares about 'wild' animals began, real night terrors which ended in sweat, screams and tears. Parents, even neighbours were alarmed. 'Somebody must have said something to the child,' suggested Erika, probably her mischievous Papi, because there really were snakes and creepy-crawly beasts everywhere, even quite large baboons, munching away in a tree; this city-child from northern Europe had developed some un-staunch-able fear.

Reini said his child was spoilt and simply wanted attention... we'll get a dog and a kitten, they will help her get over it ...'

Frowning and chewing her fingernails Erika typed *long letters* to her mother asking for advice and Mami, genuinely surprised, sent much sound advice on child-rearing to help her inexperienced daughter to cope with a soon four-year old troubled mind. 'It can be homesickness ...turned into some sort of rebellion', suggested Mami who mentioned again and again her painful longing for Knups, how much she missed her grandchild, and hearing her talk.

*****

Ten months after arrival in Cape Town came the day when the world, including Erika, Josephine, and Cölestine heard frightening news:

World War II has begun

45

Hollabrunn, Austria 1939.

Grossi with her ageing spinster daughters clear away supper dishes, settle on their uncomfortable Biedermeier furniture to listen to the radio, before it is time for bed. An interruption in the usual Opera evening from Vienna…. a solemn voice declares
…. *Germany and Britain are now at war.…*

'Appalling,' gasps Grossi, 'the Germans are fighting again. What *do* they want Poland for? Austria will not have to be involved…?'

'But we've had that Anschluss, Mama, surely you know…*we are Germany now*'….the sisters shrug, eyebrows raised, shaking their heads they look at each other helplessly. Their mother is getting on, she has lost the plot.

'Shall we telephone Magaregg? Fredy will know more about our role in all this…perhaps there is nothing to worry about. We're quite safe here, Mama, in Hollabrunn, no-one even knows where Hollabrunn is, so small and unimportant…just so long we don't lose any more money, that would be terrible…let's call them right away…'

Dr. Manfred Ragg managed to reassure his frightened female relatives. They had a long discussion about 'poor little Erika' in South Africa: 'South Africans belong to the British Commonwealth…don't they all speak English there? Du lieber Gott, Reinhold and Erika must come home at once!'

Everyone was worried, telegrams criss-crossed the globe. It was too late. History was repeating itself: the Ihlenfeldts were trapped; they were 'enemies' in their chosen new home, South Africa. Exactly like the Raggs in Woodford Green, in 1914!

The British secret service had been active long before the outbreak of this war, compiling lists of Germans who were functionaries of the NSDAP (Nazis) or those who were prominent in business or industry such as Siemens, Krupp, AEG, Bosch, Opel, Mercedes etc, or shipping. Press releases during the 2nd half of September proclaim: relatives of enemy representatives will not be interned.

It was not long before 'black Marias' appeared to carry off male prisoners to various camps in South Africa.

Erika, unusually good in a crisis, put on a brave face…

Even though her man had never joined the NSDAP he was one of the first to go. (*N*azional *S*ozialistische *D*emokratische *P*artei). Called at 10am to be ready by 5 pm for transport to Johannesburg, he was escorted by two plainclothes policemen.

Both were simple Afrikaaners, mildly embarrassed by what they had to do. As there was time before departure they escorted Reinhold

Ihlenfeldt to the station bar and had several drinks while loudly assuring him the war would soon be over and... 'Ag man, Mr. Hitler is mos bound to win, so 'Meneer Illeveld' can soon be back home'...in time for Krissmis', they suggested, wanting to prove they were kindly and humane individuals.

In Johannesburg a limousine was waiting at the station, to take internees to 'LEEUWKOP', one of three camps. 'Ag man, pr'aps the war is already over,' suggested the policemen.

A fine thought. Reini did wonder then whether this civilized treatment was in some way due to the fact that he had once been a 'consul', even if not in South Africa. On arrival he was advised by the camp commandant he could complain officially to the Chief Control Officer, Sir Theodore Truter, as only Germans believed to be 'dangerous' were to be interned.

The next five months proved to be a severe test for Erika. While her man left no stone unturned to be released from the camp by writing careful letters to Sir Truter explaining he was *the most harmless non-political man in the world, not even a member of the Nazi party, he is not amongst those who manage to be set free. Why?*

The mound of censored daily letters between Erika, Reinhold grew into a mountain. The camp was a 1000 mile train journey away, up in the Transvaal. How long would this war last? No-one had the slightest idea.

Worst of all, there was no income. With the breadwinner locked up and every penny spent on the house Erika found help and distraction by taking in lodgers. Mother and daughter slept in the nursery while two bachelors and a lady were bedded and fed in the rest of the house. It was the only way forward Erika could devise. One imagines it even began to be quite entertaining... a lot of chatter and drinking and entertaining each other. It became a busy, but also worrying, melancholy time. The pampered Gold Coast 'madam' was experiencing a rude awakening.

In daily letters Erika and her man now made frequent references to their growing estrangement and coolness after ten years of married life, something that had been developing between them and how they now regretted any unkindness and wished they could be together again.

'I so long for Europe', she admitted in a letter, absence making hearts grow desperately fond... 'I so miss you and feel we've made such a big mistake... coming back to Africa'. Her imprisoned man tried to keep a cool head and clear perspective: 'Just a few more months and it will be over...'just be brave, be hopeful...' Poor, poor Erika!

Five months later Sir Truter was finally convinced of Reini's notorious harmlessness: the prisoner was released, given orders to dissolve his home in CapeTown within a fortnight and to move to one of four smaller towns inland, away from the coast: Bloemfontein, Paarl, Ceres or Elgin. The latter, only 65 km from CapeTown was full of retired British colonial and military officers; they would surely keep an eye on the 'jerry'.

At last, a happy reunion, but with some fast action: to let the Cape Town house, fully furnished, stow away personal things, rent a cottage in Elgin and find a job with an apple farmer in Elgin...all this was just about feasible in fourteen days. Once monthly the 'new' apple farmer was obliged to report to the police-station in Caledon...

****

May 1940: German troops have over-run Belgium and Holland and the war takes a turn for the worse. South African prisoners on parole were instantly gathered up and re-interned. This time it was no longer possible to protest: Reini landed in Baviaanspoort just a few miles from Pretoria, along with 1600 German men from all over South Africa.

After several months living out of suitcases with friends in Cape Town Erika 'bit the bullet', and boarded a train to Pretoria, the nearest town to the camp. She reported in the first of hundreds of letters to Reini that their child had observed slag-heaps from the mines outside Johannesburg and declared 'this must be the place where they make mountains'.

In Pretoria Erika moved into a hotel/boarding house along with six other German women, who also wished to be in a position to visit their men.

This will be allowed once a month, for ½ an hour, separated by two high fences of barbed wire... with an armed soldier on guard duty.

Children were not permitted.

Pretoria, October, 1940

'This way, madam'! A black 'house-boy', carrying two cases and a cardboard box full of toys shepherds Erika and daughter across Church Street. The annexe to Belvedere Hotel could be reached no other way. Several German ladies had taken up lodgings in the main building. Another three, from the annex, including Erika, must, as best they could, dart across the frenzied main road, for breakfast, lunch and supper.

Erika's room opened onto a vast courtyard with a polished red stone floor glittering in the hot sun. One felt the heat streaming towards one.

A narrow covered walkway, corrugated iron held up by pillars, kept residents sheltered as they emerged from their doors to find two bathrooms at the far ends. The 'boy' put Erika's cases down and looked her up and down expectantly. Servants came from the provinces, were known as 'boys', whatever their age. After scratching around in her purse she handed him a 'tickey' (tickey= approx. 3 pence). This was acknowledged by mute nods, wan smiles from both. He sloped off.

Even further, across a roughly paved alleyway, was the only toilet for at least ten inhabitants. Next to this 'outhouse' were other brick structures, (shall we say hovels), for the black servants of the Belvedere. Two high Palm trees graced a strip of garden in the front and Canna lilies just about everywhere made the annex appear reasonably friendly...a typically South African scenario.

Erika looked down at her silent daughter. They entered, lugging, dragging, two cases onto the beds. She opened an inside door to what appears to be a larder, with shelves, and, on the opposite wall a door revealing... 'ah, a small room with a window and a bed, that's nice!' Against one wall of the main room there is a sloping metal surface and a large basin with two taps....

Then the penny dropped: 'Goodness, we're in a kitchen! It's so cheap because... *that's* what it is... tiled walls floor to ceiling. They've stuck in two beds, a wardrobe, table and dressing table with two lace doilies...'

Knups throws herself on one of the beds, sucks her thumb: 'Look up, Mutti, this is a funny house...there are windows in the roof!'

Erika brightly points out that lying in bed will be so interesting: one will see the moon and the stars and the birds flying by. Then, in her sing-song way... 'you're sucking your thumb again...don't dooo that....'

While unpacking she thinks: 'what a come-down. Still, it won't be for long'...and then cheerfully: 'here we are: a place of honour for Vati's photograph ...our cases and your toys can go into the pantry... Why not go out and see if there are other children; but don't go on or near that big road,.. promise?'

Half an hour later everything was stowed away. This was home, for the foresee-able future, and 'please God, not for too long...it will do of course, but only just... given that Reini has to share a shabby little hut in his camp with two other complete strangers -this is more or less on a par with...'

....a commotion in the courtyard, three ladies appear, speaking German: 'Guten Tag, willkommen, Frau Ihlenfeldt, we saw you and your little girl arrive so we've come to help you settle in...in this…unusual room…well, it *is* big and light! And with those windows up there' … all heads turn up, gaze pensively at the ceiling…hm, well, anyway…'I'm Pev Brinkman and this is Ilse, and here is a thermos of tea and biscuits and some flowers…wait, I'll get a vase…' Pev disappeared and returned in no time at all: 'my son and I share a room off the corridor, so I can help you get used to all this. Is the little room over there for your daughter? 'Perhaps,' said Erika warily, 'I haven't really worked it out.'

She noted Pev's wasted, lame arm, which lay cradled on her good arm.

'We'll all be doing a lot of letter-writing' Pev remarked wryly, noting Erika's typewriter ready for action on the table, 'why not come with me now and I'll show you where *my* room is and then we'll all go over to supper together this evening…the management brings cups and spoons and glasses for you…come and meet the others…no, let *me* get your cups and we will have tea first'. By suppertime Erika and Knups have met Pev's son Peter in his hand-knitted suit, all of four years old and definitely ready for bed, judging from his behaviour in the dining room.

'What a pest', sighed Erika's child convincingly, 'if *you* are friends with the lady with the floppy arm then I have to play with her boy. I'm nearly six and he's still a baby!' Erika's thoughts were on a similar track: 'well, only for a few weeks, one hopes'…

The going-to-sleep ritual was to sing a verse of Brahms' Lullaby together, then the light was switched off and Erika went to the side room to read for a while. After this unusual day she crept back into their 'kitchen'…into the bed next to her child. 'What a come-down' she thought… Still, being together was comforting. When she looked up she really *could* see the stars…

Within days the side-room had a different occupant…an Inge Müller from Tanganyika (now Tanzania). The boarding house, currently completely full, had turned her away, but when Erika heard she immediately offered up the side room, thus *reducing the rent* for her own abode. Erika knew how to scrimp and save, remembering life during the First World War. *She was simply the most parsimonious person in the universe* with a true talent for martyrdom. Even having a complete stranger walk through her bedroom at various stages of the day and night, although not entirely pleasing, made Erika feel she was not alone: she was not only doing a good deed, she was, above all, saving money.

A huge watercolour of Mount Kilimanjaro, with hints of Zebras and Giraffes on the plains below went up on the wall of the new lady. It made a great change from gazing at white tiles.

All Erika had was one framed photograph of her man. Priorities were the typewriter and her camera, (both belonged to him, of course.) With these she created a daily routine: being a mother and keeping her man posted about their lives.

One big bonus: the child was coming up for school and, in the hours of her absence there would be enough 'new' friends about, and no domestic duties. Erika never did enjoy cooking.

Her only luxury was a small Opel which needless to say greatly increased her popularity. She gave lifts to people and it was useful for getting to know Pretoria, a town with aspirations: just down the road: *the* famous landmark, the Union Buildings, home of the government, and stretching out before it a vast handsome terraced garden, always open to the public; a place to explore and romp about, especially for the young inhabitants of the Belvedere Hotel.

***

12th November, 1942. 'Bad news, our daughter has whooping cough. Rest at night is much curtailed and I'm just waiting for my numerous neighbours to complain. I can't leave her for a single moment because she starts to scream immediately. Last Sunday I pulled out her first tooth. At first she said nothing, but when she saw the blood she began to cry horribly, - surprised perhaps by her own courage.'

16 November. 'My entire life is governed by this. The child looks terrible, her face swollen, I'm glad you don't have to experience it. On top of this she has lost a second tooth, which doesn't exactly improve her looks. She coughs and wheezes and chokes, especially at night. I haven't been up more than five times a night, lucky me. During the day I let her sit outside; that seems to help. Apart from rushing across the road to eat I'm always with her.'

19th November. 'Knups' illness has worsened. It usually starts at 9 pm, she vomits all over the bed, screams, hits everything in sight and this goes on every hour or two during the night. During the day it's not so bad.'

21 November. 'I've also got it now....Knups does seem a lot better, thank goodness, we're halfway through.'

By mid December it was over. After much complaining about her daughter's 'difficult' nature Erika concedes, 'in all fairness... she is more reasonable than most of the other children.'

As always, Christmas was celebrated in the traditional German way, with every mother decorating her own tree, then inviting everyone else to come and watch the usual scenario of a German carol, followed by the opening of gifts.

'I'm ashamed of this scraggy conifer half submerged in the kitchen sink, but the draining board is now at least hidden by a white tablecloth. (I've made a crib with hay, moss, some toy sheep and a cut-out Holy Family). Parcels and presents are on the floor. The main present: a shiny leather satchel for school, one flowery umbrella and a doll's pram...

When the candles were lit Tante Inge played 'Stille Nacht' on her mouth organ'... Erika wrote to her man. The two of them closed their eyes and transmitted thoughts to each other, as promised at 8 o'clock precisely.

14th January 1941. 'A big day, your daughter went to school for the first time. Indescribable excitement: for a week before she began to enquire each day how many more days until...?

'Die dumme Kuh, (the silly moo) if only she knew how much she'll learn to hate it! I have taken photos for you so you can enjoy this event with us. I made a big 'Schul-tüte' (a German custom: a large colourful cone ending in a point filled with sweets and little gifts) and most of the *new* children were carrying one. Your daughter was one of twenty tiny people in grade 1 and we, the mothers, were allowed to stay at the back for the first hour. The teacher, an older woman, seems gentle and confidence-inspiring...but resembles a toad, hunched, with huge thick spectacles which make her look almost blind.

When we, the mothers, were told to leave I noticed Knups' lips trembling and I must admit I too had to fight back the tears. The car felt empty, the room felt empty, I've been so depressed. These poor worms must sit there from 8am till 12.30...'...

Erika's life centred on her child's welfare and on keeping in touch with her man. She discussed with him whether they could afford ballet lessons and later swimming lessons for their six year old who was beginning to show signs of poor nutrition... endless lethargy and constipation.

Feb.4th 1941. 'Three lodgers had to help me hold the child down for an enema. She became a wild animal, screaming and kicking, it was indescribable. I don't suppose she'll ever forgive me. I can't cope with this sort of behaviour. She is full of sudden fevers and un-explained pains.' Here was the old story about 'crying wolf'. Erika began to ignore her child's endless complaints and self-pitying whininess. But then she discovered an infected tooth, which had to be pulled out...

When Erika and Reini were not speculating about the war they analysed their offspring. The verdict was not great: slow to learn, did not listen, remembered nothing, lazy, rude, shy, clumsy, ferociously stubborn, morose and permanently constipated. Erika felt she recognized some of those traits from *her* side of the family and resolved to apply conscientious character-training.

The first inspired thing she did was to buy a light bulb for the outside lavatory. That awful darkness, far too distracting for six-year olds, was one of the problems. Daily prunes did the rest... so much more pleasing than enemas. From this time onwards there wasn't a month when Erika did not have to call the doctor. Her child had endless fevers, infections and childhood illnesses. During one of these illnesses the bored child studied Erika's hands: 'Mutti, why have you got such ugly hands...and your face, why does it have so many lines?'

All Erika could afford was a large pot of Nivea Crème. Poor Erika. She was in her mid-thirties and felt cheated. Her day-to day existence was dreary and predictable... she felt lonely, stressed and lost.

Would she have liked another child? On balance, probably not. More than aware of the lack of a real home, that her child was growing up surrounded by strangers, without a father, and that children *should* have siblings as she herself had experienced, and was behaving like a spoilt brat, receiving far too much attention from her own mother...no, definitely not. Some of the German ladies found employment of one sort or another. Erika soon began to regret she'd had no specific training; recalling those long letters to Reini while she was still at school in Hamburg. In those days she'd been talked *out* of studying or learning some skills, and all by the very man who was now helplessly imprisoned and unable to provide any money.

In all likelihood Erika was clinically depressed. One way forward might be ...to *teach* something...German perhaps? But who would want to learn German? Still, it wasn't too long before she found some pupils, a life-line of sorts. How pleasing it must have been to collect a few pence.

Her biggest expense was the permanent ill health of her child: something unresolved in both body and soul of Knups. Dragged from one specialist to another theories were put forward: the altitude, dietary faults,...faults in the absorption of nutrients, nerve ends, water retention; supplements and tablets were prescribed also exercise or perhaps, *less* exercise: whatever came to light was soon superseded by another theory. But the child remained morose, fearful, un-co-operative, tired, unfriendly, tearful and worst of all, a thumb-sucker.

'Motherhood is not for me,' thought Erika.

At least she was never alone. The abandoned German wives were able to socialize and support one another with picnics and tea parties. They talked about their men, and, one expects, had views on the war. There was a yawning gap here, such matters were censored in correspondence and probably not aired in front of children. According to occasional 'bioscope' newsreels, the War looked very frightening indeed.

****

Still, fate had achieved *one* notable thing: Erika's child, settled into the German school, was learning to read and write in *three* languages, albeit with spectacularly bad results. Think about it, a six-year old brain bombarded in such a way could only produce a messy end-product: letters penned by the tri-lingual offspring were touchingly, embarrassingly bad. Erika would have welcomed a better school: 'that nearby convent school which offers free *religious* instruction to small heathens, that's just what our daughter needs, but it is too expensive; besides your child becomes hysterical when faced by wrinkled nuns, even just to be taught the catechism'... Eka told her man.

There seemed to be absolutely no silver lining.

By 1942 the grown-ups had become increasingly resilient, guiding their offspring through sicknesses and health, through swimming lessons, picnics, birthdays, Xmases, school holidays and all the long daily events without any input from fathers, grandparents or any relatives whatsoever. Everything was recorded in letters and photographed for posterity. A notable event: the smashing of her child's two *new* front teeth after an unsuccessful leap down the stairs: the bleeding and screaming child was delivered by a 'big' boy (who happened to be passing) to the horrified Erika. Thanks to much clever filing by a dentist, a new Mona Lisa was created, with a mysterious tooth-hiding smile.

1942: ballet classes for Erika's lumpen offspring.

1943: exams, 'Eisteddfods'... Pretoria style, and more curious illnesses.

Dearest, you can't imagine how depressed I feel. Will this bloody war ever end? I know you'll be completely un-impressed when I confess I wasted money on a fortune teller in town. I went along and within ten minutes she told me all about our daughter and also that you and I will soon be together again, unexpectedly soon. I hope she's right. I had told her that you were 'away', so as not to give her too many clues. As for Knups....she will become 'an artist of some kind', according to the woman. She was a bit stumped when I pressed her. 'Maybe music, maybe painting, something creative....was her best shot. There's been no post from you for six days, is everything alright?'

1944. Suddenly: some wind of the 'authorities' planning an exchange of prisoners of war.... the Belvedere wives had all but given up thinking about the war, so being offered the possibility of returning to Europe seemed improbable and unwise, surely? The cinema newsreels were certainly no inducement to return to Germany.

Even so, when the offer came, halfway through 1944, to be transported by ocean-liner, *fully protected by both British and German navy*, first to Portugal and then by train through Spain and France to the ' Vaterland', most long-separated couples decided to risk it, to go home. Had they been listening to inflated German propaganda on the radio? How else could they possibly have considered leaving the safety of South Africa? The internees had endured camp life for four whole years; most had elderly parents in Germany, some already suffering frightening hardships ...no-one really knew what was going on over there.....

****

After four years in the 'kitchen' the adjoining larder contained a fair number of books, cradles, crayons, comics and even a dolls-house, made by Reini in the camp...all the property of nine-year old Ingeborg-Evelyn. None of this was permitted as luggage on the return journey.

Parsimonious Erika positioned her child on the street corner outside the boarding house, along with books, old comics, her dolls house and other toys: 'Ask passers-by to buy your things', she said ...'you're nine years old, you need your own wristwatch. Any money left can be used to buy sweets to take with us. There will be absolutely none to be found in Germany, because of the War,' Erika warned, looking her sternest.

Some days later followed an exciting 30 hour train journey from Pretoria to Port Elisabeth, where a vast Swedish ocean liner, the Drottningholm, lay in the docks awaiting about 990 Germans. The gleaming white vessel was clearly marked with the Red Cross sign and also had a green line encircling the body of the ship. This was the international signal to denote 'passage without hindrance.'

But first there were uniformed customs officials: no-one was allowed off the train until luggage and persons had been carefully searched. Each traveller was allowed one piece of luggage and £25 in cash. (British and South African exchange prisoners embarking in

Europe to return home, had similar restrictions.) There were controls, documents and formalities, the blinds of each carriage were pulled down while officials did a thorough search for hidden diamonds, weapons, illegal things, military information. It was hot and it took hours and hours…

All sweets were confiscated by S.A. Customs. Might they have contained smuggled diamonds? Erika had some difficulty getting through to her distraught daughter, who'd never been *that* close to armed, uniformed officials before, and was behaving appallingly.

Still: out there was an enormous ocean liner and somewhere inside it there would be a man called 'Vati', (which sounds terrible in English but pleasing in German), so, 'never mind the sweeties, in a minute we will see our wonderful Vati again.'

****

Women were allowed to board first. Erika, who discovered the family were assigned a 4-bed inside cabin on E-deck, ie. the lowest deck on the ship, started to get the luggage down, to move in.

She was greeted by a missionary's wife who enquired how big Erika's family was. 'Only three,' the wife exclaimed, 'we are five! Would you mind if one of our children shared *your* cabin?'

Erika smiled wanly but somehow managed an instant 'star-turn' as an ex-shipping agents' wife: a steward in charge of assigning passengers was found and she begged him to see if there hadn't been some mistake.

'But no, madam, you are down for a cabin with two children, Ingeborg and Evelyn'. The friendly Swede got one of Erika's most winning smiles as she pleaded with him to try once more: 'I know from years of experience in the shipping world that there are always some free cabins at the last minute, do please have another look'…

And indeed, a cabin for three was found. The luck of the Ihlenfeldts! They were to find themselves in a luxury cabin, with a small seating area and a curtained- off double bed for the parents.

Married men were scheduled to board at dusk. Their women stood near the gangway, screaming, weeping, rejoicing, singing, waiting to embrace their men folk, whom they had not touched, even with their fingertips, for four years…

Later that evening most children were bribed with chocolate and many loving promises, to get some sleep, while the re-united couples explored the topography of the boat and even found the bar, which was by now doing big business with men celebrating their freedom. Four alcohol-free years had gone by. The reserves of the 'Drottningholm' were soon reduced to such an extent that only beer and a few bottles of wine remained after the first fortnight of the journey had passed.

The trip to Lisbon was to take four weeks, allowing for only very modest speeds. The idea was to keep a distance from any coast, travelling more or less up the middle of the Atlantic due north. Every two hours the captain reported his position to the German and the British admiralty who gave orders to all warships in the area to leave the 'Drottningholm' in peace.

During this interminable crossing the invasion of the Anglo-American troops in northern France had begun. French partisans or resistance fighters were active, exploding bridges and closing down railway lines; the counter transport of British prisoners from France was also greatly delayed. 'South Africans', once arrived in Lisbon, were lodged in 5-star hotels, organised by the German embassy: 900 Germans took over Lisbon, Cascais, Estoril and Domingos, places which used to be homes of exiled royalty. Luggage was tagged with DIPLOMAT labels, while each family received handsome amounts of cash from the German government.

Unbelievably, in 1944, *at the height of the war,* there were British, French and American guests at other tables in the hotels. Everyone behaved politely and correctly, if in a somewhat restrained manner.

Life, now filled with daily excursions and shopping for things which were going to be useful 'at home,' was thought to be completely delightful.

The idyll lasted one month. Then, close to departure, a doctor was called: Erika was 'unwell' and must remain horizontal. All three Ihlenfeldts were assigned a sleeper-coach, to share with the patient. This was good: the one-day journey took a whole week. Bad in one way, but fortunate in another: Erika and Reini might have had a second child by mid-May 1945 but fate had decided against it.

While the loathed 'boches' edged their way through France, via Biarritz (another very royal hotel) they escaped several partisan attacks and explosions. As the train crept along, hiding in tunnels, passengers often had to change over onto coaches, but in the end there was a safe arrival in Heilbronn, Germany. Here the family was quartered in barracks for two days to undergo 'Nazi indoctrination' of 'heroic' dimensions: they were issued passports, food coupons, clothes coupons, train tickets, pocket money…

And then the Ihlenfeldts stepped out for a walk in the Heilbronn Park to discover what a bombed city looks like. In a restaurant they ordered roast venison for three, and learned (too late) they had consumed their entire months' meat ration. At night, woken by air-raid sirens, they slipped into elegant silk dressing gowns, Erika's with swans-down collar and sleeves, and appeared in the shelter looking like extras from a film-set. Reini and Eka were a triumphal success...the expressions on the soldiers' faces with their steel helmets and gasmasks hard to describe... No-one knew that only four months later the British would send 244 planes to drop 1249 tons of bombs on this 600-year-old city, decimating the place and killing seven thousand people in 20 minutes.

In 1944 the rail system in Germany was a somewhat haphazard affair. To get from one place to another was a question of sitting on the required platform and waiting. Erika was as excited as a small child before Christmas...even though she'd been sitting on platforms in Heilbronn, and then in Salzburg, for hours, (gazing at the ruins of the once glamorous Hotel de l'Europe, where she had stayed in better times). Eventually a slow, stopping train deposited the family in Klagenfurt. It was 3 o'clock in the morning. The station, partly destroyed by bombs, harboured a Red Cross office where the Ihlenfeldts slept, huddled together on a hard wooden bench and a birthing chair.

The Red Cross contacted the military station nearby who sent a messenger to the castle. Not too long after an open, horse-drawn carriage pulled up outside the station and there they were: Mami and Papi, arms out-stretched, bursting with questions.

'Why *couldn't you wait* for the war to end ...are you out of your minds coming back now...did you really *have* to....?' The older generation examined their exhausted daughter, their grandchild, the bedraggled state of the weary travellers and quickly realised only one thing was needed: no more questions, just a hot bath and a long sleep.

***

'How lovely: Magaregg in warm Autumn sunshine!'

Erika was sitting outside with a cup of coffee; the 'refugees' had made themselves at home, loving every precious moment, relaxed and safe for a few contented weeks.

'It's almost as hot as Pretoria, sitting out here in the sun', Erika moved her chair into the shade while Papi pulled his hat forward to shade his bulbous red nose. 'Jause' (coffee-break) on the lawn by the fantastically ancient Roman urn was a family tradition.

'Where is *my* Knupslein?' Mami offered Erika freshly baked Streusel cake...'I tried yesterday to explain about my sisters and

Neumarktl, but I'm not sure she was really listening, she was so surprised to see the mountains turning pink….actually, your daughter was in danger of falling from the window in the tower…not even Papi seems to know why the Karawanken blush at sunset…'

Mami had to try hard not to crowd in on Knups, who appeared to have no memory of her earliest years in Hamburg. Of course Mami admitted she was disappointed… it was hard to understand. 'But then, we've been separated almost five years. Can it really be so long? She seems a very innocent nine-year old! Has she accepted her father yet, after the camp, do you think it's all going to be 'normal' now, Ekalein? What a miserable four years you three have had, we thought about you every day, you know; but we still believe you shouldn't have returned…the Nazi's are as oppressive as ever…you will learn to keep your head down...the situation is more than serious. Do you and Reini have any idea what is going on in our country? You should have remained in Africa, Ekalein, believe me, coming back was a mistake…'

Erika, strangely disoriented and weakened by the miscarriage, felt overwhelmed by dread and sadness: 'too late, we are here now.'

Cölestine informed Erika about the recent death of her own mother: The gracious, almost centenarian Grossi had passed away peacefully, tended by daughters Grethe and by poor Valerie, the failed opera singer.

'I'm terribly concerned about these sisters of mine,' confessed Mami, 'they live alone in the house Grossi has left them and seem to be drinking too much. They want to keep the house and cling to each other even though they don't really get on. Lost souls, that's what they are. What can I do?'

There was some relief for Erika: to feel her parents were 'parenting' *her*, and that Reini was by her side. But, and there always is a 'but'…*he must move on to his own parents*, up in that small harbour town on the Baltic, where he knows he is truly needed; his own father, now eighty years old, was no longer able to run the business without help. Reini certainly did not like the idea of going off alone. The pressure was on Erika to agree to travel with him once more. A case of divided loyalties. Choices had to be made. And Winter would soon be on its way.

*Erika's man had vowed to be a **non-combattant**, carried official papers to prove he'd been locked up in a camp for four years. He'd come 'home' to be of help to his octogenarian parents.*

Erika had seen little of her in-laws, had once admitted not feeling too comfortable in their company during short visits in the 1930's. Reini understood and really could not hold this against her, if anything, he agreed, 'but I am a dutiful son, there *is* a job to be done, I *have* to go. Ekalein, will you come? Please come with me?'

How could she refuse?

Reini and Erika were either completely fearless or totally uninformed about the war. Is it at all conceivable that Germans, even Austrians, had no inkling what lay ahead in the next six or seven months?

The only sign of war near Mageregg were military barracks close by which Ingeborg-Evelyn-Knups got to know rather well: the care-taker's daughter, exactly the same age, invited the 'South African girl' to come along to a tiny class especially for children of soldiers stationed in the area, in this way half of each day was spent catching up on basic skills, reading and writing German and presumably some arithmetic.

Erika, an exceptionally intelligent adult, was also stubborn, ambitious and snobbish, but above all she tended to be extremely negative. Reini was often 'up against it' when it came to important decisions which had to be resolved jointly.

Still, her surprising decision to go to Pomerania with him was probably based on two aching facts: the memory of those four years *alone* in Pretoria and the fear that something might happen to him, another separation, or worse. Neither of them had the faintest inkling what they were letting themselves in for.

****

An adventurous train journey, almost due north: passing the ruins of Berlin; ('look Knupslein, see all those broken houses....don't forget this sight, this was once a very important town') and some two hours later the South African Ihlenfeldts moved in with two, decrepit, ancient German Ihlenfeldts in their small harbour-town house on the Baltic.

Reini wasted no time, went to work straight away with his father in the office downstairs. The double-story house, situated directly in the harbour, was separated from docked ships by ancient elms, a wide cobbled road and railway tracks along the docks.

Erika soon found her bearings: 'I've seen it all before, during happier times, on visits from Hamburg, or Accra. That spectacular view of most of the harbour, a good thing from the point of view of the shipping agent, and quite interesting, I suppose,....but what's this, on the right, a large low concrete air-raid shelter sunken into the ground...this is certainly something new.

Well, my turn to roll up my sleeves, do my bit.

Can this really be Ida, the once imposing Admiral's daughter, just look at her now, shrivelled and bent...a shadow. And this dark, neglected home: downstairs the outmoded office of the shipping agency, and up from the large entrance, the steep staircase to the second floor, just as I remember. It all looks so dusty, dingy and primitive, everything from another era...

One pulls a chord: a brass bell jingles, and when the door is opened one steps into the dark hall, the drawing room to the right, cobwebby and antiquated...across the space, by the windows stand two tall, dusty, ornate porcelain vases decorated elaborately with colourful china flowers and leaves, I'd forgotten those....and on the other side *still* that laughable spittoon and that splendid upright piano with fancy brass candleholders, a stool to match, velvet tassels festoon the cushioned part... the child will love that! Awkward to move about: the old people have pushed the dining table into the centre of the living room; it normally 'lived' in the dining room,...'(how did they do that, it is so heavy?)'

'Erika dear, it is impossible to keep so many rooms heated,' explains Ida in a quivery voice. How thin, how shrunken she'd become; formerly a proudly elegant woman from Berlin, the 'beautiful Frau Ihlenfeldt'; she'd been a fine singer as well as a skilled water-colourist...and now? Gnarled, stooping, shrivelled, without servants? How does she manage?

And here: a rusty bathroom tub with equally rusty clawed feet! And, oh God, the wooden toilet, still at the back of the garden, and those musty disturbing smells everywhere, indefinably worrying, everything dark, do they ever open windows? Ida and Alexander, both in their eighties, they must have been struggling for some time'.

Erika, torn between dismay and pity, hears the telephone and voices of the office staff, filtering up through the floorboards below.

****

Erika found time to write to her mother: 'We've survived three weeks of life by the Baltic. For the first time we are face to face with the real Germany: nothing in the shops, daily and nightly visits to the air-raid shelter, artificial fog, (smoke-screens) in our harbour area, (to fool the bombers), and now this icy wind from the North East ...Ida has loaned me a black fur coat, one that cousin Berthold 'brought back' from army service in France two years ago, 'you can keep it, Erika,' she said, 'you will need it here.' Best not to ask too many questions about that one then! But I did try it on most grace- and grate-fully. Weeks later she writes:

'With some effort we've managed a Christmas tree and carols (and another dolls-house made by Reini, for Knups) there has even been a fair, where we bought the tree and handmade wooden toys and crafts and arty things. It did feel Christmassy in the way I used to dream about during the hot summer Decembers of Pretoria...Now there is snow and ice; Knupslein is so impressed.'

Erika wonders whether her letters are still getting to Klagenfurt.

'There have been so many air-raids. Because of constant air alarms and smoke-screens to protect the harbour area, I must keep the child indoors, the school is too far from here. But I've signed her up for a weekly piano lesson with an elderly lady, about ten minutes away. Once the route has been absorbed by our eager pianist-to-be she will be sent off on her own. I'm surprised how keen she is: already there are signs of rapid progress, she sits at this piano completely in another world, for hours. Well, there is little else to do. I have devised schoolwork, to stop her, still so baby-ish and immature, from falling even further behind in the three R's. Dearest Mami, we so miss you, and Papi, of course!'

When, one day, on the way home from piano lessons, the alarms wailed and the smoke screens welled up, Knups, who had to cut through a park to get home, choose a wrong turning... 'all the bushes looked the same'...and, hopelessly lost, darting this way and that, had no idea what to do. Erika panicked for the first time: 'I stood, then I ran up and down in front of the house looking in every possible direction, cursing myself for letting her go on her own. I am a terrible mother.' Fortunately there was no air-raid. Knubs arrived home some 15 minutes later to be smothered with hugs and a few tears.

'*One cannot be too careful. I was shaken, did not even dare tell Reini...*'

****

In January 1945 Reini received a call from the local SS Headquarters with an order to present himself at 9.30 am. on the following day.

'May I ask what this is about', Reini enquired cautiously.

'You will find out when we see you tomorrow,' barked a voice on the line.

Reinhold might have been only marginally less surprised if a bomb had exploded next to him. What possible interest could the Gestapo have in a man who had come back to a near-destroyed Germany from the safety of South Africa to assist his old parents?

When called by the Gestapo one must expect anything and everything. He was more than a little concerned. Was it because he had not signed up with the Territorial Army? He did have papers issued by the highest authority in Berlin: he was absolved from military duties as an *exchanged prisoner of war*. Reinhold instructed his secretary to telephone the Chancellery in Berlin if she had not heard from him by 5pm, after his interview. She was to tell them he had been taken by the Gestapo, explaining all the circumstances and to ask for *immediate intervention*.

At Gestapo headquarters he was told to sit on a wooden bench in a corridor for an hour. Were these unnerving sixty minutes designed to intimidate candidates before such an interview?

'Mr. Lewien will see you now...' Reinhold was not sure he'd heard correctly: Levin, Levy, Lewien...there were many possibilities.

He was offered a chair and wondered about that too. First the usual questions; name, address, age, occupation, religion, and so on:

'Why are you not registered with the Territorial Army?'

Aha. So that was it! Reini explained the whole story about the oath he'd made in South Africa, as an exchange prisoner.

'An oath made in front of a British citizen does not count as an oath in Germany,' was coldly offered in response.

'I have documentation signed by the highest authorities,' ventured Reini. An extremely long, stifling, smouldering silence elapsed...until 'Mr. Levine' shuffled his papers, opened a drawer and pulled out a book to look up something. There followed another prolonged pause.

Eventually, frowning, he deigned to reply:

'Alright, let's leave it at that. But would you mind telling me why your daughter never says 'Heil Hitler' when she fetches the milk from the milk cart in the morning?'

Now followed lengthy explanations about growing up in South Africa, where no-one says 'Heil Hitler' and that the nine-year old had not yet got used to living in Germany. 'Well, see to it you re-train her at once, Herr Ihlenfeldt! It was planned to keep you here, but you had best pay more attention to matters of this kind.'

So much for Gestapo methods.

'From now on I fetch the milk myself' decided Erika. 'My daughter's adventures in Swinemünde must become even more curtailed. Although I can perhaps still let her go tobogganing in the park area by the air-raid shelter... it is within shouting distance of the house and office.'

In January and February it snowed heavily, later the frost was severe. Erika kept an eye on her daughter's movements from the veranda. She also observed hundreds of refugees coming off the ships each day, poor people carrying shabby cases and sacks, homeless, cold and starving with nowhere to go. Desperate, some came to the doorway, begged to stay the night, even if it was just on the floor of the entrance hall. It was pitiful. In return they offered a measure of flour or some potatoes from their miserable supplies, food salvaged in their flight from the Russians.

****

Erika, crouching on her haunches, scooped flour, with her bare hands from the open sack into a small clay pot from the kitchen. 'I could make dumplings with this and they go well with gooseberries', she thought, looking up at one of the refugees. 'But thank-you for this precious stuff. Are you sure you can spare it? 'The only thing Erika's mother-in-law *did* have were rows of bottled gooseberries, stored on a high shelf in the outside loo, of all places... the wooden one at the bottom of the garden.

Suddenly Erika became hysterical, frantically scratching about in the sack of flour, shaking her head, sobbing because her wedding ring had fallen off into the flour and could not be found. She had lost so much weight, her fingers were bony. Her hands were shaking...

****

'We speak endlessly about getting on a ship, anything to leave Swinemünde' thought Erika 'yet these refugees think *this* is safety.... Persuading the older generation that staying in this harbour town is a problem, well, it's a waste of time. It is something they simply don't want to hear...'

'The Russians won't do anything to us' the old people pleaded, 'we can't leave all our things...our whole life is here...'

Peenemünde, on the island Usedom, was only a few miles away. This was where the V2 rockets were developed and made. It did therefore seem surprising that Swinemünde harbour had never been bombed. The Russians were making advances on sea and land along the Baltic and, by the 12th of March could already be heard clearly in the distance. It was perhaps at *their* request that the allied forces deployed 700 American bombers to drop 1435 bombs onto the harbour and the town.....

The alarm went off at lunchtime. Reini escorted his mother down the stairs to the shelter (a Splitter Schutz-bunker), a sunken but above-ground, thick-walled concrete construct, and Erika was to follow with her father-in-law. The old man refused to budge. He sat on his rocking chair in the centre of the living room, and glowering at her he declared: 'I want to die in my own home. Go away. Take your child, Erika, go to the bunker. Leave me alone!'

Erika, by now too terrified to reason with him hurried her child down the stairs and out to the bunker only about ten yards away. The bunker door was already shut. She knocked, then banged on the heavy iron door but there was no response. She took off her shoe and hammered the heel hard on the door.

It opened, just a little. She pushed her child in and followed... then the warden slammed the door, bolted it again, pushed heavy things in front of it. Within minutes the inferno began. After each mighty explosion the bunker rocked and swayed, like a ship. People moaned, wept, screamed, held each other tight. Erika noted her child was praying. 'The nuns in Pretoria had achieved something after all...that's where we should have stayed,' crossed her mind, after the first of many crushing explosions...

One hour later, after the 'all-clear,' the door pushed open by the warden, traumatized women, children and a few ancient men climbed out, clinging to each other in a blinded, and cautious way. It was hard to breathe. Where-ever one looked there was a dense haze of dust and smoke. Stepping out into uncertainty, bits of people scattered and piled about, here a leg, there a torso, no-one could walk in a straight line, there were bodies, parts of bodies, there was rubble. The houses still stood. But where were the seven docked ships, full of refugees from the East...had they also tried to get into the bunker? Where could they be?

Erika held her child's hand as they climbed up the grey dusty staircase...the front door wide open and there, in his rocking chair, sat the eighty-year old, grinning inanely, unharmed, apart from being covered in plaster. The inside of the house was just about habitable although some window frames had been blasted out, no glass left in the windows...the place was filthy, freezing, but it stood, it had a roof. It can be sorted', said Reini, looking around. 'God, we are the lucky ones!'

*

Erika's time had come: She was in charge.

Unspeakable days followed. Over 20.000 inhabitants, refugees and soldiers were declared dead and half the town was flattened.

The park was a mess of toppled trees, dead bodies, probably refugees from ships, were scattered everywhere. All roads were blocked. Days, weeks passed until all corpses were put to rest in a mass grave on the Golmberg 5kms outside Swinemünde. What little remained of the town was completely useless, there was no water, gas or electricity supply, and no prospect of any repairs.

Erika swept and swept, pushed, commandeered her man: find candles, matches, nails, planks, cardboard, anything to stop the cold coming in,' find wood, get water in the bucket'…Reini carried buckets of water from a mediaeval pump several blocks away. Sanitation, well, that was mediaeval too. But there was wood to burn and the old stove in the kitchen was just the thing, under the circumstances. Official recommendation to 'vacate' the town had by now been posted everywhere.

It really was time to go. The Russians were coming.

The older Ihlenfeldts remained in complete denial of the reality around them. They had witnessed the streams of refugees passing their home for months now, seen stiff corpses unloaded in nets like so much dead cattle, seen children dragging the dead on toboggans to the mass graves…'*You* must go', they said, 'please, you three go, we want to stay, in our house, with our things, the Russians won't do anything to us….'

Eventually an old friend, a former Africa-captain, bumped into Reini on the street and finally managed to persuade the bewildered, old folk to accept a cabin on a freighter going to Lübeck. He was even able to contact friends in Lübeck who would arrange a room in an Old People's Home. Some days later the younger Ihlenfeldts were also safely stowed in a small cabin (nobly vacated by the ship's cook,) on a freighter to Kiel. The fire in the stove was still on when Erika handed the house keys to yet another captain known by Reini. This man offered to act as caretaker.

For the first time in months Erika felt relatively safe. God knows there was little enough reason to feel safe, but there was nothing more she could contribute to every-ones' well-being.

She had no idea what their own ships' cargo was. The Baltic was heavily mined and ships were torpedoed each day.

It was wise to move extremely slowly and only at certain times. One might be blown sky-high at any moment. When she finally learned the cargo of their boat was torpedoes she had not realise the 24 hour journey would take *nine* days.

It was slow and agonisingly dangerous progress. The family were dropped off at the furthest end of Kiel harbour, right by the railway station. Later, when they set foot in a small town called Eutin, they were met by old friends, the Heyers, from Cape Town days, who had arrived to meet them with a small wooden cart for transporting the luggage; Erika's ten-year old helped to drag it over the cobbled streets, and what a racket it made: 'blublublublu,' echoing between the walls of houses, no wonder the noisy thing was called a 'Bullerwagen'.

Fifteen minutes later Erika realised they were *really and truly* right by a lake… inside a picture-book, fairy-tale, half-timbered house: three floors up: right under a roof, three beds with big puffy featherbed covers, a table carrying a large bowl and water jug, sunlight pouring in by the window and poor Reini's head hitting the eaves and door frames every time he moved….a small price to pay…because they 'd made it, safe out of reach of the Russian invasion and far away from that terrible grey house, now lonesome and abandoned to Russians right in the harbour of Swinemünde.'

****

The name **Eutin** derived from 'Uit' and 'In', because eons ago, when it was a small settlement, it was surrounded by a town wall with two gates: 'Out 'and 'In'. Populated by people who spoke Danish, Dutch and German in mediaeval times there was and is, to this day, a local dialect called 'Platt-Deutsch' (low German') which has its charms, but sounds pretty incomprehensible. Perhaps it is a little like Danish.

Such a romantic place: a castle in a park, a church and a market; nearly every house with trellised roses growing up the walls and at the bottom of a slight hill shimmered a lake, surrounded by forests and ever more lake, in fact it was all part of the 'Switzerland' of Schleswig Holstein. After the dour depressing Swinemünde Erika felt reassured.

They also made contact with Reini's parents, now settled in an old people's home in Lübeck, about an hour's drive away.

Soon an attic room with a slightly higher ceiling was found at Bahnhofstrasse 10, offered by a distant family member of the Heyer clan: this was to become 'home' for a very long time. The wallpaper, unforgettably yellow, and covered with ornate curly roses and leaves, one biggish bed for the parents and, horrors… a prickly straw filled mattress for the child… by the door, a coal stove and on the other side a bowl and jug on a wash-stand. There were two windows. When these were opened you would come pretty close to being able to leap across into a Post Office window.

'How grateful I am, so very grateful, for absolutely everything....' thought Erika. 'It is Spring, the sun shines, the lilac on the Mahlstedt-strasse, with that indescribable scent...how lovely it all is.'

Meals and social life took place downstairs with the kindly hostess and her daughter, a large girl with huge staring eyes. Ursula was a year older than Ingeborg-Evelyn-Knups, but could not go to school because she was mentally retarded. She did everything she was told without protest. Her mother, Inge Heyer, was coping as best she could without a husband who was still at the front, in Russia, she believed.

In some ways Inge Heyer was pleased to look after refugees, and soon found things for them to do. It was all 'go' with the 'refugees'; first a school had to be found (easy, 10 minutes away) then a job was needed for Reini, (not so easy, where were the ships?) and what about Erika? As it turned out, this was the simplest thing: Inge Heyer ran a crafts/gift shop, right there in the house, opening out onto the pavement, with a window displaying pottery, brass and wooden objects... although not exactly brisk...but there always were customers, hoping to buy a birthday present or two. Erika was soon running the shop and gratefully so, for cooking was never her forte. Frau Heyer took care of meals for the entire household. She put hot meals on the table when there was absolutely nothing in the shops. She had recipes up her sleeve Erika could only marvel at: the unforgettable 'Grosse Hans', more than likely a Danish dish: if you were able to lay your hands on some flour, fat or lard and bottled pears you could shape a huge dumpling, steam it and serve it up with the heated fruit in it's own thickened sauce. Indescribably delicious! Then there was elderberry soup, also served hot, with dumplings. Erika had never heard of such delights, and indeed, when there was simply nothing else everything became a treat. Scratching about in a coop were a few chickens, who conscientiously laid very precious eggs from time to time.

One evening word got around: a military train was stuck in the station. Just four minutes along the road! After sunset, in the dark, Reinhold and two friends decided to 'inspect' the train. The men did indeed come home with sugar, butter, coffee and flour, stowed away in their bulging jackets.

'Stealing for *your family* does not count,' stated Erika, 'besides, the soldiers always have more than anyone else.'

There didn't seem to be a war in Eutin. Well, not like the one in Swinemünde, anyway...

Some weeks later, when the British advanced and occupied Eutin, and *the war had actually been declared 'over'(* May 1945), Erika's man was at last able to find something more sensible (and less dangerous) to do. He realized the Brits would need an interpreter. He penned a letter to the Commander of the military government, offering his services. They snapped him up. After enquiries about Reini's past politics and general skills (he had never joined the party) he was asked to appear for work on the following day, along with several other Germans with language skills. They were allowed into the military canteen to have a substantial lunch.

Critical events at this time were: locating rooms, halls, anywhere at all, for the constant stream of refugees from the East. Reini had to requisition homes from the good citizens of Eutin, for military personnel and for refugees. The population of this little town was gradually swelling to a 100% increase:. bursting at the seams. Medical supplies were unavailable, there was no food, there were no clothes. The workload was indescribable. After two weeks of stress Reinhold Ihlenfeldt was instructed by the Military Commander to take on the role of 'Bürgermeister' ie. Mayor of Eutin. At first he could hardly believe his ears and his reasons for refusing this honourable task were numerous. There were meetings with other possible candidates and with British officers, but in the end, when even gentle bribery wasn't making him relent ('you will be well paid, you will be respected, you only need commonsense and there will always be experts on hand when you feel you don't have specialized knowledge, the military government will requisition a suitable home for you...'), Reinhold still could not see himself in this role.

The persuasive Brits nagged on. They finally swayed him by reminding him he'd 'come back to his homeland to *help his country*,' and now was the time he was truly needed. That got to him...he finally agreed.

'I will do this work on one condition,' countered Reinhold, 'if you come across someone better qualified to do this job you will release me from my duties at once!' 'Splendid', said Colonel Gray, shaking the new mayor by the hand. On the 17th May 1945, printed notices were to be seen in all the shop-windows announcing the name of the new mayor, Herr *Reinhold Ihlenfeldt* and that all his instructions must be obeyed. Signed :

THE BRITISH MILITARY GOVERNMENT
W H. Gray .   Lt. Colonel R.M. Jones.

Erika was stunned. Here she was, in a tiny attic, sharing a bed with the Mayor of Eutin! And this was a man who had recently robbed a German military train in the dark night... *and* one who had turned down the offer of better accommodation.... Still, she was so proud of him.

With other ladies she immediately took on the role of distributing the famous American CARE parcels to refugees and other needy folk. For her child there were no civic duties until a year later, when she curtsied and presented a bouquet of flowers to some dignitary at a conference for European Unity. In a borrowed white dress, white ribbons on the ends of her pigtails, Erika's child made her first appearance in a newspaper.

Erika's 'job' got her into the midst of people far less fortunate than herself---those who slept on hay in sheds and barns, wrapped in rough grey army blankets, those who needed medical attention, and had little to eat and nothing to do but wait until 'something' might happen, whatever that might be. In those first years after the war there was little to do but wait and see. Refugees continued to flow in and out of towns all over Germany and the British, American and French occupiers had their in-trays full of chaos and misery.

Everyone had to improvise, especially the mayor's wife, setting a good example. She watched and learned how to cope with even less than she had *ever imagined possible*. She learned how one chats up a farmer for a few baskets of sugar-beet, how to get them home and even how to turn them into a sticky brown substance, to smear on bread or to use as sweetener.

In the cellar, in an old-fashioned copper bowl, large enough to scrub down the girls, one at a time,(Inge Heyer enjoyed this weekly task with mind boggling thoroughness...as there was no bathroom). This cauldron was kept in a very basic laundry room, along with logs and coal and a fireplace.

Erika would wonder about its multiple uses when a log and coal fire was lit under the pot, then filled with chopped beet to simmer, bubble and spit in a friendly way, emitting an unforgettable odour. Huge numbers of glass jars filled with the stuff were lined up on the shelves in the cellar, along with other bottled fruits and berries. The cellar was endlessly fascinating, and Erika had no idea that her daughter found it somewhat piquant but also frightening to be scrubbed *together* with Ursula in the same cauldron as those deliciously smelly sugar beets.

Hanging on bent metal coat hangers were sad stretched furs of rabbits, like small discarded coats, their former owners having given their all to keep everyone supplied with protein. In the corner, on the floor, lay a wormy heap of potatoes, and masses of shrivelled apples.

Some months after arrival a larger, more pleasing room with kitchenette on the second floor became available. Erika turned this space into a 'mayoral' bed-sit while the attic became the domain of her now eleven year old daughter. By now a *real* housewife lucky Erika owned saucepans of her own, one unforgettably, made from an army helmet. And things being as primitive as they were, the basin in the kitchenette had to do for ablutions as well. There was only one WC for everyone in the house and no bathroom. Erika soon discovered the Public Baths, a quaint affair only five minutes away, where, after a long wait, one had to pay for ten minutes in a small cubicle containing an old-fashioned bathtub with clawed feet. Did the famous Burgomaster Reinhold Ihlenfeldt ever have enough time, in those post-war years, to have a bath?

*****

As the years passed, friends and colleagues invited Erika and her man to dinner, to the yacht club and to parties in each others' homes. Just like in Cape Town and Accra 'Eka and Reini' were much appreciated and always enjoyed a busy social life.

But the *older* Ihlenfeldts, who never really recovered from the shock of their flight from the Russians, died peacefully, in quick succession and were buried in Lübeck. Sad as this was, it was a relief to all concerned

Soon Erika longed to see *her* own parents again. The slow process of the German recovery after total destruction of railways and roads made travel chaotic. She did eventually make it to Klagenfurt for a few weeks; the castle had been requisitioned by American troops but her parents were living in a small house nearby. Erika endured adventurous hardship trying to get to her parents, at one stage even travelling in a cattle truck. She was generally much given to exaggeration, but no-one was ever able to disprove this.

Her beloved Reini's greatest happiness was sailing about on the Eutiner See. He never owned a sailboat of his own but knew enough persons who were honoured to lend him theirs and the annual regattas and events kept him fit and content. Capsizing once or twice was all part of the fun. Neither of his two women were all that keen, however, with some bribery, Reini's 12 year-old spent many weekends baling out a slightly less than watertight boat while learning to keep her head down when the sail changed sides in the wind; a *valuable lesson in life's vicissitudes.*

Erika did her level best to keep *out* of sailing boats.

Life-long friendship developed between the Ihlenfeldts and Col. Reginald Jones, the man in charge of Eutin and the surrounding area in

Schleswig Holstein as representative of the British military government. The Joneses lived in Pulverbeck, a grand requisitioned house on the edge of the lake. He and his wife Betty were delighted to find Germans like Erika and Reini who spoke English and were willing to give them insights into the current situation. Such personal friendships were considered irregular at the time, but mutual sympathy carried them through any unspoken criticism, from both German *and* British circles.

At this time a painful (instantly suppressed) sadness took hold of Erika. She noticed that Reini had made a conquest at the many parties they attended and how his eyes gave him away during conversations with and about the lady in question.

Always sitting together, always touching each other.... 'how can this be, after all we've been through together,' Erika sighed, when she herself had never entertained such feelings about anyone else. 'Such a betrayal, such' ...no, she couldn't even admit it to herself. She did have her pride:

'Never *show* anyone you care *that* much' was her motto, and 'don't give anyone the satisfaction knowing you are *so* dependent', was another. All *she* managed was to turn in on herself in a negative way. Still young, she felt that terrible question endlessly haunting her: what am I doing here, and what good is it, what use am I?

An old-fashioned woman, she believed she existed for her husband, her daughter, and for her ageing parents. Yet, somehow this no longer added up. It never occurred to her that she could perhaps do or learn something new. There was no incentive. She felt trapped and depressed. She was forty-two years old.

Her man, now in his forty-seventh year, had persuaded himself that Europe was no longer the place for him: the only way forward was to return to Africa. *They did after all still own that funny little bungalow called 'Accra' on the edge of Lion's head, in Cape Town.* He had resigned from being Mayor in 1946, did some fairly mundane civil service job for the military government for two years and felt he was 'going nowhere,' achieving nothing. It was 1948: time for a change.

Erika was appalled. When it came to the crunch Africa was the last place she wanted to be. But once her husband got his teeth into something he would not give up until everything was carefully organized, every detail weighed up, corrected, planned, from every angle possible. This sounds tedious, but that's how he was, a stickler.

In retrospect his efficiency seemed a miracle. There were no international telephone calls, faxes and e-mails had not been invented.

There was 'snail mail' and also lovely old-fashioned telegrams, of course. The Post Office just happened to be right next door.

Within weeks he'd booked a cargo boat from Oslo, organized friends in South Africa to pay for it, accepted invitations from various persons to come and stay in South Africa, particularly some dear friends, with a guest farm. They were starting a business 'in jam'.

'Please, do come soon, dear 'Ihles'...the berries are ripening; we need you to help make Youngberry Jam while you find your feet in Africa... *Can you bring a large copper cauldron from Germany?'*

Of course, Reini would fix it.

A cauldron was specially constructed in Hamburg and shipped to the farm in South Africa. Other old friends, the Brinkmans, who had survived terrible air raids on Hamburg, were also planning to return to S.A....with hopes to set up a factory for 'Büstenhalter'. For those not in the know, these are 'brassieres.' The Brinkmans were no other than Pev, with her lame arm, her husband and their son Peter, the bane of Ingeborg's life in those Pretoria days, when all fathers were still in the camp.

So, Reini, dashing about, sometimes with, often without his family, organized the *great trek back to Africa,* while Erika and her child got on with normal life.

Just at this time poor Erika had the unpleasant task of explaining menstruation to her teenager. When this occurred for the first time there was that inevitable mother/daughter moment, when *things* had to be talked about. Erika was not much given to talk about 'things'.

As an enlightened and final treat Erika allowed her daughter to spend an idyllic day bicycling with a young admirer to a place called the Bungsberg, where the two youngsters swore undying love.

*****

There will be some 'fast-forwarding' now. It was summer 1949 and the Ihlenfeldts had reached Oslo by slow trains, via Denmark and Sweden. Reini's two women were sleepy and moody, but he was bubbling over: A boat trip, albeit on a freighter...and a fresh start, his favourite things...

Not *everyone* was happy: Erika, once settled in her cabin became embarrassingly withdrawn and appeared only for meals. This was her discreet way of showing displeasure. 'To be honest,' she admitted to everyone: 'living in Europe has been a terrifying adventure, but *I've* understood at last *where I belong.'*

Too late! A *good* wife must stick with her man, through thick and thin.

'You can always go back and visit', suggested Reini. Soon different problems loomed. The most pressing: finding a job for the head of the family.

After some time on a dreamily beautiful farm near Plettenberg Bay, with the most kind and generous friends anyone could hope for, Reini, ever positive, ever optimistic, set out again to knock on the doors of former contacts in Cape Town. Ten years had gone by since his last job had been so suddenly whisked away by WW2; he was nearing fifty.

It was hopeless: no one had any work for him. After several months of to-ing and fro-ing and much practical work on the farm, he began to fear he'd made *a bad* mistake. Bottling Youngberry jam was not exactly his idea of a career. And Erika said: 'I told you so'.....

Poor man, he'd left no stone unturned. Erika, on the other hand, had grown to love life on the farm and would have been perfectly happy to stay there for ever.

***

In the end something worth considering did come up: a managerial post in South West Africa, **Walvis Bay,** a small settlement in the Namib Desert with a fairly important harbour. At that time (1950) it was South Africa's only harbour on the West coast. In 1878 this natural deepwater harbour and the Namib Desert had been annexed by the British.

When the Germans acquired Southwest Africa from native chiefs in 1884 the British enclave was excluded and put under the administration of the Cape Province in South Africa. By the 1950's Walvis Bay was a miserable dump with 8000 inhabitants, some sandy roads, eight fish meal factories, a few houses and shops, many on stilts (because the place was prone to flooding), and the Railway Institute, the hub of what little social life there was.

Most inhabitants were native labourers in the harbour and factories, along with their families. Sturrock & Woker, the firm Reini was working for, provided employment for 20 Europeans and 120 Namibians.

There was also some connection with the Norwegian whale-industry which had stationed itself in Walvis Bay to process both whale meat and fish-oil. This installation had burnt down in 1950.

One day, when the newly arrived Reini was inspecting charred remains of these buildings, he found numerous cans of Arcanol rustproof paint, the brainchild of Erika's father, which had made Papi Ragg a wealthy man thirty years earlier.

What a spooky coincidence! What an omen, how heart-warming. He said he felt his father-in-law looking over his shoulder saying: 'go on, son, this is surely the right place for you.'

****

'Constant sandstorms' wrote Erika to her parents, 'the finest sand imaginable forces itself into doors and windows, however well sealed. When there is no wind the stench from the fish meal factories pervades the entire area. There is no sanitation, no paved roads. Electricity is available from 8pm-10pm via a generator from the Cold Storage Co.

So, if what you want is a cold beer, the way forward is to hang a bottle outside in the wind, inside a wet sock. After 10pm one uses petroleum lamps or candles.

No-one has a fridge, and my culinary disasters can all be blamed on the petroleum oven. Talking of machinery: Pop Kraemer's old Packard, the one used for transporting milk, potatoes and pigs, has been revamped for Walvis Bay and shipped to us,.. we really are well set up now. He more or less *gave* it to us! How I wish I had a fridge....'

Inexplicably, Erika found great happiness in Walvis Bay. Writing to her mother in that grand four-towered castle she told how she now was 'the queen of a five-room, grey breeze-block house, can you believe it dearest Mami: my own home for the first time since 1940, when the war began. I no longer mind there is only an outside bucket loo, and also only about 3 sq. yards of sand called a garden, fenced off from the worst of the blowing sand (the only thing growing is a Tamarisk tree, about 3ft tall, and an amazingly hardy Oleander plant)...it is all a challenge, I quite like it ...'

****

Very shortly after his arrival a branch of the international Seaman's Mission opened in Walvis Bay and Ihlenfeldt, as director of the firm, was able to assign two smallish rooms to this enterprise. An English reverend, along with a few boxes of books, was the modest instigator of this scheme. Erika, voted in as member of the 'harbour lights Guild' (ladies who offered tea to visiting sailors), must now sell knick-knacks from a kiosk to any takers. There were also dances and other entertainments. Before too long Erika's man was headhunted and offered the post of mayor of Walvis Bay. Erika became hysterical with laughter.

He declined.

It had to be said they soon had a pleasing circle of friends and there were always ocean liners with captains, who invited and entertained the hardy 'locals' on board.   By then the primitive settlement had progressed to a modest power station, which functioned for several hours each day.   Life was 'transformed'.

The close proximity of Swakopmund, a very German-looking seaside resort in the Namib Desert, only one hour further up the coast, proved to be a special treat for the deprived souls from Walvis Bay. Here one could indulge oneself with delicious cakes from the German bakery while momentarily kidding oneself one was 'back at home,' in some mythical Germany where time had stood still. A small 'Park' and even a bookshop provided solace from the surrounding desert, although even Swakopmund had found no way of keeping sandstorms at bay.

By the time the Ihlenfeldts left Walvis Bay eight years later there was in existence a newly built Seaman's Mission, complete with chapel, library, a hall for dances and events and a residence for the pastor and his assistant. Reini, a Lutheran in word but total heathen in deed, assisted with the building of a Lutheran church and Erika, with the help of a friend, had laid the foundations for a public library, spending much time classifying and setting up a workable system. Some years later the municipality of Walvis Bay took on the task of providing professional personnel.

All this had come to be.

Erika's daughter, now known as Evelyn, (somehow the German bits were dropped) having boarded for two years at the Holy Cross Convent in George, (where there were still many about who hated anyone or anything German) was transferred closer to 'home', to the Windhoek Holy Cross Convent. For two years she was near enough to 'home', that is *only* fourteen hours by train from her new home in the sanddunes.

Mind you, steam trains were slow in those days. Sometimes they stopped, unable to start again. There was one such ancient locomotive, often almost buried by sand storms, just outside Swakopmund. It was known as *Martin Luther*....whose words: 'here I stand, I can do no other'...when he was taken to task at the Diet of Worms in the 16th century, never failed to amuse visitors passing through the sands of the Namib Desert.s

For a full seven years the cheerful 'pioneers' seemed as content as can be. Erika, and her Reinhold, both now 'middle-aged,' ready for retirement, like two craggy ancient Welwitshia plants... had put down deep,deep roots in those sand-dunes. In 1959, when the time came to return to Cape Town it proved to be an emotional wrench.

****

It seems there is nothing quite like 'suffering' together: in all its quaint ghastliness Walvis Bay had left both Erika and Reini with unforgettable, bonding memories.

Erika boarded the boat along with her beloved black cat, the 'schwarze Peter' (the German symbol of good luck, but tucked away miauwing in a cage) and with a husband now freed from any further constraints.

This melancholy day had become a very significant one: Reini was about to take retirement.

Finally: it was high time to get back to the wonders of civilisation, for those years that were still to come.

Josephine and her daughters' zither lesson 1890s

Coelestine c 1900

Coelestine and Erika, London
c 1910

Erika in Accra 1936

Erika and Knups in Pretoria 1943

Mami's castle Mageregg c 1960

Ingeborg-Evelyn's story

What a poor start: I don't care for these names.

I can't relate to them at all. Who is this meant to be? All the others have real names, names that fit and work, but *Ingeborg* and *Evelyn*, well, they don't feel like me. Mind you, it has been useful at times, to call myself just plain Inge, and I have been an Inge and still am, to several people who are dear to me.

In my incarnation as a 'Brit' the name Evelyn has been invaluable. But just the sound of it makes me feel hot and prickly…that elongated 'eee' and the 'vil' to follow. What *was wrong* with my parents' tonal sense? They were not musical and it shows…

All that for starters, is quite uncomfortable.

Then there is that birth in *H a m* burg, another daft name…now that one thinks about it. No, only trying to be light-hearted; I must confess right now, being light-hearted is not something that comes readily.

I was treated like a princess, cosseted by at least three, if not four women, dressed, fed, weighed, bathed and potty trained, to say nothing of the baby gymnastics. I could hardly tell them apart although one was dressed all in white and wore a white cap. She did most of the work, briskly, I expect. Others came and went. No doubt the best was 'Mami', she was always there. After a month the woman who had given birth to me vanished, and a year later the nurse in white did too. A new nurse in white took over the chores. A *year* later I was visited by a stranger who was said to be my mother. I didn't care for her. After three weeks of her dressing up in a white uniform I allowed her to feed me, touch me. My father also tried to befriend me: I gave them both a hard time. People kept coming and… disappearing. Only 'Mami' was always there. And as I became bigger there was an occasional encounter with Papi, who made a lot of pleasing noise on his pianola and even allowed me to type on his typewriter. No doubt Papi was a formative influence. After all, typing is precisely what I am doing now.

But this is reaching into the future.

For as long as I remember I was a small fortunate person known as '*das* Knupslein' or '*der* Knups'. Now there is a very subtle distinction between the two: <u>*der*</u> Knups is masculine, the effect is one of a stubby, stubborn, stumpy, wilful and somehow comical person. <u>*Das*</u> Knupslein, being both diminutive and neuter brings out shades of something cute in need of protection. People should take greater care when they choose names for their children…

80

My parents lived and worked in Africa, shadowy figures who came and went, once, sometimes twice a year. I don't suppose they registered in my two or three-year old mind. I was endlessly photographed for them, so that they could at least see what I looked like. To be honest, I remember little from that time, apart from one cold, white day when I was allowed to stick a stubbly orange vegetable into a snowman's face.

***

Early years in any child's life, as the personality forms itself, are very important. Don't Jesuits say the first five years of a child constitute the entire nucleus of the eventual person?

All I can say now, looking back to the time when Erika and Reini returned from the Gold Coast, the notion that I would be in good hands, groomed to make a new start, aged nearly four, with 'real 'but totally inexperienced parents, was a very bold one. I force myself not to romanticise this. But there are some things that *do* come to my mind, things that must have left a mark, (like sins leaving 'black marks on the soul', as the nuns would have it, in my later convent education).

Erika and Reini had no experience as parents. I expect they were really quite nervous and possibly trying very hard. So, when I was quite old, that is, three and a half, we were to sail around the east coast of Africa to Cape Town.

First my mother took a train to Hollabrunn to show me to *her* grandmother. From an early letter I learned that I did not weep leaving Mami, but could think of little else than sleeping in 'a little room on wheels'. On the following day there was to be a trip on a plane. Whatever that was; 'a long room with wings like a bird?'

I have been told these things, they are not memories. Strangely I *do* remember that first flight, from Vienna to Basle. In those early days of travel by plane my mother was in a state of terror: she'd never flown before. There we were, boarding a tinny, tiny plane, which seemed vast to me…without a man to 'take care' of everything. I assume it was tiny: I have seen pictures of planes from 1938, and let's face it, they were puny things. Small wonder my mother passed out as the propellers took us up and away. 'Altitude sickness,' was the explanation.

I had a great time, walking up and down the aisle and befriending everybody. I sat on the laps of countless lovely 'daddies' while my mother got herself together again. Strangely, this is my second real memory…the snowman was the first, but this was better: loving all that attention, being fussed over by strangers. In Basle we were met by a concerned Reini, who took care of wife and child in the time-honoured way. Another little box on wheels and we were ready to board the 'Tanganjika': an immensely vast gleaming ocean liner.

What does a nearly four-year old need… apart from regular meals, warmth, clean clothes, and a soft bed? 'Tante Nika' provided all these and more: there was a nursery with trained staff and toys. Children were fed separately and food was excellent. But nowadays the answer to the question at the beginning of this paragraph and of this entire life-changing situation would surely be 'love'. A six-week journey in unbelievably hot climates does not bring out the best in people: tempers flared all round. There are photos of us sweating it out on a rickshaw in Port Said, wearing tropical helmets and looking *reasonably* cheerful, my mother languidly detached. On board I caused a flurry of excitement by telling others that my *real* parents lived in Hamburg.

It all fitted, since Erika was very quick to have her child taken off her hands, not just by the nursery but also by a young missionary lady, who seemed to 'love' other people's children. Of course I didn't understand. But somehow, as far back as I can remember, I recall the feeling that I knew better and perfectly well what these grown-ups were up to.

I must have sensed my parents' efforts at parenting were not quite of the standard I was accustomed to. I quite liked them, but they didn't get things right. Mostly exhausted, the heat was overwhelming us all.

So, time was spent in the deck pool, floating about, in a rubber ring with a net underneath. My father liked water. My mother, who had a lumpy figure never cared to reveal her body. I must assume I was homesick for my Mami and Papi, those loving, known people in Hamburg.

But exciting things happened too: every day there was a violinist who entertained passengers at noon, tea-time and in the evening.

His speciality was to encode the letters of a passenger's name in his daily program, quite a feat. For example:

Midday Concert:	
Immortellen, Walzer	Gungi
Naschkätzchen, Intermezzo	Siede
Gedämpftes Licht, Tango	Meisel
Ein liebes Mädel, Tango	Reuter
Afternoon	
Ich tanze mit dir, Walzer	Schroeder
Hochzeitstag/Troldhaugen	Grieg
Liebesgruss, Lied	Elgar
Elfengeflüster, Intermezzo	Rhode
Nachts ging das Telefon	Kollo
Evening	
Frühlingstimmen, Walzer	Strauss
Eine kleine Nachtmusik	Mozart
Liebestraum, Lied	Bochmann
Dreimädelhaus	Schubert
Tango Bolero	Llossa

Read down the first letter of each musical item and you will find:..INGE IHLENFELDT. Such an honour. Did this musician leave a mark on my soul? Did I become a violinist? Strangely... well, read on.

It is thanks to my methodical father this program was stored away for seventy odd years. I can't quite focus on it now.

I neither knew nor heard anyone else in all the years to follow, right up until my twelfth year, who played a violin. I was not taken to concerts and had not been to any schools which taught music other than singing. There was no television and we had no radio.

***

SS. Tanganjika, Sunday the 11th September, 1938. '...but *please* can I come too, Mutti, I want to put on my nice dress, just like you, and have cake in the big room with the grown-ups....all the time I have to play in the sandpit with the other children and then it's bedtime.... and I want to be pretty like you...I promise I won't talk ...'

Erika gazed at her almost four-year old daughter and shook her head: 'you're covered in sand, look at you. You'll have to have a bath first and will you really be quiet? Completely quiet?'

'Yes, I promise,' said Knups. Erika got her child ready, now very proud in a fancy new navy dress with white dots and a white collar.

A large place had been cleared in the bar, a pianist and violinist will perform to ladies and gentlemen, sitting at tables, sipping their tea. Knups craned her neck to find the waitress with the cake-trolley who appeared in no time at all to satisfy her youngest customer on this rather warm afternoon.

'Which cake would you like?' This one? No? The most colourful one?

The musicians walked on, to friendly applause. Erika had a quick look to locate the nearest exit. As the violinist tuned, the child frowned, took a swig of juice, put her glass down. The concert began. The child stopped eating, even moving.

She listened.

'Why does the violin sing when you stroke it with a stick? It sounds so sad,' she whispered after they'd come to the end of the first piece. It was a well-known song in ¾ time, smooth, gentle and romantic and Eka recited the words to her child, very quietly, after the musicians stopped. Knups looks at her gravely. 'Can I play that song one day?'

'Shhhhhh, you promised, shhhhh!

****

My parents were great keepers of letters, telegrams and photos. To be confronted with so much material is like having treatment by an expensive shrink. Could my inexperienced parents, aged 38 and 31 respectively have been treating me too strictly, too critically?

I was expected to behave like an adult, on the 'children should be seen and-not-heard'…principle. Am I kidding myself when I seem to remember not being able to take them seriously?

Vivid fragments of memory from the earliest days in Cape Town: I was almost four years old: Auntie Eve, a tall, thin lady, with an easel and tubes of sticky paint, asking me to sit still while she painted and painted …a picture of me! Her voice was gentle, funny and I loved her. Something radiated from her, such an encouraging thing, such acceptance. I can still feel it now. I *really* loved her.

Less pleasing: nightmares. Once we had moved to our bungalow I recall frightening wild beasts which made me wake up and scream. My parents came running. It happened again and again. My father thought I was being 'naughty.' He was wrong because I couldn't make them not happen. And then that circular glass-topped coffee-table in the 'lounge' which my mother liked to polish: it produced a thin whiney squeak…, she was amused because I never tired of it.

But she liked to hear me sing: she would stand me before a circle of her friends expecting me to entertain them. I did, allegedly, with great aplomb. One begins to see where all this was leading: performing on a violin, perhaps?

My father came home from work one day with a puppy *in* his pocket. 'Take it out!' he ordered. It was small, it wriggled, legs, tails everywhere, and we thought it needed a drink... Then a wee, then a chew of my teddy, and another wee...

Soon Erika was writing extremely critical letters to her mother about the difficulties with her 'exasperating' offspring. Disobedient, stubborn, wilful, lying, always wanting to be entertained, refusing to eat normal food (only macaroni was acceptable), rude to the coloured maid Lucy and even worse to the Zulu gardener, in short, I was a pest.

Not unlike the puppy then.

Letters from Mami, (sent at the time when *she* was packing up to leave Hamburg and move into her castle in Austria,) were full of good advice saying she really could not understand why 'Knupslein' was difficult, she had been like a lamb in Hamburg, and if a child was lying it was usually through fear of punishment.

Well, my father certainly believed in punishment...'if you do this, then we'll do that' approach; 'If you don't eat that meat *now* you will sit here until you do' ....and so on. One afternoon, locked in my room for some misdemeanour, I decided to jump out of the window. Just my bad luck: the man was in the garden and caught me doing it, landing on the grass. He pulled down my knickers and slapped my bare bottom.

This deeply humiliating event left an indelible mark on my four-year old psyche, the indignity of it, the cheek and how- dare- he!-feeling has remained there to this day. I mean, a clout around the ear was one thing, but the other was just too much. From that time on I suppose something inside me closed down, perhaps for fifty years ...until he died. By then he believed me to be wonderful and adored me. I had accepted him, but still only in a fashion.

Not long after my 'chastisement' in 1938 it was as well he was to be interned in a prisoner- of- war camp. When he'd gone I consoled my mother with 'never mind, we can 'buy' a new daddy. This remark was gleefully recorded in the family chronicle. As it turned out, I did see very little of him over the years. Perhaps this was a good thing: it allowed me to form closer bonds with my mother. We never discussed this, even forgot about it. But there always remained something alien between him and me: I thought of him mostly as someone who nagged and got in the way. Later, as the decades passed, I remained politely distant...while he lectured me, and demanded replies to his endless letters. I did an absolute minimum and there were always barriers. He loved writing to his numerous friends, to record his life in minute detail. When I was older, I saw him as a pedant and despised his files full of letters, dating back to his earliest days. I feel bad about this now, wish he'd drop in for a chat. But he's dead. If he hadn't done this scribbling, and kept so many pictures, well, where would my account go now?

***

By 1940 he was locked away in the POW camp and my mother and I left CapeTown for **Pretoria.** Recollections from this time are, in my case, selective, only vaguely coming into focus, in a disturbing way. Is it normal or not to remember the fabric of ones mothers' dress, a delicate silk georgette garment, grey with large orange dots, very 1930's?

Or the shine of the red polished courtyard outside our strange new abode? There are vivid snippets--- such as the day I returned with my little friend Peter, from one of our 'gold and silver' expeditions, slow, eyes-to-the-ground searches for treasures,' mostly in the slums just beyond our courtyard, where the black servants had their dark, dank, mysterious rooms. We carried with us an old jam jar in which we collected anything shiny, especially small coins or pretty stones and on this particular day, longish white balloons, which we found strewn about. My mother, followed by Peters' mother, and then other ladies, seemed much exercised by our gathering up these 'balloonies' as we called them. We were told they were dirty and that we should never, under *any* circumstances, *ever* go there again! Six and four years old, we were stood before our agitated mothers, wide-eyed and bewildered...

A more pleasing area for letting off steam was the vast garden of the Union Buildings, just three minutes away. Once we'd been coached in the skills of crossing the road, a small and very un-busy side road, we had a kingdom of lawn and rows of still young trees to play in, on, and under. We tore about, shouted as loud as we pleased, we each had our own favourite tree, which we climbed and felt happy on. Ones very own undisputed territory. Were there mothers hanging about? Perhaps they'd come with us at the beginning, or was all this later, when I was six, or seven, or eight? I recall feeling wild, sweaty, grubby, and wondrously free. There's nothing quite like sitting above ground on a branch, probably no more than about six feet up... such a seriously good feeling.

Communicating in a Babel of tongues, English, German and Afrikaans, our friendships took on an exuberant flavour of nowhere else on earth. At first I had only a few selected friends, like little Peter who spoke German; English was what we heard all day long, with Afrikaans limping along in third place.

I was the only child regularly in bed with some illness. Apart from all the normal childhood complaints such as mumps, measles, whooping cough there were bouts of lethargy, when I remember lying on my bed, sucking my thumb. This maddened my mother. At night she covered my thumb with iodine tincture and bandaged it up tightly to make it inaccessible. Only those who suck their thumbs as long as I did (up to twelve years old) will know what a primeval urge it is, this unstoppable need to do it again and again. With it came a relaxation of reality and living, a dissolving into another dimension, which is impossible to describe. I would chew and gnaw at the bandages, suffer the taste of the iodine, *anything*, to get at my thumb. What does this mean? Looking back at my behaviour I can only remind myself that we are little animals when we are young, and there are some things little animals need to do…like snuggle up to a grownup. My mother disliked physical contact with anyone and pushed me away, usually with a joke. 'Fass mich nicht an!' (don't touch me') she'd say, looking mildly embarrassed. She and my father seemed affectionate enough. This I noted in later years; in Pretoria she had only me. Her determination to shape me into a better scholar, better dancer, better eater, more amenable person, did nothing but make me more and more negative and stubborn. And yet, at school, I was nearly always top of the class, teacher's little helper and generally a GOOD THING.

I was dragged to specialists, to find out why I was so bloated, so tired, so constipated, so bad-tempered, so melancholy. If she bought a bowl of fruit I'd gobble everything up, and this she didn't like either. 'We can't afford it,' she'd say, always, every day. Boarding house food I scorned, only fish and chips and fruit were 'in'. Doctors tried their luck with all sorts of remedies but not one of them said 'she needs a home, a father, or even, she is missing her home in Hamburg,' to say nothing of her grandparents. Holistic healing had not arrived. Soon I was signed up for ballet and swimming lessons: I hated both at first, I was very cowardly, but my mother had the steely determination I lacked.

Another vivid memory is returning to our white-tiled room, sobbing, not really being able to explain what was wrong. I had been in the room of an elderly couple who liked to listen to music on their little radio. I had sat with them and started to blub. I actually remember this, a feeling not all that different from the need to suck my thumb. Something frightening, inexplicable and hopeless, the sound of a slow orchestral work, I have no idea what it was. With hindsight, the misery was probably triggered by a memory of my grandfather playing on his pianola, some arrangement of Beethoven, Schubert, possibly.

Did my mother put her arms around me? I don't know…perhaps.

A great believer in independence she dispatched me off to school from age seven onwards on Pretoria's public transport. She'd always pick me up in her Opel, but even the ballet classes were soon reached by bus. I made a huge fuss at first, to no avail, she was bigger than me. Good really: I needed that toughening up for later years.

It was customary to slap children about the ears in those days. This is called an 'Ohrfeige'. I had plenty of those! Not at school, only at home. At school it was rulers, struck hard on the palms of your hands. That happened twice in those four years. German school consisted of two large rooms divided by a sliding wall, and a playground. The classes had about twenty children in each room who were taught in three languages; German, Afrikaans and English. How this was divided up I can't recall, but I know my mother was puzzled by my curious tasks and slow progress. Although German-speaking at home I preferred *to read* English books but spelling was appalling in all languages. I hated sums but was thought to sing nicely. Reports were average, later I became teacher's pet with top marks, despite frequent absence due to illness. My mother kept me on track: homework sessions in the afternoon. I saw no fun in that and pretended to be really stupid, just to annoy her. Another ruse was to be baby-ish, to make her love me more. I desperately needed hugs, praise and affection, even protection, but she was adamantly hardened against that sort of thing. What was wrong with her? What was wrong with me, with us? There was constant manipulation, one way or the other. I needed her, she needed me, but we were not very 'good at it.' She was so critical!

In my head remains a patchwork of snippets of those four years in Pretoria, vivid, palpable and real. Just imagine the moment of disbelief, when I rose from our potty…(yes, we used one, as neither of us could face the long walk to the outside toilet adjacent to the native quarters, especially at night)..and found a bright red pool of blood.

My mother, in shock, called the doctor immediately. He guessed at a burst vein, or bilharzia, or a bladder infection. Laboratory tests confirmed an infection caused by a lung infection I'd recovered from recently. News went round Belvedere Hotel that I was on my deathbed, having some bizarre female complaint at the tender age of eight. I felt fine, but was not allowed to get up. It meant staying in bed for nine days, before the infection cleared. No problem: I was an experienced 'being-in-bed' person, having had one throat, chest, ear, tooth infection after the other for three years running.

These were 'My Treats': my mothers' jewellery box: I put on every brooch, necklace, ring there was and gazed at myself in a hand mirror. Or: provided with a tray and matchboxes, glue, paper and scissors I constructed chairs and wardrobes for my dolls house. Then the typewriter, my favourite pastime: I typed a letter to my father, not at all bad, it is right beside me now, in German, with questionable spelling, but certainly literate.

'How does she know how to type?' he queries and my mother's reply is: 'modern children simply *know* how to do this'. The equivalent of present-day infants fiddling around with computers...

For very special events I would be taken to a boiler room opposite the infamous 'balloonie' area. (This was now forbidden territory). My mother, sitting on a stool would turn my shoulder-long hair into ringlets with tongs heated in the wood stove for provision of bathwater. It must have been testing to judge just *when* to take the tongs out of the coals as there was always a memorable smell of singed hair. How I loved her attention and the transformation. I felt special. The first time I was squeezed into a frothy pale green tutu and saw myself in the mirror, with curls and pointed toes in satin ballet shoes,...well, it was the start of an astonished realization I was 'cute' in a puddingy sort of way.

But then came a hard knock: I gave up my first solo performance at the so-called 'Eisteddfodd' in Pretoria's Town Hall: my latest illness had made me so weak and wobbly that the ballet teacher cancelled my slot.

***

Other awakenings during those tender years: a short holiday with a school friend on a hot, dusty Transvaal farm, still under construction; the only entertainment was swimming in a circular corrugated iron dam, stuck right in the middle of nowhere, probably rainwater, perhaps for crops or animals: there was a tiny ladder to get up the outside and then jump in...the water murky and warm with wriggly things, frogs, beetles. Three or four of us, the boys rather braver, were putting our heads under water. Taunted by them and finally persuaded to dive under, I came face to face with a boy who planted a kiss roughly on my mouth, under water. No-one could see...

Well, the others laughed and teased us when we surfaced, shaking our wet heads, rubbing our dripping noses. Had they seen us, after all?

Later, when no-one was looking, the boy said he loved me. We were both eight, and this was my first kiss, never forgotten.

And then there were chickens on the run after they'd had their heads *chopped off.* What a nightmare! I began to miss my mother and the predictable, safe, Belvedere Annexe. Eventually returned, burnt brown and looking more grown-up than my mother remembered, I fell into her arms and sobbed how happy I was to be back at home with her.

* * *

By 1944 the war in Europe was becoming intolerably dangerous. One might suppose South Africans would take it out on the large contingent of German wives and children in their midst, but if there was any trouble I certainly had no inkling of it. There were so many children in the boarding house that the innovative manageress of the Belvedere suggested an evening show with folk-dancing and singing and a play, acted *only* by children: each child was to take part in some capacity. The play was a thriller, a murder, I seem to remember, with an Afrikaans text, and to this day I can say my line which was:' *hier is die pragtige pêrels',* (here are the wondrous pearls) although I haven't a clue who or what I was. Did Erika keep this memory alive? In later years, whenever either of us handled pearls, we'd get the giggles and say, with great delight: "pragtige pêrels" using impressive Dutch back-of -the throat gutturals.

After the 'cultural' input there were games, *with* forfeits: I had to kiss a boy *fifty* times, he was the favourite amongst the gaggle of kids, twelve years old, with a mighty stammer. I reported to my mother that the kisses had been 'lovely and soft'. She on the other hand informed my father that I would turn into a 'bad lot' one day.

And then there were the unforgettable 'little blue flowers.' Pretoria is famous for them now: Jacaranda trees were originally South American, and now there is hardly a street in Pretoria which does not turn into an enchanting shade of blue in the Spring. The flowers look even prettier after they'd dropped on the ground, both canopy and carpets so radiantly blue.

But now the crowning memory: a combination of 'little blue flowers' with the Afrikaaner ice-cream man on his horse-drawn cart.

'Jump up, missie' he'd say to me, and I'd sit with him as we ambled around the block, selling his wares. The road next to the annexe was on a steep incline, I feared for the poor horse in front; did the man have brakes on his cart? Surprising, really, that my mother allowed this...I wonder if she even knew. 'You are the nicest little girl in his

90

area', he'd say, 'would you like a job selling ice-cream?' This was not to be. My last memory of Pretoria was standing on the street corner surrounded by my toys on the pavement, price tags on each item, everything going cheap. Passers-by were kind and curious: why was this happening?

'I am going back to Germany,' I said, 'because my father is coming out of the camp'…Most said nothing, walked on. They must have known it was a death sentence. What on earth were my parents *thinking* about?

***

Blurred memories of the train journey to Port Elisabeth: the dramatic confiscation of a sack full of sweets (bought with profits from my street sales) and later that big moment when my father came up the runway. Did my nine-year old brain shut down due to overload? I don't remember. *My* first true recollection is of him ordering *ten* eggs for breakfast, all boiled. I sat watching him devour them one after the other. I was embarrassed. He was a stranger who ate more eggs than anyone else. I was no longer the focus of my mother's attention. Now he was always there and had views about me that did not coincide with my mother's. I did know I was *supposed* to like him, but I didn't.

Just to prove my independent spirit I made friends with a different grown-up man. He was an artist who sat on deck painting, day after day. We got on really well and I liked sitting near him with my own pencils and crayons, drawing while he occasionally looked over and encouraged me. He told my parents I had talent. I liked him a lot.

After four long weeks of cruising up the west coast of Africa we finally disembarked in Lisbon. Freedom, at last. There had been two 'refuelling' stops, and 'fresh provision' stops, but Germans had not been allowed off the ship.

Once installed in the Grand Hotel in Estoril, (home of abdicated kings of Europe), I gradually became used to the idea of a 'father' being around. We had a huge room; my parents could close off their sleeping area with red velvet curtains and I slept on a sofa opposite. I remember the view down to the sea. Day after day my father jollied us along to see many places: Cascais, Lisbon town centre, the beaches. There are vivid memories, an old castle on a hill with strangely shaped chimneys (Cintra?) and a shoemaker from whom my father bought leather sandals for me, made of shiny brown leather half-saucers over the toes. We walked and walked and ate ice-cream after icecream. The hotel smelled of olive oil, everywhere one went was that special smell of Portuguese olive oil…

One night I was awakened by noises. I looked across to my parents' bed. They had no clothes on, they were playing 'rude' games. I watched for a while. What they were doing reminded me of the day I was punished for playing 'doctors' with my friend Gisela, when we were caught looking at each others' bodies …a horrible and embarrassing day in Pretoria, a few years ago.' I gazed at them for a while, fell asleep eventually, dismayed and disgusted. I had decided: I would never, ever, speak to either of them again.

And I really did fall silent *for a whole week.* I was furious. Whenever possible I went out of their way and did my own thing, as far away from them as I could get. I could not smile. I looked away from them. I nodded or shook my head when appropriate. 'What's the matter?' they both enquired, over and over. I stared. After a week of this my father threatened to take me to a doctor if I didn't speak. So I let them have it…the whole sorry tale about their 'rude' games at night. I have no insight into their feelings about all this. I expect they found a way to make me feel better about it. And I did begin to talk again.

****

'Help, I had no idea we hadn't drawn the curtains around the bed, we must have forgotten…..how could we be so careless'…Erika was more upset than she liked to admit. How does one explain to a nine year old what parents do after dark, when they are in love, after such a long separation, after a few drinks?

With lame reassurances they bribed their aggrieved child, sent her off to the swimming pool with money to spend on friends and buy ice-cream. 'We'll come down later and join you, and then we'll go out together to see a castle.' Involved face-saving stratagems were put in place by embarrassed parents…largely a case of 'attention lavished and money spent on' a horribly, hopelessly confused young person. After six weeks in Lisbon the primal scene was eventually overlaid with other impressions.

Overlaid, but not erased. Such things are etched for ever. Would I really have behaved like that if I'd 'known' my father better? He seemed like such an intruder, always talking to my mother, and paying the wrong sort of attention, I felt, to me. And she was different too, now that she had him back. Why did she like him so much? I was not at all sure I didn't prefer our life in the 'kitchen' of the Belvedere Annex.

Boarding the train to France I knew this 'holiday' had now ended. For some reason we had a compartment with beds, while others had second class accommodation without beds. My mother had been taken ill in Lisbon shortly before the onward journey, it was very mysterious, she had to lie down all the time, and could not carry anything. In later years I was told she had miscarried....

First stop was Biarritz just across the boarder between Spain and France. The hotel, even grander than Hotel Estoril was right on the beach: one huge room for parents, mine, ballroom-sized adjacent to theirs contained a king-size bed with velvet curtains on a platform and a pillow shaped like a long sausage. 'So...this was how kings and queens slept...' Too scared to go to sleep alone I begged my parents to stay until I dropped off: another one of those 'etched' memories. But what a far cry from the cosy intimacies of our tiled kitchen in Pretoria!

Food was scarce in France, dinner and breakfast meagre, to say the most. Here was the first taste of hardship: watery soup, with dry bread? My father tells how we walked to the station on the following morning, sitting on a park bench next to an elderly, tiny, French 'granny'...who asked: 'what is that long train standing on the siding?'......

'We scratched together our pitiful remains of school French and gave her the required answer. The little grand-mère gazed at us with sad eyes, stood up, then walked off without a word'.... (from a letter written by my father.) The German occupiers were hated, naturally.

My parents had much to learn.

During the onward journey our train was attacked several times. Even grown-ups had to learn to stretch out on the floor when the shooting started. I was not afraid. Lying flat on the floor was uncomfortable, boring and just look how filthy it was, seen from three inches away for an interminable time. We were not allowed to budge in case a partisan (resistance fighter) would get frisky with a gun. Everything was threatening really, my father, the train, the war, the lousy food, to say nothing of the swastika flags we were given to wave out of the windows, unbelievably, and stopping for hours in dark tunnels to be safe from the partisans...'Sh....no more whispering... they might shoot into our carriage' whispered my father, huddled up on the floor, 'make yourself flat as a snake and don't move or anything,'.... 'but I must go to the toilet'.... 'don't you dare move now, we could all get ourselves shot.......'

The authorities escorted us back to Germany safely. On arrival in Heilbronn the grown-ups were taught how to use ration books, to go into air-raid shelters and, presumably, how to do the Hitler salute.

'I am nearly ten now, just a few more months, but even I can see my parents are getting things wrong: we ate food in a restaurant and used up all our 'meat rations'. We must also learn how to jump out of bed quickly, not bother to get dressed before the bombs start falling: we must run to the shelter, a horrible grey place with hardly any light, under the ground. Later, when the soldiers said 'good-bye' they stuck their arm in the air and said 'Heil Hitler' and then we went to the station and sat about just waiting, and waiting... for many hours. The idea was to get to the castle in Austria, about four or five hours by train.....'

Did my grandparents know we were coming? I remember sitting on a platform, falling asleep with my arms crossed to cradle my head, on a suitcase. It's so easy to sleep when one is really tired.

'When we arrived it was the middle of the night: we couldn't wake up my grandparents. There was a place for sick people at the station and they let my mother and me lie down on a bed. My father had to sit on a chair with a hole in it, all night. I felt sorry for him. In the morning the nurse who let us sleep also let us use her telephone. Then, at last, Mami and Papi came with a carriage and a horse. It was a sunny day; we all fitted in the carriage, with our luggage and the horse was strong enough to pull all of us through Klagenfurt out into the countryside where the castle is. I liked the ride much more than those horrible trains; people were just starting to get up and some waved to us. I was happy to see Mami and Papi but I didn't remember them at all.'

August. September, 1944. 'Another girl lives here, in a tiny house near the stream, not in the castle. Her name is Karla and she is my friend. We play all sorts of games...like going up in the attic where there are dusty trunks full of old clothes. We put them on and pretend to be someone else. Out of the windows we can see far away mountains and fields. On hot days we paddle in the stream. There was a snake slipping along the pebbles and now I'm not so keen to go back..... Karla says they don't do anything. She goes to school not far from here; you pass the gates and walk along a dusty road with very high trees on each side. At the end are more gates and small houses where soldiers live with their wives and children. There is a tiny school...I'm supposed to go every day. I have to do everything in German now. I really like Karla.

On Sunday mornings a priest comes to say Mass in the chapel in the round tower. There is just enough room for Mami, for us and the maid. Karla comes with her mother. Mass here is much more fun than in the cathedral in Pretoria, where it was so hot and there were so many people, I know I am not supposed to say this, but going to Mass is quite boring. I understand the priest can talk to God in Latin, but I really don't know what he's saying. After Mass Mami invites the priest to have coffee with us; he's just an ordinary man without his special holy clothes on. He talks to Papi, who plays pianola music on Sundays. You don't need to use your hands for this. Papi prefers it to going to church. My father also does not go to church. He says his parents belong to a different church, so he believes in God in a different way; I suppose that's alright? Sometimes I feel sorry for my Dad. I must hug him more and tell him things. He wants us to go away from here and go by train to visit *his* parents who live by the seaside. His father is very old and needs help in the office; he is waiting for my father to be there right *now.'*

November 1944. 'On a train again….we should be there in four, five hours. My father says there are no partisans here to attack us. What about the bombs' I asked, but he said 'the bombs are for towns, not trains.'

'We've just seen a horrible thing: a broken, grey town, all the buildings fallen to bits. The train went along the outside of the town. My father said: 'look, remember this for ever: this is what happens in wars. It used to be a very important place called Berlin, and now it is nothing.'

When we get to the seaside it will be cold. We will not go to the beach for a long time, only in June. I miss Karla. She has promised to write and send me her photograph… I wish I was still in the castle with Mami. She cried when we left.'

Swinemünde. December. 'My other grandparents have a dark house with a piano. I have my own room. It is next to my parents' room. We have to go up a wooden stair case. Downstairs is the office where my father helps *his* father do all the work with ships. From the balcony one can see many ships, first there is a cobbled road, then a railway track and after that the ships. It's fun to sit on the balcony because it has glass windows so one is warm and dry. We've been here for a few weeks now. Soon it will be Christmas with ice and snow. My grandmother says there is a market for Christmas toys and presents and maybe even cakes. Really! And when I looked at her piano she said *she knows a lady who can teach me to play….*

I got into big trouble last week. When I was standing next to that vase by the window, which is bigger than I am, I said to my Dad: 'one day, when your parents are dead, I would like to have this vase'. He gave me an 'Ohrfeige' and said I was not to talk like that. I wasn't sure why he hit me so hard. I suppose he doesn't want his parents to die.

He's very bossy these days. The other day I put some butter on my bread and asked if I could have the jam and he said: 'from now on the rule is: because of the war one can have either butter, or jam, but not both at the same time.' And my mother *and* grandparents agreed with him!

Soon it will be Christmas.

It was jolly cold at the Christmas market. We had hot red lemonade and spicy cake. I was allowed to buy, for my room, some wooden painted dwarves, cut out of wood and also a holy thing, to hang by the door, it is made of baked red earth and looks like Our Lady over a little bowl for holy water. I don't have holy water, but I tried ordinary water which slowly came out. I like it though. It's no good for making the sign of the cross, but I'll hang it over my bed along with the dwarves. I wonder where one gets holy water from. They had some by the chapel door in Magaregg. The market people sold candles and trees; being out in the dark was really nice.....

My new task: because I'm not going to school I have to go each morning to get the milk from the man with the cart. Grandmother gives me a tin can with a handle and a lid. I pay him. Here one has to say Mark and Pfennig; everywhere money is different. My mother makes me sit down every morning to write and also to do sums.... in German.

When I was writing with my left hand the other day my father said it was a bad sign. I'm not sure what he means, but I can write and draw with both hands. If one hand fell off I would have a spare one, how can it be bad? Sometimes I don't like my father. I will soon forget how to say things in English and Afrikaans.

Anyway, no-one here would understand what I'd be saying.

My piano teacher is very old, and gentle. I practise for a long time. I like doing it. I can already play a tune and my mother says I am quick. For a change... now that she has walked me a few times she tells me I'm old enough to find my own way. I'm happy to go out on my own. Soon I will be ten. I have no friends. There are bad things sometimes. Each day we see poor people who have come off the ships with their luggage. They are called refugees. They have no homes, they look tired and worried. Every day more arrive. My father says they are running away from the Russians, who fight and kill everybody. I hope the Russians don't come *here*...It has snowed again. Everywhere looks white and beautiful. My Dad will get his toboggan from the attic. He has not seen it since he was little.

My grandmother could sing when she was young, play the piano and she also liked to paint. Next to the piano hangs a small drawing she did of pink flowers on a branch. 'They are apple blossoms' she explained,

'..and in a few months I'll show you my apple tree with those same flowers, down in the garden'.

We must go through the garden every day, when we use the wooden box lavatory. There is a big hook on the wall with torn newspaper. At the top I see a shelf with pale green berries in glass jars. My grandmother calls them 'gooseberries'. There is also a proper lavatory in the bathroom, but it is so old it can only be used for pee-ing and we have to pour water in it, because it's broken. Lots of things are broken in my grandparents' house and some things are weird, like that large pot of sand next to my grandfather's chair. It is called a 'spittoon' and one must spit in it. I'm not sure why. The second weird thing is a small long basin with a wooden cover on tall legs by the foot of my grandparents' bed. It looks like a donkey on which you can sit; my mother said it is for washing ones bottom.

Because it is so cold the dining table has been moved into the piano-spittoon-living room. Usually it lives in a big room across the passage to the veranda. But in the room where we all do everything like sitting and playing, lessons and smoking and eating... is a huge tiled 'oven' which my father fills with wood and coals and it makes the room very hot. All the other rooms are very cold. I have one warm cardigan and a very small coat because I'm growing a lot. I get wet feet in the snow but there are no boots in the shoe-shop. My mother is cold too and she is getting thin because she has to work hard. The other day she was crying: a poor woman rang the bell and asked if she could sleep in the entrance and my grandmother said it was alright and gave her a blanket, so then the woman said thank you and let my mother take some flour out of her sack. My mother put her hand into the flour and her wedding ring slipped off and she couldn't find it, she was on her knees, putting both hands in the sack and feeling for her ring and then *she* started to cry. I didn't know what to do, so I stroked her back... she *did* find it in the end. I think my mother is very tired. I have never seen her cry before'.

'The grown-ups are arguing about leaving this house, going away *before it is too late*. When I come they stop arguing and talk about other things. They look upset.'

January 1945. 'More and more strangers come to the door every day. They get off the boats and ask us where to go, or, could they stay inside until the trains come, or something. We have nothing to give them, but they usually stay downstairs in the hallway, huddled together. They go to our lavatory in the garden There are no bottled gooseberries left. Outside is ice and snow, just like my father said, but it's not *that* good without boots and warm clothes. I play with the toboggan

97

sometimes, there is a little hill in the park next to the air-raid shelter, but yesterday a man asked me to let him use my toboggan for pulling heavy things from the ships. When he passed I saw two stiff stretched people lying on my toboggan. He has not brought it back. Some bigger boys come to play there too. I don't know them. We have to go into the shelter sometimes and it is very dark and boring.

They do a scary thing here, whenever they think airplanes are coming ...they switch on some metal bowls to blow out a white fog over the whole town. Every street has them and soon you can't see where you are, the ships are invisible, the roofs are invisible and it is best to be at home. Then the bombers fly over the whiteness and don't know what to do with their bombs and go back home.

Tomorrow is my 10th birthday. I have no friends here, so no party. Maybe, only maybe, I will have a tiny cake and a present.'

February 1945. 'Every day my father tells his parents that we should leave this place because the Russians are coming nearer and nearer...they think I'm not listening, but I am. My grandmother says, no, no, you three go and leave us here, we can't leave our home and all our things. Then my father tells them, quietly, so I can't hear...what bad things the Russians do to all women, even old ones. My grandparents are sure the Russians would never do anything bad to them. It is amazing how they all say the same things over and over again. I feel sorry for the grown-ups. I feel afraid.

12th March 1945. 'Today I was nearly killed, but the bombs missed. Nearly all the windows are smashed. We were in the shelter when it happened, but not grandfather, he wouldn't go. 'I'm tired of going there all the time' he said. 'I don't care if the bombs kill me.'

My mother grabbed my hand and we ran down the stairs, out onto the cobbled road and down a slope of grass to the shelter...but the shelter was tightly shut. My mother banged on the iron door, no-one seemed to hear us. She took off one shoe and banged the door with the heel... then the door opened a little and a man said what do you want,...OK.OK...and let us in. We sat together with my father and my grandmother and lots of other people. Loud bangs, further-away bangs and then suddenly they became very loud and the shelter rocked and shook, like a ship. I saw women who were crying and holding each other. The lights went out. I decided to pray, in case God could stop the bombs falling on us. I had my rosary in my pocket and held it hard, but no-one else was 'doing it', so I didn't either. The most frightening thing was when the floor rocked. It was so dark, just a few torches.... a few times my father said: 'that was close'...and my grandmother, who held his arm very tight, looked like a small grey mouse all pointy-nosed and shrivelled up. 'Her house must be broken by now, I thought, 'with my grandfather in it'. My mother looked straight ahead and said nothing. Then the noise stopped. We stumbled out into a fog of dust and smoke, it was hard to breathe and hard to see. I held my fathers' hand... we clambered over stones, broken trees and torn-off legs and smashed bodies. My father said 'they are dead'. We were so close to our house and it was not burning; many things were burning, but not *our* things. Inside we found 'Opa',...he had white dust all over him and was still in his chair. He cleared his throat loudly and looked silly, even his moustache was white, but seemed very pleased with himself.

Now there is a lot of trouble: my father must nail the broken windows to be shut in some way. It is becoming dark. My grandmother is finding candles, even some Christmas one; there is no electricity, it is cold. No water comes out of the taps. We have no food.....'

Today is a new day. My father and I took a bucket to find an olden-days pump; I've seen it before, it is near by... and we must go again later in the day. My mother and I tried to go along the road to see if anyone has food, but the shops are bombed or closed and there is nothing on their shelves.

People are starting to leave Swinemünde because the place is full of dead bodies and sunken ships. They go on wooden trucks pulled by horses, like on farms; they huddle together under blankets. My father has bumped into an old friend, a captain of a ship which has not been bombed. This captain says he could get us all away, first my grand-parents, then us, on two separate ships.' So that is what is going to happen. It will be nice to leave Swinemünde. I have not met a single child to play with in the five months I've been here.

Interlude **2009.**

The writer, myself, is now grown-up, in fact quite elderly. What I've described on the previous page is the closest brush with death my family had. *We were the lucky ones.*

What had been going on around us was a hell of subhuman events, of cruelty, incomprehension and fear, as though every living creature was to be crushed, ground into fragments, pulped, dissolved, humans remorselessly brushed off the face of the earth, burned, drowned, gone for good. Plans of these very events must have been dreamed up in safe clean offices by blunted bullies: and such men, on both sides, had the power to command others to do the dirty work.

No war can ever be described as good. Neither Britain nor America can claim a Good War, yet, undeniably, they *had* to engineer the destruction of that brutal, noxious Nazi avalanche which had appeared from minds of madmen. Calling themselves leaders, these stunted gangsters, little men, were led by the devil; scientists, laboratories, factories, all mindlessly producing, catering for, making possible that Armageddon of indescribable cruelty: World War 2, in all its ramifications.

Persecution of Jews and disadvantaged minorities in Germany, the cruel killing, hounding of dissenters, remains to this day the sort of thing that gives following generations nightmares for life. The slate can never be wiped clean, the cruel events linger like frightening demons, hidden, lurking in black clouds. When and where will they re-appear?

Is this *one* form of punishment? *It is not easy, being a German.* It is especially not easy even now, sixty years later, to live in Great Britain, or should I call it England? They, the British, cherish their victory, and so they should. But they do tend to forget looking inside the cracks of history, to see the countless numbers of ordinary, powerless, frightened Germans bullied as much as others by that brutal, terrifying system of the Third Reich. They would prefer to overlook there were some who never truly understood the consequences of Nazism, or the many brave ones who discovered to their peril the consequences of insubordination of any kind.

Giving the Hitler salute and all the other childish role-playing was expected of every citizen, and one saw it clearly even then: going along with the Nazi ethos, Nazi rules, was a prerequisite for staying alive. I had no notion whatsoever of what was going on, over sixty years ago. Not one single time did I see my parents raising their arms in the Nazi salute...perhaps they did when I wasn't looking. But then we were there only for the last terrible months. Only misguided milkmen, puffed-up military officials, simple-minded bureaucrats, teenage boys, may, in those days, still have had any enthusiasm for displays of loyalty to the Reich. It was perilous not to conform, right to the bitter end.

April 1945. 'Now new things are happening: we have good food like butter and cheese and cake on this small ship, but I am ill, and can't eat...curled up on a bunk, well, a sort of bench under the porthole, my throat is hot and red and I can't swallow a thing...

****

At last: we are in a new place, a fairytale town: every house has roses growing up the walls. It is called 'die Rosen Stadt.' It has cobbled roads, like the ones in Swinemünde, but no ships, only a lake with rowing boats. Nothing is broken or bombed. I don't think there even *is* a war in Eutin...it feels like a holiday place. Our friends give us food and help us settle down while we tell them about the bombs. My father talks about our raid in Swinemünde: a 'terror raid', he says, and 'carpet bombing.'

At first we live in a very old house right high up, under the roof. It was built in 1650. My father has to bend all the time. A week or two later we move to a newer house, also belonging to this same family. They are called the Heyers, one of three sets of Heyers in Eutin. These new Heyers have given us a room with a higher ceiling, right at the top of *their* house, which was built in 1930. My father can stand straight at last.

A bed for two people with shiny brass railings, wonderful! But I sleep on a prickly straw mattress on the floor; with a puffy blue and white checked feather-bed. Our two windows open up right next to the Post office, where friendly ladies sit waving and laughing, we could have touched hands if we really stretched. Our attic room is tiny, the toilet downstairs on the next floor shared with the whole house. No-one here has a bathroom. The owners of this house live on the ground floor. Their daughter Ursula has big staring eyes, she is eleven. Her father is still in the war, no-one knows where, nor when he will come home. They say things differently here, I like the way they speak and I *love* the way Frau Heyer cooks. We are allowed to use her kitchen: we are all becoming a big family, with Tante Inge (I am allowed to call her that) doing all the cooking which we eat together at a long wooden table with a low lamp hanging over it. She knows how to cook unusual things. She uses fruit and vegetables; lucky Ursula to have such a mother. Ursula stays at home, there is something wrong with her brain, she can't read or write. She can play though.

For almost a year I have missed proper school, but now I must go again. After school Ursula and I pick dandelion leaves for the rabbits. We made a dark den in the roof of the outhouse; it is full of spiders and cobwebs, but we've swept it and arranged old boxes and cloths and cushions. It is our own pretend- home......

May 1945. There were no air raids in Eutin. Once I saw dirty, ragged people walking down the middle of our road, at least five in each row. Were they going to the station, perhaps, just around the corner, about thirty or forty of them? They carried nothing and looked burnt and bandaged and ragged. My mum heard they had come on trucks from Hamburg where there'd been a terror-raid, just like in Swinemünde. So they were refugees. Somebody must have had a plan where they could go? Sometimes dirty ragged soldiers walked on our street. They also had nowhere to go. The town was filling up with refugees from everywhere. Then, suddenly British soldiers were coming. At least they weren't Russians.....

But the grownups in Eutin were nervous: would they have to fight......?

'We should spend the night in my wooden summerhouse next to a nearby lake', said Tante Inge, 'it is a long walk, but, well, better to be safe'. So we loaded up a 'Buller-wagen', and pulled it along, with bedding and bread and apples and stuff and walked for about three hours, after dark, to this lake. If the British came into Eutin in the night there might be danger ...best to hide until it was all over. Ursula and I crept up a little ladder and made ourselves a bed under the eaves of the summerhouse. The grown-ups slept on chairs downstairs. No-one heard even one single shot: it was a silent night. In the morning Tante Inge stuck her head out to see if anything was going on. The lake lay still, like a   sparkling mirror, even the birds were silent...nothing was moving.

Soon we discovered the British had entered Eutin from the *other* side and were already in charge of the town. After a day or two when we had nothing left to eat we walked back to town, feeling sheepish but also wary. It was not long before I saw my first British soldier. There were plenty of them in jeeps but this one was just strolling along. I did the V for victory sign and told him: 'I can speak English' He laughed and asked 'how come?' So I told him I came from Pretoria. He fished in his jacket pocket and gave me chocolate. (Guess what: it worked every time!)'

***

Tante Inge has decided Ursel and I need new dresses for Pentecost, a special holiday in Germany. 'We will go for a long walk through the woods and right round a lake to a restaurant where one can eat jellied eels' she told us. I didn't know or care about jellied eels but I loved the dresses the dressmaker made for us: pale blue shiny cloth with large pleats front and back and white lace collars. I think it had been an old curtain before. Ursula and I look like sisters. Tante Inge enjoys seeing her daughter play so happily. I don't believe Ursula has ever had a friend.

My new school is only 10 minutes walk from home. I love going there and all the things we have to do. The war is finished now and although the fighting has stopped there still is no food anywhere.

****

A few months later, before the winter came, my mother found me boots for the coming winter from CARE parcels she was helping to distribute. One boot was brown and the other was black but they were warm and dry. No time for vanity then.

Hand-knitted knee length socks made from thick sheep's wool scratched and prickled, but they helped the boots stay on. I also owned a new winter coat, made from a grey army blanket. The words 'DEUTSCHE ARMEE' were printed in large letters, fortunately only on the inside. For Christmas the big surprise was a muff made from rabbits' fur.

This fur had grown on *our* rabbits, the ones Ursula and I had been devotedly and carefully feeding in previous summer months.

One must learn, to 'harden one's heart', says Mutti.

But the British were super: they came to our school and we had to take off our clothes so they could decide who was too thin. I was one of the lucky ones. From that day onwards thin girls were allowed soup with fatty blobs swimming on top, as well as a cream cracker. I brought mine home, so my mother could have some too.

Eutin was such a good town: There was a convent where a nun taught me to play the recorder and piano. She was quite hunched, with a twisted crippled foot....as we had no piano my mother sent me to practise across the road: our grocer owned an upright in his tiny storage room. There, amongst sacks of flour and weevils, I sat each day, practising on his 'honky-tonk,'... I was so happy.

Sometimes happiness *is* like that: *not* knowing any better.

Soon I had friends, who invited me to come and play at their houses, or even to sleep there. This put an end to my thumb-sucking. My best friend Jutta would laugh for sure, if she noticed. So I stopped, for ever, there and then. We went to recorder lessons together. Her mum was a professional singer who showed off like mad, wearing ex-tra-or-di-nary clothes! She'd come to our house, stand outside the windows, sing a sonorous bit of opera full blast, to make us hear she'd arrived. The whole street knew. My own parents were so dull by comparison. Mind you, they had become friends with Colonel Jones, and his family, who were the British 'rulers' of Eutin. Now these people lived in an old-fashioned smart house, called Pulverbeck, with a huge grand piano and they had a car and amazing food. Going there was *really* something. They gave me an amazing book called Arthur Mee's 'Everlasting Things'.

'My parents were always out. This was because my father had become an important person, a Bürgermeister, which means everybody knows you. I was the 'Bürgermeisters daughter'. When they went out at night they just said: 'go to bed after you've done your homework and then you can listen to our radio.' It was a very little radio. I remember them listening to it, when the war ended and my mother cried.

****

They had more and more friends. One New Years Eve they felt sorry for me and said: 'Here is the alarm clock. We will set it to wake you up at midnight and we will give you a glass of port-wine and our radio, so you can listen to the music at midnight and drink a toast to the New Year.' That's how my parents were....

One morning after they'd been out to dine with friends, my father woke up, and managed, but *only just* to get out of bed and open a window. He had smelt gas. My mother was still extremely *fast* asleep. It seems I had left the gas on just enough to kill them both. After heating my supper and eating it all alone, I'd climbed upstairs to my attic and gone to bed.

This was *one* way to learn to be more careful. They were not cross at all.'

I had long thick pigtails in those days. Strange, I don't remember washing my hair very much; maybe one doesn't need to when one is only eleven or twelve. My birthdays were fun too: I was allowed to invite a few girls from my class to come to my attic where we giggled and laughed and ate cake and drank lemonade.

The lemonade is much better now... during and straight after the war German lemonade tasted vile. I can't imagine what it was made of. Anyway, it was pink.

I also learned about old customs like walking two-by two in procession, while carrying a paper lantern with a lit candle and singing:

'*Laterne, Laterne, die Sonne Mond und Sterne, Brenne aus mein Licht, brenne aus mein Licht, Nur meine kleine Laterne nicht....*'

This was to mark November the first, a gloomy day for so many reasons and yet the happiest for young children in Schleswig Holstein.

In the icy winters I built up fond memories, wearing my new winter coat with fur hem and a fur muff, going to midnight Mass in sparkly snow, and yes, I *did* remember the rabbit, but it felt so lovely wearing this, especially at night. Unforgettable too, just a few months on, was Spring, with snowdrops and carpets of primroses and later that scented lilac along the way to school; how lucky I felt.

104

Tante Inge liked to sunbathe in her deckchair in the backyard; she'd go really brown, already in May. Chatting to her, baking in the sun, I had my first brush with psychic matters.

'When will my husband come home from the war?'…she asked and I replied, (chancing it, I knew): 'in exactly four months from today. Surprisingly this is what *really* happened. Now I had acquired a reputation for soothsaying. I never succeeded again. Mind you…curing warts in the Schleswig Holstein way might just fall into this category: *If you wish to cure a wart, first wait until full moon, then sit outside under the moon, but it has to be midnight, then, allow a slimy snail to creep over the offensive growth.* Mine fell off three days later, not just one, but a whole nest of them on my left knee.

In summertime everyone's attention turned towards the beautiful lake, the Eutiner See, where there were long wooded walks around the shores, sailing boats and regattas and, passing over a small wooden bridge: an area given over entirely to swimmers. Each summer a patient, bronzed man in swimming trunks held onto a fishing rod *at the end of which was a child*, learning to swim… probably an especially strong construct, with a harness to be strapped around the prospective swimmer. I so wish I'd been taught that way, so safe and comforting. It has to be said that swimming in natural lakes takes some getting used to: there are ducks and 'bits' and slimy things, unlike the Pretoria swimming pool. Lakes have a strange odour, which changes with the seasons, and when certain algae take over… even I refused to go in.

Those four years in Eutin were the richest and happiest: *two* parents, real friends, real seasons, excellent teachers, adventures of a kind that I had not had before. One 'adventure', never revealed to my parents, was the day yet another 'Tommy' promised me some chocolate. 'Come to the barracks, not very far from your school, I'll be there, I have some in my wardrobe, just come along and I'll get it for you.'

'My lucky day' I thought, 'to talk to this nice young man, who has enough chocolate to *give away.*'

When I got there he was waiting, ready to show me in. No-one else was there. 'This is where I sleep,' he said, 'you can sit down here,' patting the blanket covering his bed. We sat down and chatted, 'how old are you, what things do you like doing', things like that.

At last he went to get the chocolate. Then he put his arm round me and stroked my upper leg. His hand went under my skirt…Grabbing my chocolate I pulled away and ran out shouting: 'you are very rude'….and ran and ran, looking back, again and again until I was sure he was not following…

Admittedly there were few chocolates, treats, new clothes, only that intangible thing called 'culture'. This sounds so pompous:

One was learning to savour and appreciate the things that stay with one for life: smells, tastes, poetry and songs, classical music, art, theatre, even a brief bit of ballet, school excursions, friends who were weavers, potters, painters...metal-workers, a total life experience. As soon as the war ended these creative activities sprang back to life.

Most adults we knew were *making* things, useful things, such as thickly woven sheep's wool rugs, or prickly knee length socks: these admittedly, I came to loathe. We knew potters, furriers, tailors and the most indescribably medieval shoemaker who worked in a dark 'cave-like' cellar to the right of the Rathaus on the market. Another regular was a man who beat brass into ashtrays and wall hooks and ornamental candlesticks. In those dark years after the war, when there was *nothing* to be found in the shops, these wonderful creative persons were the salt of the earth.

Right in the midst of *general renewal and rebirth* I also *began* to understand about dying: my grandparents in their dismal old age home died one after the other. I say that glibly. One doesn't understand until one gets old oneself. Poor Ida and Alexander had become two ancient, grumpy persons, with an unpleasant odour and nothing but complaints. The flight from the Russians, leaving behind their lives, home and possessions, had broken their spirits. At that time there was very little we could do for them.

I can only suppose my father was relieved when their suffering was over. They died about one year apart, in 1947 and 1948 and were both buried in Lübeck. An organist played Handel's Largo, both times. To this day I can't hear this without thinking of dismal wintry funerals...mixed with guilt that I'd felt no love for them at a time when they most needed it.

*****

My 'best' friend Gabriele lived on a farm. She invited me to spend time there; amazing because of the good food, the horses which were 'mating', the family's own small lake where we swam in the nude,...the golden glow around all this early sensuous awakening of the most innocent kind.

We played recorder duets, folksongs, little pieces by Bach, Telemann. Once I'd left Eutin we lost touch. I liked her name so much that I swore I'd pass it on to my own daughter one day. But my very, very 'best' friend was Jutta. I wish I could remember why. It was complex: we were classmates; she had this loony singer-mother. We too played recorder duets. We roller-skated, with great gusto; I fell and broke my right arm in three places. This was established only one day later, when I had been dragged along to visit the ailing grandparents in Lübeck, all the time moaning about my arm. Of course my parents assumed I was trying to get out of going. But the following day an X-ray revealed three fractures. My arm was in plaster for months.

How quickly one learns to do everything with the left arm; my teachers were impressed by both handwriting and drawings.

During all these events Jutta was always around. We gave each other confidence, advice, and exchanged secrets. Almost grown-up, private ones, as we had become teenagers who were now called 'Fräulein'; for the first time. We no longer had to do a 'Knicks' when shaking hands with grownups, (a 'Knicks' being a small curtsey). Another first was a crush on a boy. This was no ordinary boy, he was a superb violinist. His name was Uwe.

By then I was a pianist of roughly Grade VlII level, but, only by the very end of four years in Eutin, a beginner violinist. I'd been roped into a group of young musicians who were being rehearsed to play Haydn's 'Toy Symphony.' I was the 'cuckoo'. What an honour!

Uwe was the concertmaster. I sat at the back of the little band assigned to my *vital* task. This meant I had to count carefully and come in with the lamentable 'cuckoo' at just the right split second. If ever there was a task I was not able to fulfil, this was it. I soon learned to fake the counting and came in, *often* in the right spot, by ear. Story of my life....

But this is when it all started. My l passion for the violin, inextricably mixed with admiration for our 'concertmaster', was born.

I pleaded for a violin. My parents managed to track one down. It was 'mine' on an indefinite loan from the kind Heyer family who owned one, stored away for at least 50 years in their attic; a lovely thing it was too, with a glowing red varnish, frayed gut strings and a carved scroll in the shape of a lion. I was in heaven.

Nearly all young violinists in Eutin had lessons with a gaunt old lady called Lila Kroening-Devantier. (She was actually the first female violinist to be employed *professionally* as rank and file player in a German symphony orchestra.) To get to her I had to walk up Bahnhof-Strasse, turn right past the station and the old windmill... and at the end of the road was her ancient house with low-beamed ceilings, a sanctum of magic mystery: the sound of violins. I was not taught in her large dark music room with mysterious objects and pictures, but in a tiny, sunny spare room. On the wall a beige cloth wall-hanging with embroidered and appliquéd Egyptian figures of the antique variety, entered my subconscious then and has just resurfaced, as I write. I worshipped this teacher…and everything about her.

Within four months she invited me to perform at one of her prestigious pupils' concerts: I played, with piano accompaniment, an arrangement of a song by Mozart called 'Komm lieber Mai'. One of the three Frau Heyers present told me afterwards that the violin sounded wonderful and that she was proud of me. As it was really *her* violin I was gratified she was so fulsome. My parents could not come for some reason. After the concert I was accompanied home, with a longish detour, by Uwe. On this walk we promised each other to correspond when I'd got to Africa and that we would *never* forget each other. I was just 14 years old. Four of the happiest, and also the most dangerous years of my life were over. We left with many tears, said goodbye to vast numbers of friends and got on a train to Oslo, to catch a freighter sailing for CapeTown.

I was numbed, leaving behind my first boyfriend, my friends and my violin-teacher. Life no longer seemed worth living.

My mother was sulking too. How could we possibly share my fathers' vision of our future in Africa?

July 10ᵗʰ, 1949. The Bay Beach Hotel, Seapoint, CapeTown.

Dear Uwe, my parents are spooked by a coincidence: they have the same room number as in 1938. It's nice here, very windy, as we are just by the sea…I see it from my window. Every day my father goes to town to look for a job with various former colleagues, but so far he has no luck. I search in the newspaper each morning to see if I can find one, for him, but it seems I'm not old enough to get this right. Most friends from before the war have gone elsewhere, even their favourites, the Kraemers, who now live on a farm many miles from here. We are going to buy a car and drive there. I miss everyone in Eutin and all I can do now is practise my violin, but quietly, as we are in the hotel.

It is hard for my parents. Perhaps it will be fun to go to that farm. I can't remember the Kraemers, he is called Pop, she is called Eve. Please write to me at the farm next time. Will I ever go to school again?

Searching for work in Cape Town was fruitless. The only way forward was to stop spending money on the hotel, to borrow a car and drive off into the unknown.

'Heidehof', a farm very near Plettenberg Bay, about 5 hours' drive from CapeTown, belonged to a German friend who had bought the land in 1940. He and his wife Eve had then built their own house, in the style of an old Cape Dutch farmstead, along with a few outhouses,.. had established wheat fields, youngberries, bees, helped of course by black workers and learning new skills as they went. A brave venture….and what a kind offer, taking us poor refugees in.

These were the nicest things: to live in the 'bush', surrounded by breathtaking scenery, plants, birds, all the business of daily chores, the space and sounds and smells…unforgettable, priceless. Eve Kraemer, a painter by profession (and farmers wife by necessity), became my adored grown-up role model. She was so gentle, funny, positive and kind; I was reminded that ten years ago we had loved each other just as much, in that painful Cape Town era, when my father was locked up as prisoner of war and these same Kraemers had befriended us.

'Auntie Eve' takes it upon herself to mother us, feed us and to stop my parents from despairing.

We are given jobs to do…woodwork for my Dad, cementing stone steps, building a rondavel; my mother and I learn how to open beehives wearing helmets with nets and glove; we harvest youngberries and grenadillas, we cook jam to be bottled and sold. It is satisfying, fulfilling, bonding and exhausting… and after all that work we sit on a wide covered veranda and allow our eyes to scan an expanse of shrubs and trees dipping down into a valley framed in the distance by the mysterious Tsitsikamma Mountains.

Just 15 minutes' drive down a winding road lies 'Nature's Valley', the most glorious, still little known, beach in South Africa. In no time at all we have turned into *new* people, *new* South Africans, forever spoilt and unfit to live anywhere else, for we are now in paradise, underscored with a permanent chorus of crickets, birds and occasional ominous rustlings in the tall grass. My poor father, still hunting for a suitable post in the world of ships, is already close to 50. No-one seems to want him. Instead the Ihlenfeldts appear to be on the point of becoming 'farmers,' just like the Kraemers. This pleases Erika…but Reini voices his doubts. As much as I love it here I can't quite believe we'll end up as farmers. My parents are far too unpractical. I have no faith in their skills whatsoever.

Months of idyllic farm-life come to an end.

I am to be 'kitted' out for the Holy Cross Covent in George, about two hours drive away. The farm food has built me up somewhat. I have no idea how or where a beret should be placed on my head, without making me look like an idiot. Two stupid pigtails, long black stockings to be attached to a suspender belt, along with four pairs of voluminous navy bloomers, shirt, tie and a pleated uniform complete the picture.

Who *is* this unbelievably gross, lumpen creature I ask myself, standing before a full length mirror. A good thing Uwe can't see me now.

Mother Superior, in her great wisdom, decrees I must sleep in the junior dormitory, as my English sounds unconvincing. I should also attend lessons with juniors, until acclimatized.

I recall my first night in the dormitory, surrounded by 'tinies'. I was not going to show my dismay being with them, but when the lights went out I burst into hysterical tears. Someone reported this. I was questioned.

On the following day I was established with girls in my own age group, and within days all was going swimmingly. Well? *Quite well*........

One of the hardest things was to be woken at six by a nun ringing a bell: we, the fast-asleep girls were expected to leap out of bed, kneel down and pray. Unforgettable: that semi-conscious slithering out of bed onto ones knees...putting ones head on the bed to imitate prayer and yet sleeping another sixty precious seconds. One or two early risers could be heard murmuring prayers but I don't think I ever managed. Thirty or more beds were then required to be made up by us unfortunates and then to be measured by the same nun now armed with a ruler; she'd lean back, close one eye, judge the alignment... *everything had.... to be.... perfect.*

There were *lurking* difficulties...not to do with language or bed-making, but with the simple fact that I was German. WW2 had not been forgotten in South African schools... most nuns came from England or Ireland. One or two really had it in for me. Someone, not a nun (of course), stole my tuck box, a miraculous gift of assorted goodies, sent to me by a friend of my parents in CapeTown. I felt crushed on all fronts, battling with all the holy stuff such as Mass first thing before breakfast,... daily prayers of the Angelus, when the bells rang...all this was so alien and yet, as a Catholic, I had to conform. I felt trapped. Later during term there was 'retreat' for the Catholics, which meant *no* talking, *no* school work, for three whole days. I was speechless, (which was the whole idea, of course) but became resentful and unfriendly.

When I pointed out there was all that catching up I had to do, that I was hardly able to afford spending three days reading improving tracts about saints, my comments were not appreciated.

'Behaving like a bloody German'....is what they thought, without a doubt.

On Saturdays there were 'etiquette' lessons. One was instructed what *not* to say at dinner parties (*never* talk about religion or politics) what *not* to wear (nothing too short or shiny) and which books to avoid.

There were all manner of humiliations on a daily basis: nuns inspecting ones fingernails, ones closet, ones bathtub, bed-making skills and woe to anyone who was not towing the line. On Saturdays: dry-cleaning your school uniform with a damp rag,… shining shoes, a discipline similar to that in the army, only more ferocious, with feral nuns giving black looks with unfailingly sharp eyes… endlessly chalking up black marks. All-powerful and constantly breathing down ones neck: they were the enemy. I kept my head down at first, becoming more outspoken as time went by. My only comfort was the splendid music hall, where I spent as much time as possible, practising both violin and piano. This was my salvation: the nuns soon softened when it appeared I had won several gold-medals at a regional Music Competition, bringing glory to the school.

None of the initial troubles were relayed to my parents. Our letters, written under weekly supervision, were censored. I had the advantage of writing in German of course, and doubted any of the nuns could cope with that. Still, one never knew…..I even managed a correspondence with Uwe in Germany; changing his name to Ewu seemed to fool the nuns. In this way we stayed in touch, even under these most trying conditions. Innocent letters told him about my first experience of Gilbert and Sullivan's "Mikado", studying the role of Katisha, the ugly sub-heroine. I had memorized all my arias and soon found myself on the stage, feeling self-conscious and silly. My 'operatic career' was short-lived: I was conscripted into the orchestra pit instead, my voice, allegedly, too soft to carry more than about three yards.

Playing the violin in the pit did me a lot of good. I had only been at it for about a year after all.

***

While all this fitting in, adapting and adjusting was going on my enterprising parents had set themselves up in the Namib Desert, doing much the same. My father had left no stone unturned, and of course he found a right worm under one of them: a posting to South West Africa, in a god-forsaken harbour called Walvis Bay. The job came with a grey breezeblock house, and loo, out in the sand-dunes. In 1950 the Ihlenfeldts took up residence in their first real home since 1939, and there they remained, happily, for eight years.

Yes, indeed: Walvis Bay *really* was in a desert, complete with almost daily sandstorms, no electricity, no sanitation and one main road. A Railway Institute, used by desperados and drunken sailors, provided entertainment.

To visit South West Africa from school was a three-day / four-night train journey both ways. Because of the great distance I was eventually moved to another Holy Cross Convent, in Windhoek, only about 12 hours away from Walvis Bay, run by same order of nuns, in a rather less 'frightening' establishment, or perhaps I'd just got used to boarding schools by then. The pupils were a mixture of German, English and Afrikaans speakers, the nuns as before, mostly Irish or from England.

I did not miss the George Convent, so cold and wet….and so very strict. Windhoek Convent, instead, was hot and dusty, with a swimming pool and daily siestas during the hottest part of the day, offering a great deal less holiness than the George Convent. Things were more relaxed. One began to feel in control of ones own destiny.

Only two more years and I would go to university somewhere, perhaps even back to Europe, to my mother's sister in Vienna. That was the plan.

How nice to be sixteen, to begin noticing ones body, ones hair and clothes, to make friends in a more meaningful way. School seemed a doddle, I had chosen the easy way out and there was in any case nothing seriously difficult to contend with: the nuns taught neither physics nor chemistry, so I left out maths, my worst subject, and coasted along on English, German, Afrikaans, history, geography, botany and music. This was a huge mistake. I realized, six months before my final exams that maths was the very subject one needed to study science at University.

Still, at first my new school was perfect and I made meritorious advances, even to being nominated prefect for several terms.

During my final year I was allowed out of school to take private violin lessons with a local professional, now sorely in need of a more methodical approach. My teacher, a German aristocrat who, unforgettably, had a small gold crown painted on his car doors, not only had high standards, but was also very kind. Whenever I played badly I blamed it on the lousy food at the convent and he invariably took the hint by inviting me into his kitchen and offering me salami or delicious German liver sausage on bread-rolls.

Several events stand out during that time:

We were starved in more ways than one: girls of 16 and 17 feel the need to befriend the opposite sex. I was beginning to gaze at priests or altar boys, or anyone in trousers, in a somewhat hypnotic way. It was surprising the nuns allowed me out to spend time with the aristocrat violin teacher. But we both behaved immaculately. This was the time when 'attachments' might have become both troublesome *and* pleasurable.

My class teacher, Sister Dympna, who could speak German, was a large ungainly nun, palpably unhappy in her own skin who wandered up and down in our senior dormitory saying her rosary, restless as a caged lion, when we were trying to go to sleep. She had a crush on me; I found cream cakes in my desk and she insisted on making me a brown taffeta party dress...only God knows why. I suppose she enjoyed taking my measurements. It was all very proper, and nice for me, to be thought so wonderful by a poor, dumpy, disturbed nun. Hormones could be troublesome, even to the brides of Christ.

During holidays teenage hormones were on the rise as well. My group of boys and girls met up on bicycles and somehow managed to enjoy life, despite the god-forsakenness of Walvis Bay. There were long afternoons in a beach hut, reached after much heavy pedalling through sand-dunes, (horrible if not impossible,) where we'd sit about, picnicking and flirting. We met in each others' homes, listened to strange songs like 'I'm a lonely little petunia in an onion patch,' Charlie Kunz creations and pop songs of the forties such as 'Always' and 'Yes, my darling daughter.' The infamous Railway Institute showed appalling films; in desperation we saw each one through. There was little else to do.

My *special* boyfriend, Patrick Hamilton, was also keen on Elaine Bramwell, who had a rather handsome brother called Leslie, whom I fancied as well. We all fancied each other. And, oh yes, the local baker's son, Karl-Heinz Maischatz, how could one ever forget such a name, he fancied me for my musical skills, a kindred soul, a decent pianist. His father baked marvellous pastry. This bespectacled boy was not part of our bicycle group...., a much too studious and earnest fellow, who, I heard later, died very young.

Then there was a German boy, who fell madly in love ...he had a memorable way to remind me of his feelings: his first job in the new Power Station allowed him to send me nightly greetings by switching off Walvis Bay's power supply in three short bursts at 10pm. He also had the deplorable habit of visiting my mother, when I was back at school. He'd sit and sit, wanting to talk about me. At first she felt sorry for him, later she decided to be brutal, and sent him on his way.

So, a pattern emerged: innocent gadding about, no drinks, no drugs, only simple clean fun. We were 'good' children, and very well controlled by the strict morals of the time. I'd as good as forgotten Uwe in Germany, although we did still write occasional letters.

There were new attachments, nothing too serious, and for us all an imminent reversal of the state of dependence on parents to the state of 'going out into the world'. Of all these young persons I was the only one to go to university. I was still a very immature and babyish person. My obsessive violin playing, after only four years, was not quite of a high enough standard to take up further studies.

'Don't even think about a career in music' was my parents' advice and 'it is not 'done' for a woman to play in orchestras. Besides', said my mother, 'you'll never find a husband with this terrible scar on your neck...do you *have* to practise all the time?' (Parents: they have such antiquated, annoying ideas.)

'Why not become a scientist, like your grandfather,' they suggested, meaning well.

'But it's only six months before my 'matric,' I pointed out in horror, 'one needs maths for that!'

Suddenly there was no choice: without further ado I settled down to catch up on a subject I hated and had successfully avoided for over a year. A dedicated Irish nun took it upon herself to sort out what little maths I had, adding the missing bits in record time.

It was she who discovered I needed glasses, as I sat frowning at the blackboard. (I did pass but, disgracefully, only with a C, when all other subjects had been A's or B's....a portent of what was to come.)

My life's story so far...*always catching up, learning at great speed things that others have done long before me:* English and Afrikaans aged five, then sorting out German once settled in Eutin, discovering violin aged fourteen, (a dead loss starting that late if you're serious about it,) endlessly changing schools, countries, friends, ...*nothing but hurdles and more hurdles......*

Well, I managed the maths. Now the next hurdle: a degree in science: three long years. Uselessly, feebly submissive, I was a push-over, a door-mat.

'You can have violin lessons too,' the fond parents said. What a hope. Without one single physics or chemistry class in my life I would soon be attending first year lectures. The only preparation for this was a small book I had exchanged for a voucher I'd won in an essay competition in South West Africa. There it is, on my bookshelf to this day: 'Die Welt in der Retorte,' a modern Chemistry for everyone, with 180 drawings and 16 charts. It did not help that it was in German, but reading it proudly, carefully, I believed I'd have a fighting chance as a serious student.

Ironic: the prize-winning essay had been on the subject of my greatest love...the violin. It was no big deal winning the first prize in South West Africa in 1952: in such a huge country there were very few schools. Touchingly, inside the cover it gives my address: E. Ihlenfeldt, P.O. Box 18, Walvis Bay. Why is this so moving, half a century on? Hidden among the pages is also a 'holy card', the sort that nuns give their favourite pupils on special occasions. It reads:

Unum est necessarium: Nosce te ipsum!
In sua voluntate, nostra pax.

Growing Up.   Know thyself: 'nosce te ipsum'.

It is fair to say I can't be sure I do. I know I've burnt my school books, I know I am 18 years old and 'reside' in Fuller Hall, the official residence for 200 girls on campus in Cape Town. My mother was in tears when we said goodbye. I can't bear it when she cries. I know she loves me. I love her too.

Everything, everybody is thrilling; I feel so excited! We all have our very own rooms, part of H Flat, there are nine of us and we're mostly from *distant* parts of southern Africa...Nyasaland, South West, Transvaal, Eastern Cape, Southern Rhodesia and Natal.   What a collection of travellers: It will take me 3 days and four nights to get back home by train. My parents are a thousand miles away. I am classified an *ex-enemy alien*, which means I must visit a police-station every three months to show what I am up to. What if I forget? Too bad I'm still on my father's passport...why can't I have one of my own?

Why do I have to be a German?

Perhaps 'freedom' is over- rated, this is one thing I'm not sure about yet. By my modest standards (penniless, the War, convents etc) I'm on a roll and simply can't believe my luck. 'Freshettes' like myself must pin a green bow to their clothes, for three months. This is *one* of the rules our delightful lady warden, Mrs. Emmett, tells us to obey. We are also expected to sign out whenever we leave the residence, stating time and destination, have to be in by midnight; only one night a week though, having told the warden with whom and where we are going. Modified 'freedom' then, modified rapture for a while. And yet, I feel elated.

Should one dare infringe there is a house committee, who are very strict indeed; one would probably be 'gated'. Still, this isn't at all bad: it is sheer heaven compared to the convent.

At night I lie in bed and listen to the distant roars of the King of Beasts...the Groote Schuur Zoo is only 500 metres from where I am housed; instigated by Cecil Rhodes who had a fondness for lions... now I must listen to their unhappy calls.

Compared to the other lovelies in H Flat I am a true Cinderella: *everyone* has *more* and *better* clothes. Some of them even use make-up. And they have loads of pocket money. Here I am, in a navy-blue convent skirt with one of my Mum's hand knitted pullovers. She makes all my clothes and they are terrible. Do I mind? Yes. But my parents pay for my fees and residence, so I try not to. As for music lessons....no, there are far more pressing things to worry about: getting to lectures in the morning, practicals... most afternoons. Signed up for Physics, Chemistry, Botany and Zoology leaves little time for much else. I have white lab coats, regularly laundered by the coloured maids; slicing up smelly dogfish or peering into a microscope, all this is much better when one wears a snowy white lab gown: it goes with the job. It's all rather fun. For dinner we don black academic gowns; mine is venerable, has seen many previous owners. The effect of wearing all these garments is subliminally empowering.

Then reality sets in: the worst is Physics. Sitting far back in one of those sloped lecture theatres I try to grasp what a remarkably shrivelled old manikin is talking about, and simply cannot find the way into a single sentence he utters. There are no tutorials. No-one knows of my agony and disbelief. I have never been faced with something I couldn't at least understand just a little. I try and try again. I take notes and look at them. It is hopeless. I am too proud to tell anyone. No-one else in H flat is doing physics. 'So much for convent education', I think,' what shall I do?'

Anyway, there are more interesting events. Like Rag week, and the fun of staying up all night with the men from Smuts Hall across the road. For once there are no restrictions. Our float is called A BAD 'UN .... Everyone dressed in Arab clothes. I cannot work out what we are portraying. Each year wearily patient Cape Town-ians put up with mad students begging for money, waving hysterically from their floats parading through town, all for good causes, naturally: like helping coloured people and poor black children.

I am the 'freshette' chosen to go and chat up the Mayor of CapeTown to buy raffle tickets during Rag week. Why me, I wonder when I see my picture in the 'Cape Argus'.

My parents in distant South West Africa are amazed and proud.

Cape Town University has always been liberal and emancipated, compared to others in South Africa. Totally un-awakened politically, I have no views on the lot and lives of other races. Nuns never spoke of such things, *nor did my parents,* so now, when other students invite me to join various action groups I prefer to refuse. In my closed-in way I need all my time to myself. I have also learnt to be wary of 'being German'.

Looking back I would say I had the social conscience of a twelve year old. This comes of spending four years under the tutelage of nuns: history was a collection of stories in a book.... ancient Greece, the French Revolution, the Boer War, all interesting events to learn about, but I don't remember ever taking on board how to assess and judge anything. 'Never talk about religion and politics' was what our 'etiquette nun' had advised. This suited me just fine. I felt safe with that.

****

Kolbe House, Rondebosch.

One of my first brave ventures was to explore the Catholic Centre situated down a steep hill from my new 'home'.

I wandered into Kolbe House and noted times for Sunday Mass in the chapel and other activities which sounded like fun; the first one was to attend a tea party on the lawn under a venerable tree. Mrs. Spring, the housekeeper, had prepared a lavish spread for about twelve new students and I offered to help pour the tea.

This immediately identified me as 'a leader'. Soon I was roped into all manner of things I really did not want to do at all.

Moral: never offer to pour other people's tea. However: Sunday Mass in the chapel turned out to be a very good way to befriend other students. Over a friendly cup of tea in later months I heard a strange tale from twins called Helene and Thérèse: 'our brother mentioned he'd seen a 'freshette' at Mass and that he just *knew* he will marry her one day. Only *seen*, not even spoken to her!'

How romantic was that! Who could it be?

By then I'd settled into Botany studies with great gusto. It was even moderately interesting. Months later, during a practical in a laboratory I noted one of the demonstrators peering down my friend's microscope. Inside his tweed jacket I imagined broad shoulders, bearing silent witness to protective, caring kindness. I cooked up some questions to ask him, hoping he would peer down *my* microscope as well. He did look vaguely familiar. Later, strolling down the steps in front of Jameson Hall, to the residences, where he'd parked his car, he told me he was called Pierre, that he'd seen me at Mass, had graduated from Science last year, and was now studying for a BA. A tiny gold crucifix on his lapel told me he was very religious. He had beautiful black eyes with enviably long eyelashes. We both felt very shy.

I signed in, went to my room, and thought about 'my' demonstrator.

Another nice boy, also Catholic, seemed equally impressive. This one was an Irish redhead, with sticking-out ears, studying law, very witty and amusing. I liked him a lot. He never so much as noticed me; he was obsessed with another girl. I began to think I liked him even more than Pierre and more than the very rich Jewish boy, who also had a car and stood to inherit South Africa's Peanut butter industry. Now this one was very earnest indeed and decided I *had* to meet his parents: 'they are curious about you', he told me. 'O God, here we go', I thought.

In Bishopscourt, one of the smartest areas in town, in an intimidating mansion, over dinner, *his* parents questioned me about *my* parents and the War. They seemed satisfied with my account. Once their son had me back in his car to take me out some place he became somewhat demanding. I was very unfriendly about even a single kiss.... so this little episode came to a sudden end. I had hurt his manly feelings.

How difficult it was to get these encounters right! I didn't mean to hurt him, only to wriggle out of any sort of physical stuff ....this seemed top priority in those truly innocent post-convent days. And yet there *was a* bit of lust...like when I saw my Botany demonstrator in his tweed jacket. How does one describe such virginal, innocent 'lust': no more than a wish to be noticed and admired and perhaps, held, *briefly*. Perhaps I was just a tweed fetishist, unknowingly?

Somewhere in this new phase of existence was a first year science student, trying to keep up and feeling, surprisingly, in control of her social life. Those three years ahead seemed like an eternity of new delights and experiences, all waiting to be lived.

When I presented myself at the College of Music the authorities decided I was to be signed up with Maria Neuss, who in turn had studied with the great violin pedagogue Carl Flesch. Originally Czech, she enjoyed an international concert career. This means a great deal to a violinist: studying with her was a passport to violinistic respectability. Unforgettably, she always had a cigarette between her lips while demonstrating; the ash would become longer and longer until it fell on her instrument and slid down into the *f*-hole. All her students were waiting for the day her valuable instrument went up in flames. She was the wife of bushy-bearded conductor Fritz Schuurman, in charge of the University symphony orchestra. My place was soon to be at the back of the second violins. I had never played in a 'proper' orchestra before and found it very hard. 'The Mikado' in George did not count. This was terrifying, the steepest learning curve, ever.

To be honest, the thing I loved more than anything was walking down the hill to *attend* the rehearsals, to be part of the magical atmosphere in the revered College of Music and the feeling of being actually accepted by real music students and their teachers who formed the 'band.' No doubt they despised me, a mere science student. One learns to keep one's head down in such a group.

Those were the days when it was still safe for a young lady to walk home alone in the dark after rehearsal, all part of being 'free' and grown-up. The fact that my path home took me past Kolbe House, where my handsome Botany demonstrator lived, became an added pleasure. I could call on him, he would walk me up the hill. The road between the College of Music and Kolbe House was aptly named 'Lovers' Walk'. Now don't get this wrong ...I *was* a convent girl.

Pierre quickly brought me to a part of life that was completely undeveloped: literature and theatre. He already had his B.Sc. and now was *his* time for English literature. His tiny student's room was full of books, both French and English. He was fluent in French and eager to involve me in all his experiences. I assumed he had French origins. First he made me read Baudelaire and then Graham Greene. The days were not long enough to fit everything in. I wondered about his father, who allowed him to stay at university for yet another three years, 'he must be so well-off,' I thought, 'Pierre even has a car.'

He loved all theatre and took me to the Labia Theatre (named after its patron, Count Labia) to see a controversial new play called 'Waiting for Godot'. This was puzzling, material for much speculation. Pierre was always taking me out; we were getting fond of each other. There was so much to talk about. When the time came to visit Walvis Bay for a few weeks I had already become a much more conscious creature.

Strange, my parents seemed to disagree with me about almost everything.

Pierre and I wrote each other many letters. My old friends were still about, but I felt I'd moved on, being with them seemed different now. Stuck in Walvis Bay for six weeks, what a punishment...

'Unspeakably hideous, smelly Walvis Bay,' was all I could think, so I consoled myself listening, endlessly, to a recording of Bach's 'Chaconne' for solo violin. I was obsessed. This was music for being alone, for dreaming. I was also committed to play a Mozart 'Divertimento' for an event in our Common Room in Fuller Hall, at the beginning of next term. It gave me something to do. Other students got themselves holiday jobs to earn pocket money, but this possibility had not yet dawned on me. I must have been a real drag, mooching about for so long.

Fortunately I was not alone getting to Walvis Bay and back to CapeTown by old-fashioned steam train: other students joined in Windhoek and places further along the tedious trek southwards, with endless stops for picking up more coal and water. Sun beat down on the carriages and dust and soot flew into the windows, open because of the uncomfortable temperature. We consumed vile food and prayed for nightfall, when the cooler air made it possible to collapse on our bunks. Needless to say, depending on the company, there were raucous goings-on.

Tucked up with Graham Greene and Baudelaire I remained one of the quieter passengers. Was it four days and three nights, or the other way round? There was a lot of Africa and it all looked the same: dry shrubs, dust, small flat-topped hills and distant karakul farms, the odd dreary town...poor ragged black children running along the tracks, shouting, begging.....

The first thing after the return to University... was a hot bath. I have no memory of being picked up by anyone at the station. How did one get back to 'Uni' on the other side of Table Mountain? There is no memory, besides I would not have liked anyone to see me after such a trip.

The only thing in my Residence cubby-hole: a letter from Pierre, what joy!

Ndola, Northern Rhodesia.   *January 16ᵗʰ 1954*

Dear princess, I want this letter to be waiting for you when you arrive. I so look forward to see you; my so-called holiday, as you know, has been quite demanding ...Dad seems to think I need to know more about the business. He insists I stay as long as possible, which is why I can't pick you up from the station. No doubt your father has managed to send one of his friends in CT to get you back to Fuller Hall.

As soon as I arrive I'll take you out and we can have a long talk. How about the Drive-in at Sea Point? We'll have our favourite: Banana and Bacon toasted sandwich! Love from Pierre   Ps It's my birthday today!

After this separation we both realised how much we cared about each other; our delightful round of cultural explorations continued.

Soon exams were hanging over us: hard grind was now the only way forward and studying together was more fun than swotting alone. Armed with lecture notes, books and rugs we set out whenever we could to combine duty with enjoyment of beauty spots around the mountain, and on rainy days, Pierre's 'digs' were an interesting prospect.....

This was a tiny cottage in the gardens of Kolbe House shared with a troubled fellow student obsessed with issues of race and injustice, an Afrikaaner who carried South Africa's pain on his shoulders. One day we found him staining his skin brown and getting together torn and filthy shirts, trousers and worn out shoes, in order to be like a poor coloured labourer, looking for work. He then set out for the harbour to do research on the treatment of blacks and how it might feel to be one.

I didn't know what to think. No-one else I knew wanted to do such a thing. Pierre stood by, concerned, interested, but mainly with the worry that all this would backfire in some way, like the police finding out ...possibly the greatest fear in apartheid South Africa. Leanings of dangerous sympathies for coloured people were the perils that got one locked up in prison. It was all terribly hush-hush, best not talked about: there were spies about. We were sworn to secrecy.

My own awakening about bigger issues was a long time off, absorbed as I was by lectures, laboratory practicals, lessons at the College of Music and the attentions of my devoted boyfriend. Still only friends, physical proximity began gently, slowly, surely. He confessed to being an 'experienced' man, who had slept with prostitutes in Beirut, and this information I, an innocent convent girl, took on board with due interest and curiosity. Both Catholic and wary of getting into 'trouble', Pierre hinted darkly on several occasions that we had to 'talk'...that there was something I *really* needed to understand...and I replied guardedly: why yes, of course,' not knowing what he was on about.

Perhaps he wanted to get engaged? Perhaps he had picked up some ghastly disease, or, perish the thought, was there someone else? When he finally worked up the courage to tell me what was troubling him I was none the wiser. We'd devoured our favourite Banana and Bacon toasted sandwich at the Seapoint Drive-In when he revealed he was not French, as implied, but...*Lebanese*. Embarrassed, (I had never heard of 'Lebanese', and there were so many things I'd never heard of,) I said: 'I don't mind, honestly! What exactly *is* Lebanese?'

I'm not sure he believed me.

Nevertheless, I was given a long spiel about 'Liban', and the Cedar of Lebanon, and Phoenicians, and Arabs... and how his family always spoke French. Somehow he managed to convey that there was something wrong with coming from Lebanon, and that I, being German, would mind, would think him an Arab. Deeply concerned for him I was only at the very bottom end of a slow learning curve about such things.

All I knew was that I cared about him, would hate to hurt him. At that time I still had no idea that *anyone* might 'mind'.

'Why did you say you were French?' I wondered, and his reply was: 'because I speak French, because I love the French, and Lebanon belonged to France once.' What he could never bring himself to say was: 'I could pass for a French, Italian, Greek or whatever Mediterranean you'd like, but please *don't think of me* as an Arab, or Syrian, or Jewish.' He needed that little golden crucifix on his lapel, he needed his golden-eyed German girlfriend, he needed his Belgian cousin (*his* uncle Mansour had married a Belgian woman, Marthe, their child was therefore 'Belgian...')

This was a case of racial inferiority-complex and I began to understand how he saw me, on some sort of pure-race pedestal. All this brought out my missionary instincts: he was so vulnerable. I would help him, be his crutch, and to hell with all this incomprehensible thinking. For a long time we avoided the topic. It was deeply embarrassing, not only for him.

Year One of B.Sc. studies flew by and I found myself sitting the first University exams in Jameson Hall, or 'Jammie' as we called it. Pierre flew off to France and Belgium to spend time with his 'Belgian' cousin while I trekked for four nights and three days to languish in the Namib desert dump, Walvis Bay.

Romance on a train in the Namib Desert (a true story)....a dusty, tired girl student is accosted by a young man from Stellenbosch University, both on their way home for the holidays. Attracted by her violin case he enquires about her studies, her destination...they end up in the dining car as the train chugs towards a tiny station in the midst of nowhere. The sun has almost set: 'Tot siens', he mutters, looking deeply into her eyes...all those watching observe him being picked up by a farmer's truck. He turns, waves....the train moves on.

That night she sleeps badly, wakes up early. It is hot. She stands in the corridor to gaze across the expanse of dry dusty shrubs, turns her face to be caressed by the cool morning air. In the far distance she spots a horse, a rider, trying to catch up. How curious, he seems to be waving his hat, shouting. Gradually he catches up and she hears his shouts; 'Ek kan nie eet nie, ek kan nie slaap nie' (I can't eat, I can't sleep), 'can I visit you in Walvis Bay?' She shouts back: 'I have a boyfriend already, forget about me'....she sees him kick his horse to keep up.

Poor beast, it was exhausted. The rider waved and waved. The rider became smaller and was soon invisible.

****

Mercifully the exam results arrived in January:

I had failed Physics and Chemistry, and the re-sits were scheduled for March. For the first time ever I had to eat humble-pie, I was a spectacular failure…

1954 turned into a year of wrestling with fate, the odds against me. Pierre had returned from his holiday in Brussels and Paris laden with gifts of French perfume and frilly sexy knickers. Still crushed by my disastrous failure I was certainly kept out of mischief trying to pass *both* failed subjects without help from anyone. I did manage Chemistry but to my dismay Physics was a write-off, even the second time. Another year then, of my least favourite thing, and no escape. Having progressed to dissect, with trembling hands, such specimens as Dog fish, frogs and the nervous system of locusts, I now had before me the arm of a *real* corpse for my Zoology course, in the famous Groote Schuur Hospital. This made a deep impression.

Pierre of course passed everything and was always there for me, taking me to shows and balls and lovely drives all over the Cape Peninsula. We were known on campus as a 'starry-eyed' couple, madly in love. I was still a virgin, and remained one for another year at least, but cut off from real life, politics and the big world. It was like living in a bubble. Inevitably, they have a way of bursting. You can't see it coming, but it's a foregone conclusion.

I think it was an unglamorous year, but in the end I managed to get on to the final year of Microbiology, which was what I had been aiming at all along. One so loses track of goals when one has to take so many small difficult steps.

We had become secretly 'engaged' by the end of this time and somehow this closeness and security superseded all the science I was trying to absorb. I was nineteen years old. My trouble was I had absolutely no vision of what I really needed or wanted.

That 'violin-thing', my great passion, had withered. 'Science' was an unequal struggle, and there was no love at all.

Pierre? Well, he was my rock. What other reality was there?

By this time my parents knew all about the French / Lebanese boyfriend. Prudently they said very little, but the implication was that they'd had experience of Syrian traders during their many years in Accra, mostly wealthy diamond smugglers, or at least shady in some way. I suppose they were trying to influence me. They hoped this was a passing infatuation.

It never occurred to me my parents might be even remotely xenophobic. They'd lived in the *native* town of Accra, *not* with the whites in their own township, they had many Jewish friends, my father had enjoyed the favours of a pretty black mistress in his bachelor days, ...

By the time I started my third year my parents came to Cape Town and took us, Pierre *and* me, out for a drive near that spectacular bit of beach facing Table Mountain. I believed he'd won them over. Little did I know that, behind the scenes, there was an exchange of letters between the mothers: Pierre's mother had invited the Ihlenfeldts to visit Northern Rhodesia for Christmas, to break the ice. My parents' reply, although polite, was utterly negative: they had no wish to build any bridges; a marriage between a German and a Lebanese: unthinkable.

Pierre and I survived another two longish holidays apart. I even got myself my first job in a fish meal factory in Walvis Bay. The work was measuring the percentage of moisture in shipments of fish meal in a special laboratory: if any sack of the stuff was too dry it might ignite in the hold of a ship and cause death and destruction.

This was perhaps the most boring and smelly way to earn some cash one could ever imagine: there I was, in my white lab coat, piercing every bag of odorous fish meal with a special hollow needle containing a hygrometer, and then recording the result. Every *single* bag, and there were many hundreds, had to be pierced and accounted for.

My parents did appear to be proud of me.

I couldn't imagine why. Back in Cape Town, working in the Groote Schuur Hospital laboratories was part of the Course: mainly testing Petri dishes full of bacteria and working with X-rays during microbiology practicals. The most interesting part of my three-year course was potentially the most dangerous; now there was little time left before our final exams. Suddenly three years of study had shrunken to a few remaining months......

As far as the great love affair went we had, after some discussion, decided to take a very big step: I was to 'lose' my virginity. It was I who wanted this...'we just can't go on the way we have for so long. We are grown-ups,' ......and so on...

Why we decided to do it the way we did is a mystery now.

We went for a walk at dusk along a private mountain path, behind the University, somewhere below the famous Rhodes Memorial where, standing up, leaning against a sloped and uncomfortable rock of the 'Devil's Peak', Pierre 'deflowered' me. It was cold, calculated and less

124

painful, (he hoped,) for both, and appropriately scientific really. No mindless passion, nothing sexy at all.

Even worse: We both missed supper that evening.

****

Another dusty, interminable journey to Walvis Bay, more 'work experience', and, after six long weeks of so-called holiday I had a secret arrangement to meet Pierre on the train journey back to CapeTown, stopping off at a ghastly railway junction called De Aar. We so needed to be together, alone and far from prying eyes. CapeTown to De Aar must have taken at least a day by car, and Pierre had arranged for us to stay the night in De Aar's 'finest' hotel.......

One never forgets high emotions. Both exhausted, he from the long drive, me from the filthy train, our happiness to find ourselves together and completely alone in the middle of 'no-where' was, finally, an overwhelming dream come true.

We frolicked in a hot bath, dropped into bed and slept, intermittently. We were indescribably happy. It was our one-night honeymoon.

****

September 1955. 'Help...,my periods, they're late! Probably because of all this travelling...and being in Walvis Bay... my body reacts to such things, even at school I missed periods, like in George, only every three months....perhaps I'm just exhausted and also worried about Pierre and all that... If they don't come soon I'll find a doctor...I know, I'll ask Mrs Emmett to tell me the name of some-one. If I'm pregnant....I'd be kicked out of residence, and where would I go..., I'd better tell Pierre.'

While the doctor poked about inside me I heard his words... 'signs of early pregnancy'. I could feel the blood draining from my head.

'To be certain,' he said, importantly, 'I'll do another test. I'll let you know, in a day or two'.

'I'll call back' I assured him, and fled. I didn't want him phoning the residence.

Two days later: the results are 'positive'. Pierre, solicitous, strong, collected me in his car and drove me up into the mountains to Bain's Kloof, where UCT's wooden shack for Botany student research was to be home for a night and a day. I wondered if the bumpy road might not solve all our problems. We discussed our options: abortion, unthinkable, getting married at once: but what about our finals, parents, where would we stay? I could not think at all, let alone 'straight'. Poor Pierre abandoned me to 3rd year Botany students, to hard wooden bunk-beds in a log cabin and to the 'convivial' evening around the log-fire. The course was to begin in the early morning mists. My closest friend Marilyn became my confidante. Devastated and sleepless I considered gin or jumping off a cliff. It was too humiliating…'please God, let me have a miscarriage. Oh, to be an unsullied, un-pregnant me again, studying for that wretched B.Sc.'

After the Botany camp I made an appointment to talk to our warden, the kind Mrs Emmett. To my surprise I was embraced, congratulated, advised not to be dejected: 'just send a telegram to your parents, my dear, as quickly as possible! You can get married quietly,' she said, 'and stay in residence until after the exams are over, in nine weeks' time.' Well! Just like dissolving morning mists, the shock of what I'd got myself into floated away, to be replaced by acceptance and courage. Unexpectedly everything appeared straight-forward, the most natural thing. Common sense prevailed. I breathed again.

Mrs Emmett had only one request: that it all should remain secret. Whom had I told, only Marilyn? Then she too must be sworn to secrecy. I could have one night out, on the day of our wedding and was to sign back into residence the day after, return to the fold as if nothing had happened. But the news must not get about… it would set a precedent…

So here was this bombshell, a thunderbolt: an unspeakable event which was to shatter the cosy existence of the Ihlenfeldts. Their only daughter had become pregnant, with her long-time Lebanese lover Pierre, and they were about to be married. In 1955 there was no alternative: this was what one did.

I almost killed my mother with this blow to the family pride, honour, you name it. When the telegram arrived in my fathers' office he left work early to break the news. My mother passed out. The doctor was called…

It doesn't bear thinking about, their disappointment, shock and disgust with me and their own shame at having to tell friends and family. I knew how my father felt, he'd made it all quite clear one day when he explained that 'when different races mix the end result will be an unhealthy, unattractive, half breed, just look around you, look at all these poor 'coloureds' in South Africa.' He knew no better, I told myself, it was the handed-down wisdom of his age.

Shocked by his ignorance, saddened to realize he would never understand I despised him, ignored him. Did he have any insight into the appalling state *our* relationship was in?

My mother, more cunning and less outspoken, never came out with unscientific twaddle such as his, and eventually managed to put on a brave face. It must have been a learning curve for my parents too... It is fair to say that I felt totally distant, for a very long time. I hated them.

Years later I found the following letter from my mother to her parents in Austria.

Es schmerzt mich, Euch eine unerfreuliche Nachricht mitzuteilen. Vor wenigen Wochen kam ein Telegramm von unserer Tochter, dass sie ärztliche Bestätigung hätte, sie erwarte ein Kind. Der Vater ist angeblich dieser Pierre Attala, von dem wir Euch ja schon berichtet hatten. Eure Hoffnung, (unsere auch) dass sich das Verhältnis mir der Zeit verwachsen würde, ist hiermit zerstört, sie sind bereits kirchlich getraut. Knups studiert dennoch weiter und hofft ihre Schlussprüfung zu bestehen. Ab Mitte Dezember wird sie nun mit ihrem Kamel-treiber in Nord Rhodesien leben. Wir sind am Boden zerstört mit diesen Ereignissen.

It pains me to give you bad news. Some weeks ago we received a telegram from our daughter that she has been confirmed to be pregnant. The father is allegedly this Pierre Attala, about whom we had already informed you. Your hope (and ours too) that the relationship would die away in time is therefore destroyed; they have already got married in church. Despite all Knups continues to study and do her finals. From the middle of December she will live in Northern Rhodesia with her camel-driver. We are gutted by these events.

After our 'quickie' wedding in the Catholic church in Rondebosch, with a tiny gathering of close friends, we drove to the 'Red Sails' in Hout Bay, a small hotel near the beach, where we spent the night, listening to the waves and the wind. Joy and pleasure seemed to have vanished: I was depressed and silent, Pierre was not himself either.

A married couple, just for one day, then it was back to 'swotting' for our finals, in separate lodgings. What a relief to get back to Fuller Hall, where life continued as if nothing had happened, even after this upheaval.

Poor Pierre, he must have wondered what he'd let himself in for: an unresponsive, depressed 'wife', furious in-laws, another six weeks of studying and then...?

November and December flew by. I failed my finals, Pierre passed his. He, the practical one-- and the person with funds, rented a tiny house in Pinelands, a windy, bleak suburb where, for a few weeks, we learned to live together and to meet our respective parents who had all decided to come to Cape Town. It was our first Christmas together. I had never cooked before. But this was the least of my problems.

Parents: when they arrived from Walvis Bay they took the line it was their duty to kit me out for my role as a wife...'the trousseau', in other words. My mother dragged me around Cape Town's Adderley Street to find a flowery nylon dressing gown and some respectable nightgowns. I was already blossoming and needed a loose-fitting maternity smock and one of those skirts with a hole cut out in the front for an expanding tummy. How ridiculous I felt. How unglamorous! My mother was at least *trying* to make things better for me, but the tension was indescribable. My father offered us £100 pounds, to help with the expenses: my dowry. I suppose this was the equivalent of £1000 today (2010).

Pierre's stepmother Josephine, a woman of great warmth and poise, showed neither stress nor doubt when *she* dined with us and my parents, in our small rented house in Pinelands. With great sweetness she made light of everything I had produced, either burnt, overcooked or not cooked enough, but the wine was good and so the ice broke, just a little; my father even took a photograph of the occasion, a sign for sure that he had been won over by Josephine's undoubted charm.

For me this was the start of ten years of trust and deep affection for a woman who really understood what being a wife and a mother was about. We called her 'Nana', and she looked after me as if I was her own daughter even though she had two of her own: the toddler Danielle and Jacqueline, a convent-girl in Southern Rhodesia. I learned from Nana how to be practical and positive and to have standards in home-making I'd never come across before.

Pierre surprised me too. He returned from some outing with a huge sack, filled to the brim with bran, which he deposited on the kitchen floor. 'This is for you,' he announced. 'My mother says pregnant women get very constipated and I wouldn't like that to happen to you. You must take at least three large spoonfuls every morning.......'

'My God, this sack will see me through the rest of my life', I thought. I had never tasted anything more disgusting in my life. I was not even half-way through this pregnancy, the correct official birth-date should be in July. I gave suitably vague replies when people asked questions.

In the fifties one minded about such matters.

Soon we were to leave Cape Town for good and settle into our *real* new life in Northern Rhodesia. Still on my father's German passport, I now received my own and *it was British*. Pierre, a resident of Northern Rhodesia, had a British passport. I became British, by marriage. How bizarre: by marrying a Lebanese, (who wished he were a Frenchman) I, who had been an under-age passport-less German, had become British. My new surname 'Attala',..... 'att-allah,' means 'gift of God'.

We flew, of course. No more god-awful train journeys for me. I had felt the baby 'move' once or twice in Cape Town, and so now there were the three us, in the clouds,.......for a while. We were on our way to a British colony, somewhere above the tropic of Capricorn, but below the Equator: a protectorate of the United Kingdom, administered by the British Government.

1950's **Ndola** was a very small place indeed,...the terminal of the Rhodesia Railways system, a shed for an airport, a few small shops, one hotel, a bar and the 'Bijou' cinema. At a rough guess no more than 3000 whites lived with Indian and Coloured people in this town. The entire country had a population of 37,000 Europeans, some 2 million native people lived in townships, or out in the country, 'elsewhere'. Some came to work for the white man in the towns, others were employed in homes.

The Attala home, a stately double story mansion, with tennis court, swimming pool and terraced gardens was serviced by several servants permanently on duty; they lived in small quarters in the back garden.

****

Pierre and the 'new missus' are welcomed as befits the only son of the house. Two black men in starched white uniforms carry our luggage, upstairs, then stand by to take orders from Pierre as to time and extent of dinner later on.

Two Siamese, 'Emir' and 'Emira', purr around our feet as we are led upstairs to a large bedroom overlooking tumbling terraces of flowers in the garden. There are high, leafy trees. They make me feel small, alien and displaced. I was Pierre's 'booty' and this had to be fine by me.

'Intimidating,' I thought, 'everything so richly luxurious, purple velvet and dark pink satin, foreign, substantial, outmoded,' but then I saw, with delight, a gleaming grand piano, a major feature of the living room. Beyond it was an airy garden-room and next to that a 'ping-pong' room.

Other than put my swollen feet up, or wander about outside, inspecting the pool, the tennis court and the plants, there was little to do. Nana had an excellent vegetable garden which she tended herself, along with the Northern Rhodesian gardener, I was told. The rainy season was well underway... earth and air had a muggy, musty, damp smell.

Soon tired and looking forward to getting into that huge, maroon satin-covered bed I noted all opened windows had metal gauze to let in air but keep the 'bugs' of Central Africa out. This was a comforting thought....

Unpacking took less than five minutes: I owned very little. There was a new green leather vanity case, a gift from Nana for Christmas; apart from a gold necklace, given to me by Pierre, and a few modest baubles collected over the years there was a comb, a tin of Nivea and a tooth brush. After dinner and a hot bath, followed by a dab of cream on my face, I pulled back the sheet and blanket on my side of the bed to find an enormous furry spider crawling hastily from underneath my pillow.

I screamed.

My knight in shining armour came running from the adjacent bathroom, from his shower, advance fearlessly, but dripping. He brandished a towel. My mood of enchantment now somewhat diminished, I insisted on stripping the entire bed, just in case of hidden sibling spiders.

Not some sort of dreadful alien omen, I hoped.

The days were long. Pierre drove to the office after breakfast and I looked about for things to do. I was allocated a small car....Pierre had taught me to drive in CapeTown; 'life in Central Africa might be intolerable without that skill,' he'd warned. As always, he was right.

Northern Rhodesia gets to be very hot by midday: despite its altitude walking about is no fun. There were really only two roads one needed to know: 'Broadway' for going down hill to the family firm, Border Motors, a General Motors agency with numerous branches on the Copperbelt,... and 'Cecil Avenue', cutting across to the right. This was where there were several shops, a Post Office, one small supermarket, and a tiny dress shop, 'Rivoli,' run by an Italian lady. Most of Ndola was quite primitive, but then it had only been founded in 1900.

My new husband behaved strangely, now he was back: he drove me around reeling off a never-ending list of things he wanted built, changed or developed in the area. Nothing he saw was good enough. I became dizzy and weary from all his energy. Always glad to be back in the big house or to float about in the pool, I thought about nothing at all. I *did* practise the piano every day, in a desultory way, Chopin Nocturnes, Haydn, that sort of thing.

When 'Nana', tiny Danielle and Pierre's father Antoine, returned to their splendid home Pierre and I set ourselves up in a small flat in 'town'. A second-story apartment in a newly-built complex of offices was soon ready: black sofa, black curtains with an abstract flower design, two armchairs and a pine bookshelf... why did I choose so many black things?

This was the view: glaring sun, dusty cross-roads by a large yard full of second hand cars....further along, the famous Dam, where I once spotted a crocodile crossing the road, then scuttling back into the water.

Using up my dowry on whatever was needed I began to enjoy 'nest-building'. Nana had given us quite a few things from the big house *and* we employed a delightful man from the Bemba tribe called Tom to come in from the 'township' each day. He cleaned, served lunch and was kitted out in a tassled fez and white gloves, whenever we had guests. Tom did pretty much everything.

I learned to become a proper 'madam'. This is what everyone did.

And what *did* these black men think of us white 'madams'? I cringe with hindsight when I remember the fez and the gloves but Tom seemed pleased enough with his uniform at the time.

He was gentle, experienced, discreet, polite and kind.

*

My twenty-first birthday was celebrated in the 'big' house by a gathering of Pierre's cousins, all from the Lebanon, all employed in the business.

I now had a father-in-law. We stood shoulder to shoulder. He examined me with his close-set, intense eyes; I examined him back. He was portly, with a very long nose, spectacles, darkish skin offset by snow- white hair brushed back over his large skull; a chiselled Arab-looking face. Eye to eye he presented me with a gold ring bearing a large ruby. 'Your eyes are the colour of 'jaune caca'' he announced, gazing into them, 'this is a Lebanese ring, for you, an antique, *especially* from Beirut'. I was touched while the others grinned...for the cheeky 'jaune caca'.

'How kind' I thought, 'such an exquisite ring...perhaps I've won him over.' I was aware he was not *too* keen on a German daughter-in-law. He constantly inhaled medication from a bottle with a pump, carried it with him all the time; a nervous man with troublesome asthma. It seemed he had plenty to worry about.

His favourite place was by the phone in the garden room. Here he sat ringing up all his friends in Johannesburg. On Saturdays, permanently by the phone, he placed bets on horses or dogs, or whatever it is possible to bet on. Betting was his passion. He both won and lost large sums. I was in no position to be judgmental but could not help remembering (and instantly repressing)....my own father's so-called 'shady' Syrians.

My gracious mother-in-law proudly introduced me to all her lady friends. She had a way of making me feel special. One of these ladies, hearing me practise, said knew a ballet teacher who needed a pianist...would I like to have a go....

Suddenly a small door had opened, allowing me to start an independent activity in a field I *should* have been pursuing for the past three years......and so:

'...there I sat, fat, hot and sweaty, with swollen feet, gazing jealously at dainty bodies, kicking and jumping in time to my piano skills. For the next three months there was something to do, something that took my mind off my strangely constricted life opposed to my hideous expanding shape. This was a life-saver: I decoded I would take up ballet as soon as the baby was born. In the meantime I waddled about with swollen feet wearing Pierre's shoes. I felt more and more bovine. The heat in the flat was intolerable. I imagined the burning hot sheets of corrugated iron above our ceiling. I turned on the cold taps and lay in the bath for a very long time, to gaze at my disgusting, swollen body...aha, I felt a twitch, 'it' likes being cool, just like me.'

But...'it' hardly ever moved. It was a placid creature, like myself.

Our only cinema, the Bijou, was on the other side of the road and quite well served with the latest films. We went there often. That really seemed all there was to do in Ndola. Pierre, not into drinking in bars or playing sport, preferred reading or writing poetry or listening to a few records we possessed. He taught me to love French chansons: these we played regularly...*and* he taught me the words of 'J'attendrez, le jour at la nuit, j'attendrai toujours, ton retour...' I did so learn to love those songs.'

'We'll visit France *and* Beirut one day soon, *and* we'll drive to Elisabethville just across the border, where Uncle Mansour and his Belgian wife live. French delicacies are flown in and there are nightclubs; life in the Congo is nearly like that in Europe! You'll hear the songs, Imagine...all this,' he promised...'imagine, just six hours away by car.'

Pierre wasted no time, he bought some land in and around Ndola; one was a corner plot just five minutes away from the office, up a hill called North-rise, the other some 10 miles out of town. He wanted to create some wonderful place, somewhere, somehow. Bursting with ideas and energy and creativity he loved driving there armed with hat, sunglasses and a spade, to turn up the baked earth and study plant life, drink from his thermos flask, making plans. I staggered along, wearing *his* shoes, because of horribly swollen feet, dead from the heat, hobbling about unhappily in fear of snakes and creepy-crawlies, not knowing how to survive until he'd had enough. It and I…we were no fun at all.

He wanted me to enter into all his plans; I was incapable of keeping up. There was an uncomfortable feeling between us at this time. I was not at all sure who or what I was, or who I was becoming. Still kidding myself the baby wouldn't arrive until July I found myself, on the 29th of May, in hospital, with a long lonely night ahead. The timing was absolutely right, perhaps a few days overdue. Was it customary in those days to get on with giving birth on one's own? Or, being me, had I requested it? I *think* Nana suggested she'd stay with me, I can't remember now.

Abandoned on an uncomfortably high, hard, clinical bed I was left to get on with it. 'I'll come and see you from time to time' a nurse said.

'Fine', I thought, 'I can do it, just like everyone does.' By two in the morning I was screaming loudly, waking up everyone in earshot.

The Ndola hospital was tiny, perhaps twenty patients, if that. One patient told me later that she'd been kept awake by my noise for hours and that she had prayed for me. The nurse kept herself to herself. I couldn't understand why she was unable to do something, anything, to make it better. I began to call Pierre's name. No-one heard.

From two until dawn feels like a long time, when you're alone on a high hard bed, screaming. Eventually the doctor arrived and sliced whatever needed opening: a huge baby boy emerged. I had lost too much blood and needed a transfusion… it was horrible, all of it…when I'd been so confident before. Now I was like a dead thing, for many hours.

Later Pierre arrived with flowers; the room and the corridor outside already full of bouquets from all of Nana's friends; I had never seen such flowers! He sat with me. Our son in the nursery cried a lot, I was told. Maybe that was a good sign, a boy who made a lot of noise. I was curious to see him.

'He is big,' Pierre told me proudly, 'a new Attala, our 'gift from God'.

On day two I got up, trying to go to the baby, but collapsed in the corridor. Nana had just arrived; she helped to tuck me up again. Then my baby was brought to me and encouraged to suckle, but he just wasn't interested yet. I stroked his large head, his black hair and looked into his blue-black eyes: a real Attala. But most of the time he cried, or whimpered. Nana and the nurses felt there was something wrong; no-one knew for sure. The baby lay very still. Could he be so exhausted just from being born?

I certainly was.

On day three Pierre and I had a good look at our 'Luke', who for once was peaceful. He gazed at us as we undressed him, we wanted to see all of him. I was startled to see his huge genitalia. But he still refused to drink.

Nothing changed. I remained in my flower-filled room, Pierre and Nana came every day, the baby was examined by the doctor who had several views...that he might be 'mongoloid,' as there were slightly slanting eyes, or that there might be some internal problem. An X-ray was scheduled for day five. The result: Luke had broken bones all over his body, even his skull had broken and reset, in the womb. He would never be able to walk, he would be a cripple. It was thought to be an extremely rare condition called Osteogenesis Imperfecta.... perhaps one baby in 20,000... something like that... 'Brittle Bone Syndrome'.

The poor thing: he cried so much because he was in pain whenever he moved. We were devastated. How would it be if he lived?

At the end of day five he was in an oxygen tent, after that I never saw him again. Nana took care of everything: she informed everyone, consoled Pierre, got all the baby things out of our flat, she called the priest to baptise Luke and on day six she dressed the dead baby in one of the baby outfits, for his funeral. I remained in my room, still bedridden, and was told later about that tiny white coffin carried by Pierre to the Ndola graveyard...

There was plenty of time to reflect while I was recuperating. I could not cry. I seemed to be an onlooker in someone else's show. Nana had kept my parents informed by telegram. It was now up to me to think of some views and feelings that I could readily share with *them*, without allowing too much bitterness to creep in. What had caused this terrible event? I remembered my father's nauseating views on 'mixing' races. What were *his* thoughts? 'I told you so?'

On a more scientific level I remembered my work in the X-ray department in Cape Town, wondering whether this had somehow managed to damage my ovaries. It was the time of several atomic bomb tests in America; had some harmful fall-out landed in Walvis Bay? No-one knew the answer.

Recent research (2006) on brittle bone disease has identified a new gene known as the cartilage-associated protein or CRTAP that, when mutated, is likely to prevent fully functional collagen from forming. Collagen provides the framework on which bone and tissue are built.

Re-installed in our flat, the nursery cleared of baby things, Pierre tried, with infinite patience, gifts and kindnesses, to cheer me up.

I had been ordered to remain in bed a little longer (sitting down was excruciating). He played me all our French chansons, read to me and brought gifts and food. Never ever had such a fuss been made of a young wife.

As always, Nana acted far beyond expectations, in touching ways: she took over our flat with four or five friends, to give me a massage. She also washed my hair, and brought me exquisite handmade Lebanese chiffon nightgowns, flowers and magazines. To cheer me up I was presented with a five carat diamond ring, which had belonged to Adèle, Pierre's exotically beautiful mother, who had died when *he* was born.

Soon the whole sad business began to fade and I focussed on re-inventing myself, my figure, my hair and my clothes. Hideously stretched and marked I was a mess whichever way you looked at it.

I wanted to set about becoming a new person. This involved dieting, dyeing my hair… (black), re-discovering my violin, taking ballet lessons, and … trying hard to accept the fact that my parents wished to visit us.

This was a shock at first. It also provided some incentive for turning the nursery into a guest room, trying harder in the kitchen, and generally learning to become what felt like a 'grown-up'. I was twenty-one, after all.

The Ihlenfeldts arrived and were made welcome, first by the gracious Nana and later by Pierre and me, in our little flat.

We drove them all over the Copperbelt showing off what little there was to see: anthills, the copper mines, the business branches, and somewhere, en route, we collected an adorable white kitten from friends. It was almost a substitute for a baby.

My parents never said what they thought of my new life. But an equilibrium had been established. My father resumed his careful letter-writing with endless, meticulous accounts of their dull social life or plans for retirement. I replied, but not as frequently as he wished. My mother's illegible scribblings were witty and amusing: I much preferred those.

For me the time had come to *enjoy* being young, and perhaps, to learn new things, to expand in different, new and unheard-of ways.

Even with my body trimmed down several sizes, my hair dyed, I was still in greater need of 'stylishness'.

Soon followed a series of journeys: first by car to the Belgian Congo to meet Pierre's uncle and family and also, to learn how far Africa had 'come' under the Belgians: I found black men wearing shirts and ties and actually working in offices. What's more they spoke immaculate French, miles better than mine. The shops were tempting, with imported goods from Europe and all this only a few hours by car from the Copperbelt.

Unlike South African Apartheid the Belgians seemed to have got it right. Or so I thought at the time. Northern Rhodesia as British protectorate felt no different to South Africa. I liked being in the Congo very much, but for the fact that I was acutely conscious of being a 'Pomeranian Peasant' compared with Tante Marthe and of course Miriam, the beautiful Belgian girl, married to Pierre's cousin, Jacques.

The Elisabethville Attala's had a different feel to them: one had to be on one's toes all the time, not unlike visiting an embassy. Tante Marthe, dressed in the latest from Parisian couturiers, drank nothing but champagne, even for breakfast, Miriam ate only the daintiest morsels of fillet, smoked salmon and asparagus, in order to be as slender as a pencil. I tried not to get depressed.

In no time I was discreetly told off for wearing 'unsuitable' garments. At first it didn't seem too bad, as everyone communicated in French.

But for an official opening of a new motor agency branch in Salisbury (now Harare), where we all met up some weeks later, I was reminded again that there were rules about what one wore and when.

I had bought an exceptionally pleasing dusty pink slim skirt and long-sleeved top for this representational event, with Pierre's approval.

Tante Marthe, however, took me to one side and lectured me: 'mais Evelyne, tu dois porter a tailored suit, avec un hat et gloves…and what about your shoes and bag…they don't even match!'….well, both crushed and resentful I fled to our hotel room for the rest of the evening.

Pierre offered practical help. In future I would receive, from Paris, a monthly fashion magazine and he would advise me whenever I bought anything, or had things made.

This was helpful, at first.

At this time I realized something had gone wrong with my insides: months passed without periods. Even worse, I was growing little hairs in places I didn't care for. I was not pregnant, besides I lacked all desire for procreativity, which left Pierre disappointed.

Nana insisted I saw a lady doctor, a friend of hers, who diagnosed, with much psychological insight, a female complaint which manifests as a thickened covering of the ovaries, thus preventing female hormones to be released. Her theory was that I'd been traumatised by events and that my body said 'no more of this!'

Nowadays ovaries can be put right with a course of hormones, but in the 1950's it meant: 'the knife'. A Lebanese specialist in such matters was found in Johannesburg and poor Pierre took his non-functional wife for urgent 'repairs'. The surgeon removed two thirds of each ovary, as well as an appendix (just in case) and wished me luck. 'There are no guarantees' he said, 'you may or may not conceive again.'

My wonderful mother-in-law was not going to take this sitting down. She set off to Lourdes in February 1958 to pray. Staunchly Catholic she appeared to have a direct line to heaven: soon I was pregnant again!

The next nine months Pierre and I began to live life to the full. How unbelievably fortunate we were: we were making a new start. The big black cloud had gone. Pierre amused himself with a new hobby: he took flying lessons. One afternoon each week he did the required number of hours to obtain a pilot's license.

I stayed on the ground and applied for work in the hospital laboratory. To my surprise I was offered a part-time job analysing blood and other bodily samples; someone actually taught me to extract blood from people's veins. (The hardest thing is getting the needle *in.....*)

While spending several hours a day in a white lab coat again there were many chances to observe unusual events: like an autopsy on a youngster who had killed himself on a motorcycle, by not wearing his helmet. The sight of this vulnerable-looking corpse having its skull sawed open caused me to pass out on the floor. It soon dawned on me that working in the hospital was something I could do without.

A much better idea followed.

There was nothing in our way: we employed an architect to design a house for us up in Northrise, so as to get out of our hot flat, and out of 'town'. This young South African arrived from the Congo, where he had been working for Pierre's uncle, to meet us and to discover what sort of customers we were. Here was a meticulous man who needed to know every detail about our likes, artistic leanings and our philosophy of living. How very pleasing to be taken so seriously.

Do all architects take such trouble? He was a Corbusier fan who showered us with pictures of the latest developments in Europe and

America, while cleverly forming his own plans. After several consultations there was a spectacular end result. Money was not mentioned; this creation was one of the most involving, bonding and fulfilling event in our lives so far.

Wallpaper, fittings, furniture, everything was ordered from various parts of Europe and shipped with astonishing efficiency to this distant part of Africa....just for us. The architect and Pierre became close friends and Pierre invited him to live and work in Ndola. A delightful old house quite near to Nana's place was offered to him and his family, also to an assistant. The population of Ndola was growing rapidly, almost trebled, in ten years. Soon this young man was getting work all over the place.

While his amazing design of a pre-cast concrete roof was under construction I tried to keep myself amused by teaching infants at the Ndola Convent; it has to be admitted I showed little ability and even less affinity to small people who were to learn to count and heaven knows what else. They were noisy, they wriggled about and I had no idea how one copes with six year olds. I lasted about three weeks and declared myself defeated.

The kind nuns seemed to understand and were reasonably gracious.

Instead Pierre came up with the splendid idea that we should go abroad to Rome, Venice, Brussels, Paris and London, before we became parents. He arranged everything, as always. All I had to do was pack, and go. The Grand Tour was to begin in Venice where we experienced a whole week in the most romantic city in the world. It rained mercilessly, every single day.

Pierre, the tough rugby player, was determined to visit everything of note, happy on foot from morning to night, dragging me along, mostly full of complaints. I was after all, three months pregnant. How could I possibly match his energy? Here was a poetic, unstoppable, dynamic person, bubbling over, off-set by a solemn, cool, Nordic mother-to-be, who needed to sit down and take it easy. I did what I could but tended to retreat to our little hotel quite often. Once, walking about in the rain on my own, I found a tiny boutique catering for pregnant ladies and bought a lovely orangey-red broderie anglaise 'tent' attached to some slightly stiffened frame. In it I resembled a giant traffic-cone, successfully hiding any bulge, current and future. It was dramatic enough to wear when taken to La Fenice to hear Maria Callas sing in 'La forza del destino'....a lavish show with real live camels (or was it horses?) on the stage. We emerged, dazed, at 2 am.

Next stop: London. I had never set foot in England before. The overall impression was of greyness and darkness, incredible busy-ness and much drab dreariness. It was here I first began to realize how Pierre loved the theatre. He knew about the latest, most up-to-date trendy plays and managed to get us tickets for any work that came from the pens of people such as John Osborne and Arnold Wesker----- 'angry young men' ... it seemed Pierre was one of them. How had all this scorn and disaffection managed to reach us in Africa? Newspapers, obviously: Pierre had British papers flown out to Ndola each week. We had no television yet, nor any radio worth listening to.

The London shops were stunning. In Harrods I purchased a maternity garment, an elegant voluminously-shaped coat, a 'Givenchy copy,' no less. Even in June London seemed a chilly place to a person from Central Africa, so I trudged about gazing at the usual things like Buckingham Palace and St. Paul's, wearing my very expensive coat.

At Liberty's we bought a Danish white leather sofa, to be delivered to Northern Rhodesia, as soon as possible...hardly realizing then quite how posh we were.

London nightlife, quiet, grey, damp, dark and dull, led me to have high hopes for Paris, our next stop. I had become disillusioned with London, especially after sunset.

Pierre's cousin Jacques with his Miriam, were to join us in Paris making a cheerful foursome, albeit with one small snag: *my* French had a long way to go. I made great efforts to keep up. We saw films, plays and went to the 'chansonniers', where the sharp and smart French kept up with the latest in politics and gossip. It was all fairly impossible for me. I did the best I could. Jacques, Miriam and Pierre were fluent and well used to the French, I was on a steep learning curve even when it came to food. Only the very best and most unusual would do for the Attala's.

Unforgettable: a Rabelaisian restaurant which made sport of serving up dishes in shapes of male and female anatomy along with life-like imitations of indescribable human excretions, all edible of course. We laughed, pretended to be shocked, and swallowed everything.

If one kept ones eyes shut it was all quite delicious.

And then there was Vienna, where *my* delightful aunt Dagmar took us to a disreputable nightclub, even more wicked than those in Paris. Eventually came the daunting task of facing my grandparents in their castle. They were charming. It felt so good to know Pierre had been shown to, and accepted, by everyone in my family, by all those who mattered to me.

Rome was too hot for comfort. I couldn't wait to get back to Africa.

By the time we returned to Ndola our new house was nearly ready, causing a stir amongst the white population on the Copperbelt, and also in architectural magazines world-wide. The precast concrete roof hovered over the second story like a nun's starched hood and our talented architect and builder kept their fingers crossed: it looked as though it might take off and fly away. All timber and fancy interior fittings arrived in good time: we were able to move in a few weeks before I was due to give birth. One week before the birth, Pierre's father Antoine was killed in a car crash. Pierre was now in charge of the entire business.

He could afford to be even more lavish.

Gabrielle Toni, born a week earlier than expected, on December the 24th, weighed 7 lbs. Although she had chosen this approved and celebrated date for her birthday she was an instant misery. Nurses put sparkly Xmas decorations on her crib and on two other Xmas babies…

After three days we returned to our lovely home. Gabi cried and cried. Nana assured me she'd settle down and recommended gripe medicine. The screaming continued. I became afraid of this very hungry baby and gave up on breast-feeding. A 'trained scientist' needs to *know* exactly what is going *into* a permanently screaming open mouth.

'Why do women want babies?' I wondered. It seemed no fun at all.

Wisely the new Dad flew off to Johannesburg on business and left 'the women' to sort out this problem. He returned with special Lebanese gripe medicine, used by Lebanese babies in Johannesburg. Gabi tried the stuff, spat it out and took some time to accept life in her new house, with her somewhat nervous parents.

1959, a predictable year; in comfort, even luxury but nevertheless yet another steep learning curve: not used to babies I turned into a fastidious 'according-to-the book' mother. Dr Spock was the fashion in those days so I got by without asking too many questions. Our by now bottle-swilling Gabi soon did what was expected, enjoying mashed bananas, fresh vegetables, sitting, crawling, walking and learning social skills when other babies came to call. A large circle of friends now invaded our lives every weekend: there were other mothers and babies to compare ourselves with. The big draw was obviously our lovely house and glamorous swimming pool.

Pierre's mother, a woman who did things in some style, had invited the Bishop of the Copperbelt to come and bless this newly built home. A picturesque event, a bishop in full regalia, incense, holy water splashed about in generous quantities and much muttering in Latin, made both the 'house-boy' and the cook very anxious. Already sensing that Catholicism was much like 'Ju-ju' in African villages, when I was asked to go to church with my new-born to be purified, (some ancient practice of the church I knew nothing about), I bristled with indignation...I mean, what exactly needed to be purified? Once the bishop had left and I'd dried up the splotches of holy water I began an inner dialogue with God, made a deal with him even...he could strike me down if he wished but I could no longer continue with this 'mumbo-jumbo'.

From then onwards I refused to go to Mass.

God didn't mind. Instead of Mass, every Sunday there were guests with prams, children, towels and picnics and we all became very attached to one another. The men, architects and lawyers and the wives 'just' wives, young, pretty and enjoying colonial life, such as it was: lovely weather, servants, tropical fruit and good vegetables. We didn't know it yet, but the daily existence under these very pleasant conditions made us restless and, in my case, bored. It was all quite delightful. It was the 'sixties'....a time of some notoriety... We partied, drank and danced into the early hours. When it was hot we swam, also at night, sometimes naked.

Daily life was easy, too easy. But increasingly there was talk about politics. One worried about Africa and the reality of living there, being part of the great black/white divide. It felt all wrong... and now there was this talk of 'freedom', of 'independence,' of 'equality'.

Occasionally, when I was shopping on the main street, I was jostled and even pushed off the pavement by young black ruffians. White people were beginning to feel uncomfortable. I was one of them. When it all toppled, how would it feel to be part of a small white minority?

For me the most unsettling time was early morning; often before sunrise: despair and loneliness, staring out of the window at the early foggy garden of the rainy season, birds pecking on the lawn, the anthill still just a faint outline by the pool.... while Gabi drank her bottle. Mothers are supposed to feel fulfilled and content. I can't describe my misery. During the long hot afternoons, minding my child in the garden, I felt bored, trapped and lonely, wishing I could be elsewhere. CapeTown! Could this the answer? My parents had retired, settled very near my old university; there had been invitations to come and stay, anytime. We had made our peace. My mother would look after Gabi; I could have violin lessons at the College. Retrieving my violin from some recess, I began practising; I'd almost forgotten how to play.

In 1959, with a one-year old in a carry-cot in one hand and my grotty old violin-case in the other I flew to CapeTown to be welcomed back into the bosom of my family. I was twenty-four years old.

Our 'great estrangement' was never discussed. Gabi basked in their attention: Erika, suddenly a granny, loved having her around.

My father invited all their elderly German friends: we were on show. It made a nice change, for a few weeks. But soon I started missing Pierre, and the house, and all our young, trendier friends in Northern Rhodesia.

I'd had a few lessons at the College of Music where Stirling Robbins, former leader of the LSO, worked me very hard, for a very short time with, among other works, the Bach 'Chaconne', my great favourite.

'If only I'd got my hands on you five years earlier' he said. 'I could have done wonders with you.'

After a month of this, I felt ready to cope with returning to the Copperbelt...but now with a goal, and a daunting, exciting task.

***

Ndola was not such a backwater after all: a shining cultural beacon had appeared in my life: Elsie Fraser-Munn, who ran the Central African Conservatoire of Music. Once she realised I was someone who could actually play a violin she immediately invited me to take part in all manner of delights: performing, with organ, for example, the entire Handel's 'Messiah', as solo violin. As I had never done this before (had anyone?) I entered into the spirit of things and survived the ordeal.

Assigned to teach at the conservatoire (a private house with a large drawing room containing a grand piano) I had been roped in to take singing lessons myself. Mrs. Munn, a homely lady from the north of England was an irresistible force who never took 'no' for an answer. The fact that I had little more than a 'rusty' Grade VIII diploma was neither noted nor discussed.

When one lives in Central Africa different standards apply.

'Do you realise, my dear, you would sound *just* like Kathleen Ferrier, with a voice like yours....all you need is to train for a while, here you are, listen to these exercises'..., which she then proceeded to demonstrate, showing her memorable teeth with a huge encouraging smile.

After 45 minutes of excruciatingly embarrassing vocal gymnastics I fled, promising to think about it.

Obediently I returned for another lesson and was given important-looking books, including Schubert Lieder, and sent off again, feeling hopelessly trapped, with a strangely sore throat. My doctor saved the day by writing an official note to Mrs. Munn certifying I had fragile vocal chords and should not, under any circumstances, try to sing with them.

I suppose she must have seen through that. It was the end of my 'singing career.' Mrs. Munn insisted however that I begin work on a Diploma from the Associated Board, this time for the violin. Wise woman…

Pierre was also getting involved in the Copperbelt cultural life such as it was. His passion for theatre was fired by local amateur dramatics and he began directing shows, most memorably Wycherley's Restoration comedy 'Tis pity she's a whore', which was entered for adjudication in an all-Copperbelt competition.

The adjudicator, one Peter Hall, arrived from London, just at the beginning of his now illustrious career. Sadly Pierre's show did not win; nevertheless, theatrical events can be a lot of fun. Peter Hall came to dine in our wonderful house and showing him around he took me into a quiet corner and asked: 'what on earth is a person like you doing in a place like this…why don't you live in London?' It was plain he was not much taken with the delights of Northern Rhodesia.

I thought about this more than was good for me.

Most days I was alone. Pierre, a *night* person, who liked to go to work very late in the morning, was mostly out or up until 2 a.m., rehearsing amateur groups or 'working'. I never enquired. He would return late for supper and disappear again. Obviously there were days when we went out together; leaving Gabi with a babysitter was always more my concern than his. My days were long…

He wrote poetry and also a play, which I remember not liking. In it was a line I recall to this day: 'I smell Negro sweat'… uttered by a white person who sensed he was about to be attacked…just a small hint of the fears of the white man in those days…..

It was in this time that a fondness began to develop between our architect and myself. He dropped in once for some reason, heard me practising and said: 'I wouldn't mind having that noise going on while *I'm* working,' or words to that effect. On Sundays, when all our friends drifted into our garden to swim or just to hang about we'd spend time on our deck chairs talking to and gazing at each other. At parties we danced Calypsos, all the rage then. Sparks began to fly.

One afternoon, during Gabi's siesta time I heard the familiar noise of his Volkswagen on the driveway and knew at once why he had come. No one disturbed us and this time of day became dangerously ours, for many months. He taught me to like my body again. But such things are painful and cause pain to others. When he admitted to Pierre that he loved me my husband replied: 'yes, I *know*. So do I….'

The architect's wife was not *as* benign and came to call for a woman to woman talk. It did not go well. My excuse was that I had no wish to take her man away from her, just to 'borrow' him for a while.

'Why not borrow Pierre, he's nice too'...was the best I could come up with....

This worked for a while. By swopping partners, just occasionally, after parties, we all appeared to get on famously and for several months we enjoyed the ongoing social events without turning a hair. There were other people involved in this miasma of behaviour, but it becomes a little too shocking to go on about it.

I became pregnant. It was my secret hope then that my next child would be the architect's.

Pierre knew about my doubts, but was, as always, completely in control. 'I will love it, even if it is not mine...' he said, knowing there was a strong possibility it was his own. What a splendid man. How could I have been so ungrateful and disenchanted with all he had to offer? Our closeness seemed to have vanished as far as I was concerned; he was a great believer in 'freedom' and put no pressure on me. On the plus side was Pierre's back-up of kindness and generosity, on the other was my immaturity: no grasp what life was about. Life felt all wrong. I was spending too much time navel-gazing.

I would not like to admit, even to myself, that my parents may have been right, but for all the wrong reasons...

All I knew was that I was twenty-five years old, having my third child and 'knowing' two men.

Tormented by thoughts about *who I was and what was I doing*, a hand-writing expert informed me I was suffering from a 'Madame Bovary' syndrome. As I had not read the book this did not mean too much. One day, at a party, a woman who read palms announced I would leave Pierre and be very rich one day. This gave me a jolt: up to that moment I believed I would never do such a thing.

As soon as 'we' were pregnant again Pierre and I left for Europe once more, to enjoy a last chance of being free enough to get away. Gabi stayed with a Danish friend, Birte, a few houses away, whose small daughter was Gabi's closest friend. I set out on an earlier flight so that I could visit Salzburg, a place I'd always wanted to see, and then took the train to Klagenfurt, to stay with my grandparents in their castle. My own mother would be visiting at the same time, as well as all her siblings, who were scheduled to appear from Vienna and Italy. What a to-do: The entire Ragg clan assembled in Schloss Mageregg. After getting to the ripe old age of twenty-five without ever spending time with my family I would suddenly be surrounded by them. It was the summer of 1960.

One hot morning, shopping with my mother in one of Klagenfurt's busiest roads by the famous dragon in the marketplace I slid to the pavement, unconscious. My poor mother! When I came to my senses she put me in a cab and took me to the nearest doctor. I began to realize there was bleeding, some sort of painless miscarriage. When the doctor was told I was three months pregnant he was reassured…'some hormone tablets and three weeks in bed should bring all this to a satisfactory conclusion.'

Three weeks in bed…what sort of a holiday was this going to be?

One month passed. My only cherished memory of this time was being driven up the Loibl Pass in my uncles' car surrounded by my mother and her sisters right up to the Yugoslav border, where we stopped to drink Slivovitz and gaze across to the mountains and valleys where the Raggs and Klanders originally came from. We were on the famous Karawanken, last mentioned over one hundred pages ago.

Meanwhile Pierre had postponed his trip so that I was fit enough to accompany him for a few days in Nice and later on to Denmark to look into the furniture business he was hoping to set up.

When we met at the station in Nice he had rented a snazzy sports-car and smelled, no, stank strongly of sweat and perfume. I remarked on this and he confessed he'd just spent the night with a girl he'd met in a nightclub. I was intrigued. Nothing Pierre did *ever* made me jealous. We were both like that. Wherever we were on this holiday Pierre went out to nightclubs and amused himself and I went to bed early. A strange set up really: we still liked each other. He assured me I was 'completely free', he truly believed in this. I don't know if either of us were happy. The innocence of our great love at CapeTown University had slipped away and left us as friends, extremely liberated ones.

Poor little Gabi: when I returned she would not leave my side. She was plainly disturbed by my two-month absence and it took at least three months to reassure her. I had no idea children minded being left so much.

Locked into another pregnancy, life proceeded gently, inexorably.

There wasn't much to do, other than keeping everybody fed, clean and happy. Did I read? I can't recall. When Gabi had her nap, I did too, when she watched the Flintstones, so did I. Having a television service in Northern Rhodesia was the very latest addition to our rather spare cultural life, if one can call news and adverts and the Flintstones 'culture'. Our black and white TV set was no bigger than two shoeboxes on top of each other. We had a record player and a small pile

145

of records. These things helped to pass the time: even knotting a dreary beige bedside rug helped, for a while. We saw our friends socially.... but the mad parties had ground to a halt.

The architect's wife was also pregnant. There were three of us 'Sunday swimmers,' all with big bellies.

When Pierre was away on business trips he left me with a small white pistol by my bed 'just in case'. There were many reports of crime in those days. He taught me how to use it. I was tense and afraid. One night there was a prowler in the garden. I observed him.... peering out from the dark bedroom, armed with my pistol, my heart beating fast. Would I have shot him?

He sloped off undisturbed.

In these changing and troubled times the white population of Ndola was delighted to have access to such wonderful things now available in a classy bookshop and a smart outlet for imported Danish furniture. All this was thanks to Pierre's good taste, high standards and astounding energy.

In February 1961 Lucienne Erika made her first appearance. One careful look and I knew she was Pierre's.

***

The early sixties were a time of unrest and steady erosion of colonial rule in many parts of Africa. Northern Rhodesia, neighbour of the newly independent Congo, had its share of protest against Federation with skirmishes and attacks on whites and Pierre, along with other liberal-minded young men, did his best to steer a course by taking part in political gatherings of black party members and leaders.

One of these was Kenneth Kaunda, then a charming man in his twenties, who came to our home on several occasions. He strummed on Pierre's guitar and played with my children. Having been recently released from prison he was now the president of UNIP (the United National Independence Party) and with civilized black persons such as him about there was surely little reason for unease. But needless to say, many whites were beginning to feel and fear the famous 'winds of change.'

Uncertainty grew in September 1961 when Ndola got into the world headlines: Dag Hammerskjöld, the secretary-general of the United Nations died in a plane crash just outside the town. He had been engaged in negotiations in the Congo crisis, across the border. This crash was controversially revealed, some years later, to have been caused by a fighter plane attack, but it was hushed up at the time, and

146

remains a mystery to this day. Hammerskjoeld's coffin was placed in a church in Ndola for viewing when Belgian families poured across the borders in convoys to pay their respects, filling up the town. A photograph in the Northern News, revealed Pierre and me walking solemnly past the coffin.

By then motherhood was so much simpler the second time round…I knew how it all 'worked' and Luci soon turned me into a doting mother.

With the appeal of a tiny mischievous monkey, clinging, loving and quick, I adored her….while Gabi had some adjusting to do but was soon also won over by this quirky new person. They became the best of friends, in a curious way. As soon as I felt up to it I took my little daughters to CapeTown, to show them off to my parents.

Why am I going into so much detail? To examine how curiously, laboriously, a relationship changes… until one sees only ONE way out. What Pierre and I had was so very strong at first, strong enough to cut me off from any feelings I had towards my own parents. But now? We seemed to be able to manage without each other. After only six years.

I planned to return, of course. But not until I'd had some more lessons. I certainly had no plans to leave Ndola for good. My new baby helped to fill my fairly vacuous existence….I missed the architect, if I missed anybody, but even that was tailing off …to be honest.

The Marriage of Figaro.

Mozart took over our lives in 1962: the Central African Conservatoire had mustered sufficient numbers of singers and musicians to give a run of performances, after many months of rehearsal, all over the Copperbelt. I had engaged a nanny, so that I could devote myself to higher things. The wondrous Elsie Fraser Munn ordained I should 'lead' the orchestra which consisted of piano, 3 violins, a cello and a flute. All missing parts were incorporated in the piano score, so no worries there.

The Conservatoire was agog: the large living room filled from one end to the other with chorus, soloists and 'orchestra'. It was a hot, humid day, after heavy rains all morning.

'A tight squeeze,' I thought, trying to get in, clutching my violin case, and wishing I'd made an effort to arrive on time…what a racket, with everyone chattering or warming up. How am I supposed to get into the orchestra area and who on earth is *that* ….why has he spread all those magazines around himself on the floor, …he must be the flautist

Elsie found in Luanshya....he's looking at me ...*and* he's just winked. Well! No-one has ever winked at me like that before...'

His music-stand was behind my chair. Once settled I turned around to greet him and take another look, noticing his scruffy clothes and dandruff covered shoulders.

'I'm Evelyn, I said 'and you are....from Luanshya?' We looked at each other. 'Charles', he mumbled, removing his pipe from his mouth. 'I suppose I'll have to put this out now....'

Mozart's 'Marriage of Figaro' needed many rehearsals and I was frequently prodded in the back by Charles' flute with a quiet hiss: 'help, I'm lost, where are we?'

Plainly Charles' 'counting' was even worse than mine.

How delightful; here was a character unlike no-one I'd ever met before, casual, nonchalant, funny. He was British, I liked his voice and his devil-may-care approach. He mentioned he was a District Officer, working for the Colonial Service. I only had the haziest idea what he was talking about. We had plenty of time to get to know each other, even with my back turned to him for hours and hours. Meanwhile our producer and musical director were driving themselves into darkest despair. Opening night was only a few days away and both stage and acting were laughably dreadful, so bad in fact that our director resigned.

'I have my reputation to take care of', he said. Indeed.

The orchestra crept off home. Later, soaking in my bathtub, staring at the turquoise mosaic tiles, while Pierre, for once at home, was taking a shower, the cosy setting triggered a useful idea: 'how about *you* offering your services to Elsie Munn, you're always going on about the theatre? *You do it...Mozart needs you!*'

To my surprise Pierre agreed at once.

Another late rehearsal and some of us dropped in by the only hotel, to have a drink. Pierre, still busy with the sets, stayed behind. It was someone's birthday and there was dancing in the lounge. Charles danced with several young ladies and finally got round to me. After he brought me back, politely, to my seat, someone whispered in my ear: 'Do you realize Charles has a wooden leg?'

I had noticed many things about Charles, his shabby clothes and unkempt appearance, but I thought people were teasing me. He was witty, he made me laugh, he was tall and handsome. I have a weakness for tall men. My excuse is that women who had insufficient fathering always look for tall strong father-figures to make them feel looked after. Charles was very sure of himself and his posh British voice pleased me enormously. I knew nothing about public school boys in those days.

In the meantime my not tall but oh-so-dynamic Pierre came, saw and rescued the 'miscarried' Figaro. What he achieved in three extra rehearsals was little short of a miracle. I felt so proud of him. Hundreds came on the first night and on the second night people had to be turned away. The Northern News wrote enthusiastically and the phone went all day; the show was even re-scheduled for another event in Mufulira. The entire Northern Rhodesia Copperbelt seemed to be agog.

After the final performance Charles offered to run me home. As he pulled up outside our house I looked at him closely and stroked his face...in a tender sort of way....just for one second. At that moment our big front door opened and Pierre, who had got home earlier, appeared, lit up by the lights in the hall. I wondered if he had seen us.

Charles and I arranged to meet in the Ndola Park, to talk more frankly and unobtrusively. Nobody in their right minds went to the Park, which was hot, sandy and bleak. I had Gabi and Luci with me, just so Charles would know that they existed. He was a natural with children, doing with them what people do in parks: swings, slides...that sort of thing. I'd never seen a man doing that.

After two or three more innocent meetings, once, at my house, when he looked around proclaiming I was *not* to take him too seriously, he was just a 'ladies' man', having recently recovered from an affair with another married woman, I became determined I would conquer him,....it was almost a challenge. With great ease one enters the world of lies and deceit, of fabricated dreams, full of new hopes and schemes.

At the same time there were further theatrical events at Ndola's Lowenthal Theatre: Menotti's 'Telephone', Bach's 'Coffee Cantata' (presented as a mini opera in costume) and TS Eliot's 'The Wasteland', all produced by Pierre with sets by our splendid architect. I was to recite T.S Eliot, sitting in a rowing boat on stage.... and remember feeling acute embarrassment. The Bach was more my style and Charles played his flute again. We were all in it, together, hilarious! The triple bill took people by surprise: it was of a standard never before achieved and described as 'worthy of the West End'.

More sobering, for a further cultural event, I had been cast as an ant, in a play called 'The Sycamore Tree'. My costume consisted of a green swimsuit, tights and a green bathing cap with much boring sitting about in dressing rooms.

Not 'my thing' at all ....

****

149

In 1963 the Federation of Northern and Southern Rhodesia was dissolved. It was the year of breaking free: I, who had been kept and led and cosseted and overwhelmed....became a person who needed a new identity. I prepared myself for that Licentiate examination by passing, first: the general Paper for Teachers' licentiate and after that, the practical of the Associated Board. I was ready: I had visited London and taken lessons with two well-known British players, David Martin and Frederick Grinke, both teachers at the Royal Academy.

Charles wanted *me* to visit his mother; a very English lady, bemused by my background, but nevertheless kind. It was all beginning to look like a serious step - in the right direction. Her husband, Charles' stepfather, flirted with me. I was used to that. Most men flirted with me. I took it for granted. Perhaps it happens to all women? Even Charles' *god*-father took me out to dine and propositioned me. I'd heard that English men were somewhat repressed but maybe I was giving out the wrong information? Perhaps he was just out to test me...did I live up to the highest standards to enter the Chadwick clan?

Back in the safety of Central Africa I was asked to perform on Northern Rhodesian television, some unaccompanied Bach: a nerve-racking experience, but there has to be a first time for everything. Soon after came the important examination and I certainly was well-prepared for that. My examiner, visiting Africa for the Associated Board pronounced me *a sensitive player, with a sound knowledge that should make her a delightful, sympathetic teacher.'* I was chuffed.

During this time there were frequent trips to Luanshya, to spend time with Charles, who managed to slip away from work unnoticed. Or so he thought. It was a poignant time; overwhelmed with loving and protective feelings for him, I tried to leave my mark by sorting out his home and his clothes and by admiring the novel he was writing. We even had a little dinner party for his friends. Our tiny Central African mini-scandal got about and before we knew where we were Charles was 'posted' to Mwinilunga, some godforsaken village hundreds of miles away. Had the District Commissioner heard about Charles' affair? Did the Foreign Office have 'emergency moves' up their sleeve when staff got into trouble? Whatever it was, we were separated. Letter writing was our only life-line, for months and months. I opened my own post-box in the main Post office, just for Charles' letters. I sent him parcels of nice things, even a record player, as he'd complained that his had broken down. It cost £15. He promptly sent it back, saying it was not the sort of sum a District Officer could spend on luxuries. I was dismayed.

He was then removed even further, near the Caprivi strip next to Angola. I fled to CapeTown with my children and we planned meeting there. When he came to the house my parents were not remotely pleased with this pipe-smoking Brit. 'What *do* you think you're doing? You are a Catholic, Catholics do not divorce'…that sort of thing. I didn't have a leg to stand on. In the past they'd always said I should marry a German or an Englishman. Yet here he was, a 'pukka' Englishman and they disapproved again.

Charles and I spent a week together; he stayed in a hotel nearby and we went out with the children every day; they both adored him.

For some reason he became involved in an ongoing debate I was having with a fellow violinist, who had offered me her fine violin to buy; she was upgrading to an even more expensive one, which she needed for her increasingly professional playing. Charles insisted I should have her instrument and that he would buy it for me. I suppose he was showing his commitment to me, why else would he have done this. We're talking about a lot of money here…enough to buy a sensible car. Remembering the fuss he'd made about the £15 record-player I should really have asked Pierre for the money, but couldn't, under the circumstances, and my parents even less.

So Charles paid for my first 'good' violin.

He had to return to his job a week later, this time to Lusaka, but I stayed in Cape Town for three whole months, thinking, scheming, planning and practising…and learning to touch-type and tabulate. 'Perhaps, soon, I will need to earn some money to keep myself and my children…'

Returning to Ndola I discovered Pierre had given many parties, other women had worn my clothes, even slept in my bed. I threw a plate of hot tomato soup at him, in fury.

I minded only because he'd let them wear my clothes…the rest didn't matter.

But the time had come to consult my mother-in-law. Standing in her bedroom, while she was getting something out of a carved, scented cedar-wood trunk at the foot of her bed, I gave her a somewhat sanitised version of the truth. We stood looking out of the window. She advised, with her lovely French accent: 'Evelyne,…men *are* like that…just *let* him, why not, what does it matter…?'

Although I had not disclosed *all* scandals, nor my relationship with the architect I *did* tell her about Charles. She showed no sign of discomposure, gave no reproach, to my surprise. After that I loved her even more.

Only a month later Charles was recalled to London for a course at the Foreign Office. I asked Pierre if he would mind if I went to London, with our children of course, and he said, 'why should I?' So I flew over, first on my own, found a basement flat with the help of an agency, arranged the delivery of an upright piano and a little teak desk from Heals and then returned to Africa to pick up my clothes and my daughters. Sounds easy, and in some ways it was. Apart from the fact that Pierre supplied the funds I was *beginning* to think for myself. 'I've left him, for a while', I thought. 'Who knows, perhaps for ever.'

***

Having gathered together a few pleasing objects for 18 Hillfield Park, Muswell Hill, the place soon felt more homely. By Attala standards, my chosen flat was, well, not exactly a slum, but a little depressing, if it hadn't been recently painted and cleaned up. Just outside the window was a pile of rubbish, (which remained there for as long as I did) and the garden in the back was completely neglected, a tip. I was not used to such things, but somehow it was all part of my unbelievable adventure. My mother had been born just a few miles from here, imagine that. I was becoming British. She'd approve, for sure.

Everything in London appeared more interesting than what I'd left behind. Dirty, grey, busy, wet, teeming with life, and such a thrill!

The owners were incredibly welcoming: I soon had their tiny basement flat looking more to my taste with the help of a couple more extravagances from Heals. Pierre had dispatched one of our Persian rugs, as well as my favourite painting of an old fashioned little girl, which we'd bought in Hamburg. More importantly, he was generous with a monthly cheque, to pay for everything.

'I have all I need, I can afford a good private school for Gabi and Luci, just around the corner, as well as ever more music lessons, this time the piano. I will soon able to keep myself teaching piano *and* violin, if necessary. Never have I felt more carefree and independent. Guilt? None at all. Missing the luxuries of home, pool, friends? Not for a moment. Twinges of regret about Pierre, about Africa? Well, no, nothing.

But then, who was I kidding? There was this Charles, who had not yet 'declared' himself, other than buying me a violin and presenting me to his mother. I suppose that's quite serious? His stepfather had actually warned me against Charles, saying the man was moody and unstable and not a good bet at all. I did not believe him.

The children, cheerful enough, only occasionally asked about Pierre. Luci started wetting her bed... a bad sign. The headmistress announced she was the worst-behaved child she'd ever had in her school and also the only one who ate her meals *under* the table. As Luci was only three and a bit I did not take this too seriously, and hoped the bedwetting was a consequence of the strict school rather than the new life in England, away from her father.

Behaving like an independent spirit gives one a great buzz... I hardly worried about a thing. I never considered how lucky I had been that Pierre was so generous with his money, nor that I was *stealing* back my freedom. Charles was established in a small rented room in town, but at first we saw little of each other as he was on a course run by the Foreign Office, to do with staff-training in the newly independent Zambia.

His step-brother, a well connected ex-BBC man, took a great interest in Charles and in the new lady friend. We were frequently invited to glamorous parties in Kensington and before I knew how it came about I had been asked to submit an essay on 'Women in Africa' and a polemic on 'Race relations in England' to the BBC. What little I knew about the woman's role in Africa was discreetly added to a learned piece written exclusively by Charles' pen. The piece on 'race relations' was a different tale. I had certainly noticed, when making calls in London, that mentioning my surname *Attala* was not altogether helpful. People on the other end of the line were suspicious of foreigners. Reverting to my German name seemed even less wise. I noticed other things, mainly to do with black or brown people. In London it was *not good to be anything other than properly English.*

A 'class' thing, perhaps? Less travelled, less educated, less worldly, Brits were suspicious of foreigners. It took me a while to gather facts; my piece, part of a program with Enoch Powell, the 'wayward wizard of Wolverhampton,' was broadcast from Bush House to the world. I managed to catch just the last bit of it, clutching a portable radio to my chest. I had to stand outside to get better reception, a bizarre moment, hearing my own voice! The actual recording had not been a problem: I did rather enjoy the novelty of finding my way about in the warren of corridors in Bush House, but when I was asked back for a live discussion at a later date, I sat silently, frozen in terror of saying the wrong thing. I was never asked again.

Yvonne, my land-lady from upstairs, had two small boys of her own. She seemed to like my girls and generously offered help with baby-sitting whenever required, so I was soon busy spinning a great web of connections and events, all of my own doing.

I had been given the name of a modelling agency in Shaftsbury Avenue, by a distant acquaintance in Ndola and when I turned up there, as suggested, I was immediately taken on as a prospective model. All one needed was a set of photographs called 'contacts' and once I'd survived that my face could be seen in a flashy magazine called International Model, for the benefit of...I'm not quite sure now, advertisers and film-makers, I suppose. All this was very surprising, gratifying, still, it was not quite what I'd come to London for.

Just a little bonus, one might say.

Someone advised me to go to the City Literary Institute, to sort out my piano playing. This venerable institution had provided adult education, with excellent teachers, at a very reasonable cost for about twenty-five years and I was immediately placed in a class with earnest amateurs wanting to become more accomplished, just like myself. Our lecturer, a pianist of stature, assigned each of us to learn a Mozart piano concerto, as well as the piano reduction of the orchestral part to accompany another student. My concerto was the "Coronation", and we were invited to return the following week, having learnt the first movement. I was willing, I tried, it was a struggle. Despite his high standards the teacher remained charming. He wanted to help. I was questioned, 'why was I doing this, what was my background', and when he knew the lot he suggested I try a private teacher, a Canadian, who lived in Swiss Cottage. This was the best thing that could have happened; I cleaned up my act and soon I was practising works for another Royal Schools Teaching diploma, as well as taking lessons in theory and counterpoint.

Why is one so happy when there are things to overcome? Why did I not enjoy my Science courses, years go? Something had changed. There was this huge motivation to be a musician, even though I was nearly thirty and had produced three children. Now I burned to improve myself.

None of this could have happened without Pierre's money. He came over at one stage to see his children, even took them off to Torquay for a few days. I bought them smart little 'going away' pleated skirts and jackets, with matching hats for this great event. He invited me out to dinner and a show. While we dined he grinned and staring at me said I still had no idea how to put on make-up correctly. I was instantly cured of any residual friendliness towards him.

Charles was babysitting for me, that night.

Not long after there was a call from a law firm. It was to do with divorce proceedings. 'Well, now it's happening', said my inner voice, 'be strong, be calm.' Inner voices keep one on track in times of stress.

When I opened the door to the solicitor he looked at me in genuine surprise: 'I thought you were a black woman, because of your name'...

We sat opposite each other and I filled in the papers. The man kept looking at me, then ventured, sympathetically: 'If I had a wife who looked like you I definitely wouldn't let her go.' The only kindness he could offer was a little flirtation.

He had also brought instructions: I was to go to an address near Regents Park to return the five carat diamond ring I was still wearing. It was the London home of my Ndola doctor, a friend of my (now) ex-mother-in-law. She was to carry it safely back to Africa.

'So be it, closure of a decade as an Attala. What have I done?'

It felt strange. The ground under my feet had vanished.

How curious it seems now: by any standards life with Pierre had been remarkably privileged. When at first I knew his weaknesses, very soon he had become my rock...arrogantly sure about *almost* everything.

I did *so* care about him, years ago. Why on earth did I need to get away? All those new beginnings there had already been, throughout my life...never before had I spent ten whole years in *one* place, spoilt, cosseted, indulged...what finally prised me out of all that, and above all, out of Africa?

Could it be all that sixties talk of 'Freedom?'

Not only black Africans but also whites hoped for just that: hippies, suppressed Communists, artists, architects,...shackles and constraints were falling everywhere, while all become bolder, looking for greater fulfilment and wider horizons. A white skin in Africa had truly begun to feel uncomfortable; being stuck in my golden cage scared me. A white woman had recently been burnt to death by black men on the road to Luanshya.

Not far off thirty years old I hoped there would be more to life than feeling trapped, or even terrified. How to get back to Europe, *with* my little girls of course, perhaps, one day, to make it as a professional violinist, that had become my seemingly impossible new dream.

Then, out of nowhere there was this 'new' man, with his roots in England, his lively literary mind, his wit and charm. *And* he liked my children. He worked for the Foreign Office, and that too, was surely a very good thing? What could possibly be wrong with that?

Not that he'd suggested marriage... but I had *some* faith in my ability to bring him to his knees.

Once in London for one whole year I turned, every day, a little more, into a would-be British person. In January 1965, when Churchill's funeral cortège was shown on television, (those cranes in

155

the Thames harbour bowed in mourning...) touched and saddened along with British people I caught myself almost forgetting I had been on the 'other side' during the war. Where were my loyalties? I wasn't sure. *I suppose I never quite knew my own identity, where I belonged. I would re-invent myself. All I had so far was a new sense of freedom.*

Charles, the most archetypal Brit I'd ever come across, his family and friends, knew exactly who they were. My own parents said nothing about Germany; whatever thoughts they had about Germans, other than their relations, was totally suppressed, kept to themselves.

In London I swiftly, bravely, made contact with musicians, teachers, BBC people, fashion and modelling agency persons, several famous photographers and people from the world of film, actors and dancers..... as well as ordinary folk, such as the milkman and the hairdresser and so on, all Brits with their revealing voices and views of one sort or another.

My own accent, still that well known South African variety, I became increasingly aware of ...while hoping that lying on the same pillow as Charles might have an improving influence. But there was more to becoming British than sorting out an accent: I knew practically nothing about the English, their history, the class system, their political parties...all those subtle distinctions.

The few months Charles and I had together, before his return to Lusaka, Northern Rhodesia, were packed with (his) family events, and I was included in them all. It seemed I was accepted, just as I was, glamorous, ignorant, different, naïve. We were going to be married!

'You do realize, Evelyn, Charles will never have any money,'...my very kind prospective mother-in–law was obviously testing me.

'I will try to earn some too,' I assured her, 'besides, I really don't mind. Soon I'll have my diploma, follow Charles to Lusaka, fully equipped to teach and play both violin and piano....I will find pupils...'

If only Lusaka were a little further away from Ndola: we would be only six hours drive away from my former life. My heart sank, the idea of returning to Africa drove me to despair...still, 'my future is with Charles; we will not be there for long, surely, in a year or so we return to London, become Londoners, and never, never, never have to live in Africa again.' Those were my thoughts.

Then came doubts...on more than one occasion:

Quite early on I had sold a diamond necklace, a gift from Pierre, in order to be kitted out in some expensive clothes: a tweed jacket with a fox-fur collar and a matching hat, mainly to look smart whenever I 'play-acted' being a London model, like calling on my agent for example. How unwise of me, to go shopping in Bond Street, of all places, for such things, especially when we were about to live in the middle of Africa…

****

We had arranged to meet for lunch, but when I arrived in this new outfit he looked distressed, hissed at me furtively: 'take off that silly hat, and *why are you dressed like that?'*

My heart sank. I thought he'd be proud of me. I was so wrong.

The second occasion seemed more serious. After another glamorous Kensington party I drove him back to his rented room somewhere near Oxford Street…he was plainly drunk and I was quite glad to see the back of him. No sooner had I got into bed in Muswell Hill the telephone rang…it was Charles, in a pitiful voice: 'Come and get me, I've locked myself out and I really can't wake up the landlady.'

I took a dim view of this. 'It is 2 a.m. The children are asleep. Find a cab', I suggested.

'But I have no money in my duffle coat…'

'Come on, I'll give you some when you arrive…'

So I sat up, half asleep, waiting. Huddled in something black, without trousers on, in fact, quite naked under his coat, he finally appeared, on the doorstep, looking completely ridiculous, Never did one see a stranger thing than one white skinny leg and another more sobering 'artificial' limb sticking out from under a shabby old duffle coat. He stank of vomit and of whisky. I was disgusted. There were *lengthy* explanations…how he'd got undressed, been sick, and how he'd suddenly remembered to put the milk bottle out, accidentally locked himself out, how he'd phoned using a few coins in his coat pocket from the phone booth on the corner. I listened, eyes shut, very weary, crept into bed: 'have a bath, for God's sake'…is all I could think to say. When he crept in next to me, still disgustingly smelly, my thought was: 'I can *never* marry this man.'

Might I have seen the funny side, had I been less earnest? Plainly a bit low on the humour stakes… my German genes, perhaps?

Another moment of pain - certainly nothing to laugh about – happened one afternoon, in my miniscule kitchen. The brothers were making preparations to leave London again, Charles to Africa, William to Canada. I heard strange sobbing noises and found Charles, with his back to me, leaning against the sink, weeping in loud frightening gasps. I could think of nothing other than putting my arms around him.

'We'll soon be together again', I tried, but he pulled free and spat out, with real venom: 'you stupid bitch, I'm crying because of my brother, because I will not see him again for years... you think *everything* is about *you*!'

Stung, I walk away, to hide my tears. My new world had just collapsed. How was I to know he was sobbing about his brother? Why did he need to lunge out like that? Had he been drinking? No-one had ever called me a stupid bitch before.

***

At last, a pleasing interlude which cheered things up a bit: my agent called assuring me I'd hit the jackpot by being chosen for the 'Drinka-pinta-milk-a-day' girl. It was my wholesome looks, my clean complexion! They will send the dates for filming in a few days. 'And congratulations' he said, 'this really is the Big One. Your picture will be *everywhere*, all over England.' Great. On second thoughts, embarrassing...

No sooner this was in the diary a letter arrived from the Royal College, confirming my Diploma Examination...on the *same* day as the filming. A case of Sods Law, no one would budge, I tried both sides.

My agent had become steely and unpleasant.

Charles' view was: 'forget the milk-ad, the Diploma is surely more important: then we can be together, in Africa.' Alas, he was right.

With considerable regret I cancelled my near-encounter with true British fame. Shortly after Charles left I did my piano diploma...and failed. Sod's Law, again. But candidates were encouraged to try again, three months later....so, not the end of the world. Once again alone in London I was able to work a little harder at my piano, under the vigilant eye of the excellent teacher who was also very sharp: A different Haydn Sonata, a different Brahms Rhapsody, a more pleasing contemporary work.... 'you may be able to *fool* them into believing you're a pianist' she suggested...

I had *learned* to enjoy her laconic style.

The agency forgave me when further jobs came in. One was for ENO's Fruit salts (as an attentive secretary to an executive racked with indigestion), the other: a 'Persil Mum', with two dirty little boys. The only reason I was chosen for the latter was because I was a lot *less* glamorous than the much younger ladies who had lined up at J. Walter Thompson, the famous modelling agency. A 'mum' with two little boys, hanging up her snowy white washing, had to have a slightly withered look. I fitted the bill. It's what happens to you when you get divorced, practise all day long.... and fail examinations.

One <u>unusual event,</u> the kind one might perhaps see in a film, stands firm in my memory: a young black actor - dancer, whom I had met at the afore-mentioned glamorous parties in Kensington had telephoned repeatedly. I tried not to encourage him at all, but he would not give up, pleading to see me again. He knew I was 'engaged' and shortly to return to Africa and still he telephoned.

'I want to know more about life in Africa', was his line....

In the end I gave in, went to his very 'arty' flat, where he had prepared a meal for us. He asked many questions. We listened to music from various parts of Africa I did not know. He was extremely likeable. We talked, we ate and listened and when the conversation dried up I made a move to go home. 'Why not dance with me first' he asked. I assured him I was a poor dancer. He then suggested he'd like to dance *for* me, and turned on some special lighting. I could hardly refuse, besides, I was curious.

His room was large, decorated with exciting masks and ethnic objects; everything happened in it, cooking, sleeping, eating...and dancing. I sat on his couch, expectantly. Soon he emerged from behind a screen, but now completely naked. Before me, only three meters away was this very beautiful black man, with a huge erection, twisting, turning, gyrating in a trance-like state, for what seemed like a long time...and just for me.

'How can this be happening? Wait 'til I tell Charles!

After a while he danced nearer and then even closer, until stretched out on the couch he implored me to sleep with him. I must admit I was tempted. He tried to remove some of my clothes, tentatively, gently, perhaps he hoped I wouldn't notice...he moved seductively, silkily, to make our bodies touch. I'd had wine and was 'entranced', but...I *did* notice......

....and thinking about poor Charles, sitting lonely, just he and his dog, in his little government house with a corrugated iron roof, in Lusaka...on the other side of the globe, I had to convince this unreal, seductive creature that I wanted to be faithful. Even though he was probably the sexiest, most beautiful man I'd ever seen.

So I kissed him, chastely, *with care*, then dressed and walked away, with a tortured smile. Virtue triumphed. Neither of us said another word...

He didn't follow. I wish I could at least remember his name.

Three months later I managed to 'fool the examiners' of the Royal Schools of Music, just like my piano teacher had suggested.

With an ARCM added to my LRSM I was equipped to do my thing, wherever I might be, an 'associate *and* licentiate' of the Royal Schools of Music.

****

Zambia, Lusaka, 1965.

At last, back in Africa. I have joined my chosen English-man. A small voice in my skull drones on, assessing, understanding, remembering:

'… a week already, getting used to all this is taking a while…that pong of wood-fire…still, I've seen and been in such places before,…that corrugated iron roof, the polished red floor and the government furniture,…just hadn't really imagined actually living like this…oh well… And the kitchen? How primitive can things get: massive wood-fired stove, hot as hell, no fridge, just a wooden box with gauze-covered doors for ventilation…come on, get a grip: my mother had one of these in Walvis Bay days, so if *she* could cope…

…I do wish he hadn't bought these terrible curtains for the girls' room, awful cartoon characters in tacky colours, what will it *do* to them? And the curtains in the living room are ghastly too; his mother's hand-me-downs…I'm not going to let myself crack up now…Charles seems very pleased to see us and goes about admiring, as he puts it, 'all these *female* things', meaning my toiletries in the bathroom and some of the objects from Muswell Hill… such *little* things can be put right.

But a much *bigger thing* has been upsetting, disgusting: some Zambian woman has seduced him, 'a black parliamentarian' he says proudly, while I was stuck in London. I don't think he has crabs anymore, the oil is working. He claims she is *not* pregnant. I still love him, just as before, but if he still wanted her, if she *were* pregnant…

I must stop these thoughts.

'Lusaka only has one main road, it feels slightly more important than Ndola… layout is better, the buildings are bigger, it is the capital, after all, hot and dusty. Does Kaunda, now he is President of Zambia, still keep in touch with Pierre?

Pierre comes here often enough, to oversee the running of another large General Motors outlet and, I have to admit, a *most* appealing shop full of wondrous things from Denmark. He took his children back to Ndola for a few days. I've asked him for my piano. He said he would like to keep it but would let me have a smaller one instead, He'd have it sent by a local piano shop. No point quibbling, I haven't a leg to stand on.

160

Charles hates Pierre, he doesn't want me to have *anything* of Pierre's. Flattering, in some ways, but so unreasonable …

There is a huge Mulberry tree in the so-called garden, a dry dusty plot of dismal neglect…quite hopeless I should imagine, but then I'm not a gardener. Wood-fire smoke emerges from the servant's shack. Charles' peculiar car, or rather a van… known as the 'Old Lady' and also his beaten-up Hillman, are parked there. He is fond of wacky, tacky things, or, I assume, he simply doesn't mind. His factotum, Morrison, has been all over the Copperbelt with him; a Zambian who tolerates my arrival but takes a dim view of any changes. And then there is 'Blotto', the mad Dalmation. He likes chasing cars down our road. Gabi and Luci are taking all this very well. Soon they will go to school, Charles will drive them there on his way to work. I have nothing to do until they return. I could practise…find pupils, go swimming somewhere? Or shopping?'

'Wer A sagt muss auch B sagen' (who says A must go on to B) is one of my mother's sayings…and what about 'Plus ça change, plus c'est la même chose'? I have asked Charles to wait a bit, before we *actually* get married. *Just in case we are making a big mistake.* I do feel a bit ill-adjusted after the revelations and the blazing, terrifying row we had. It seems right to 'just live' for a while, see how it feels.

Life in Lusaka isn't that bad really, considering. There is an ex-pat population of pleasing cultivated Brits, and there are even some musicians of quality amongst them.

In no time at all I am fully engaged in the most delightful way: not only is there a first-rate cellist two houses down our road, but he comes rushing round when he hears Charles practising his flute in the lunch hour, and then discovers, with delight, my skills on violin and piano; he is quite bowled over. Light in the darkness! Arnold Zelter, the enthusiastic cellist: an anchor in my new life. He knows everyone in town, and through him we are instantly part of a new circle of people and, as happened later, life-long friends. His parents, (Arnold is still living with them, has just finished his studies in England) are the kindest, most gentle, thoughtful people, the sort one often finds in Africa: emigrated from Europe before the war, and wholly entered into the spirit of Africa in their youth. First settled in Southern Rhodesia, the older Zelters have a deep involvement with black Africa. Known to be Communists, personal friends of Doris Lessing, they are liberal, enlightened company in every way. We feel honoured to be with them. Zelter senior owns a fairly ramshackle import / wholesale / retail business…. bales of colourful cotton cloth in one of the dusty back streets of Lusaka. What fun to drop in and purchase some material….I make good use of his shop. Within two weeks I have bought some thick brown-red denim and 'constructed' curtains for our front room.

What a difference! I find marvellous African prints and make cotton frocks for my children, and a matching tie for Charles. Creativity, always a good *sign*, seems a cure for all ills. Gradually, slowly, life in Lusaka becomes and stays a good time, a happy time.

The talented young cellist was also interested in woodwork and made a fancy music stand for us, under somewhat bizarre circumstances: Pierre had suggested I take my former dressing table from Ndola off his hands, he would send it to me in a van. I was delighted. But the van, not in the best condition after the long bumpy journey from Ndola, turned into our road, drove too close to a ditch and turned over in front of the cellist's home: out, and into the ditch slid the dressing table and disintegrated into a heap of exquisite firewood. Dear Arnold: he gathered it up and made, amongst other things, a double-sided music stand, for our wondrous flute and violin duets.

Well, it had to be said that Charles and I were, by now, now playing marvellous duets, and not necessarily musical ones.

But we had not yet 'tied the knot' officially. Charles' father, who worked at Oslo University and who had also married a German, some years after *his* second divorce, now took pains to write to his son with some serious advice: '*Do* get married in church', he said 'it's the *only* way for a good marriage.' Although particularly touched by all that neither of us was inclined to much 'holiness'. Besides, in the eyes of the church I was still Pierre's wife, until death do us part.

So, with assistance and encouragement of new friends, who were in Africa working for the British Council, (whatever *that* was?) we decided on a date and made arrangements for a simple registry office event. For some reason Charles didn't even want a ring, but I did not let him get away with that!

Wearing a crumpled, bespattered tie an old Etonian with an even posher accent than Charles' declared us 'man and wife.' Witnesses were the British Council representative and his wife, the latter a violinist like myself. My daughters, aged seven and five, in special garments with matching handbags, were our bridesmaids. It was all over in a few minutes. We drove on to the best hotel to celebrate with a modest luncheon and chilled champagne. I felt overdressed in a white silk coat, bought specially in London for this great day.

There *never* was another opportunity to wear this very elegant garment.

Now, after my 'British' wedding, celebrated on a steamy hot day in the middle of Africa, I had a *real* British name to put on my already British passport. From *that* point of view this was a truly historic day.

Not long after my parents arranged to stop off in Lusaka on their way from CapeTown to Austria. We put on a magnificent show for them: the children sang a song or two, Charles and I performed flute and piano duets, some of the raciest Badineries and Sicilianos from the repertoire resonated into the dark African night and my mother remarked we were 'absolutely listen-able to': a very grand compliment coming from her.

On the second evening my father invited us to dine at the hotel and we dressed up for the occasion. I recall wearing a somewhat fancy pink chiffon number, which made Charles feel uncomfortable; still, it was a lovely evening, being wined and dined, and seeing my parents gazing at us with approval. It had been ages since I'd been taken to a smart place to eat…to see, to be elegant, to *be* seen. Whenever, in much later times, I suggested to Charles we do it again, his standard reply was always: 'yes, yes, when we have something to celebrate…'

There would have been only one thing worth celebrating in Charles' life and that was to become a published author, his one obsessive dream. He and his typewriter were 'an item', it went wherever he did and life was incomplete when he was not working on something. I suppose it was one of the few things that had kept him sane when posted to the outposts of the Empire in his District Officer days, his own special 'something to celebrate', constantly in the back of *his* mind.

Out in the bush he had cleverly taught himself to play the flute, and later, while on leave in London, had even taken lessons. But *there* was no big dream, just talent and pleasure. *His* field was literature, his great joy were his books, his pipe and his writing, a self-sufficient man…and why not?

While Charles and I were getting used to one another a huge historical event occurred on our doorstep. Lusaka is not far from Southern Rhodesia and this is where Ian Smith was causing a stir by announcing his Unilateral Declaration of Independence. It was November 1965. The response was swift: Rhodesia was placed under the first United Nations Security Council sanctions. These forbade most forms of trade and financial dealings.

Within weeks we felt the effects, even though Northern Rhodesia had become the fully independent Zambia in January 1964. Planes which used to bring goods to Rhodesia no longer landed in Lusaka either, trains stopped running, shops became empty. Bakers had no flour and soon we were all baking our own bread, and eating extremely healthy local produce. Where did *we* find the flour? Did the embassy provide it? At first it was frightening, but we soon adapted and anyway, one of the most pleasing things is baking your own bread, with that smell wafting through the house. Later, before Christmas, I baked traditional German biscuits together with a new Swedish friend, who lived just around the corner. Why was this such a pleasure, that gorgeous spicy smell, the giggling, the end results... we felt like little girls again.

It was becoming unbearably hot. Charles and I decided to take a week off, while my daughters stayed with their father. We had planned to fly to Malawi, get ourselves up Zomba mountain to a famous guest house, the 'Ku-Chawe Inn,' and to celebrate a belated honeymoon.

Up in the cool fog and forests of the mountain life turned into a picture-book of delights. One morning we bumped into a fellow walker, just as it began to rain. We followed him to a shelter; he was a pleasant older man, who revealed, casually, that he was Glyn Smallwood Jones, the Governor General of Malawi. He omitted the 'Sir'. 'Do come and dine with us, our lodge is not far, I'll send someone to pick you up,' he said.

I was on my very best behaviour. Surrounded by silver, crystal, and liveried servants, even in their holiday chalet, the Governor General and Charles held the fort talking politics, while I managed some small talk with Lady Smallwood Jones. 'My first brush with diplomatic life', I realized, 'quite intimidating...' wishing the evening to end. One can only hope the Governor General and his wife were pleased to have company, stuck up there in the damp mists of the mountain.

We walked a great deal, reading wonderful novels in our log-cabin and drinking hot chocolate every night. It was then and there a tiny embryonic creature began to take shape.

The following nine months were well spent. Elisabeth, the British Council friend, who was a somewhat better trained violinist than I, became a regular contact, someone I was always delighted to visit and play music with. She was not so keen on performing in public but we did put together several events in churches and at the University, most memorably a 'run-out' to a place called Broken Hill, home to a lead, zinc and silver mine opened in 1906 and only several hot, bumpy and dusty hours away from home. Broken Hill is where the eponymous skull was found in 1921, (now known as Homo Heidelbergensis.) said to be 130,000 years old.

We had worked hard preparing a mixed program of solos, duets and trios, with a pianist to accompany us… something to bring 'culture' to the hardworking miners and their womenfolk. The performance was arranged in the local theatre, the posters were up.

Bach, de Falla and **Bartok**, they proclaimed.

On the big day, after a filthy journey (no such thing as an air-conditioned car in those days) and thankful arrival in the darkened theatre, slightly cooler than outside, we began to rehearse.

Halfway through the 'run-through' our organizer appeared, wringing his hands: 'we've not sold a single ticket so far, I'm so sorry,' he said.

We, the hapless musicians, looked at each other, and at him. 'Perhaps they'll come flocking tonight,' he suggested, crestfallen, but admitting his doubts. 'Still, I have just had an idea' he mumbled, then shuffled off.

Apart from our loyal husbands, hanging around in the auditorium, and a couple of cleaners, there appeared to be not one music lover in this miserable, un-prepossessing dump. We gritted our teeth and said: 'the show must go on, after all we've worked hard for weeks and weeks.'

'It keeps us off the streets', as Charles liked to say.

At the appointed time we walked onto the platform to gaze down at a sea of cheerful black faces. It appeared there'd been a change of heart in Broken Hill. But what about those armed guards by the exit doors?

Our audience was the Broken Hill Prison, its inmates the most attentive audience we ever enjoyed. We did so hope our music-making was no worse punishment for them than languishing in a lonely cell. Halfway through one of my solos the power failed and there we were in total darkness, surrounded by 'wicked' jailbirds. We tried, for a while, to continue in the dark, feeling increasingly nervous, but memories failed and so we left the stage. The audience never stirred.

However, the British Council must have been pleased with us, bringing German, Spanish and Hungarian culture, as we had…to the masses. Just one of the things they did in those days, although they would have preferred British composers.

From all this grew an excellent idea:

Zambia, about twice the size of Britain, with a population of only about 3 ½ million Zambians and 74,000 ex-patriates, had a flourishing broad-casting station. With the help of Zambian jazz musicians who had been coming to me for lessons in note-reading and basic harmony, I got myself an introduction to the Zambian director and tried to plead a case for European classical music. Luckily the man in charge of cultural matters had been to London, by courtesy of the British Council perhaps, and had received training by the BBC. When I told him I'd broadcast (*once,*.. but I didn't mention that) from Bush House I was offered a weekly slot of 45 minutes of classical music, to be discussed and introduced by myself. What a coup. Provided with a typewriter and a stack of vinyls I could set about bringing classical music to the whole of Zambia. My aim: to win the country over and away from all that dreadful pop stuff everyone seemed to like so much.

With borrowed recordings from all our friends this wonderful Odyssey began, and lasted an entire year; a pleasing way to keep my own memory alive in Ndola, given that many former friends there would take note of this wheeze of mine, and what a great way to pass the months of pregnancy. Charles, the writer in the family, corrected and advised me on my scripts and we both learnt a great deal: there was the timing to do, and of course my own 'delivery' to rehearse. As for my English accent, it *must* surely have been improving. One has already made a great leap forward when one says 'Bayt-ovun', not Beethoven......'Mow-tsart' instead of Mozart, and then there always is 'Baark'.

The nine months of this, my fourth pregnancy, were certainly not dull. Charles fell ill several times, with pneumonia and tick fever, but he was strong and recovered well. It was his task to de-tick that impossible Dalmation from time to time, which caused the fever. Blotto was altogether more trouble than he was worth. He was genetically programmed to adore all persons, good or bad, and to hate cats or cars in motion. If a burglar attempted entry at night (as happened often in those days) Blotto's tail beat the floor in delight and anticipation of a 'visitor'... and the robber was left to do as he pleased.

One night a burglar actually entered the bedroom, I woke up to watch him rummaging in my handbags, lined up neatly on a shelf.

'Don't move' went through me, (too terrified to move), while Charles snored on beside me. But as soon as the man crept out with several bags I flew into an indescribable rage, put on my slippers, and tore off behind him in a flowing white nightgown, using my remaining shoulder-bag like a lasso swirling above my head. A Valkyrie could not have been more terrifying, while one-legged Charles managed to hop to the open window shouting the loudest and most terrifying curses, shattering the sleep of the entire neighbourhood. The burglar ran faster, dropping my bags as he fled. There had been no cash in them anyway. It was surely Blotto's job to see off burglars, not mine.

However, Blotto *did* have that 'thing' about departing cars and the unforgettable sight of Charles, on many occasions chasing the enraged beast down Surrey Road, dog barking, his master shouting loudly and waving a walking stick aloft, is etched in our minds. He would beat the animal mercilessly; the children were distraught. The dumb dog wasn't worth having.

Like all expectant parents we had fun discussing names. 'It's a boy this time, I'm sure' I said, 'John and Thomas' sounds nice together'...puzzled by Charles' grins. One has to be properly English to know such things. *He* was keen on 'James', and as my grandfather had recently died in his castle in Austria I suggested 'Manfred' for a second name. James Manfred has a manly ring to it, I thought, although it was a small reminder that my British son would have *some* alien genes. Also, it would please my mother. We were already planning to spend Christmas in CapeTown that year, with our as yet unborn child, while my daughters were to join their father.

We were 'doing' alternate Christmases. They loved going to him and always came back full of news of the wondrous goings-on in Ndola, bringing back new toys and clothes....and ideas. I did think that having two very different influences was enriching their perceptions. 'Daddy said we can do this and that, and daddy gave us'...and so on....well, to be honest, all that was hard. By far the worst occasion came when they returned with a cage containing two white rats. Charles, who was never at his best on Sundays, usually recovering from a heavy dose of whisky on Saturday evenings, took one look at these pink-eyed, pink-nosed creatures and said: 'Out, out, out! They are not staying in this house, I will not have rats here.'

There was an anguished cry from my little girls: 'But we love them, they are so sweet and they won't bite you...and Mr Kaunda gave them to us...' Pierre had been to visit the President, with his daughters, and Kaunda had indeed bestowed the rats. Charles was adamant.

Whose side was I on? My daughters said they hated Charles and wanted their Daddy. And I was trapped, wanting to, but unable to please anybody.

Charles got his way. My memory has suppressed the fate of the rats. Guinea pigs, a cat and a dog had been part of the household for many months, but the decision over the white rats was the start of a very 'twisted road' I should never have taken.

One never can please everyone. It takes time to learn this.

Again and again I reminded myself that my children had every right to enjoy their fathers' largesse, that I was behaving according to the wisdom of King Solomon, remembering Charles and I (and the new infant) would, could... shortly become a separate family. There was also an element of selfishness; I needed Charles all to myself. It was self-preservation as well as a hardening of the heart mixed with the need to 'wipe the slate clean' and start again. He was such a very excellent stepfather, with his stories made up specially, like 'King Murgatroyd' which he read to them at bed time,… they so loved his ability to engage with them, to make them giggle and to stimulate them. He was much better at parenting than I was. I was almost jealous. Well, just a little.

All this was the early part of that 'twisted road' mentioned above.

I was barely conscious of it at first. The girls were away more and more. I did my broadcasting, prepared some successful concerts with Arnold the cellist and a superb American pianist, and, hardly noticing, became extremely pregnant. One concert, a trio recital of Beethoven's 'Ghost' and Schubert's marvellous 1st trio, took place only two days before the birth of our son.

James Manfred was a skinny thing, about two weeks premature and delivered in the record time of twenty minutes. The doctor never even made it to the hospital. Poor baby, I was ashamed to show him to anybody, with those stick-like arms and legs. Charles was very happy. He said 'I love you' and drove off in a trance of joy to see friends and celebrate being a father, having a son.

Two months later we took our infant to CapeTown, to experience a German Christmas with my parents, while my little girl-VIP's flew to Ndola. It all felt quite normal… but it was that twisted path.

According to Sören Kierkegaard *'life can only be understood backwards, but it must be lived forwards'*.

It is easier now to see where and how I began to take the wrong approach to my daughters. Like all children they wanted to be the centre of our lives but they gradually fell between two stools: the VIP life in Ndola and the ordinary family existence with Charles and me.

And now there was a baby, which added *some* interest to their lives, but also took the focus off them. They gave no impression they felt left out.

Of course life was much simpler when they were in Ndola. With a new baby there is much to do. I moved out of our bedroom, Charles must not be disturbed in the night…'the sleep of the breadwinner is sacrosanct' I thought, and he never demurred…and I *did* wonder about that…

After our short holiday in CapeTown we were informed by the Foreign office that time in Africa was up: next step was a 'home-posting'. My broadcasting, concertising, having servants and lounging-by-swimming-pools life had finally, definitely, at last…. come to an end.

London, 1967.
April Fools' Day: is this a joke…it is snowing at Gatwick airport. A few bumps on landing….our five month-old grins toothlessly over my shoulder, amusing the fellow-passengers. Oh dear. I am weary already.

Packing and travelling almost over now; tired thoughts flutter about: 'my girls abandoned in Africa, this time for longer; while Charles and I become Londoners…they might not even *like* to be with us once we are organized…just look, rows and rows of identical homes, how *do* people find their way about in a place where everybody has the same houses?…, poor Gabi-Lu, (as they are increasingly called by us) at least they are safe for now in Pierre's beautiful home,…their home too.'

However much one looks forward to a new life, the change-over can be disconcerting.

I am a creature of habit: moving into a dingy flat in London felt like yet another come-down. Charles' brother had booked us a temporary home in a basement in Belsize Village, just to get started. Even that corrugated-iron roofed 'government' house in Lusaka had now assumed a glow of exotic splendour.

'No-one here to help carry our cases, but someone has left milk and teabags… that Asian shop, just five minutes from here, I saw it, it was open when we passed… oh well, here we are then, England. At last…..'

One needs a knack for nest-building: just one or two deftly placed familiar objects, a vivid tie-dye painting, a potted plant, some bright cushions help to distract me from a depressing, hideous flat. Once the tacky window-less so-called kitchen has a brighter bulb and I've scrubbed down the sticky equipment the first visitors begin to call: William and family, Charles' father from Norway, his stepbrother, his mother. Not at the same time, of course, so I can enjoy them all, in their different and splendid English ways.

Charles' father endears himself by calling me 'a slip of a girl'. I've never heard *that* before, it sounds so slimming and lissom, all the things I wish to be, so that no-one might think of me as a post-natal mother of three…well, four actually, counting the first baby.

My man has much on his mind; he seems depressed.

What followed was no help: within a few days of her visit to us Charles' mother tried to commit suicide by taking an overdose. An ambulance was called, just in time, her life was saved. Charles did not say much. I never found out why she had done this; it was not talked about, just a veil drawn over the happening, a dense tactful silence. English people tend to be like that. Why would she do such a thing; this elegant, lively lady, with seemingly no care in the world? She'd looked so pleased to welcome us, to inspect her new grandson. I felt close to her, because I loved *her* son so much. Years before, when I first discovered Charles had lost a leg in Korea aged only nineteen I was appalled, just imagining   *a mother's* feelings when her child's leg is cut off...

Our numerous tasks were challenging, stimulating, enlivening but also exhausting. Apart from entertaining placid James, the easiest-going of my children, there was much to do: getting him a cot was pretty urgent, he was doubling in volume every day, or so it seemed. In the baby-shop our eye was caught by a new contraption into which you harness an infant, suspend it in a doorway to allow the happy creature to bob up and down, thus strengthening its leg muscles.

There he was then, our son and heir, limply dangling and staring in a helpless, puzzled way. 'Jump', we cried, demonstrating, to the best of our ability. We got ourselves a good aerobic workout, but our son was not amused. Despite all efforts he never got 'the hang of it'.... a picturesque way to describe the problem.

However: hanging over *me* was a black cloud of worry... it would not go away. With some difficulty it was all spilled out before a friendly doctor in Belsize Village...the perplexing fact that my new husband seemed to have no desire for physical closeness any longer, that he had 'gone off me' as they say.

The doctor's theory made *some* sense: that a new father would see his partner in a different way for a while, more as a mother figure, and that she might find herself on some pedestal, to be loved in *a different* way. I tried to settle for this, but the worry remained; after all, it had not been my experience with Pierre.

 After much determined house-hunting in the Hampstead, Highgate and Belsize area we found a modern 'chicken coop' on Denning Road, over four floors, with a large basement leading out into a narrow garden, just a few paces from Hampstead Heath. It was brand-new, light and *clean*. How fit I was in my thirties, up and down those timber stairs all day long... so house- proud, polishing them by hand, all thirty-six of them. The girls shared a room on the ground floor. Pierre had brought them to us, they settled into our simple lifestyle without any problems. The convent school was 15 minutes walk from home and Charles, as before in Lusaka, dropped the little uniformed girls off on his way to work.

The older one, now a small maternal figure, (just like Cölestine and later Erika had been to *their* sisters) guided her little sister through the terrors of nuns and their restrictive ways. One contemplates all those nuns casting spells over generations of females in this family.

My role was to pick them up each afternoon, wheeling Jami along in his pushchair, often in the rain, and then to do all the things my servants in Africa had done for me for so many years. Where did time go? In this pram-pushing, nappy-washing phase my only relaxation was shopping for groceries with James, who, furiously sucking a dummy, found himself buried under several days' provisions in his pushchair. Once we got as far as Selfridges in Oxford Street, using public transport, but the sheer physical effort was too much; I knew I'd never try that again.

I had certainly become a real Londoner now…washing nappies in the old (second-hand) twin-tub was the worst thing, then drying them, draped all over the music room, weather being the way it is in England.

One Saturday afternoon Charles set out and returned with the latest thing: *disposable* diapers, what seemed like a year's supply of them, the entire back of the car…piled up to the top. No more nappy-washing - how remarkable was that.

Gradually the novelty was wearing off. I began to look around for something outside the domestic sphere, like opening my violin-case, trying to play something, anything. More sensibly, I went for violin lessons, which could be done in the evenings, with Charles baby-sitting. He was good about this, generously forking out the going rate, £2 an hour. I recall feelings of guilt spending all this cash on myself. Two well-known professionals got me started with a new regime of serious work on my technique. Our neighbours, a French couple, must have been less than thrilled to hear my never-ending practising through inadequately thin walls. Taking up space in the basement was a jaundiced Canadian maple baby grand, an even *more* noisy instrument to torment the persons on the other side. How musicians and their neighbours suffer *in semi-detached houses,* the only factor we had failed to consider when we bought the place.

Only one more year, then James could be started off in a nursery school; I'd at least have the mornings to myself.

***

What does it mean to 'become a professional', being an 'amateur', having a 'calling'?

With 'a calling' there is the implication of something not of your own choosing. It also implies a gift, something you carry around with you: use it or lose it.

Let's assume an individual has this gift, has a reasonable desire to perfect the gift, but has not been blessed with sufficient training. This is the province of an amateur, who is not judged, nor needs to earn his bread with his underdeveloped skill, who is nevertheless content with what he has achieved and sleeps easy in this knowledge. He is fortunate.

Then there are those who have this same *calling,* but who get to the right teacher at the right time (for violinists that is about age seven or eight), who learn to practise correctly so they pass through the early grounding, say to Grade Vlll (the British system of gradation) by the mid-teens and who are then admitted to advanced studies, to absorb advanced technique, repertoire, performance. The next logical step is Music College and going abroad for further studies with famous teachers and performers, competing with other whizz-kids in international competitions.

Only such players *may* become professionals. Working single-mindedly for a good ten to twelve years, strong, with healthy nerves, the constitution of an ox, and *if they still actually enjoy music after all that,* they will earn their bread with fine orchestras or as soloists, but that only if they are very special, have exceptional gifts.

By the time I was thirty I was probably half-way, perhaps not even that. With dogged perseverance I did all I could to advance my skills. *Unlike* that Great-Uncle Sepp in Neumarktl, that zither virtuoso, a Wunderkind from birth….(in those days I knew nothing about him). I was no Wunderkind, only a hopelessly late 'starter'. Nor had I any concept of the distance still ahead of me. If some well-meaning person had told me straight that my obsession was just too late, that there was no chance of getting to the top of the tree…would I have believed it?

Probably not.

The sixties.

Everything was changing, Africa, Europe, the world, was changing. Britain too, with Harold Wilson newly at the helm, was a country in crisis. Even so, many ex-pat British were cutting their losses and returning to England. In Pierre's case, he still kept the magnificent house in Ndola and of course the business, which was run by two of his cousins. My 'ex' remained a 'bwana makubwa', which is Swahili for a big or powerful man. Now, owning a new home in London meant he was near enough to see his daughters whenever he came from Zambia. He had custody over his children and continued to pay a monthly allowance for their upkeep and schooling; according to our divorce I had been assigned 'care and maintenance.' Fair do's. That's what Welsh and Scots people say.

It was nice to have his cheques every month.

This was the time of 'Oh Calcutta', of Hippies, wherever one looked, and of strikes and demonstrations. On the news was a battle outside the American Embassy, policemen on horses fighting demonstrators against the war in Vietnam. I felt sorry for the horses and pleased I lived in the safety of Hampstead while observing the goings-on in central London. Mr. Wilson was not popular and his policies generally led to severe restrictive measures.

Not knowing much about British politics I found myself confused. I'd got the idea about Empire, and how it was all falling apart, but Charles' view of his country seemed to me quite different from the reality.

'The British *value* black and brown immigrants', he said and 'Unions are good'...and yet, looking around, there seemed to be nothing but trouble. I still see and smell the mountains of rubbish bags on Denning Road, waiting to be collected by dustbin men who had a grievance and never came. There seemed to be strikes everywhere. In Africa nothing quite like *this* happened.

'Well, it takes time to understand British ways,' I consoled myself; not that I understood *anybody's* ways then. Charles, whenever possible, was pleased to spend whole days watching cricket, another mystery. Poor man, he explained everything patiently and probably became resigned to be living with a German person blunted by living in Africa or generally from some other planet. Glamorous, perhaps, but I needed a lot of help to keep up. Shakespeare, the latest plays and novels, politics, sports, very little seemed to 'hit the spot'.

I tried to become, at least, a domestic goddess of sorts.

As we settled into life in England there was a chance to join an amateur orchestra in Highgate. I also found myself a competent pianist with whom I patiently waded through mountains of repertoire for performances in music clubs here and there... paid 'gigs'.

By 1968 and 1969 we had taken trips to Stratford-on-Avon, abandoning James with his grandmother, and later on to Margate *with* James, where it rained every single day. I even dragged Charles over to Hamburg and Eutin, determined that he should see a little of *my* homeland and believed he quite liked that. We lived it up on the infamous Reeperbahn in Hamburg and Charles flirted with the kitchen help in Eutin so that I began to feel life with such a good-looking man, smoking a pipe all day long, was proving to be a trial. The ladies always noticed him, of course he responded whenever he got away with it, as men do. Once I spotted him leaning out of our bedroom window whistling appreciatively at a girl on the road. She was, apparently, someone who went on the same bus route as he.

'What is he doing, flirting with young girls.... when I've given up a life of luxury for his sake to take on motherhood, the subtlest servitude ever devised, and now his drudge in England,' I sulked, constantly on a knife edge with jealousy. He liked talking about the 'typing pool' and watching the 'dimpled thighs' of the young girls playing net ball in some park, near his office in Holborn. I felt threatened. 'You're ridiculous,' he'd say ....in a huff. Why was I so unsure of myself? He made me feel old and undesirable. Perhaps I really was? Here was that black cloud again.

My mother's advice had always been: 'Never show a man how much you care, he'll only take advantage of you.' The idea was to have some pride and self-respect. Did my Mum learn that from her Mami, and did Mami glean this wisdom from Josephine? I wished he *did* take advantage of me, but it was a rare thing. What exactly did 'advantage' mean, in this context?

'More than likely it is a case of the 'mills of God, grinding exceeding fine...my punishment for having broken the rules,' I reminded myself. In the eyes of the Church I still belonged to Pierre.

*

On the day our podgy son turned two I persuaded him to chuck his dummy into the bin, for ever, and took him to a Nursery, where he was as happy as can be and, under the eye of a stranger, became potty-trained overnight.

My regained freedom turned into a frenzy of practising, inspired by my handsome teacher's ravishing playing. In Hampstead there were famous people and musicians wherever you looked: one bumped into Jacqueline Du Pré and Daniel Barenboim regularly, the cartoonist Hoffnung's widow lived opposite and wherever you walked you heard voices of singers and players at work; *just* the inspiration needed to get my act together.

When I'd heard the Dvořák Violin concerto played by an Austrian girl in the Queen Elisabeth Hall... I so wanted to do that too, more than *anything* else ....*I'd close the music room door and enter into my all absorbing task. My poor neglected children were beating their fists on the locked door, pleading for food and love and attention. I cared only about myself.* I have been accused of it all. Still in my early thirties, I worked as hard and long as I could muster.

Memorably, but only once, I *did* abandon the entire family to go all the way to Aldeburgh for a lesson on the Mendelssohn concerto. My teacher was working there at the time of the Festival and I was dedicated enough to travel that far. Charles dined out on the tale of *his* dedicated baby sitting, which included taking all three of them out on the Heath and later, cooking fish fingers for dinner.

How gratifying to get away for once, have a Sunday to myself. Not many husbands would offer themselves up in this noble way in those days? I don't suppose he got much writing done that day. He'd already had the bitter taste of rejection of some of his work but, like myself, his determination knew no bounds. Not just dogged determination... obsession as well. We were both driven and never questioned our pursuits.

If a man could walk on the moon, as had indeed just happened, then so could *we* succeed in *our* chosen skill.

****

By the time we'd become used to life in London we were posted to Nairobi.

'Back to 'bloody' Africa'...*my* words, certainly not Charles'...

'I've said goodbye to Africa for ever,...we *can't,* surely not, we'd even asked for 'No More Africa', how can they do this to us, and anyway, what about the girls, can they go to school there?' I was beside myself.

'I'll have a word' said Charles, grandly.

'You *know* we are 'globally transferable' and have to go where we are needed. But, (chewing his pipe) I'll get advice on schools, don't worry'.

The Foreign Office informed us Nairobi schools were of a poor standard, the girls would be best left 'at home', especially the older one, in a boarding school. Would we consider separating the girls? 'There is a special advisory body for parents: ask for an interview and they will offer many options to suit your children.'

The Advisory Body quizzed us about our children's abilities, interests, talents and hopes for the future. At the tender age of eleven and nine one can detect trends, not much more. We said we were looking for a *happy* place, with a bias to the humanities and arts and, most important, enlightened kindly staff, who would take great care of them, *just like a family.* Nowadays all this would have been fed into a

175

computer and out would come pages of info about the requested establishment.

After some thought our experienced advisor told us he would send us the prospectus of a place called St Christopher's, run by Quakers. 'Your daughters will love it', he promised, 'we have excellent reports, it all absolutely fits the bill. They will learn to be truly independent, challenged and stimulated.'

The girls' father was informed. We all studied the prospectus. Charles drove me there to see for myself and to meet the staff who would be taking care of my children. It seemed fine, in a 'mouldy' sort of way. To me the British boarding school ethos of plain living appeared depressing beyond belief: it all looked so shabby and Spartan. Charles assured me that *all* British boarding schools were like that; I tried to imagine how my spoilt Attala girls would react. 'They've never seen such tatty furniture before, they'll hate the place', I thought. It would take some getting used to. I felt uneasy. 'But thank goodness they have each other… and now there is a good chance they will see Pierre more often…'

I thought of them a lot at first, clinging to the idea that the older, the sensible one, would help the nine-year old through this huge adjustment.

Trying to overcome my own resistance to yet another stint in Africa, here it was again, my twisted path.

It was 1969. Of seven generations under the looking glass there were now four living, (Mami, Erika, Evelyn and Gabrielle), one gone to another world (Josephine) and two further links in the chain, yet unborn.

After the sale of her castle Mami lived in Vienna in an elegant Retirement Home. Her mind was clear, she took coffee with fellow residents, she could read English fluently, she went for walks, discussed books…she was a lovely old lady.

 Erika only rarely came 'home' to see her mother…all the way from Africa, a fact that tore her apart. She missed her family, especially her Mami, for whom she had nothing but the tenderest feelings.The words 'Mami, Papi, Klagenfurt,' cast a magic spell. Erika, bi-lingual now, never gave up her German passport (by marriage) for a South African one. Until her death she received a small pension from the German government. How she longed to be in Europe, near her family.

Two generations were now in Britain, getting to know the British, not quite taking in it was, even had, become 'home'.

For my part, living in so many places, some not even mentioned yet, had turned me into a melancholy thing. Constant change meant pain, again and again. One tries to become 'new' and whole... and then, after embracing a new place one wonders where one is coming from.

Was it even remotely possible to become truly British?

My eldest, only a teen-ager at the time, complained that 'nothing ever stays the same', coming to that conclusion long before I did. As we all moved from home to home, never *quite* belonging, just like wild geese, the irony was that each painfully acquired new home, new existence, perhaps even new persona, would probably be lost again, eventually...

In the end one had to learn to let go.

This was perhaps the true start of my 'Wanderjahre': Goethe's famous concept of getting out into the world to learn, understand, and 'find oneself'.

Kenya, 1969.

Nairobi, one of the largest, fastest-growing cities in Africa, was a very pleasing place indeed, 'home from home', like most ex-British colonies. In the fifties Kenya had been in a state of emergency arising from the Mau Mau rebellion against British colonial rule. By 1963 the country was independent, with Kenyatta at the helm. All was well.

When we arrived for our first British Council posting we settled happily into a flat-roofed house with a large garden, employed a Kikuyu maid 'Njere', and adopted a Collie called 'Cavalier' and a Siamese cat called 'Roundhead'. To *my* greatest delight there was a nursery school two houses down and the homely Lavington shopping centre just around the corner: a motley collection of Asian-owned one-story buildings, arranged in a U-shape under tall Eucalyptus trees. They offered all that was necessary. Soon we could say 'Jambo' and 'habari' and 'asante sana,' which is Swahili for 'hallo', 'how are you' and 'thank you very much'.

Daily life thus completely organized I had time to devote myself to my violin. Still inspired by London, with ambitious works to be practised and performed I was absorbed into the 'right' musical circles, all expatriate then, (with the exception of two Kenyan trumpet-players) into the Nairobi symphony, a decent amateur group. There were several good pianists, and in no time at all I was taking part in improbable events all over the capital.

There's nothing like being a big fish in a small pond, it gives tremendous courage. Soon in demand, even with a chance to perform the Mendelssohn concerto with the Symphony Orchestra I took part in never-ending events, all of *some* quality. The Goethe Institute, roughly the equivalent of the British Council, doing its bit to bring German culture to Africa also latched on to me, an 'ex-German', involving me in several interesting projects, such as performances with Franz-Peter Goebels, an eminent pianist from Detmold, Germany.

How lovely to be with Germans again, to speak, dine with them and be re-acquainted with a part of me which had been quietly slipping away.

Charles and I gave numerous dinner parties; the correct term was 'being representative'. Our silver wine goblets did look very splendid on such occasions, so much so that Franz Nagel, the Goethe Institute representative, raised up his goblet...and then broke down, revealing, with an anguished face, he had been a Jesuit priest some years back. A profound silence followed. Playing reams of Telemann on the recorder, with or without other players, was *his* hobby now, and he was a dab hand at arranging impressive cultural events. We liked him very much. Later there was just a small snag: I had made an unexpected and unwelcome conquest. I received an embarrassing call from his wife: 'do you realize my husband is obsessed with you, writes poems for you and is completely miserable. I don't know what to do.'

Poor woman, I had no idea. He pulled himself together and recovered...as one does.

Becoming more ambitious than I had been in London I persuaded one of the local pianists to work with me in order to present ourselves at Nairobi's National Theatre: my first solo recital! Hard work of several months practising together paid off, the hall was full and the audience generous with applause and praise.

But, my pianist had also fallen into a passion; *his* distressed wife, traumatised, came to Charles, to cry on his shoulder at the British Council office...while I fled back to London to have more lessons with the handsome teacher, who had come to mean rather a lot to *me*. Again, something I did not see clearly at the time: the smitten pianist resembled my violin teacher in London, who in turn resembled Pierre. All three had black hair, beautiful eyes and medium build. Does one have genetic predispositions that get one into trouble from time to time? There was something 'in the air' in Nairobi, that wonderful climate, vegetation, the gracious lifestyle...

In 1971 the Lusaka Musical Society, in the form of our dear friend Arnold, (the cellist who lived on our road in the Lusaka days) sent me an official invitation to return to Zambia to give a trio concert with a young, imported Czech pianist, destined to stardom: Ivan Klansky.

I was delighted. The only snag was four-year old handful James: who would take care of him for a whole week? He and our collie, Cavalier, were inseparable. In the end his father took time off work and stayed at home while I had this unique opportunity to fly to Zambia, rehearse with a superb pianist (who was to have a big career and is now someone of great eminence in Europe) and give two performances, all in one week.

****

Many have fallen in love with Nairobi and with Kenya.

The beauty of the Rift Valley, Lake Naivasha or Mount Kenya, all accessible by car, got us out of town, especially at the start of our 'tour'. From time to time we drove to the Ngong Hills just beyond Nairobi, now famously linked with the writer Isak Dineson, who had lived on her nearby farm as described in the novel 'Out of Africa'.

Standing up there in the tall, dry grass, gazing out toward the Rift Valley, my constant fear, being unarmed, was the possibility of a stray lion wandering about... or Charles' pipe dropping ash in the breeze and starting a bushfire of unmanageable proportions. But there was nothing to fear. Our lives were protected, pleasant enough although...even *there...,* were those 'black clouds', following me around.

Charles, a loud snorer, kept me awake most nights. Since he showed no interest in me I began to sleep on the veranda. By the time I came to life he was already on his way to the office. Other husbands would spend Saturdays and Sundays at home, going shopping with their wives or making trips around the country, but Charles *had* to go to the office every weekend, or so he claimed. (In retrospect I think he must have gone there to do some undisturbed 'writing'.) I resented that and felt he was avoiding being at home.

Somehow the boss got wind of our estrangement. He, and his wife, urged us to take a weekend off, to visit a swish hotel near Mount Kenya, where we would enjoy the sight of white peacocks on the lawn, a log-fire in our bedroom, even an attempt at horse-riding...in short a romantic time together. Did it work? I can't remember. Did he snore? Probably.

It is true that I seemed to attract male admirers. Even the ten-years-younger cellist in Lusaka had presented me with a gold brooch, his soulful eyes professing helpless devotion. But it was Charles I *really did* want...he however appeared to fancy everyone *but* me. I was nearly forty by then and although he was proud of me, of my music, my presence, other things drove him away: my jealousy, my aversion to cooking and entertaining as a British Council wife, and, I suspect, the absence of sound, literary conversation. Charles and I were, allegedly, 'larger than life' and much admired by everyone. This was nice of course; lucky no-one knew what was happening or *not* happening, behind the scenes.

One day the smitten pianist invited himself for a coffee and a talk. Would I marry *him* if he divorced; would I divorce Charles? I told him I'd gone through all that once before and that divorce was horrible and that I had no intention of doing it again. He dissolved into thin air. He wrote poems. I still have one, written in great pain, just for me.

My daughters came to stay twice in the three years, on their way to holiday with their father in Ndola. It was always fun to have them with us although the space was tight: they shared Jami's tiny room and slept on a borrowed bunk-bed, on loan from a kind Asian family across the road. We made a point of taking them to see some of Kenya's splendid sights, the Rift Valley, the Game and the Indian Ocean. They were so very close now, endlessly entertaining themselves (and us) by singing pop-songs in the car. Their little brother James adored them both.

We stayed in a memorable hotel, old colonial style, on the shores of Lake Naivasha, saw the pink flamingos and also spent Christmas in a hotel on Mombasa beach, where the heat and humidity were unbearable. Charles suffered on the veranda with his typewriter, being creative, as always.

Although the ocean looked spectacular we all preferred the pool; the beach sand, glaringly hot and full of prickly things, sea water just like a tub of tepid bathwater laced liberally with prickly *plus* stinging creatures, menacing in equal measure. Everyone, apart from Charles, was in the pool from morning to night; James learned to swim, thanks to his sisters.

It was difficult to work up any sense of Christmas, despite the visitation of a special hotel Santa, complete with white beard and hot red coat and hood. Five year old James was agog. The girls made the children's room 'Christmassy' by decorating palm fronds with cotton-wool 'snowflakes'. Christmas doesn't really 'work' in Africa. Well, just once it did: when Luci clambered up on the roof armed with wrapped presents for James and dropped them through the chimney…the small boy was so excited he never even noticed his sister's temporary absence.

When 'Gabi-lu' left us Luci was in tears. But her tears, unbearable to take, were for our collie, Cavalier, whom she loved more than any of us. I remember feeling sad: we were definitely becoming estranged. 'Do they weep when they leave Pierre', I wondered.

We discussed this problem with the boss, whose wife was concerned and puzzled I saw my girls so little. Her husband tried to convince headquarters in London to pay air-fares for my daughters. We were told 'step-daughters' were not entitled to taxpayers' money. If Pierre had not retained his home in Zambia I suppose Charles would have had to pay the fares himself. Fortunately for us Nairobi was on the way to Zambia.

Again, the 'twisted road' from earlier times: I accepted certain facts…that the girls were Pierre's responsibility, certainly financially. He was, after all, 'the richest man in Zambia'. The girls seemed happy. Why complicate things? But were they really content? I had no way of knowing.

When, to my greatest surprise and dismay we received news of our next posting, to Lagos, Nigeria, it never occurred to me that headquarters had also discovered a way of economizing on air-fares for my children: we would see the girls since they were coming to Africa anyway… on a regular basis.

No, surely not, there must have been some other reason they needed us on the West Coast.

My destiny: yet another three years on the continent I so wanted to get away from. The only chink of hope was 'home leave' *every* year, for one month, since the climate on the West Coast was, allegedly, so appalling.

'The white man's grave' is what people used to call Lagos in the old days.

****

Once again: a brief *re*considering of the generations currently (1973) drifting through their lives:

Cölestine, still befriended with an elderly gentleman; they go for walks and have chats over dainty Viennese cups of coffee.On the 9th of July she dies from a cold which had turned into pneumonia. *Two of the seven women are gone, two are, as yet silent, unborn…*

Erika, in Cape Town, rushes to Austria for her Mami's funeral, desolate to witness the body of the ninety-year old buried in the same grave as Papi, up against the wall of a tiny, ancient village-church. 'Schrecklich,' she whispers. Erika's misery is slightly dispelled by the realization she is about to inherit one quarter of the proceeds of the castle…and quite a bit of family silver. Carried back to Cape Town, it is polished every week by the coloured maid, Abigail.

Evelyn, beginning yet another 'new' life, this time in West Africa, hears about her grandmother, feels vaguely sad. Memories of those first four years with Mami are based on hearsay, photographs and old letters. There is only one recent souvenir: a very good recipe for Strudel, typed out on Mami's rickety old typewriter in Mageregg, where all the family met in 1961. Her colourful, teenage <u>Gabi</u> jets about with Pierre's 'other' family to visit either Beirut, where they now have a handsome house quite close to Pierre's twin sisters, or to Ndola, still an option in those days,...or just the two girls to Lagos, one of the least acceptable African cities. Normally she is still at the boarding school recommended by the Foreign Office, along with her sister, whom she has learned to control and manipulate, taking on the role of a mother-substitute.

'All is more or less well' I believed. It was the time of sexual freedom, drugs and wild music, the time of the Hippies, but 'my daughters are *safely sheltered* from all that,' I told myself. 'No doubt their father, with *his* high standards, makes sure they are successful in all they do.'

Nigeria, 1974.
Charles flies ahead, James and I remain in Nairobi for another week; I am involved in one last Goethe Institute concert and there is the packing to supervise. Yet again!

Friends and colleagues remind us that we are 'so lucky' to be posted to *such* an interesting part of Africa, a place with a history and culture...never mind that awful climate, everything will be air-conditioned and there is the sea,... of course.

Poor James: the hardest thing was parting from his dog. Cavalier had been his best friend for three years; they were mostly found wandering about together...there was a strong bond between them. Now the dog lay by our collection of suitcases, head on paws looking thin and miserable, refusing to eat. He 'knew' all about suitcases: he'd been left before. We stroked him, trying to make it better...his tail registered our love, but so weakly...it was heart-rending.

Poor, poor, dearest Cavalier...

Both pets would be allowed to remain in their home, but with a new owner. We were not so worried about Roundhead, the mad cat, who was really an acrobat... merely *disguised* as a cat. Mostly found on top of doors or shower-rails Roundhead would gaze down at the passing show, taking a philosophical stance.

Lagos is located on a group of islands, endowed with creeks and a lagoon. In the 1970's it was already an overcrowded, shambolic city, now, thirty years later, the population was 13 million, second only to Cairo on the African continent. In the 15th century it had begun as a small fishing and farming settlement, a Portuguese trading post. By 1862 it was a British colony and in 1960 it became independent.

Unlike Nairobi there seemed to be nothing British about it, even after one hundred years of British rule. It was chaos from the very start: the first hurdle, the infamous Ikorodu Road, was a dusty artery leading into the centre from the airport. Our haphazard and sporadic progress was impeded every few yards by traders, often young children, determined that we should buy, or at least haggle over a huge variety of goods. They climbed onto the bonnet to get the driver to stop: imploring faces, young and old were squashed against the car-windows.

I was terrified. Our driver, arm dangling nonchalantly from the car window, contemplated his bit of the road, there was no other route into town, the crawl was hot, slow and forever. Everywhere, tumble-down shacks, squalor, poverty, litter, nervous skinny goats and scrawny dogs, dust and dirt, lorries covered with colourful pictures and curious injunctions appeared to be bussing people. 'These are mammy-wagons', informed the chauffeur. He added to the chaos: drivers had one hand on the hooter at all times: desperate cacophony for miles around accompanying the dismal scene. There was no alternative: we had to adjust to this novel experience. Charles took it in his stride; he'd already been in Lagos for a whole week.

The first days were spent in a block of flats on Ikoyi island where newly arrived British Council Officers stopped off until their prospective homes were ready for habitation. From a veranda could be observed the comings and goings of a fleet of six or seven Mercedes belonging to a rich Nigerian; a man with as many wives. Lagos had many such resplendent people, in impressive flowing embroidered robes, fingers weighed down with heavy gold rings, but in even greater numbers were beggars and cripples, often missing limbs and creeping around in the dusty dirty roads, hands stretched out. They were sometimes treated in a kindly manner by locals but more than often one saw harshness, kicking and curses.

My violin 'fame' had travelled ahead: I was immediately involved in a concert in the cathedral, arranged by the organist Ken Jones, an Irish builder of organs and harpsichords. When I returned from this event my family had disappeared. Neighbours informed me that James has fallen off a swing … nothing serious.

At 2 am. father and son re-appeared from Lagos General Hospital, after a long wait for an X-ray and the inevitable plaster cast, full of horror stories about conditions in Nigerian hospitals, with rats scuttling about under the chairs.

Our spacious, 2-story house was newly built, on Turnbull Road, Ikoyi Island. Not far was Ikoyi Park, famous for a sign near some soggy ponds which read: DO NOT SKATE ON THE ICE

Ha!…How consoling, this miniscule remnant of British colonial humour from times long past, what pleasure to read this in temperatures never below 30 degrees Centigrade and 100% humidity day and night. On paths basked ugly blue-ish pink lizards, doing never-ending push-ups in the sun. We only went there once, maybe twice; walking in Lagos, with clothes sticking to one's back just wasn't very pleasant. Generally a smelly place, with open sewers and drains running by the side of roads, occasionally the dumping place of corpses, one saw beggars and deformed, helpless people and wherever there was a space, a stall with some hapless trader, mostly women, selling whatever came to hand.

Within days we learned that officialdom and most, if not *all* problems, can be solved by way of 'dashing'. This was a system of bribery: exchanging a desirable thing such as a bottle of whisky, or cash, for a service which you would not normally receive without a very long wait, such as having your air-conditioner fixed or your tyre pumped up.

Society was totally corrupt in the 70's. Organized crime seemed part of life: all homes employed night-watchmen, poor fellows armed with machetes, threatened with all manner of evil if they did not stay awake through-out the night. Also in our employ were a large cook who lived on the premises with wife and sons, and a 'houseboy', who cleaned up after us all. The garden was so new there was nothing to do or look at. A gardener did get a coarse stretch of lawn going after much travail… I took no interest until we'd rigged up a net for the occasional sweaty game of Badminton.

Indoors, praise be, was air-conditioned in every room, except the kitchen. Generally avoiding activities in it, I once entered the cook's domain, and found him almost completely naked, glistening from the heat, stirring something. I never cooked a thing in three years. Eating wasn't much fun either: we lost weight. 'Chop (eat) small'- no quench (die)', was our motto…the Brits had left their lingo alright! And our Hoover was called 'dem snake dat chop dem dirt'.

Air-conditioners: with a normal 18 degrees Centigrade and tolerable humidity indoors, things like books, shoes and other leather-goods were preserved from growing mould and disintegrating completely.

It was not unknown for violins to dissolve into ninety-two individual parts when left in their cases unused for a while. This actually happened to a friend who was holding the British Council front in Accra, Ghana, the friend who had played concerts with me in Lusaka, with whom I enjoyed a friendly rivalry, when it came to violin technique *and* life in general. We kept in touch. Hilarious correspondence kept us amused during our West African postings, comparing our 'hardships', the odds this time *truly* against us. With the humidity outside so very high, condensation formed on the cool windowpanes, as if it were permanently raining, while one felt safe, dry and cool, gazing out.

In order to play a violin in hot churches the trick was a generous heap of Baby Powder on the left hand otherwise you'd be stuck to the fingerboard from the sweat. Wearing anything other than cotton or silk was a punishment. The direst punishment was the electricity failing, especially in the night. This happened with maddening regularity: a sudden silence as the gentle hum stopped. Waking up at once one groaned 'oh no, the power, please God, let it come back. Instead there was instant, insistent whining of at least one mosquito searching for a gap in your net, or already inside it. None of us learned to fall asleep without that reliable hum which promised gentle, cool, dry, sleep, minus mosquitoes.

Silence meant suffering, sweating, and total misery.

The British High Commission dominated our social life. Staff had access to the swimming pool and that included us, the British Council. We did spend time at the beach, during Gabi-Lu's visits, but the sea was dangerous so no-one went in properly and besides, more often than not, there would be corpses carried along on the shoulders of bearers, rolled in sisal carpets with feet sticking out...this tended to dim any flickering enthusiasm. James was haunted by the sight of a dead body he'd seen floating in the harbour by the embassy.

There was a bad feeling at the beach; everyone knew it was the place for public executions...allegedly to teach the 'criminal element' to reform. My father had once attended such an event in his younger days, while working in Accra. Carrying his camera with him he was able to capture and describe the feelings of the assembled multitude, all taking a keen interest, listening to the last words of the miscreant and the officiating priest. There was a cheer, when the deed was done, when the 'price' was paid. It *must* have been a learning experience to some. Apparently Lagos too found these hangings a valuable deterrent to increasing crime in the city.

The embassy launch would take us Brits out to another beach, across the harbour to a remote place, quiet and safe, where picnics and social life thrived in a more British way: with umbrellas, cool boxes, gin and tonic and slices of lemon. Entertainment could be found elsewhere: an adventurous embassy official got hold of old films and created events on his spacious lawn, under the African sky. A lovely idea, but sabotaged by the insect life: I regularly emptied out giant cockroaches from my handbags. They liked crawling *into* things.

One evening, back in London on 'home' leave, we learned the insects had outwitted us. Returning from a night out at the theatre, we turned on the light in our kitchen to find before our very eyes crawling beasts, scurry-ing off in all directions, into corners, over and *under* things. The following day 'Rentokil' informed us that we had imported eggs and larvae in our suitcases, having recently arrived from West Africa. We were evicted for a day, while they did clever things to free us from these unwelcome immigrants.

Lagos ex-patriots stuck together. So it was refreshing that one of our neighbours, employed by EMI, was on friendly terms with one of Nigeria's most famed musicians, Fela Ransome Kuti, the pioneer of Afro-beat and known to be something of a maverick, as far as politics of his country were concerned. Having studied at Trinity College in London his music was a fusion of Jazz, Funk and African chant. He was revered by a large international following; he created a concert hall known as the Shrine, a baking-hot place with a rattling corrugated iron roof and started a commune of like-minded musicians, with a colony of nubile women, raising eyebrows of the uninitiated.

He went a step further and created the Kala Kuti Republic, with its own laws, which needless to say, did not go down well with the Nigerian establishment. His popularity grew and grew as he sang about local political realities and created Afro-beat, which consisted of political messages presented in a blend of Yoruba music mingled with jazz. It was not long before he was feared by local politicians for stirring up rebellion.

We would never have dared go to the 'Shrine' if it had not been for our EMI friend, who made it possible to find it in a part of Lagos one was unwise to visit without a local guide. Pointless to say it was hot, because it always was, but inside it was even hotter. Surrounded by a heaving mass of excited fans, assaulted by the sheer volume of Fela's band, I sensed the vibrations beating against my ribcage; I could barely breathe…, feared I would pass out. It was unbearable. We didn't stay long, felt we'd heard all we ever needed of this *so* famous person.

Lagos also had a symphony orchestra. It too was like no other.

I first heard about it well into our appointed three years. It was after a performance with the famous Franz-Peter Goebels', a program especially devised by the Goethe Institute and presented in the Italian Embassy, where there was an air-conditioned hall with a splendid grand piano and an assured, appreciative following. As I looked down at the audience just in front of me I noticed four Nigerians, splendidly dressed in full national costume, gazing up at me, sitting by my feet... seemingly studying my armpits, my every move. I began to worry about the sleeveless evening gown, 'had I shaved my armpits ...these people are intent on my every move'? They stared, they barely moved during the entire performance. I was terribly conscious of them.

After a successful evenings' playing the entire group, poised in full regalia, came to meet me. 'We have been sent by the Apostolic Faith Orchestra,' they said, 'please come and hear us play... we so need someone like you to help the string section, we have no teacher...'

****

Picture a hangar the size of Heathrow's Terminal 3, then a symphony orchestra on a platform at the far end, dressed immaculately in formal black and white evening dress. Seated in the auditorium were eight hundred Nigerians. All in their best exotic finery this was an impressive audience by any standards.

We were guests of the Apostolic Faith Orchestra, but we'd been delayed along the infamous Ikorodu road. And now,...just a little late, having missed the overture, we were escorted to the front of the hall, disturbing everyone...those familiar rhythms of Beethoven's First Symphony...'but, was there some distortion,...what on earth were these strange sounds... still, it's just recognize-ably the First Symphony....they *look* good, seem to hold their instruments correctly,'...we were dumb-founded: was it possible to perform such a work, without anyone having learned to play remotely in tune? The audience were loving it and roared with pleasure.

But the players *knew*.

What could/should one say afterwards? I had been invited to help, now it was over to me. I followed up initial cautious praise with an offer for violinists to come to our house, for a 'sectional' rehearsal.

At the appointed time two vans full of musicians piled into our front room, bringing music stands and music. In no time at all I had discovered that none knew how to tune their instruments, nor could many of them actually *read* the music. They must have learned the entire concert by rote. With such numbers of them I soon felt the only way forward was to take a few of the better players and teach them individually, in the hope they could then help the others. Instruments and music books had been donated by the Apostolic Faith Organization in Portland, Oregon, who dispatched everything to Lagos but had forgotten the most important thing: a teacher. Wind and brass were rather more advanced and I forget how this had come about, but I did feel helplessly 'up against it'.

The orchestra's gratitude was overwhelming. I was touched.

My own recitals were repeated in Ibadan at the University, and yet again, further north, in Kano. I believe we flew the rest of the way, as Kano is almost up in the Sahara desert, indescribably hot and more exotic than anything seen so far: small thick-walled mud houses, camels, turbaned men in long dresses ... very little vegetation, and vendors selling marvellous objects like footrests made of camel-skin, and heavily embroidered gowns. There was temptation at every corner.

There were other musical events: an invitation arrived to present myself at yet another university, this time in Enugu. A friend from Nairobi, who had taken a teaching post at Enugu University offered me two concerts, one mostly for his students and another, more prestigious, in a concert hall, or was it the local town cinema?

The Governor of Enugu Province was to attend.

Having just experienced local 'fame' by recording a performance on Lagos television, (a dire event, which took all of seven hours to get done, due to technical problems, power cuts, machinery not working, miscalculations in the lighting)…I was feeling good about my playing and decided to offer two programs, one of shorter works, typical violin repertoire and another: *three* violin concertos, accompanied only by piano, alas.

I had been working for ages on the Bruch, the Mendelssohn, had even performed them in Nairobi and now felt the urge 'to do it again'. Preceded by a short Vivaldi concerto I launched myself into this, for me, dizzyingly huge concert….and got away with it, a resounding success, with all the trimmings, flowers, photographers, the 'media' taking an interest…there was a broadcast the following day: to perform live and to be interviewed on air, by a ferocious Nigerian lady, who questioned me, mercilessly, as to the relevance of events such as the performance I had just given.

I tend do go into overdrive when pushed into tricky situations. Here I was, a British Council wife, 'live on air,' in the middle of Africa, having to defend Queen and Country as well as Vivaldi, Mendelssohn and Bruch. I surprised myself. Some other 'being' had taken over my mind. I came out with overwhelming evidence that *all* culture was relevant to the brotherhood of man, to the enrichment of our souls…and similar eloquence I had truly never known before.

I was momentarily 'possessed'.

Possession of another kind overcame us all during one of the holiday visits of my teen-age offspring from England: they mentioned, in passing, that one of their classmates had a Ouija board, allegedly useful for fooling about with 'spirits' enjoying the afterlife.

There was never a lot to do after supper in Lagos, and for want of entertainment we found ourselves around the polished surface of the dining table with our fingers lightly resting on an upturned glass. This was a novelty. My younger daughter was appointed 'scribe' while Gabi and I felt the glass pulling towards the alphabet in a circle; we'd written the letters on cardboard and cut them out. There was a flickering candle in the centre, James was in bed, Charles was upstairs with his typewriter, all normal activities. The cook had gone home to sleep.

At first I felt bored, telling myself to relate to my visiting daughters somehow... 'what harm can it do, it's just a bit of fun?' Before long Luci started complaining the glass was too fast, she couldn't keep up. So we stopped. 'Let's see what she's written', we gasped. We saw lines and lines of letters, without divisions into words.

'It's all rubbish,' I proposed, 'let's read books instead'.

Then one of us mysteriously began to see some sense by clustering letters into words,...then phrases,...which in turn seemed to become someone else's thoughts, instructing us how to proceed. Something spooky here, I thought. At this point Charles appeared, wanting to know what was going on. He disapproved, said we were mad, all three of us and 'stop it at once, you surely don't believe such nonsense.'

But we were 'hooked'. We tried again, on another evening, and begged him to join in. Protesting, he did. Soon he too felt that strange surge, suction, under the fingers on the glass. Luci remained the scribe, did her best to keep up. We did not look at the letters, just allowed ourselves to feel like zombies in a trance, while the glass whizzed about. We were hooked all right: in our midst there seemed to be a character called Ted Bolkin, a postman from St Albans, who had died in a car-crash, who was (dead) keen to answer any questions we might have. We had many...

Night after night 'Ted' instructed us about the future and especially about life after death.

We soon accumulated a great wodge of papers, and without wishing to appear too eccentric I even told some ladies at the British High Commission about this. After the school holidays had come to an end, when Gabi, by then miserably in love with the High Commissioner's son...(who barely knew she existed...) was safely back in her boarding school, several of these genteel ladies came to the house for a 'coffee morning' hoping for a demonstration of 'this Oui-ja thing'. So I set it up, though it's not quite the same at eleven a.m., without a flickering candle, and bewildered-looking servants wandering in and out. But, after an initial embarrassing refusal to move, the glass began to spin about; soon two of the ladies took fright and begged to be excused, one of them very pale, saying she 'didn't like it'. There was some talk in later weeks, with looks askance, was 'I still *doing* it?' The answer was 'yes', with a neighbour, a beautiful and rather fey lady, with whom the glass went completely wild.

Well, the long and the short of all this was: whenever I had to perform I would call on 'Ted Bolkin' for super-human energies and there's nothing like a bit of 'juju' to lift the spirits and one's skills to a higher level. The human brain is a wondrous thing. At the time it worked for me.

We got in touch with the *Society of Psychical Research* in London and read a huge amount of extraordinary literature. Sadly it gets one nowhere. The entire business, the spirit world, remains a tantalising mystery.

One statement from 'Ted' was that Charles' novel would be published *one* day. We queried all his rejections, but, when pressed further, our ghostly friend Ted stated: "ten bird pecks end midnight". No-one managed an explanation for that prophecy. Thirty years had to pass before his book finally appeared in print. So what was all this about: is extra-sensory perception something to be cultivated, something useful? It certainly passed the time in steamy West Africa.

***

Colleagues, hearing about the wonderful French cuisine of Dahomey, suggested a convoy of Brits drive up to the neighbouring country about 100 miles north of Lagos, for a long weekend.

The Kingdom of Dahomey had been a powerful and extraordinary West African state, founded in the 17th century, surviving until 1894. It borders on Togo, Nigeria and Burkina Faso, the seat of government in Cotonou. From 1960 - 1975 it was the Independent Republic of Dahomey, then renamed Benin. Everyone has heard of the famous Benin Bronzes, now to be found in the British Museum. In earlier centuries Dahomey expanded and flourished with the slave trade and was very unpopular with neighbouring peoples because of its extremely cruel practices.... it was the home of human sacrifice and 'fetish'. The Yorubas from Nigeria were pleased to assist in bringing on the Kingdom's collapse in favour of French liberal rule, but despite the disappearance of the Benin kingdom the Yoruba people continue to produce art-work inspired by the royal art of Benin. Our goal was to get to the lake-village Ganvie.

This lies *in* a lake near Cotonu, and now has a population of 20,000 people. We were taken around in a boat, carefully navigating through the stilt houses. Thought to be the largest lake village in Africa it was established three, possibly four centuries ago. We learned that these were dwellings like those found in the Neolithic or Bronze Age in the Alps, or in South East Asia. Needless to say the main industry is fishing and fish farming in the shallow lake. One is more likely to get stuck than drown. To James' delight we bought a large, ornate tin sword in a scabbard, both lethal and decorative, and a fearsome grass mask, from a trader with an eye for the tourist trade. I wondered about the bacterial cocktail in the waters all about us. How it all works is quite beyond me. One hopes there is a river flowing through. Still, an unforgettable sight!

Flying to and fro between London and the west Coast every year was a real plus as far as I could see. In London the small, blond, sunburnt James would be sent up the hill in Hampstead, to school, while Charles could write, or watch cricket and football and I was able to take lessons and 'keep house', something one tends *not* to do in Africa. This I found pleasing. So much so that, when Charles went back to Lagos early, James and I stayed behind, to enjoy life in England a few weeks longer.

It was during such a spell that I succumbed to the charms of my favourite violin guru, an emotional upheaval all of my own doing, which gave me the energy and inspiration to continue battling with my endless quest to become a better musician. I did not feel guilty. My feelings for Charles remained as strong as ever, although tinged with a kind of doubt and wish that we could be closer and more romantic together. Ironically, we were…for a short while, after our reunion. I kept my infidelity to myself though.

On another return trip, this time all three together, we stopped off in Accra, to call on our local British Council colleagues. I was tremendously excited to return to the place of my parents' happiest days; their house was still standing and easy to find. Near it was a European-style church. We headed for that, to get out of the hot sun and also out of curiosity, noticing an elderly Ghanaian up a ladder, cleaning a window. He climbed down, greeted us in a friendly way and I told him we had come to find the house of my father, who had lived here in the 1930's. The man took my hand and said, warmly: aaah, 'you must be Mr Ihlenfeldt's daughter.' He'd instantly made the connection.

I was haunted by this. Forty years had passed, since my father left Accra and here was the *first* black man I spoke to...*and he actually remembered my father's name*. Too dumbstruck at the time I did not think to enquire how he knew. I've kicked myself for years. Still under the spell of our encounters with the world of the spirits, I believed I had been guided *to* this very man, by some friendly other-world being.

We envied our colleagues their Accra posting, altogether a less stressful place than Lagos, more settled and bearable. After the return to Lagos we began to feel the time was coming for a renewed move. 'What do headquarters have up their sleeve this time,' we wondered.

But first there was a memorable evening at the British High Commission: a huge reception for Harold Macmillan, by then retired from government, but 'doing business' for his family's publishing firm.

At one stage we had both fled outside to the cooler air on the veranda, where I found I had sole responsibility of entertaining this venerable personage. It wasn't too bad: his next stop was CapeTown and I could at least be knowledgeable about that, besides, he seemed well pleased to be gazing down my décolleté, while chatting about this and that. Such occasions were the most worrying in my 'British Council wife-career' ... I never quite knew how or when I'd put my foot in it. Some high-powered diplomat had said to Charles that I was 'enlivening' company: I worried for weeks what on earth I'd said.

****

Soon the news came: we were to fly directly to Brazil, destination São Paulo, a place with both hot *and* cold weather, a country where one spoke Portuguese. There was only one problem: we had no language training, and only the flimsiest summer clothes. Charles refused to make a fuss, he couldn't bring himself to badger headquarters. He'd rather pay the fare himself, so I was sent off 'home' to England to bring out required warm clothing, to take across the sea to South America.

I felt pretty cross he refused to speak up, but in the end it was *his* problem. I also felt very resentful being sent to Brazil without at least *some* language preparation. Having no Portuguese would be a real pest.

The saddest people in Lagos were our cook, our cook's son, (who was James's best friend) and the Apostolic Faith Orchestra.

The ladies of the string section surprised us with handsome gifts of black velvet garments, shirts for the boys and a long kaftan for me, richly embroidered in traditional white embroidery. Without taking any measurements they had cleverly judged our heights and widths. They

192

also appeared en masse at the airport to wave good-bye. I never thought I'd feel so melancholy leaving Lagos.

It was the one place where I could think of nothing better to do but practise my violin. For three years my technique was pushed to Paganini Caprices, Concertos, unaccompanied Bach, struggling with 'impossible' feats in order to expand my range of skills.

I was already pushing forty.

Brazil December 1975

Any melancholy thoughts evaporated as we landed, early in the morning, through the clouds, into sun-drenched Rio de Janeiro. The bay with the Sugar Loaf, jutting from the sea, the beaches and the inviting lay-out of the city nestling against the low hills made an overwhelming impression. I saw at once that this place resembled Europe...not at all like Africa, therefore: instant heaven.

The local representative put us up for a few days while I wandered about with my son, taking in dazzling sights and the general atmosphere of inviting, pulsating life. Here it was, the famous Copacabana beach, a great playground, physical perfection on show, where drinking just one 'Caipirinha' sent one into a state of spectacular intoxication and confusion....the 'cidade maravilhosa' instantly more divine, the giant statue of Jesus on the mountain more terrifying...

Charles took a day off work and up we went in the cable car to the famed Sugar Loaf to immerse ourselves in spectacular views. I wanted to stay forever. But no, on we flew, to the most populous place in the southern hemisphere. Soon we saw surrounding mountains enclosing a huge grey smog-filled bowl: this, we were told, was our new home.

<u>Sao Paulo</u> is indescribably vast, unknowably, mind-bogglingly gigantic, in all directions. We needed a chauffeur throughout our stay; getting to know such a city is for experts, takes more years than we had to offer.

Rotten timing: we had arrived on the 23rd of December. Our house was not quite ready and on the advice of colleagues we were packed off to a hotel in the surrounding hills, to spend Christmas as best we could. Fortunately I'd packed a few gifts for James and a tiny collapsible Xmas tree for 'festivities' in our room.... a dismal start to our new life.

Not being able to communicate with anyone we sat or wandered about in the gardens, feeling cut off, un-Christmassy, unsettled. The only entertainment was a masseuse, attached to the hotel, who, for a pittance, offered a whole body massage... so for want of anything else to do both we 'treated' ourselves to a relaxing pummelling, not without much prior to-do from Charles, who had never heard of such a thing. I imagined the raised eyebrows when he wrote home to his mother....

****

The British Council, dealing as usual with scholarships and cultural exchanges was linked, in Sao Paulo, with an organization called the Cultura Inglese. Charles' official title was the Superintendant General of Cultura Inglese: a powerful man called Pinheiro Neto was the President. Right from the start this was a testing arrangement. Charles felt uncomfortable with Pinheiro Neto and their dislike was mutual.

The Cultura Inglese, a South American institution, was a massive enterprise, with at least 12,000 students of English enrolled in Sao Paulo alone. The accent was on British culture and in the time we were there we had visits from Sir Michael Redgrave, and the Actors Company with several top-notch British actors performing Pinter, Shaw and Ayckbourn to overflowing audiences. Pinter was treated with special enthusiasm, as son of a London East-End tailor of Portuguese-Jewish ancestry (da Pinta) the Brazilians considered him one of *them*, not a real Brit at all. They loved his verbal acrobatics, his inconsequential everyday talk, easy to follow but nevertheless conveying much sinister content...just the thing, especially if English is a second language. Not to be outdone, the Cultura in Sao Paulo put on a show of their own, with Stoppard's 'Rosencrantz and Guildenstern are dead', and Charles, a magnificent performer of Polonius, led me to believe I was married to a man of hidden talents.

To me, our tour in Brazil felt, at first, lonely, isolated. A neat small house in the suburbs, reasonably close to the British school, allowed James to be transported on school days by the same chauffeur who took Charles to work. Thus abandoned each morning to the daily company of a wiry, hyperactive Brazilian maid, I communicated in sign-language at first, gradually picking up essential phrases. She was an obsessive cleaner, who shone copper pans with lemon and salt until they looked like new. She also hosed down the tiled bathrooms from ceiling to floor every other day, literally. With greatest difficulty I was able to persuade her once a month was more than enough for this upheaval... 'even once a year, or once a decade would suffice,' I assured her. But no, she'd strip, first herself, then the room, down to bare essentials and got the hose out, again and again. 'Something to do with the air pollution in Sao Paulo', she explained, 'it sticks to wet walls'...

With a small car and a map I was left to get on with shopping and finding my way about. I 'fast-tracked' basic phrases in Portuguese. It was a challenge. I was not pleased at first. Much of my time was spent practising, and keeping James amused after school. I gave him piano lessons. Local Brits were helpful, friends were found. James was soon 'in' with a gang of Brazilian boys at the end of our road, all budding Pele's of course. In fact, he could get about in Portuguese in no time at all because of his new pals: he'd bring them home and served refreshments, with an enviable ability to communicate. Half amused, half glaring I stood by glowering at the mess and spillage, unable to contribute at all.

I forget how it came about... some helpful person put me in touch with a young pianist who had been studying in London. Paulo Gori, an outstanding talent, already taking part in international competitions but also messing up his life with drugs, had been sent back home to Brazil to 'chill out' and to practise. He was persuaded to play a recital with me, he needed the money. In some ways he was crazy, but also splendid to work with. We decided on a sophisticated program, Debussy, Prokofiev, Mozart and Beethoven.

The venue was one of the most prestigious in Sao Paulo, the Musée d'Arte, an art-gallery with a concert hall attached. Here was one of those occasions when I did not quite realize what I had let myself in for. Not only was there a second concert, in a nearby town, Campinas, but also publicity, TV and the general hullaballoo when a young star is made a fuss of. Let's get this right: HE was the star and I was, at most, a vapour-trail, doing the best I could. As far as I could assess, the first performance was as good as I was able to do, being swept along by Paulo's incredible playing. However, a BBC producer in the audience came to see me later enquiring in a somewhat underhand way whether I had ever *seen* myself play... on film?

Did I realize I had no *presence* as a performer?

I think I had been totally eclipsed by the splendidly-trained piano wunderkind. Competent...but outshone, the review said as much. I had much, much more to learn (and suffer), as an 'artist'. But the Brazilian audience was so warm and wonderful, all trying to embrace me (and him) and so emotional after the concert, the Green Room full of bouquets and cards and excited chattering. One gets a taste for all that.

Before any further concerts, I took to performing to myself in a mirror, just to get a measure of what was coming across. Learning to be objective, to believe in oneself, is the hardest thing of all.

There were other pianists I performed with, but in the end Isabel Mourao became the most important. 'What, you have not performed in the Wigmore Hall in London?' she exclaimed, 'that's terrible, why not'? To her it was the most natural thing…'just *do* it', she said. It was all because of her then, during a short leave in London, I presented myself in the Wigmore Hall, in January 1977…

None of my family could come: Charles was needed back in Sao Paulo, James was with a friend and my daughters lived with their father, now in Canterbury. Only Charles knew what this concert meant to me and how important it was for my future as a violinist. My agent (this sounds very grand) had invited fifteen critics. Not one came.

Just as well. I'd put together this event in only three weeks, with a pianist recommended by my latest guru, Emanuel Hurwitz. He'd said kind things about me in a newspaper, 'that I would have had a very big career had I started a bit earlier', which was a *fairly* pleasing way of being damned with faint praise. Some one at BBC Radio London got wind of this 'human interest' story and came to interview me at home about my 'debut' at the age of forty. Almost forty-one, but I kept dates to myself. Fate and Fortune were kind and had kept me looking 'youthful.' I saw this event as an initiation into the rigors of becoming a pro…not unlike killing one's first lion, if you are a Masai warrior.

*****

Despite advance publicity, an advert in the Times, an interview by BBC Radio London, an article in the 'Ham and High', the audience was small, just about one hundred people. Charles lost a lot of money.

Playing in London is expensive; an altogether questionable thing to do without a sponsor.

Apart from that it went quite well, considering. I was scared, not *quite* out of my wits, but exceedingly brave. Good friends came to support me although I'm sure they thought I was not brave, but foolhardy. My teacher's wife, also a fine musician, gave a positive report to her husband. Later, when he'd listened to the tape, along with some other 'eminent' violinist, whose name he could/would not reveal, he told me it was decided I was *no ordinary violinist.*

I still have the recording of this event. For me there was always that nagging doubt: am I good enough, can I really play the violin like a pro? Have I caught up? I had become a hopelessly self -absorbed person.

I so needed to be alone,…to such an extent even, that when my daughters arrived to see us, while on leave in London, I can honestly say I have hardly any memory of them. The fact that both of them were wearing a lot of make-up is the only thing I took in. Gabi had just turned eighteen, Luci was nearly sixteen.

As far as I knew they were happy and I saw them as practically grown-up. I'd last seen them over a year ago in Lagos; there had been little communication since then.

There it is: that 'twisted path' again.

They must have stayed with us, as did my parents, who had carefully planned a holiday in England to coincide with our leave. The latter inspected the Wigmore Hall with us, when I was trying out the acoustics, with various splendid violins on loan from the famous Charles Beare, London's top dealer.

Back in São Paulo I played the tape to my pianist; she was delighted. Now my most loyal and helpful advisor, Isabel Mourau got us a run of concerts funded by São Paulo State. We worked up a program and flew about performing all over the place.

One of the last concerts with her was in Salvador, where a local violinist and teacher from Russia informed me my playing resembled that of Yehudi Menuhin. Now that was a very kind thing to say and I lapped it up. On the other hand…Menuhin was known to play out of tune…perhaps he was telling me my intonation was questionable… but then I'd had that standing ovation? So, an artist is never sure, nor satisfied. The smallest remark can knock one right off ones pedestal, shatter one's confidence, for ever.

Still, in very many ways, being a 'British Council wife' had huge advantages. Like the visit of one of Britain's greatest pianists, John Ogdon. This occasioned an informal luncheon in one of São Paulo's superb restaurants.

The gentle shambling giant was accompanied by his wife, who had the responsibility of making his concert career possible at all: he suffered from a condition which made him turn in on himself, locked into an interior world, where no-one could reach him. At certain times one could get some response, but mostly his form was present, his 'person' elsewhere. It was a surprisingly difficult situation especially for a long-suffering, devoted wife, a pianist of note herself. We lunched and chatted with her, while *his* head hung down close to his plate, seemingly fast asleep. Occasionally he took a bite of whatever was put near his mouth. I don't believe any of us had realized he was in this parlous state. It seemed improbable he could play the piano at all. And yet, as he ambled on to the stage in the evening, took his bow and sat down to perform one of Beethoven's monumental works, he transported us all with him to another plane, transfixed by the power of his vision and abilities. I wept, it…he… was indescribable. Afterwards, thanking him for the performance, I took both his hands in mine, wanting to make him feel how much I revered them, and him. I so hoped he could feel something outside of him. He smiled, I think…..

Other luminaries from England visited Brazil adding further dimensions to our privileged lives. There was a great deal of cultural activity in this crazy city. There were no dull moments. The Cultura Inglese kept us all on our toes.

Once or twice, when I could prise Charles away from his typewriter, we took off to see other places, like Curitiba, Santos and Brasilia, the latter a surprise to even experienced travellers like ourselves. When you fly over central Brazil you will see it, shaped like a large butterfly, in the savannah below. A planned project, built in 1956, it had led to intense debate on what modern urban life should be like. Some of the world's most famous architects had been involved. We felt dwarfed and estranged from real life being chauffeured from one splendid building to the next. The distances from one place to another were vast and living there must surely be a nightmare as far as petrol consumption is concerned. It could not have been more different from Sao Paulo, like landing on the moon, strange and unreal; I certainly longed to get back 'home'.

*****

One unfailing delight was going out to shop, back in our São Paulo. Brazilians know how to enjoy themselves: they serve free 'cafezinhos' in supermarkets, in order to make shopping an almost 'air-borne' activity. Having drunk a small sweet cup of strong, hot coffee, hyped-up shoppers *fly* around the place, buying everything in sight; all the while their ears filled with enlivening hip-swinging Brazilian popular music. I too was carried away, aroused by permanent caffeine overdose. Most people in Brasil were poor, out of work, yet unusually smiling and easy-going. It *must* have been the coffee.

One day I took my cleaning lady home to her 'favela' after she'd finished her tasks, so I could learn more about *her* life. It was suitably chastening to see the conditions in such a township: slightly more substantial 'dwellings' than those of South African townships and better organized, even so, primitive by any standards. Yet she appeared clean and cheerful each day, and above all, I believed, honest and very wise. Everyone was Catholic. She had children, but no husband. While my servant earned the money, her mother took care of all their own domestic tasks. There were some men about, mostly sitting on their doorsteps, doing tapestry….a favoured male pastime in Brazil. Unemployment was huge; men played 'futebole' or soothed themselves

198

with tapestry. I too became hooked, not on football but on tapestry: one could buy all requirements in the famous supermarkets where, crazed by a 'cafezinho,' there was a wide choice of vibrant designs and coloured wools, irresistible. One of my creations has accompanied me in my violin case since 1977, now over thirty years old it protects my instrument while reminding me of the excitements of Brazil.

Language skills had got me far enough to understand that *all women* regularly had massage in saunas and that it cost almost nothing to do so. My maid showed me where to go and I became a regular, just like her. Less pleasing, she took to 'borrowing' my clothes. I had lent her a special garment for a wedding she wanted to attend, but as the months passed she started helping herself, without telling me. When this came to light I realised I'd become too easy-going. There was now a tiny dent in our relationship. But exchanging language skills was indeed a strong bond. We survived reasonably amicable, until the bitter end.

This came all too soon. Charles had aroused the displeasure of Pinheiro Neto over some financial matter and headquarters put an end to the posting and sent us back to London.

Whatever it was, we were all somewhat surprised to be 'home' so soon, having stopped off on the way in Lisbon, just to see how Portuguese *really* sounds when spoken in Europe. For a few days he and I could test enough of our Brazilian Portuguese to realise we could get by.

Curiously, learning Portuguese had totally wiped out my fairly adequate French. I kept hoping it could be revived: but no luck…it was gone.

And (I believed) I had made it (sort of) as a (serious) violinist.

London, 1978
We're home, Charles in a somewhat parlous state. He's exhausted, I think. Various plans come to light: to find *and* settle James in a boarding school. Our stroppy ten- year-old seems quite in favour of this idea. We also consider taking 'leave' (let's *see* England, I've never been further north than Nottingham…) and above all, let's enjoy life a bit, let's *talk*…we really *must* talk…

First: we dropped the restive offspring at a summer camp for young musicians; he was to improve his piano skills while we would be able to talk, undisturbed. There's nothing like a long car journey, sightseeing aimlessly, in the Lake District… balm for the soul, stimulating, and also soothing. Second: we spoiled ourselves, stayed in a luxury B+B, serving gourmet food, all for £25 a night, a huge sum in 1977,..called in at Wordsworth's house, saw all there was to see. I was happy. The only nagging doubt, the usual problem...impossible to put right: how was Charles?

Standing on a hill with a sweeping view of beautiful English countryside, sunshine, cloudless, I put my arm round him and, full of affection, pleaded for more physical closeness.

He shrugged me off, embarrassed, annoyed, I could not tell, and made it clear there was nothing to talk about. An ominous and threatening moment... I sensed for the first time a real danger, a situation which was out of *my* control.

There was only one way forward: both of us had to get on with our 'efforts', now that we were home. He had his job; I so wished I had one too. With the help of various contacts I wrote the usual letters, applying for auditions, for concerts at music clubs, for anything at all that would further my non-existent career. A promotional leaflet with photograph was designed and printed for this purpose. It's what one has to do to 'get on'. Charles helped me.

All I could do for *him* was clean, shop, cook and hide away rejected manuscripts which flew in and out of the house. I felt compelled to do that because Charles became so upset every time the rejections arrived.

Stupid really- he had to have them sometime....I chose those awful moments with care.

But the time for rejection is never right. In despair I telephoned one of the agents, without Charles' knowledge, to have a longish chat with some friendly man, about 'my husband who is not able to find a publisher, what exactly did they think was wrong with the manuscript?' I had no idea how ridiculous I sounded and how angry Charles might be, if he knew. The literary person on the end of the line offered this pearl of wisdom: 'if the manuscript comes back more than twenty-five times it is best to *give up*, as there must be something seriously wrong.' Or words to that effect.

But one day there *was* a reaction, and Charles found himself invited to lunch with a very reputable publisher, who began to talk about 'film rights' and such matters. However, time and time again the verdict ended with 'very well written, but not commercial enough.'

Poor Charles. I went up and down the emotional ladder with him, and he did the same for me. I sort of believed in him, but wasn't *quite* sure ....and I truly doubted he was in any position to believe in me.

Neither of us had a clue, really.

Matters became even more testing when I began to present myself at auditions for major orchestras, like the BBC. The big hurdle was sight-reading. An hour spent playing to Harry Blech, conductor of the London Mozart Players, also led to a non-committal reaction. I slunk away with my tail between my legs, so to say. I had neither pupils, nor a job, the only thing that kept me going was learning new repertoire with an elderly scientist, John Bateman, also known as 'groper' Bateman, who insisted I perform difficult contemporary music with him in various venues such as the Oxford and Cambridge Music club, a grandly-named amateur organisation in London. This stylish host, for he had regular concert-parties at his home, kept me sane, when my mounting disappointment in London got the better of me. I was so desperate I began to find little things on pavements, several silver pendants: these I interpreted as omens of my impending better fortune, little silver horse-shoes, suns and stars. Why were there so many of them, lying about?

Nine fruitless months in London, it was the black night of my soul, the 'The Slough of Despond.' I was becoming a crazed creature.

***

One morning I was caught wheeling a trolley out of a department store, laden with two bags of groceries paid for earlier, next door, plus a diary, a *fitted* sheet and a blouse for my mother, *not* paid for. My husband had been complaining about our sheets, always having to be tucked in.

Why had shop-lifting become an option? I was clearly out of my mind. The fine was £75 and I had to ask Charles even for *that* money. It was mortifying. I had to ask him for money every month, ('what, again...?') but this time he was kind and concerned and decided I needed my own account, with a steady income from him. I blush to my roots just remembering. Alas, it is true. How humiliating, to be forty, to have to ask for money, even more so, to pay a fine for stealing. I still don't know why I did this. The lady judge was kind, said that menopausal women often found themselves in this situation, offering me a glass of water when I broke down sobbing. I do believe she was trying to console me. Besides, I didn't think I was menopausal yet. I think peri-*menopausal* is the term used nowadays, and even that was a way off!

*****

Life is strange. Just a few days on there was a call from the 'fixer' of the London Mozart Players, they needed a deputy, for a three-hour rehearsal in Kensington, with a concert in the Queen Elisabeth Hall. My lucky break, the day my life changed! On a late summer afternoon, taking a rest from rehearsal in the gardens surrounding the Brompton Oratory, I became a *new person, content to be alive.*

Music comes from what is in your heart…I believed, naively, in those days…and as a soloist this may be partly true.

Sadly, but importantly, in professional orchestral music-making what is in your heart is second to whatever technique you've acquired during years of training. Playing with other precision players I managed, but only just, to keep up. It was a case of being totally focused on those little black dots in front of you, and God help you, if you are sticking out of the body of sound created by the orchestra.

The London Mozart Players were a tiny group: I started as a 'second' violin and there were sometimes only four players in the section. My blood pressure was rising to dangerous levels, knowing that one mistake too many might ensure I would not be booked again. And the boss, Harry Blech, believed in challenging his players to keep up the standards. During a casual chat on the telephone he enquired which *concertos* I had performed so far, and since the Sibelius was not on the list: 'would you like to learn it and come round to play it to me?'

Not one to be intimidated I took advice from my current guru Manny Hurwitz. 'It'll take you two months to learn,' he said.

Spot on; taking an accompanist along, I performed the Sibelius to the conductor in his home in Wimbledon. He was appreciative and later told the leader of 'the band' how well I'd played. My confidence grew, I enjoyed the feeling of being accepted without any criticism…beside, the cheques were, to my mind, very handsome. My account was building up pleasingly.

****

Charles had worked hard to find the correct school for his son, subjecting him to all sorts of IQ tests because he was not progressing properly, but finally discovered what appeared to be the correct place: 'Broomham', near Hastings, would help James to prepare for entry to secondary school. He could be a boarder and, to be absolutely honest, we looked forward to that.

And yet, it *was* a wrench: Sussex was two hours away, and when it came to the crunch my son wasn't brave at all; we *all* suffered, tearfully, in our different ways. A puzzling boy: James was wise, but lazy and not academic.

Neither of us knew how to get the best out of him.

I never got the 'dedicated parent' thing right. I needed to be alone, with my new music life. All my children had to let go. Was this a case of 'man hands on misery to man', as Larkin proposes ?....I abandoned all three of them, for *my and their* own good, as my mother abandoned me for nearly five years, and later on for seven more, as Grossi abandoned her little Cölestine in Neumarktl. And 'abandoned' is ridiculous. I truly believed everyone was in good hands.

My big daughters certainly astonished me. Appearing occasionally from Canterbury I would pick them up from Kings Cross station, two bouncy, lively, affectionate young women in colourful clothes and full of chatter and laughs. The younger one did a cartwheel on the pavement; I could hardly believe my eyes, such extrovert behaviour! She was still at school, distinguishing herself with A's in everything. What was to become of such a talented young woman? The indulgent elder sister was ready to go to University. Life seemed one big excitement; they made *me* feel very dull, staid, old and uncomfortable, perhaps it was more jealousy: living with their father had turned them into unusual, exotic creatures. My influence on them was plainly zero.

Just as well. I remembered how they'd used to giggle, in the past, when I tried to speak German to them: 'don't talk funny, Mummy' they'd laugh and 'your name is *in a bog....*' *(Ingeborg).*

They had shown little interest in the rigors of classical music. Now, ten years on, they were intimidatingly up-to-date in fads, fashion, pop music, TV programs, while I felt I'd dropped in from another planet. My British-Lebanese-German daughters, were they Hippies, or what? They were fun alright. But, we were 'estranged'....a chilling, frightening word that, to be *e-stranged.*

Turned into two exotic birds I would have to re-capture and get to know them. We tried the ouija-board again, but they now seemed timid and refused. I detected them looking at me in a disapproving way, as if I were either dull, mad or just plain old-fashioned. Their father was filling their heads with all manner of interesting concepts, like FREEDOM, and ADULT CHOICES, and somehow I felt *I* was being examined, judged and found wanting. Charles took the easy way out...flirted with them; I became jealous, wary, weary and confused.

Whenever they left I felt they were pleased to escape, as exotic birds do.

Once or twice they re-appeared with young men in appalling jackboots and other frightening punk gear, which led to tension, stress and revulsion from me; I had only one wish and that was for them to go away. I *should* have been asking questions, about drugs, about birth control, about their euphoric states of mind. And about their future!

Like a coward, I remained silent. Once they'd gone I felt safe again, eagerly waiting for the next phone-call, from them, but even more, to be quite honest,... from *anyone* who had a 'job' for me.

****

For the first time in my life there was a diary, filled with dates that got me out of the house and into the world of London classical music.

Once I was accepted by the LMP other doors seem to open without me having to do a thing. I was soon invited by orchestras such as the New Mozart Orchestra and the English Sinfonia, meeting and performing with illustrious musicians, people whom I had only ever seen from a distance or on record sleeves.

It surprised me to find how many of my orchestral colleagues admitted to feeling bored, tired and underpaid. 'Oh, not that again', said one of my desk partners, when Mozart's G-minor symphony stood on the music stand, or the general groan at yet another concerto, recently performed in some other city. We travelled a lot, mostly by car, sometimes by train, or coach, all over England. The soloists were inevitably famous musicians, but the hours were long. Just a few names, to add glamour to this account: Henryk Szering, Paul Tortelier, Cristina Ortiz, Mayumi Fujikawa, Alfred Brendel, Janet Baker, James Galway, Iona Brown, Nigel Kennedy...... one needed the constitution of an ox to recover from one 'gig' to the next.

After only a few months I was struck with the fact that orchestral musicians were very dreary indeed, the conversation mostly about fees, overtime, mileage, and the weather. Life, darting from 'gig to gig', can be, *was,...* stultifying, and the glamour of full evening dress on the stages of fine concert halls became, like everything in this life, a routine to deal with in the most efficient way possible. Returning late at night, from wherever I'd been, Charles would ask me if I'd enjoyed myself and I had to admit the truth was 'not *really.*' Of course there were lovely moments, fleeting ecstatic phrases, sublime soloists, and we all supported each other, getting to the performances and back late at night, but it was hard work. Inevitably men made advances, some people had affairs, but I kept clear of entanglements. Looking back, I was very lucky to have experienced it for three years, but the glamour of such slavery is overrated.

Other surprising events kept me working hard at being a good musician: fairly eminent relatives who lived in Lübeck heard me play privately, when I visited Germany before. Not exactly household names, they lived as professional musicians all their lives, he a flautist, she as pianist. They ran a concert series in the beautiful ancient St. Annen Museum in Lübeck and immediately invited me as 'guest violinist from London'.

A step in the right direction: I performed a concerto by Tartini, with members of the Nord-Deutsche Rundfunk Orchester from Hamburg, and on a later occasion, some unaccompanied Bach; we also did various trio concerts in other towns like Bremen and Bonn, even crossed the North Sea to Heligoland.

These were unusual concerts, and a lot more pleasing than being a small cog in an orchestra. The fact that I had to go abroad, to play concertos in Germany, resonated well with the 'fixer' of the Mozart Players and my prestige grew, especially when I'd been booked for a trio concert in Detroit, America. Imagine: 'Evelyn has to fly to Detroit to play a recital....' Yes, my colleagues were looking at me with renewed interest.

*****

Somewhere, in the midst of all this busy-ness we moved from our 'chicken-coop' to a basement flat up the road. I'd spotted the FOR SALE sign, and as the relationship with our neighbour had become too strained: *her* booming quadraphonic speakers at 2 a.m., my daily practising, and threats of court cases and police intervention made no difference, we sold the place and had an architect re-design a neglected Victorian flat, for a *new beginning*.

What a shame this flat was not filmed on first inspection: to find a dwelling in the middle of London's fashionable Hampstead, in 1980, in such a derelict, foul and primitive condition was truly worth recording. The 'poor old thing' who had ended her days among at least a dozen cats had obviously escaped the notice of social services.

By the front door hung a romantic bell-pull, as you crossed the thresh-hold there was a coalhole, still in use. The potentially handsome front room, with a boarded-up fireplace was dark, damp and foul with broken old chairs and filthy objects. Nowhere was there any sanitation other than an outside loo, the kitchen a tiny corner on the way out with a miniscule brick-oven, and a small tin basin, with one dripping cold tap; the garden a formless thicket of impenetrable weeds under a mighty ash tree. Plumbing? Whoever had lived here was still a Victorian: there *was* no bathroom. One very small inside room, without ventilation, was filled knee-high with discarded junk, even a WW1 helmet. The smell of pee (cat, human?) was rank, the grime indescribable. It would have been no surprise to find rats. Small wonder the place cost only £15,000. Puzzling; no-one had helped this old person. Didn't she have children, did no-one care? Perhaps she was bad-tempered, feral. We discovered later that the entire house, built one hundred years earlier, had belonged to Marie Stopes, the pioneering family planner and eugenicist. Our basement was where the servants had lived; perhaps the former owner had been a parlour maid, who served Marie Stopes, and had never got away.

Originally, what had *actually* caught my eye, was a sapling, about five feet high, growing out of brickwork next to the bay window. I marvelled at its ability to grow out of a hole in the plaster. Each time I passed I admired its will to live. I felt this was some sort of message for me.

And then, unexpectedly… there was the FOR SALE sign. I'd already bonded with the place, because of that incredibly tenacious plant. I suppose the old woman was rather like the plant, hanging on, surviving on very little. I wish I'd seen her, taken her in; there *were* such bent old neglected women, struggling along on Hampstead's arty pavements.

We spent much money on renovation: the flat became beautiful, in a dark, old-fashioned, classy way: two and a half rooms, a kitchen the size of a broom cupboard where the coal hole had been. But we loved it and it was a bonding experience, a happy upheaval. I sold my nasty Canadian Maple piano and used the proceeds to find a Blüthner, with an exquisite tone. Charles used to play some works by Chopin and Mendelssohn so well in those days, that once or twice I thought his performance was a recording on the radio. He loved that piano. He also loved good pianists. There was one on our road, you could hear the endless practising as you passed. Hampstead was like that.

At this time my black clouds were to become even blacker.

How confusing it all was, looking back, memories tinged: my own niggling dissatisfaction with my violin technique and with the even stronger sense of having failed in other important ways. Underpinning our uneasy marriage was Charles' frustration with *his* writing but also with *my* reaction to *his* work. Not having any experience or training in literature, apart from reading and usually enjoying, *some* authors, Charles wanted feedback from me, whenever I was asked to read the novels he wrote. I was terrified of saying that I found them 'pastel' coloured, a bit quaint, possibly boring, …floundering about, but always of course 'how well he expressed himself, such marvellous prose, so sensitive, so cultivated'. Somehow, as the years passed, his inability to find a publisher seemed to become *my* fault, a result of *my* negative views.

Had I just simply said 'how wonderful' and left it at that we might have been happier, closer... who knows?

Charles was away frequently, never more cheerful than when he was packing his case to travel to distant countries as an 'election supervisor'. He'd whistle cheerfully just before he left, something that never happened at other times. When the Southern Rhodesian elections took place in 1980, he was away for three months. During such absences I always hoped things would improve between us.

Quite the opposite: much given to visiting my favourite fortune-teller in Camden Lock I was dumbfounded by his pronouncement: 'I see your partner, desperately involved with someone, it could be a male person, it could be female...I can't see this clearly, but it is a very young person, jeans, a bike...'and *I* thought, for once, the fortune-teller was surely completely bonkers, Charles was much too busy with his job for such a thing...but my antennae were out, I began to see how thin he was, always in his garden hut, scribbling away, looking pale and wan. One morning I found some partly burnt love-sonnets in the garden. I then began to remember insinuations: the old Irish woman upstairs who had said, out of the blue: 'but Mr. Chadwick is a GOOD man, isn't he...such a good man...', looking straight at me in a questioning way, and a well known agony aunt, Anna Raeburn, who lived two doors away, had stopped me on the road asking what were my views on 'male fidelity'...I'd just returned from a concert, carrying my violin, and felt too tired to get into a long dissertation on the topic. All these (cowardly) ladies were trying to tell me something that I was not picking up myself: Charles had been seen with *another* woman.

She was Nicola, a piano student at the RCM. She *always* wore jeans, *always* travelled on a bike...which explains how the fortune-teller had picked up the 'androgynous' signals.

Explains? I really wondered about such things: how does fortune-telling come into being, what do these individuals do, to 'read' such information? I knew nothing about Nicola when I went to Camden Lock. I had hardly noticed Nicola, she lived in a basement flat and somebody's bike was always tied to the rails of the gate on the pavement. I did know Anna Raeburn upstairs, just from one or two neighbourly chats. All this remained a mystery. I truly didn't see how any fortune-teller could have been reading the 'Nicola topic' in *my* mind. This was when 'the shit hit the fan'. What a terrible and corny way to describe what follows:

I had returned triumphantly from Munich, after three successful and well-reviewed recitals in Germany. Charles announced we had been offered a posting to Canada. Did I want to go?

I said I wasn't sure, there was my 'work', my pupils; how about his own feelings? He hedged for a while. For some days I managed to keep quiet, but soon I could bear it no longer: I told him I'd found partly burnt pages of his poetry and tried to get him talking: had he fallen in love with someone?

'What's it got to do with you' he said huffily, '...a poet needs some inspiration, it's not serious....'.but yes, eventually he conceded he was *besotted* with a little piano student two houses away, and they had been 'seeing' each other, but it was entirely platonic. I said I understood, and of course, 'this happens', mentioned the fortune-teller episode, and finally confessed my own infidelities, with assurances that I had never stopped loving him and 'what about us....we've stuck it out for over fifteen years, and what are your thoughts about that.' He was non-committal. But Nicola: he just couldn't help it, 'we've been together for so long, and of course, I love you, but that sex-thing....well, try to understand and stop worrying', he suggested. I even enquired if he was perhaps homosexual, but he didn't think so. He was so *not* jealous about *my* confession, it was not only puzzling, it was hurtful.

****

Suddenly a posting to Canada seemed like a very good idea. I could think of nothing else but my husband's infatuation, as he played it down and even became amorous with *me*, for a change. Nice as that was it made things even *more* trying. It was so very easy to imagine how he felt about such a beautiful and talented young thing, and the fact that he was simply transferring his pent-up passion to me instantly put me into a state of feeling 'second best'. I couldn't eat. My colleagues thought I'd gone on some terrible diet; both of us became haggard and wan, from all the stress.

But we had opened up and were at last able to talk. With such tumultuous emotions the only trouble was I couldn't believe most of what I heard him say. He was too quick and slippery with words. Round and round we went, trying to sort out our feelings and our future. He was 49 and this was his mid-life crisis.

My colleagues in the orchestra suggested I stay in London and send him off to Canada on his own. After all, it would be hard, even impossible, to get back into the profession, if I went away for several years. 'Goodness, you must love that man', opined the wife of our concertmaster and I remember thinking how strange it was to be seen as a 'tragic' figure. But I was not tough enough to be parted from him. Besides, with all the excitement of packing, and buying new things for our next posting, and having somehow, at last, found a way to be closer and more open with each other, Canada appeared to be our salvation.

Before we left I confronted my demon(s) by calling on Nicola, the pianist who had bewitched my husband. She looked quite uncomfortable when she let me in, fearing perhaps I'd come to make a scene.

I offered her all my piano students, and mentioned, in an offhand way that I had been out of London quite a lot, giving concerts, and that it was obviously not a good thing to leave one's husband alone for *too* long.... just to show her I had a sense of humour. And I did notice: she was extremely beautiful.

There is a sub-plot to all this. It has to do with my daughters. It's quite difficult to remember what they were up to; another sign no doubt of my inadequacies as a wife *and* mother.

Gabi must be 21. Super-clever Luci is 19 and refuses further studies.... plainly in a state of anarchy,...she and her young man in Punk boots, they want to rebel even more and see the world, travelling and busking with a group and 'being free'. But they must have money, they need a 'home'. They already have sexual freedom, presumably drugs and wild music...nothing but negative thoughts from me ...as far as that goes.

Charles says 'wonderful' and gives them £2000, a down payment for a little cottage, somewhere. Good move. But they buy a double-decker bus, a 'mobile' home.... I'm not amused. It's the busking idea that gets me down. Putting a hat on the pavement and hoping for some cash to appear in it. It's not 'begging', it is 'giving a performance', they say, to be rewarded with money. This is their view. 'Just like gypsies,' is mine.

Do 'Flower People' radiate love and compassion because they are permanently drugged, I wonder. What about the £2000?

'Ah, we will sell the bus and buy a home, later.' Charles is not fazed by all this, but I am. Perhaps he behaves like this because Luci is not *his* child. I am furious with him for trying to keep on the right side of my daughters' views, instead of playing the strong step-father figure. And what does Pierre think?

Not wanting to antagonize absolutely everybody I keep my mouth shut.

Gabi, still a student, seems more staid, less faddy. Why can't Luci be sensible, like her sister?

Ottawa. 1982

I've stepped off the plane, straight into The Future. Just see the 'Pomeranian peasant' now: new full-length sheepskin coat, fur hat, dark glasses and dainty boots. I pick my way through the snowy, icy landscape, feeling like an actress on a film set. Everything is larger than life...the roads, buildings, the shopping centres and cars, you name it...what a shiny, clean wondrous planet am I on..? Except for the telegraph poles, anomalously primitive, crooked logs, straight from the woods, all shapes and sizes.

Mogs, the inherited cat in 215 River Road is at least five kilos heavier, six inches higher, than any British moggy. Canadians are cheery, friendly: the taxi-drivers, who compliment me on my 'lovely' British accent, think I am British. French Canadians have an altogether peculiar accent, something from another age, another place.

Our house looks out across a road, over a strip of now bare park, on to a frozen river. There is a distant bridge. The view is gorgeous. But Charles declares the place has 'no ghosts,' and is plainly not impressed. His view of it is coloured by the fact that he studied Literature at Toronto University, after his leg was blown off in Korea; he feels he knows Canada well enough. Having turned down a place at Cambridge to come here, he *must* have liked it then....

Such abundance, opulence even.... Brent Cross in London is a poor wee thing by comparison. And he's so wrong about 'no ghosts'...there *are* historic buildings in town, near his office on Elgin Street, and some remaining 19th century architecture in Sussex Street: one still, just about, senses the fact that Ottawa was once the centre for the Canadian lumber, milling and timber industry, for the whole of North America. It might even explain the poor-quality telegraph and electricity poles. The place is full of rivers and canals.

It is small enough to get to know well and I am so happy to be here.

We are making a new start. All is well.

An American Steinway baby-grand is on order, and our house, large and beautifully heated, comes with a Portuguese cleaning lady and a larger- than- life stripy cat; both of them very assured and on the bossy side. The cat comes to the bedroom door at six a.m., makes a huge fuss trying to open it. Apparently our predecessors allowed this.

Well, Mogs, think again: we are locking you into the basement tonight.

Mogs' resting place in the basement is declared my music room, where I keep all my books, stands, instruments and where I can practise undisturbed. Mogs loves the metronome and sits on the table, with his paw stretched to touch the moving inverted pendulum. Once the Steinway is installed upstairs the cat shows he understands about such things too and sits patiently next to me while I play. Then it is *his* turn, he tries one paw, then both and eventually walks along the keyboard daintily, considering his massive frame. It sounds suitably '20th century' and New World. Mogs, my first Canadian pupil!

In the basement is a ping-pong room, where we have a television and a big cosy couch, and also buried below the ground-level, a huge guest suite, bathroom... and a tiny bedroom, for James, when he appears for school holidays. Upstairs are two large bedrooms, bathrooms, a grand suite of drawing-room, hall and dining room, the biggest kitchen I've ever seen apart from the one in Mageregg... and a tiny study, for the smoking, typing, poring-over-Canadian-Literature man of the house.

One soon grows into such a space. We already have. We've also acquired two second-hand bikes and some skis, the cross-country variety. I will learn. And Canadians, they really understand heating: downstairs rumbles a vast boiler, big enough to fuel the Titanic The heating is on, night and day. Thank you, the British Taxpayer! While Charles drives out of our double garage each day, across two bridges, to his office in town, Mogs and I are as warm as can be. A huge cosy bubble forms around me.

The social round begins: one dinner party after the next. I will have to invite all these persons back in due course. The Portuguese ambassador, a keen music-lover, is already planning a soirée with classical music...he knows a good pianist and a cellist. This is the way forward: meeting musicians.

I have never had it so good.

'Have a nice day', is what everybody says, where-ever you are, in a smiley, open-to-chat kind of way. Why are they so friendly? I was told Canadians were boring, but no-one mentioned their kindness. Our neighbours come over with a 'welcome' potted plant, they are Quebecquois, offer help and friendship. He is someone important in Parliament (Ottawa is the capital of Canada) and she is a university lecturer at Ottawa U....that's how they say it here: *ah' dah' wa' yooh*. I find myself trying to pronounce things in the Canadian way, feeling laid back. 'In the summer you must come and swim in our pool', they say, 'we have no fences in Canada, please come over, anytime. And we are used to looking after Mogs whenever you travel.'

It's all too good to be true. The sun shines, icicles glisten and Mogs frolics in the snow. The cold air makes us frisky. I have seen icicles the size of elephant tusks. Truly. They drip and build up, over time. No sooner are we all settled than we pack our bags to take a week's trip across Canada, visiting major towns, and while Charles calls on Universities and Council representatives I lounge about in 5-star hotels and explore, on my own. I learn to have eggs 'sunny-side up' and note the joys of blueberry muffins for breakfast.

The best way to get to know any place is to walk about and just look. A bit lonely sometimes, but there is always much to talk about later, when Charles returns from work, if we are not invited out.

The first major town we visit, Vancouver, named after Captain George Vancouver RN in the 1700's, has everything any human could want, mountains, the sea, beauty and wealth; apart from numerous Chinese I am struck with the comical British-ness of Vancouver Island: Union Jacks on display, London buses for transport.

Elsewhere Canada has a neutral orderly feel to it, plain and good. Winnipeg: dusty, bleak, wind-swept in a primitive wild-west sort of way; Edmonton, more groomed, Calgary, flashy.

The big surprise are Montreal and Quebec, two bustling French cities of elegance and style, very different from the rest. Even Ottawa has a totally French twinned city on the other side of the Ottawa river: it is called Hull and I am finding out about the two unhappy factions...French Canadians and English-speakers, like two jealous siblings, vying and quarrelling endlessly, while they try to define their identities. By the time Charles and I return to Ottawa I have seen much of the country, apart from the North, the famous Banff in the Rockies and Newfoundland.

We have bought two power-steered cars...no-one in North America bothers with gears - and special tyres for the winter. I can barely believe the amount of snow Canadians put up with each year. In Quebec City it is piled so high along the roads that the houses behind are invisible from the road. As soon as the stuff floats down the snow-ploughs come out of no-where, de-snowing every road. All shopping centres, both above and below ground are fantastically heated, in fact if you don't fancy being out you need never venture into the cold. Temperatures of -10 to -25, even -30 degrees Centigrade are quite normal in January and February. The condensation from your breathing turns into tiny ice crystals which settle on your eye-lashes and eyebrows. The cat reappears with snow-laden whiskers; he likes the great outdoors, at any temperature, but not for long.

*****

An Ottawa violin teacher has died a short while before our arrival and some of his pupils are finding their way to me. Within weeks I have a budding musical life. With the prospect of professional fees I gladly relinquish my 'diplomatic status' and scheme and plan how to fill my days for the best. Like in London this means 'auditions'. The most prestigious orchestra in Canada, based in Ottawa at their National Arts Centre, is my first target, they hear me but decline…possibly because they know I am a diplomat's wife and will not be there for long. This is a blow: it is the best group far and wide. I soon meet many of their players, in other, less prestigious smaller orchestras, but not being with them on a regular basis rankles.

Having set the scene for life in Canada the problem now is to deal with seven years of events: two fat diaries about the ups and downs, the myriads of memories, without becoming tedious. It also dawns on me that *capturing reality* is an illusion. Whose truth can I tell? …Only mine.

Even *that* shifts and moves about. How about Charles', or that of my children'? How depressing, how frustrating it is.

Somewhere, while all this is going on, Erika, my poor little mother and my father are beginning the run-up to the end of their lives. I never thought of this at the time; one believes parents will be around forever and both seem hale and busy and taking a great interest in our new life, even threatening to come over to visit. Erika's youngest sister lives in South Bend, which as any Canadian crow will tell you, is due south, not far from Ottawa.

Canada= 'kann er da?' (can he, there?) was my mum's little joke, not that I'd ever let her in on our marital problems. Who knows what she was alluding to, she was quite fond of making rude or plain 'dirty' jokes. Austrians are like that, scatological. See Mozart's letters.

As for my daughters, …a somewhat delicate issue, with the eldest living first alone, then with a friend, after she'd spent a few weeks with us in London…we'd sort of pushed her out into a state of independence, and it was plain from the start she didn't like it at all. To cope with life I once found her locked in the downstairs loo, on the floor, chanting 'Om, Om, Om', which is allegedly a form of eastern meditation. Without this she felt she could not cope. She'd found a secretarial job with a handicraft magazine, she had to get to her office in Soho by Underground each day, she found it stressful.

The younger one, infected with the wish to be free, to rebel against society, and totally under the thumb of her boyfriend, the one in the 'bovver' boots, was travelling without any funds, busking her way across Europe. This was, to me, so unthinkable, so shocking, that the only way forward was to suppress the whole idea and get on with my own life. What did Pierre think? Was he still endlessly on about freedom? He, by now, had so many other children, he was probably quite pleased to have shed the first two, according to my calculations, 24 and 22...or possibly 23 and 21 years. They were much on my mind, entering the school-of-life, doing it the hard way. It was only a matter of months before the eldest had ditched her job and joined the Punk buskers. I could hardly bear thinking about it.

***

Just imagine the dainty teacups, coffee-cups clattering at Ottawa diplomatic ladies' coffee-mornings: ...'and your children, Mrs Chadwick , also at Oxford ...or still at school......?'

I got out of 'telling all' by changing the subject, even better, by not attending coffee-mornings: I had to 'practise for recitals', or 'go to rehearsals', any excuse would do to get away from diplomatic ladies. In their company I did tend to feel like a 'Pomeranian peasant' anyway, even without revealing my children's peculiarities. It's not so easy for me, being properly British. With a treble-whammy of being German, brought up partly in South Africa, divorced from a Lebanese, it was simpler to suppress my potentially eye-brow raising background.

A Woman with a Mysterious Past, German background, on top of all that: hippy children. Representing Britain abroad is not quite like being an ordinary Brit ...one has to 'try harder', put one's best foot forward,(if one has one) and wave the flag, *all* the time.

On April the 2nd, 1982 Britain sent a Task Force to the Falklands.

A group of Argentinian scrap metal merchants raised an Argentinian flag on these islands, which was considered an offensive action and the now famous amphibious attack launched patriotic sentiments and much debate everywhere. Not usually deeply involved in world affairs, Charles and I became hotly embroiled in our snowy Canadian outpost, so much so that I began to feel divorce was the only solution for us.

As time passed, I began to realize how very *many* views there were on this episode, and yet another storm in our relationship passed, ebbed away, as we battled on.

****

Everyone had heard of the iconic Glenn Gould, Canada's starry, eccentric pianist. He stood alone, completely special.

214

On the way to perform my first public recital in Ottawa, on October 4th 1982 there was an announcement on the car-radio that Glenn Gould had died from a stroke.

Canadian musicians and lovers of music must have been stunned.

By some bizarre chance I had included an Elegy for unaccompanied violin by Stravinsky in my program, dedicated to the memory of a French musician. I steeled myself to make a special announcement.... then played this very appropriate piece with real sadness. This first recital was to be a successful start to seven fulfilling years of performing in Canada.

From the end of 1982 each day was recorded in my diary.

William, Charles' brother, a drama professor from Waterloo, Ontario, arrived for the first of many Xmases, bringing along one of his students, a silent twenty-year old. They were in love; he wanted to 'shed' his wife. I was saddened. On the 25th December my diary said: 'We are learning to play darts. It seems one has to look hard at the target and then allow the dart to fly to it. Perhaps all of life is like that: *know what one wants...then, relax'*.....I *did* wonder what *my* husband was thinking.

Canada provided me with two roles: that of the British Council wife, helping her husband do his job...(why, *some* of us asked ourselves, should we have to be involved in this way...being 'representational', which meant official entertaining and let's face it, a lot of work...) and the secondary role of continuing to be a violinist.

There were many 'starry' events, such as entertaining David Wilcox, who was conducting the Ottawa Symphony with local singers performing Carmina Burana. On another occasion I had the honour of sitting next to Yehudi Menuhin during an Embassy dinner, or an exceptionally high-powered evening with the visiting Royal Ballet, when we had drinks and dined with the Thatchers and Princess Margaret. While the Princess chatted appreciatively with my good-looking husband, both of them downing numerous gin and tonics, I was stuck with Denis Thatcher who told me the entire saga of his wife's secrets...how she managed on four hours of sleep (special minerals from the Dead Sea, flown in each week), and how she never stopped working, as she was doing indeed at that very moment: Mrs Thatcher worked right through the break, signing documents with her male secretary.

The rest of us were simply idling about, trying hard to say the right things to the right people, and somehow to enjoy ourselves.

To his credit, Charles was always supportive and eager I should have every opportunity I could get. He really needed another wife to do the 'representational' bit. Occasionally, when I was tied up in a run of performances for some show or other, I arranged for expensive caterers to take over. This would use up rather more of the 'entertainment allowance'…not good. I returned from a performance one evening to be told the salmon I'd bought had been only large enough to feed twenty of the twenty-four guests….Such unpleasing events added further strain to our already frail relationship.

I was alone at least two weeks in any month, while Charles travelled all over Canada, at first taking me with him. Later I visited Toronto, and Newfoundland, landing on Prince Edward Island covered in snow. On the way to Charlottetown, by car, we walked (briefly---brr in minus-God knows- what- temperatures, in the wind) up a snow-covered sand-dune to view the sea, that is, the ice, solid waves and drifts….no water visible. Cute shingled houses painted in tasteful pastel shades, a tiny quaint town nestling in the snow…a Hilton, surprisingly sleazy-genteel, graced this little island. Confederation Centre, with art galleries, theatres, a library and restaurants, could this be the 'saving grace' of the place? After a five-hour drive to a ferry-ice breaker on which we travelled, crunching and churning up the frozen sea …, cracks like flashes of lightening cut across the white expanse, shattered ice thickening and piling up, as the ferry got slower and even slower… Eventually we made it to New Brunswick to see ever more pretty, undulating scenery, pines, snow-covered farms and a glorious red sunset, and to pick up a flight in Fredericton.

Such experiences were the perks of life abroad, and Canada provided many: getting to know the territory was part of 'being representational'. Frozen rivers and lakes were challenging prospects in Canada…. apart from the obvious ice-skating and encampments over drilled holes for fishing…. one could wander among fantastic ice sculptures each year, some of them works of art, created in a competitive spirit to be awarded prizes just before, sadly, the weather changed.

Shortly before all that I had witnessed an annual event which scared me out of my wits. We'd been told the Rideau River, just 25 meters from our house, would have to be opened up, or else the force of flowing Spring water from further up country would break the ice causing flooding all over *our* part of town. Early one day I woke to hear explosions, not unlike the sounds of the Russians advancing during the war…and leaped out of bed… Charles was away, to find poor Mogs cowering behind the sofa, his hair on end: outside municipal workers in special orange gear were cutting small squares into the ice, then dynamiting it all along both banks so the water could flow freely down into the larger Ottawa River. This usually continued for three days at twenty minute intervals. No-one had prepared me for the shaking walls and rattling windowpanes of 215 River Road. On the plus –side the locals informed: this was always the sign that Spring was 'near'.

But Canada *has* no Spring....it goes straight from 'covered in snow' to 'covered in filthy sludge' to 'covered in Dandelions'. These plants, the bane of my existence, had roots the size of healthy carrots and one developed an obsession about pulling them out and admiring them. They must have been lurking there, under the snow, for weeks on end. I spent hours on my haunches, in the suddenly hot Canadian sunshine, ridding the newly revealed lawn of these villainous weeds. Mogs took a keen interest, as did an elderly retired gentleman, a former military man who took regular walks along the river while deciding he was in love with me. I called him the 'spy'...He told me he'd once been one, and took to bringing me flowers. In Canada there are no fences, no garden gates: if you are gardening you are fair bait to any passers-by.

Still, it made a change to be stalked and admired, even if only by a relentless, ancient, lonely 'spy'.

All Canadian cities had a unique flavour... loveliest of all was surely Quebec City, the only North American fortified city north of Mexico. It is one of the oldest towns in North America. The aboriginal Algonquins gave the place its name, Kebec ...meaning 'where the river narrows', the river being the great St Lawrence. The Old Town, its restaurants and lifestyle and above all the history, made it truly memorable. Equally wonderful was/is Montreal, nestling at the foot of 'Mount Royal', also on the St Lawrence; this town is now one of the largest French-speaking cities in the world, after Paris. In the northwest of the city is 'Hampstead' where the nouveau riche lived and 'Westmount,' where the *very* rich live. Also up there is a famous Oratory, festooned with crutches donated by persons who had been 'cured' by Brother André, a French-Canadian holy man. They are very Catholic, the French Canadians. The Confederation of Canada remains bi-lingual and I loved that, it added so much colour, stimulation and interest, but alas, also a fair amount of bickering and distaste, distrust. There was this endless 'thing' about the 'Canadian Identity'...one side scoring off the other.

St. Lawrence Iroquoians had a settlement by Mount Royal at least 2000 years before any Europeans got there. But in 1535 a French explorer claimed the St Lawrence Valley for France and needless to say, as the decades, then the centuries passed, the settlers from Europe had much to fear from the Iroquois wars and raids.

Even further afield, in April 1983....halfway across the world.....we found ourselves one night on Hudson Bay at a place called Rankin Inlet. A small shack, the airport, was decorated with antlers and signs in Indian writing,.... outside a glowing full moon and lots of chattering Indians in soft sealskin boots and parkas, carrying away large cardboard boxes or relatives on 'skidoos'.....motorcycles on skates. Incredibly, this tiny spot had supported a population for about 4000 years; it was mentioned in Norse Sagas as Helluland, the 'land of the flat stones'. We were on our way to Yellowknife, arriving there late at night ....the capital of the North West territories. 400 km south of the Arctic Circle it used to be famed for its goldmines, now closed. Instead, diamonds were found. Even in April I saw nothing but a few buildings sticking out of piles of snow and snowmobiles. I was a very, very cold place!

Other high spots: two visits to Banff, both unbelievably glamorous: one for several days of an international Quartet competition, where we feasted our ears on the best young string players from all over the world. The second event was a TV film festival in June 1985, during which one stayed in the ultra glamorous Banff Springs Hotel, the place of stars and royalty. All these events have become so extraordinary in retrospect: at the time the reality seemed quite ordinary... I was becoming incredibly spoilt and unquestioning. What had I done to deserve all this? Charles and I usually had so much to chat about, to be grateful for.

But there was always a distance, an invisible fence around him.

Niagara Falls, a one-off visit, regular trips to Toronto for cultural events – these were often of the literary variety, the ones that most pleased Charles....our calendar of events was endlessly, gloriously and improbably interesting. I can rattle off lists of *some* of the famous persons we had the honour and pleasure of meeting in those seven years, from Prime Minister Pierre Trudeau to Maggie and Denis Thatcher, Princess Margaret, Gillian Weir, Margaret Drabble, William Golding, John Mortimer, Hanif Kureishi....Yehudi Menuhin....Trevor Pinnock, David Willcocks, and many, many more.....

All in a day's work, but seriously, this was good. No, better than that, it was marvellous. And, talking of 'work'...I actually performed in front of 1000's with Bob Hope and Dionne Warwick. Crowning that: I played two lavish gigs with Liberace. Our instruments were electronically amplified to make sufficient noise in vast Conference centres. This was 'big-time,' high on adrenaline.

Through sweltering summers, frosty winters, opulent travelling, entertaining and lavish shows and my own delightful 'business' of teaching and performing, there were three overall concerns which pressurised and changed both Charles and me, *and* our expectations: *my* music, *his* writing, *our* children. Then there was the fourth, unspoken one, and the most frightening…our relationship.

However, what 'exercised' me on a daily level, was the never-ending wish and need to push my violin-playing way beyond what it had been. When I began lessons with the now famous Mauricio Fuks in Montreal, who diagnosed the need for a fundamental change of my bow hold, (a very hard thing to do when you are nearly fifty,) the struggle paid off, after a while. In the past, I had got by despite my inadequacies…I was 'easy-on-the-eye' and could put on a good show….but finally I had a better grasp of tone production, and from this gained security both as performer and teacher.

Occasionally the telephone rang, or a letter arrived, with a cry for financial aid from either Gabi or Luci, still swanning around on a bus, busking and, as the years passed, parading around their babies on the streets of Spain. Luci had a daughter, and Gabi, not to be outdone, had a son a year later. Unmarried, no money, no homes and no prospects, both my daughters had given birth to my grandchildren. There were two letters and once even a phone call from Pierre; I think they were about our children's latest escapades. With no more than a fleeting acquaintance with Luci's partner and no idea about Gabi's man, I was horrified.

I wanted *no-one* to know. I wished I hadn't even told my parents: they would be equally dismayed. At this first stage of grandmother-dom I could not connect with either Gabi or her sister…'they are grown-ups' I kept telling myself, 'this is what they have chosen to do. It is not my business…' while a niggling little voice queried: 'is this all my fault? What does Pierre think of his daughters now?'

It never occurred to me he was the ring-leader. I was so ashamed of their hippy-ness. I really didn't understand. I had frightening nightmares about them, strange sinister dangerous scenes, described in my diaries in those times.

***

Now an Interlude……we fly across time and land on the 24th October 2007, at 14:37...when Gabi tells me in the course of a flurry of emails:

'I'm fascinated by your 'hippy-children-shame', what a huge thing for you, not to mention us….Poor you, poor us…it all seems so crazy in retrospect but the feelings, they are very real. I'm so interested to know more. It's odd to have lived the other side of it. Your reaction was something rather abstract to us. Strange, being older now, having lived that experience and now seeing it from a different perspective. To us it was something to be proud of if you can imagine that. We were identifying with a whole generation of people, not just Dad, but songs, books, plays, films, it was a whole cultural movement. Remember the musical 'Hair'? We knew every word by heart!

Dad wasn't the only idealist. There were much worse ones than him roaming the planet, longer hair, smoking pot! Now it's a piece of history, all that... some of the old hippies are very creative and productive on all sorts of green issues. It is probably all those ex-hippies that will 'bust a gut' to save the planet....'

I tried to consider a more flexible approach. It was hard, if not impossible, for me. I was not moving in circles that were exposed to hippy-dom. We never saw 'Hair', but heard about it. Goodness, what will the young get up to next?

To me such things were not *real* life. *Real life was still about 'trying hard' and 'getting somewhere' in life. Hopping about naked and being generally rebellious was not for grown-ups. Well, you could see this in nightclubs.......And these 'flower-people', making LOVE not WAR....* yes, they were sweet, but this was not 'real' either......

By then James was about to go to Music College in Cardiff and needed sorting out, so I flew over, rented a room for him, set him up with the necessities of student life. He'd never lived alone before. All in all I had little faith in the activities and choices of my children, but who knows, maybe, with any luck, James would become a 'normal' chap.

****

Serving for so long in Canada we saw two High Commissioners take office and became particularly friendly with the second couple, Sir Derek Day and Lady Sheila.

There was hardly a month when we were not invited to Earnscliffe, a Victorian manor overlooking the Ottawa River, since 1930 the home of the British High Commission. Lady Day's butler was called Mr Dear; she would summon him during posh social occasions: 'could you bring the Port, Dear'.... and 'more coffee please, Dear', which never failed to amuse the guests.

We saw a great deal of each other. They were warm and understanding, not even remotely pompous. I felt accepted by them, more than by many of the other 'higher echelons'. Appreciating my musicianship they asked me to perform on numerous occasions, even

220

for the Canadian representative of the Queen, the 'Governor General'. I was beginning to feel very much part of the British establishment in Canada; the Days knew nothing about my 'anarchic' daughters....although I don't suppose they would have minded. Charles was admired and loved by everyone. When, in 1985, he was awarded an OBE, I was disappointed he wanted to be given his 'gong' by the Governor General in Ottawa. Gone was the chance to go to Buckingham Palace... Charles had turned it down.

During all this time there was the flickering flame of our marriage. We could have been so very happy I always thought. But I sensed that Charles had absolved his brother divorcing and marrying a much younger woman and probably longed for a change; perhaps he needed a more literary, more truly English person by his side.

I had no idea he was still in touch with Nicola. To me, she stood on a pedestal, radiating youth, beauty, talent, while I had become 'old hat', just a friend, a housekeeper, a sister. Not that I felt undesirable...I had numerous offers and opportunities for going 'astray', and indeed, on two and a half occasions.... I did. One half-an-occasion was my sex-crazed dentist, a sad, if not comical memory. The other two were one old and famous person about whom Charles was apprised.... and a young man half my age, so very touching, if not extremely flattering. My husband never showed any sign of jealousy. This was quite painful... he just didn't seem to care. This was worse torture than if he'd beaten me up. I *wanted him to care, I wanted him to want me. He could not.* He just laughed when I told him...then asked: does he want to marry you? And at the next opportunity, he went straight up and shook the man's hand. As if to say: 'well thanks, mate, why don't *you* just take her off my hands and look after her for the rest of *your* life....'

****

Beside regular trips to Toronto and Montreal we also managed one 'home leave' with a visit to Vienna and Milan, and for me, two weeks in CapeTown. By then Head Office had informed us that another, final posting was being planned, this time to Poland.

When I told my father he instantly mapped out *his* visit to Warsaw. I had mixed feelings about him coming to see us there: as an elderly German who had lost his beloved Pomeranian homeland to Poland after the War he would surely forget himself and come out with something tactless...but I kept my thoughts to myself. Dark as they were they proved to be unnecessary: three months later he was dead.

'I'm going to be 100 years'...had been his mantra...but, his time, aged only 88, was up; he'd been a heavy smoker for much of his life. He'd recovered from an aneurism *and* from prostate cancer. This time my father wept when I left, something he'd never done before. Were his tears at the airport some sort of premonition of that sudden and brief lung cancer which carried him off? I flew to Cape Town to support my mother.

Handel's Largo during the cremation service made me sob on cue beside my Mum who, with a sideways glance of her pale-green eyes, expressed... 'what's this, I didn't think you really cared...' surreptitiously slipped me her handkerchief. Afterwards the Lutheran Pastor invited everyone present to come to tea in the Ihlenfeldt's garden on Paradise Road. Erika Hermine Josephine, a shrunken, scatty, brave person, was, as always, able to put on a show. Never a believer in public demonstration of sorrow she managed, graciously, to host the reception. It was *she* who should have been a diplomat's wife.

A few days on we carried his ashes to a rocky beach near Clifton on the southern side of Cape Town and, clambering over the rocks, I was to throw them in the sea, as designated by my father.

'Schrecklich, schrecklich'...I heard my poor mother say, again, quietly, to herself: that terrible reality: her big, strong, good-looking Reini turned into ashes, now in a cardboard shoebox. For a few moments time stood still, while flecks of foam flew up onto my black skirt leaving a permanently bleached mark on a prominent front pleat....no doubt a reprimand from my Dad for not checking the direction of the wind.

Now, for the first time, Erika, now 81 years old, was in charge of her own life. I suspect, secretly, she was excited by this idea. For a while...

I felt so responsible for her. Even though she still had many good friends, all were elderly and kept doing that 'disappearing trick'. The only people who could offer advice were her sister in Vienna, and myself, her only child, stuck halfway between Ottawa and Warsaw. We both visited and stayed for longer spells, trying desperately to get her out of the house and into a place where she could lead an independent but more sheltered existence. Erika was as stubborn as a mule. Nothing seemed to suit her and we simply had to wait until she saw reason.

After a year's tug-of-war, the 'mule' was won over by a posh establishment opposite the President's residence, 'Whitehall Court'. Erika Hermine Josephine felt she could settle for leading the existence of a 'dowager duchess,' surrounded by other elderly folk, even some lonesome old gentlemen, lounging about. She always noticed them.

There followed three weeks of mother-daughter team-work: we worked out exactly what she might need in her New Life, then announced a Big Sale, to friends and former colleagues. For three weeks, I trimmed down her possessions; a painful, terrible time for her. Once, getting it really wrong, I cleared out a drawer in the bedroom, which included what I assumed to be my fathers' false teeth. Within a day or two she was asking for her 'spare teeth'. I had no idea she even *had* false teeth. The rubbish bags had already been picked up and I never had the guts to tell her. Fortunately she was becoming rather forgetful. While she slept I crept about like a thief, stealthily emptying possessions into black bags and hiding them in the garage, or even out on the road. Car-loads of books and records went to the German Old Age home, also shelves of kitchen stuff, items accumulated over the decades, bedding and all my father's clothes.

She quite liked it when she got a good price for her furniture; she loved having money and enjoyed adding up how much she'd 'earned' so far.

'You can afford some nice new teeth,' I ventured. Her wrinkled face lit up. In the meantime my father's banker had come to call, to explain she was now a wealthy lady and could have anything she wanted. Erika, the arch-scrimper and saver, survivor of two world wars and one major recession, showed nothing but dignified delight.

Eventually she was settled in style: a one-bedroom flat with a tiny balcony...viewing the Presidential gardens and the back of Table Mountain. Surrounded by her best things, her Persian rugs, favourite pictures, photograph albums and her silver, with china and glassware in a smart little kitchen for private entertaining, I felt we'd done really well. She owned a car, in garage no. 23. There were lifts to the elegant dining room and the place was full of very friendly, quiet, retired persons. She even had to 'dress' for dinner. She liked all that, at first.

******

For me, after seven years on the North American continent came the pain of packing up again. An even worse pain: I could find no-one who would take on our ten-year old furry personage: wise beyond the usual, the only cat I knew who would go for stately walks with me, who attacked children dressed as mice at Halloween events, who thoughtfully brought me exotic birds dripping blood over our marble floor and who recognised the image of himself on the lid of a butter-dish. Standing on his hind-legs, paws on the table, he'd gaze at this striped pottery cat, make pitiful sounds, his tail swishing to and fro. I loved his spirit.

When a vet was called to give him that final injection, I held him in my arms, with a strip of favourite mozzarella cheese near his nose; he kept very still. I think he knew. He was carried away in a black bag. How I deceived him, and oh, the pain of it all!

Sandwiched between seven years in Canada and a new 'Life behind the Iron Curtain' were a few months of preparation for the final posting, back in London. Equipped with Linguaphone cassettes already in Ottawa, (fearing the challenge of a Slav language) we hoped to become better than ordinary mortals if we started in very good time.

The opinions of a Rumanian violinist, a Polish cellist and a Russian violist, with whom I had shared numerous musical events, were: that we would detest it… warning, in heavy Slav voices: 'don't go, Evaleen, you cannot 'leefe in Kommunist kahnntry…you ahrr meking beeeg mistake…daire iss no foot, eet iss daark and daire iss no vork, de shops ahrr embty….'

However, the very first phrase of Polish the cellist taught me was: 'dsijai jest wadne, słoneszcnie dzien'.. (today is a lovely sunny day)……'it will be useful' he said, 'it will cheer you up'. He corrected my pronunciation, patiently, for several weeks; he was, as in everything, a perfectionist. Charles and I vied with each other, repeating such phrases as 'kwiaty na parapecie' (flowers on the windowsill) and other amusing Linguaphone offerings. 'When will we be able to say *that* to anyone?' This, if nothing else was a bonding experience.

I got into the habit of telephoning my mother every other day. She kept asking me to come and stay with her: 'what shall I do all day', she asked, like a child. I was conscious of having to 'mother' *her*, so depressed, confused, and helpless. Getting her settled, while darting down to Cape Town from time to time, learning Polish and living in London again gave me little time to worry about Charles. I was away quite often. He assured me he was no longer interested in Nicola. Like a fool I believed him.

Once our time in Canada had ended and we were back in our basement in London, Erika treated herself to visit London and to make a pilgrimage to Woodford Green. Dewy-eyed she claimed to 'remember' the roads. We found Snakes Lane, but the house of her childhood memories was no longer there.

'I wouldn't like having to keep an eye on *him*,' she stated one evening, completely out of the blue…..when Charles had gone off for

'Polish lessons'...she still had an eye for a good-looking man. Did she sense, with a mother's instinct, what *we* were going through?

Somehow, just living alone, had became a huge problem for her. Not only for her, also for everyone who cared about her.

There was no way I could have taken her to Canada or Poland. And there was no way Erika could return to Vienna....she was too much an 'African' by now. Feeling her fate closing in on her, sensing the misery of lonely old age she had become an eighty-five year old 'Poor Thing'.

***

Gradually, going to Poland was becoming a reality.

Someone 'in the know' had arranged for us to meet Adam Zamoyski at a luncheon.

This distinguished historian and internationally best-selling author just happened to be a Polish Count from a family which, for 400 years, had been one of the most glorious and influential in the country's history. Tall, slender, distinguished, in a black coat with velvet collar and a flashing diamond ring on his hand, he told us some of the more relevant facts we needed to understand Polish ways.

'What a burden', I realized, 'to have to come to terms with so much history.' Educated in England, an Oxford graduate, despite such a background he was all about the immersion into the thousand years of conflict in Eastern Europe. After this meeting I began to realize just how much *more* reading and learning lay ahead for me.

Where is the Truth? I've studied the diaries: they are full of complaints, miseries and disappointments. So, why have memories assumed a golden glow of happiness, good fortune and gratitude, twenty years on?

Does current contentment have an effect on past sadness?

Poland 1989.
I tried to see as much as one can from our BA flight to Warsaw. We were over the Baltic, I saw the island of Rügen and just a few moments later, just to the left would be Swinemünde... just as predicted in my Atlas. Through scattered clouds I saw a verdant Pomerania; an isthmus, shimmering lakes...then on due south another 200 miles in the direction of Warsaw; ETA was four pm and this time there would be no great adjustment: the so-called Pomeranian Peasant was coming 'home'...

'Don't kid yourself, get real...just because those Ur-Ihlenfeldts were fashioned here, grown from this earth down below, are buried in it, this will never be home...this is the dreaded Communist Poland' spoke the small voice, the one that always tells the truth. Maybe I just *wanted* it to be home. 'Po mare' in Polish means nothing more than 'by the sea'. My father's beloved Pomerania, and the Baltic: this he regarded as his very own land and ocean he was devoted to it all: many of his ancestors had tilled this land, spoken the dialect and known its customs. He loved it, but not enough to stay ...to be honest, in the end he thought of it with a mixture of fondness and distaste...the small-minded backwardness of it.

Church records show the earliest *Ihlenfeldt*s were laid to rest more or less where our flight is crossing now. This unusual name may well go back to ancient knights in Mecklenburg or Nordic invaders: there are *Uhlefeldt*s, *Ahlefeldt*s, and *Ihlefeld*s in Sweden and Denmark. Swedes occupied and terrorized this entire area for at least one hundred years. Poor Poles, poor Russians, poor Germans, all these tribes being pushed around and made homeless, over and over again.

For one hundred years there was no Poland whatsoever. At the end of the Second World War Stalin was granted much of the borderlands in the East of Poland and in its place Poland received a large chunk of East Germany, including my father's homeland. Before the end of the war we had to flee: I remember it only too well, when the Russians marched in. Only one half of me is rooted here...I remind myself. The other half is from the west side of high Slovenian mountains, a much happier, sunnier place.

28 May. On the runway militia with guns and *bayonets* were waiting for us; 'is this how it will be here, with *the Communists*?' I hadn't yet disembarked, was bristling already. But I was seeing things: the supposed bayonets were walkie-talkies with long *antennae,* how silly of me. I reminded myself: 'stop seeing problems when there are none.'

Being British diplomats usually had advantages... but no, we were not exactly *whisked* through Immigration; under dimly-lit neon tubes sour-faced officials in the dismal, peeling building made heavy weather of the formalities. Eventually safe in the office car there was nothing but indescrib-able drabness, dark high-rise apartments, absolutely identical everywhere. Only later, further into the centre, there seemed to be   more stylish, but crumbling, neglected European-style architecture. 'What wide roads they have here, and generous pavements, look at that, cars seem to park *on* the pavement, diagonally, side by side, so they can slip out backwards into the traffic. Clever, that, if they are careful, said Charles. They could easily bump into these antiquated trams'....We tried to take it all in. Pitiful window displays reminded me of Ndola in the 50's. A sinking of the heart: I had heard the warnings of my colleagues in Ottawa…but this was truly dreadful, not unlike the worst black and white films about World War ll.

Sunset is that soul-heaving time when most new places seem hostile..the 'unknown' brings that sinking feeling. Is this why the Brit's invented the sun-downer? A good dose of gin and tonic unlocks the flow of positive thoughts and adds delightful release, blissful relaxation……

…from a window on the 13th floor of the Forum Hotel I confront the Palace of Culture, built by Russians for the Poles as a peace offering. It dominates everything.

'Roads are being dug up everywhere…Warsaw will have a Metro, to be finished in about five years, in the meantime there is this mess,' we are told.

We've been granted an hour from arrival at the hotel before we are picked up to dine with our predecessors. They return to Britain in two weeks, their personal belongings already packed. We are shown round: what we see in the house is what we'll get, along with our own sixty packing cases from Canada. This will be our last, *final,* new home, before retirement. Not much to say about it: an ugly, grey, three-story box, on a road called Rożana, in an area known as Mokotow; plain furnishing with some valuable British art on loan from head-quarters. My heart is not 'singing', but, as my husband was given to say: 'in for a penny, in for a pound.'….. We talked with our predecessors about the hand-over, both official and domestic. The only amusing thing was their corgi, wearing a large white cone around his neck to stop him biting or licking some part of himself. The beast barked non-stop. Charles wittily pronounced him to be a 'pièce de résistance', but this joke required knowledge of Polish (*pies*=dog) and French (*pièce*=object) *pièce* has same pronunciation as pies…oh well. (dog of resistance= a watchdog)

We were told we would be watched and bugged *'all the time'*… across the road were antennae directed towards this house and whenever we went out we would be followed.

Does one get used to all this, I wondered.

29th May, 1989. Swarms of shifty men hovered around the hotel entrance. We were being followed. Charles fell for a pestering Pole who was offering a favourable exchange rate, and we *did* need some zlotys! '7000 zlotys to the £' we heard and there was a great flurry of zlotys for the £20 pound note we offered….we should have had fourteen 10,000 notes. Feeling guilty….it was all so quick, and under-hand, we didn't dare check. But when we did we had *one* 10,000 note on the top and all the rest were 20 zloty notes! This supposedly illegal act was the quick way for Poles to get their hands on foreign currency which they could then use in Pewex shops where western goods were available. *Now* we were learning!

The Deputy Representative took us sightseeing round the Old Town, completely reconstructed after the War. This is the lovely part of Warsaw, like a film-set in its newness and colourful perfection. I felt moved: I was in Europe again and it felt so good.

At the end of the day we decided Warsaw was not unlike a grey, derelict Vienna, almost totally without the niceties, alien, not to be trusted. Speaking of niceties: one must always bring flowers when visiting in Poland and gentlemen generally kiss the hands of ladies, both on arrival and departure...

These were the customs in Poland I totally warmed to.

As our baggage from Canada and from London was not to arrive for another five days we were packed off to do a reconnaissance trip from the top of Poland (Gdansk) to the bottom Wrocław (Breslau).

30th May, 5.30 am: Warsaw Central Station, a cavernous, clean place right by the famous Palace of Culture. We did not have far to go.

'Warsaw is so clean' noted my husband. 'Roads, subways, no litter, no graffitti, just remember the filth in London'. There was much scaffolding, apparently not so much for repairs, more for keeping rubble from falling on your head as you passed by. There was a desolate post-war feeling.

In the station we inspected two Russian trains, dark-green, old-fashioned, complete with lace curtains and fresh flowers by the windows.

Settled in our compartment we soon gazed at Poland: flat, some oak-forests, primitive farms with horse-drawn ploughs and reapers with scythes and horse drawn carts. We'd returned to another century.

Charles noticed him too: at one of the rural stations there stood a man who resembled my father…same shape of head, same hairline. I'd never considered my father as 'Slav'. Was I 'seeing' things?

Wrocłav (Breslau) I did find it difficult to think of Breslau as anything but German, as if one had to think of Köln as French or Hamburg as Danish. It used to be the capital of Silesia, situated on the banks of the Oder. A terrible battle in 1945, a three month siege during which something like 29.000 civilians were killed, apart from military casualties and 40.000 prisoners, estimates vary, but these were events I had to think about now. It was not helpful. I found myself sighing a lot.

First call was a wondrous late 17th century building: the University. Students were on strike but the Rector entertained us with a multilingual luncheon during which we 'glittered' in French, German,

English. For once even I was useful: there were two German publishers at the table who spoke only German. We were shown the famous Baroque Hall, the Aula of the university, where Brahms conducted the first performance of his Academic Festival Overture.

Poles play down German history. The Rector spoke passable German and we heard it on the streets as we wandered about in the old city with its beautiful Gothic buildings and Protestant churches, now converted to Catholicism. After a mere 24 hours we had convinced ourselves that Wrocłav was a very pleasing place, *much* nicer than Warsaw.

Another train journey brought us back to the north, to Poznan. Our modern hotel was out in some fields. I was woken by the local cuckoo, on a warm sunny day. Didn't some relative of mine come from here? I must find out. I felt good and yes, I knew, it's all in the mind, this thing about 'belonging.'

The freshly painted Orbis Hotel (a chain of Polish hotels) seemed more prosperous than the one Warsaw, so stuck in its dingy, neglected image, as I thought back. Someone explained *this* town has a groomed appearance, attractive shops, because it is near the German border and the prosperity was due to the annual Poznan Fair. While Charles saw to his work I visited an 'Instrument Museum' with impressive old clarinets, oboes and fortepianos, also some named stringed instruments and two of Chopin's pianos, used by him in his youth. There were many folk fiddles and I learned that Poland considers itself the *land of the violin*; folk fiddles are crudely carved and hugely in demand...I had no idea what they sounded like.

June 1st Gdansk. 'I smell the sea air. From the window on the 8th floor of another hotel I see distant shipyards. Last night we took a post-dinner walk around the block, through dark streets and past St Brigid's church where Lech Wałensa goes to Mass. The place was deserted, lifeless, no sounds, no pubs, no traffic. Gdansk looks rundown and neglected, dusty, dreary, even worse than Warsaw. Where are the Poles?'

The hotel dining room was filled with Japanese, Germans and other foreigners, like ourselves. Pork knuckles and sauerkraut for me... Charles averted his gaze. Polish beer was terrific.

When one goes to a Polish loo in a public place such as this restaurant you must pay the attendant 30 zlotys who will tear off a modest length of loo-roll... then you proceed.

Plainly, a Toilet Paper factory is needed as well.

After Charles' official duties with charming Rectors in old-style Universities and Polytechnics we were free to inspect the mostly reconstructed Danzig, the ancient Hanseatic Baltic town, full of heart-rending, moving tales of the distant and not so distant past.

There was the lovely Mariatzki, the most beautiful of many 'old' streets with below-street level shops selling Baltic treasures, art and amber in every shape imaginable… and cavernous brick churches, just like the ones in Lübeck. It is impossible to know what is Polish, what is German; a touchy subject. I objected to ancient inscriptions on German grave-stones, deliberately made illegible by Poles. If *my* great-great grandfather, an admiral in the German navy, had been buried in a local church and commemorated with a carved stone on the floor of a church I would surely be allowed to feel aggrieved, if *his* dates and name had been removed. He was born here, and he *did* work in Gdansk. He died somewhere in Pomerania in 1882, long before the Nazis.

Charles reminds me of 'collective guilt; I feel uncomfortable, then moody.

This is where it started, that 'guilt thing': It is difficult to be a German *anywhere*, but even harder in Poland. Warsaw and Gdansk have shrines on every street where candles are lit and flowers are left on a daily basis, to recall the murdered Poles during the War. At first I am amazed, then shocked, then tearful, finally resentful. I am truly sorry that German soldiers did brutal 'unforgivable' things, Russians, as well. Should I put a candle down? *I'm collectively guilty.* I honestly don't feel guilty but I am supposed to. How does one handle all this about 'the sins of fathers visited on their children'…who said that, anyway? I don't want to know and yet I must. *I must.* I try to imagine these cruel events. But guilty? If my father had committed crimes, would I feel guilt? I think 'uncomfortable', certainly, wondering why he'd done it, wishing he hadn't. But committing crimes would have been *his* decision, not mine.

Besides, my father had been in no-one's army, had lived, locked up, in an African Camp during the entire War. Thank God, at least, for that. So I walked past sad flickering candles and tried to focus on other things. Like the wars which had raged over this ancient Hanseatic town.

Being here was having a disturbing effect.

2 June. Non-stop from breakfast till dusk: first a call on yet another Rector and the usual chat, seated on old carved chairs…charming, they always seem to be. We drink hideously strong coffee, munch delicious poppy-seed cake and I have time to enjoy the rectors beautiful clear Polish; even *I* can understand. Later we see the Old Town and then lunch in a grand hotel, memorable for the scooped out irradiated ice

cream containing a lump of glowing sugar. (The sugar-lump is soaked in brandy, then lit... a must-try recipe...)

At dusk we are taken to Gdynia, the harbour area and to Sopot, with its elegant pier and holiday hotels, the Baltic turbulent, the swans looking uncomfortable. Swans? Strange, I don't associated swans with waves and oceans. Do they like salt water? Perhaps the Baltic is not salty, just polluted. Bathing is forbidden.

Another very early start, we had to catch the train back to Warsaw at 6am. On the platform I said: 'hmmm... look forward to a sturdy Polish peasant breakfast on the train: hot bread-rolls, ham, cheese and coffee, aren't you?' Charles nodded.

Blearily I took his briefcase, so he could deal with the small suitcase, and entered the carriage before him, vaguely aware that *he* seemed to be held up by a sudden knot in the flow of human bodies trying to board, I heard shuffling and 'przeprasczam' (excuse me, sorry) and calls from men to one another, it all took a while before Charles re-appeared, sighing, bemused and ruffled. Settled for our three-hour journey I had placed his briefcase on his seat. The train moved while we discussed the commotion and discovered to our delight an English-speaking Pole sharing our carriage. He was a guitarist. We chatted. The attendant asked to see our tickets. Charles felt first in the usual pocket, then the other, then his briefcase...the wallet...where was *that*...?

Robbed, in broad daylight, Charles hadn't so much as noticed.

We'd been warned *not* to speak English in public places, and I'd forgotten to keep my mouth shut. The Warsaw/Gdansk train-robbers were famous for their skills; the Polish guitarist saw it all, telling us about their cunning wickedness and offered to make a written statement to the police at Warsaw station and also to the police in Gdansk.

Later I wondered if he was perhaps part of the gang, the man employed to soothe ruffled British feathers with his excellent English.

Never did three hours on a train pass more rapidly...it was not so much the cards nor the money, more the fact that we'd not even cottoned-on to what was happening...two of the three men still on the train protesting innocence, the third vanished of course...very clever,.. on top of everything, no breakfast, 'skint' as we were.

'Mother-hen' British Council was almost directly opposite the Station. We rushed back under her wings, were plied with coffee and reassurances...'it happens to everybody, don't worry, we'll take care of everything'.....cluck, cluck, cluck......I had not yet seen the office...a magnificent place, easily the most impressive I'd come across, with a hall for receptions, a small cinema, a large library with reading room.

Tomorrow was to be the <u>Big Day:</u>

June 4. Polish Elections: The world was watching: would Communism be vanquished? Having passed muster we'd re-located to the top floor of our new home; our predecessors were still living down below, but about to return to England. I stared out of a window hoping to see crowds on their way to vote, but Warsaw was quiet, deserted. To see some action we were taken to lunch at the British Country Club, but there too all was quiet....dark clouds, mosquitoes, later some drizzle. In the evening we were treated to a visit to the theatre: two amusing short plays by Václaw Havel, enjoyable, but we needed 'help': actors spoke faster than our Linguaphone tapes...

5 June. With help from our predecessor's wife I was learning about useful shops on our road, also how to get onto wobbly, antiquated trams: incredibly cheap, 30 zlotys, about ½ pence a ride in any direction, that's Communism.... We called in at the Embassy shop which measured 5x3 yards and stocked sensible British basics ...enough for very lazy British staff to survive if they were too timid to look around Warsaw markets. Our Ambassador was paying for a packet of aspirin at the till...

I found markets out in the open, a huddle of covered tent-like stalls where one saw fruit, flowers, smoked eel and imported goodies from Germany, cheeses, olives, biscuits and other luxuries, costing 1000's of zlotys, in line with prices on the other side of the iron curtain. Colourful, full of life, but few Poles could afford this; I felt guilty buying things there. Back home I was introduced to my cleaning lady 'Dorota', who was intimidatingly lovely. She spoke a little English, enough to break the ice anyway. She used to work for a Warsaw newspaper, now did house-cleaning to supplement the family income with dollars. If ever there was a so-called 'representational' female, she was the one....*she* should be married to Charles and I should be doing the dusting.

Dorota has promised to help me with my Polish.

Later: on to the Embassy Club to meet staff, followed by a dinner party at the Deputy Representative's, with a collection of interesting Poles, ministers, poets, a conductor and a flautist...people are elegant...I shall have to try a lot harder.

6th June. Have trammed and walked over huge tracts of this city. Typical on every street-corner were Ruch Stalls; 'Ruch' is Polish for 'motion', 'traffic' or 'movement.' Here you purchased newspapers, stamps, tram-tickets, matches and shaving cream as well as the more intimate necessities of life; also typical were columns with little red domes, displaying posters of cultural events.

Mysterious archways led to courtyards, a common feature of architecture here, to me an endless delight; what was it about a dark tunnel leading to unexplored territory? It was quite usual to find nothing but overflowing dustbins, but often there were little gardens around a religious statue or benches under a tree, in bigger spaces perhaps small shops like milliners, shoemakers or silversmiths. Bras and corsets could be made to measure, judging from the stunning Amazonian encasements with stout circular stitching in a shop-window behind the British Council. Out in the residential areas it was still usual to have frames in these courtyards for carpet beating. In the early evenings, after tired wives return from work one could hear the thumping of rugs being beaten, reverberating between the surrounding walls. Or was it the Polish husband who did the beating? Large overflowing dustbins, usually left overturned, while cats, immense black crows and pigeons rummaged together, the cats skinny and feral, no cat-lovers here. Pedigree dogs were the thing, not a mongrel in sight. Dogs on the street were always muzzled.

Some things had not changed: an ancient horse and cart frequently passed the house, delivering coal or soil, or whatever. Coal was dumped on the pavements in front of apartment blocks and eventually shovelled into basements to fuel collective hot-water systems for entire building(s), socialist style. Today I'd bought chives and cottage cheese (instructed *not* to buy Polish milk products but I reckon if Poles live, so will we) and also a huge tin of Greek olive oil, a real bargain....On closer inspection, at home, it proved to be Russian and not much better than cat's pee, no wonder it cost so little, but the cottage cheese was delicious. Big reception at the B.C Office for us...not dull, and food from the Country Club.

7th June. Blackest rain, non-stop. 'Just what this place needs, a good wash,' I said. Appalling to see, even now, so much evidence of the last War: walls riddled with gunshots, so much neglect. *That* war ended 45 years ago. Hazardous pavements, bleak empty shops....in an underpass in the town centre I came across five cheery old men on accordions and violins, playing pops from the 20's and 30's. They were amazing but their hat was empty. They were the generation that knew the War, perhaps fought in the uprising. I was so moved by them.

If they had known I was a German...

'Still caught up in a social whirl: dinner at the Embassy's second in command, where we were introduced, amongst others, to Count Zamierski, a Princess Radziwill and the author Kapucinski, famous for his writing about Africa. There was an impressive mountain of caviar on the table, I've never seen anything like it.

8th June. Last big drinks party for a while. We still haven't received the air-freight luggage, nor our crates from Canada. Even worse: part of my tooth broke off while eating in a restaurant. So much for that Canadian dentist...I must have swallowed it; I did think the rice a bit granular. 'Local dentists are not recommended' say our colleagues. 'Fly to Berlin, or Vienna, or back to London to have it seen to...'

Fly to Berlin for a filling? How can this be?

9th June. 'Knowing the luggage has not arrived and that my mum is in Vienna I have hopped on an Austrian Airways flight to kill two birds...see my Ma...get that tooth fixed. It makes sense. Departure from Warsaw airport worse than arrival...lengthy and suspicious scrutiny by guard, along with arguments and queries about a piece of paper which had been removed by the first one, while I am stuck between two hostile Poles...,awful not to be able to talk...I thought they were supposed to be so nice. Not on this level, they're not.

I must be honest: I am glad to be out of Warsaw and back in civilization. My cousin Fritz has brought my Mum and *his* mum, Dagmar, to meet me, but has to rush off, so a rented limousine gets us back to Vienna's District III and we talk and talk and have tea, and supper and then my aunt walks me round the block to a monastery, where I sleep under a huge crucifix in a monastic cell. 'What's happened to the monk who normally lives here? And how does one get across the corridor to the loo and shower in a flimsy gown without frightening some holy person?

10th June. During an enlivening breakfast seated opposite a music critic from Tel Aviv (whose surname is Frankenstein) my family comes to pick me up. Numerous calls to dentists have been made: they do not work on Saturdays or Sundays. I will just have to give up smiling, until I find someone. (Why does Frankenstein sleep in this monastery...? I am resolved to find out...) We walk through some of Vienna's smartest streets and visit an exhibition of Klimt, Schiele and Kokoschka. Klimt is and always will be my favourite artist. After a treat in an elegant ice-cream parlour we take the U-Bahn to Heiligenstadt, where my beautiful cousin Hanna drives us up the mountain to view a Polish church. It was built to commemorate Sobieski's famous victory over the Turks 300 years ago. He came to Vienna, like good neighbours do, along with Polish troops to help get rid of the infidel.

11th June. Sunday. We go to the Augustiner church and hear Beethoven's C Major Mass, followed by an open-air lunch. I've had plenty of time to study my mother: she is reasonable in the morning, but by late afternoon her perceptions become unfocussed. She's not on drugs, she's not drinking...but she's not sure if I'm her child or her sister. By nightfall she is mad. I am alarmed. Has she come to the end of her usefulness? Dagi admits she hopes her sister will die rather than live on in a state of madness, asking the same questions over and over.

We whisper behind my Mum's back, aghast. How can she even travel alone, like this, having lost 'so many of her marbles?'

12th June. Sunny in Vienna, raining in Warsaw, we are just 55 minutes apart. It appears our air-freight from London has finally arrived, after two weeks transit. Even an oxcart would have been quicker. Still, here I am, brooding about my mother, also unpacking, with the first stirrings of home. I've smoothed my chipped tooth with a nail-file....

13th June. Rain....taken by charming young Poles from the office to the Customs shed where a huge amount of time is spent hanging about, waiting. It is chilly. There is nowhere to sit. Eventually our cases, packed in Canada and in storage ever since we left, are weighed, unpacked, examined by unimpressed officials. It takes hours and is 'bardzo nudny' (very boring). I imagine my husband, warm and dry in his smart office...why must I do this, surely this is 'men's work'?

14th June. And here they are, all fifty-seven boxes, some of them already in the rooms where they will be needed, kitchen, dining-room, many alas, on the landing...total chaos. Canadian packers have wrapped every single object in at least one square yard of white paper, every book, each spoon, imagine the work and I've been at it all day. *Alone*. But how re-assuring to see our things again! The big wooden head from Nigeria is nowhere to be found. This house still feels strange.

15th June. More and more of our things emerge as I slice open cardboard crates and plough through mountains of white paper. I'm collecting the paper to give to the little shops when I next go shopping...surely they'll be delighted to use it instead of newspaper. Meanwhile it feels like a bizarre, nightmarish, solitary Christmas: a new iron, new kettle, dishwasher, dryer, washing-machine.

My Polish cleaning-lady is helping.

I'm supposed to be going to the Queen's Birthday party at the embassy, so I try the tiny hairdresser around the corner. She uses beer as a setting lotion. No–one speaks a word of English. I experiment in Polish, no choice really. My hair looks good. I reek of beer but am ready to go to the embassy. It seems the office has forgotten to pick me up. Dorota calls a cab; like a fond mother she tells the driver where to take me.

16th June. My wondrous machines are hooked up and humming; the embassy electrician has had a busy day. I'm setting up a music-room in the basement, rather like the one in Ottawa, but with a higher ceiling and better acoustic. I have sorted and filed all my music...to think I've played all this stuff. We've bought a monstrous turn-of–the century upright piano from our predecessors, it's huge and black and Austrian...someone will bring it down into my den. Haven't touched my fiddle since May 26th, is this a record? Finally got rid of that mountain of white Canadian paper; at first the greengrocer seemed non-plussed, even a little hostile... then graciously accepted one half and sent me to his friend up the road, who sells groceries, with the rest...I am immensely proud of my Polish!

17th June. Warsaw's telephone system is totally antiquated: one can barely hear what is said...we make an agonizing call to our son in Cardiff. It takes hours to get connected ... apparently not overhauled for half a century. At noon our first visit to Lazienki Park: what a marvellous surprise, gorgeously varied landscape, very close to where we live. (Actually there are many lovely parks here, although not as groomed as we have come to expect in the West. I do believe they mow their lawns with scythes.) Transcendental delight: to be drawn in by the strains of distant performance, open-air, of Chopin's piano music...to find, in an expanse of red roses, under a huge improbable *stone* willow, next to an artificial lake...an amplified grand-piano. Each Sunday, under this statue, Warsaw's best pianists sit for several hours, playing one Chopin work after the other...'free' music, in the fresh air, dogs barking, children trying to be quiet and adults sitting or walking in a state of quiet bliss. How well-dressed the Poles are, even the children, all in their Sunday best. The birds are joining in too. I feel as if touched by a magic wand. And tearful.....*this is the moment I'm totally won over.*

19th June. 'First the ecstasy...now the agony, I speak of my first experience of SUPERSAM, a caricature of a supermarket, unimaginable in the West. One must line up for a small basket, (oh my...there are about 35 people before me)...never mind, I'm getting there, slowly, towards those baskets, security cameras are pointing at us, directed at the queue, every 5 feet, this hall, dingy-er than any place I've ever shopped in, a dark brown ceiling... designed by the same architect as the airport probably. Haphazard, rickety, grey metal shelving, rows and rows of the same stuff: pickled cucumbers in glass jars, shredded pickled cabbage known as Sauerkraut to us Germans, small grey or brown paper packages of unknown things...lentils perhaps. Damn, I've not brought my pocket dictionary. I feel nervous about picking up a package and looking inside....those cameras are probably checking my every incredulous move. Aha! Here are small cardboard boxes containing a semblance of cornflakes...and here, fresh brown bread. I'd better join a different line-up for meat and dairy products....to be served individually.   Thank goodness, I've done my homework, know what to recite: *potrzebne mi, tego mi potrzeba...* I need... eggs, bread, pumpernickel, 1 kilo butter, buckwheat groats, a Swiss roll, sour cream, one jar kefir....'*co to jest*' what *is* this? Everything is stowed in brown bags, laughably cheap: my Polish shopping spree adds up to roughly 50 pence. I am proud of myself. Cakes in Poland are outstanding and so unbelievably low in price I am constantly shaking my head...there are definitely *some* plusses when it comes to Communism'. Preferring to remain car-less, use trams, except on *serious* shopping days I run Charles to the office only on Fridays, then make use of the Embassy shop and from there to the 'diplomatic' petrol-pump, where there is no queuing.

We're settled now, I think. I must stop this blow by blow account of first impressions. Everyone has been unhesitatingly kind and helpful, my cleaning lady, for example.   It's her day off. A great relief not to have to appear fully dressed and made up, to play-act my role as lady of the house.   Our gardener, very gentlemanly, talks a lot and I smile winningly and say 'dobrze' ('good') from time to time. He knows what to do.

Keenly aware of the huge barrier due to lack of communication I am determined to learn by watching childrens' TV with a dictionary in my lap. Watch, listen, write the word down, find it in the dictionary.... I am keeping a record, alphabetically. How anyone can come here and not learn Polish is beyond me, but people do. As there is nothing to do apart from walking about on the streets I make great advances stumbling about on my own; the pavements are not the most even in this place. I hunt for interesting things in little shops, trying out my best 'shopping' phrases, I found three smoked ducks on display, so I bought half a one: it was delicious. I rushed back: too late, they'd all gone.

Poles stand patiently in long queues, nearly every small shop has several persons hanging about outside; a form of social intercourse, perhaps, or just a way of making sure they are not losing out. Totally startling: a farmer was selling a pig's head, amongst potatoes and cabbages, propped up on the pavement, flies buzzing around it. How would it feel to boil such a thing? You'd need a huge pot. What would it taste like? I did consider it, but no..... I was not quite ready for that.

*****

Pan Paderewski, a pianist who lives nearby, has been recommended as accompanist. (Pan=Mr.) He appears, stays a very long time; this was hard work as we speak mostly in Polish and broken German; I begin to fear he'll never go. But we will play together next week, on a trial basis.

An honour, of course, he is not only the grandson of the *great* Paderewski, Poland's famous concert-pianist and composer (as well as Prime Minister) but also the Head of Chamber music at the Warsaw Academy. Now this will get me practising again......

A few days later he calls again, with two well-behaved spaniels. I have noticed how frequently Poles walk their dogs, all of them the most pedigreed creatures. His animals sit quietly while we play through a few things, feeling our way musically...he's very good, has made numerous recordings with 'prizewinning' violinists. He suggests we prepare a recital for October, to take place in the Academy Concert Hall and wants to make a recording of my party-piece, the Elgar Sonata.

This sounds good to me...we'll see. First he has to go to Europe for two months, for some concertizing and for a holiday. Both re-assured and intimidated, but I try not to show the latter.

This is not going well. My account of the lives of seven women is turning into a manic account of travels and experiences of just one of them. The others are there, of course, in the background: poor Erika, now totally in limbo, on the verge of dementia; her loneliness does not allow her to enjoy her wealth or even whatever there is to be got out of life when one is eighty-two years old.

Ingeborg or Evelyn, or Knups, the Pomeranian Peasant, is caught up on an undertow of madness. *This madness rests on many things: beginning to understand the horrors of European History, of German iniquities, gradually seeing, accepting, the ever-widening gulf of relationships going and gone wrong; the feeling of estrangement from her children...sensing the finiteness of life.*

Time passes quickly.

There is much loneliness. The madness described earlier is not unlike the start of a new but painful love-affair, rather a total involvement ... realising the terrible suffering that has occurred in this part of the world. Shorter surges of 'love' can come from everyday, often ridiculous experiences, like finding a corpulent lady dentist in Warsaw who has 'access' to American materials and needles. Having inspected my nail-filed tooth she sent me off to an instant X-ray, a Dickensian attic up three flights of bent wooden stairs to a dingy, cluttered flat-let housing a retired doctor with ancient 'retired' apparatus. I had the X-ray in half an hour, the entire process cost 10$, then having proof that the remaining tooth was sound, repairs with good American materials could take place. A case of *very good* 'Polnische Wirtschaft,' a contradiction in terms of what this famous phrase really means, an adventure, even a delight!

After only two months in Poland we had already seen Poland from top to bottom. Now we drive 'across,' to Radom, one of Poland's oldest cities, and Sandomierz, also ten centuries old... then down to the Ukrainian border, roughly an eight hour journey. When you go on a journey in Poland you are wished a "szerokiej drogi" which means a 'wide road'. It makes extra good sense here, where it is unwise to be in a hurry because of horse-drawn carts or even the odd combine harvester. We see old-fashioned motorbikes with side-cars like in war-films.

In Sandomierz there was a rebuilt market square and an old vicarage-museum, filled with a hotch-potch of treasures, catalogued and lit, of course, it felt like stumbling into a dusty old attic. Then on to Lancut, where we attended Summer master-classes for violinists and a guided tour of the Palace with an incredible inlaid parquet floor and a dream library for the count-of-the house....even the latest English, French and German papers and periodicals...all poignantly coming to a sudden end at the outbreak of WW 2. In Poland it was never far away, that terrible, terrifying war.

Only two hours from Warsaw is Poland's most eastern city, Lublin, on top of a hill, looking down on a former suburb called Maydanek. Partly restored, the old town had an Austrian-Italian feel, but the rest was a crumbling ghost-town, laced with tacky new high-rise buildings. At the foot of the hill was the 'Memorial Museum' of Maydanek.

The first thing one saw of this former concentration camp was a concrete monument by the roadside. The eye was drawn along a path to something resembling a huge chalice, silhouetted against the horizon about ½ a mile away. Between these two structures were the now familiar barbed-wire fences, observation towers and rows of low wooden barracks. We wandered about in this area and imagined, or *tried* to imagine, how it might have felt to be trapped, branded, de-loused, de-haired, de-humanized, terrorized and starved....until you were shot or gassed. Three successive barracks filled with hundreds of thousands of blackened rotting shoes collected by the Nazis for re-processing become part of this sickening experience. Eventually, having forced ourselves to look at absolutely everything, we got close to the vast concrete chalice seen on arrival, from the roadside. It stood next to the crematorium and had an inscription in huge letters:

OUR FATE YOUR WARNING

The chalice contained ashes, found on the site. We were drained, tearful and tired. Through no fault of mine I was part of this inhuman crime. Not Charles. Only me. How must he feel, married to a German?

I was at least able to hide behind a mantle of British-ness, my English name, my husband's work. We drove back up the hill to Lublin and sat down beside a fountain, ate our sandwiches, without enthusiasm. There was no consolation... unless one counted driving home. This had only been our first viewing of such terrors.

On Sunday the 20th of August the first free parliamentary elections were to take place in Poland. Everyone knew how it would be: the Solidarity-backed candidates would win 99% of the seats in the Senate. There could be only one man for president and it would surely be Lech Wałensa, even though he was only a 'lowly' electrician.

*****

The British Council was up to its ears in the 'Know-how Fund', Britain's contribution to helping Poland back on its feet. Charles had never been so busy. I hardly saw him; we slept in separate rooms and he left for work very early. This is nothing new...we'd slept apart for years. He would come home haggard and drained, to change and then out again for receptions, dinners, concerts, films, a busy social life. At first I tried to keep up, later I often stayed at home. I was good at being alone: it comes from being an only child. Sometimes, on week-ends, we did things together. We took walks through streets and parks, I showed Charles around, like a tourist guide...the sight of battle-scarred buildings still unrepaired since the War... our own little park in Mokotov, with two monuments to the slaughtered dead of our suburb just south of the city centre. It was close to the 45th anniversary of the Warsaw Uprising, an event which had caused the total destruction of the city; currently all memorials and shrines had fresh flowers and candles. Now, almost 50 years on, when the rest of Europe was all done up again, Warsaw still festered on and on in its peculiar way: the wounds do not seem to heal.

Don't misunderstand, the Socialists had done their bit, restoring the Old Town; they'd built their Palace of Culture, and much of the centre of town was respectable, there was also a handsome ceremonial route along Lazienki Park, the road of the embassies. But traces of World War 2 were everywhere. One could of course go to Poland, and try not to think about the appalling events of sixty years ago. Some people made that choice. I needed to absorb these distasteful events, caused by persons similar to my father, my uncles, my grandfathers.

My mind always faltered with such thoughts. It was all completely real, true, yet unthinkable. What a thing to inherit!

We visited Auschwitz near Krakow, we visited Treblinka, just one hundred kilometres from Warsaw. Ausschwitz, the Nazi's Final Solution for Europe's Jews, gave an unsuitable first impression: a *pleasant* modern building offering refreshments and ticket counters... modern and westernised. This felt all wrong.

However much you need a cup of tea or an ice cream, you should surely not be having them here, on this damned spot. Everyone had seen the camp in documentaries and films, but despite inner preparation the reality hits hard. You can't 'shut down' to protect yourself and it is best not to try to speak, because you will be weeping. Even writing about it now I weep. It is irreparable.

Treblinka was an even more 'internalised' experience. Situated in the countryside, amidst woods and shrubs one saw a railway track, which ended suddenly...then a small field with smallish rocks, standing upright, like so many calcified persons...and there was no-one to be seen anywhere. The place was silent, even the birds were silent. It was a grey day... misty, drops of rain... if I had not read the history...well, I might not have understood. I told myself nature itself was trying to eradicate the loathsome, unspeakable acts that had taken place here.

To grow up with this history must have a powerful effect. It may explain something about Poland's visual arts. Remembering cultural events of the late eighties, early nineties,...installation art, paintings, theatre, posters, I had an overall feeling of basic, hard-hitting, utterly brutal realism... making one feel one had never understood, or been honest, about life before. This art oozed straight out of fear, pain and cruel suffering. Nakedness, sack-cloth, blood, destruction, filth, chaos, silence, fear, darkness, deception, raw cruelty, often with oblique reference to the political yoke of Communism, this thorn in the flesh, now falling away, had been overpowering: there was an urgency in art I had never seen elsewhere: sickening, frightening and shocking. This shock after those seven years of suave, bland and blatant luxury in Canada could not have been more extreme.

****

There are other places of pilgrimage in Poland but nothing can be more Polish than the 'Black Madonna' of Częstochowa.

According to legend St. Luke the Evangelist painted this picture on a cypress table-top of the Holy Family. There are frequent miracles attributed to the 'blackened' portrait of Our Lady; just like Lourdes it is a 'Must See' for any Catholic in Poland. During one of our son's brief holidays from his Music College we took him for a drive south and stopped off to join the throng of visitors swarming to catch of glimpse of the famous painting. He stood before it for a few seconds and probably requested success in his chosen career. No doubt his father had similar thoughts: in *his* case she's done him proud. He can't complain.

Doing the whole tourist 'thing' included the Salt Mines near Krakow. These were up and running in the 13th century. We began to appreciate their awesome-ness after a descent of 200 meters by stairs to a chapel carved entirely from salt by the dexterous miners themselves. Ancient pictures show hooded figures at work, a reminder of the Seven Dwarfs of Snow-white fame... the entire experience like a dark fairytale. Later, getting to know the lovely old town of Krakow itself, we found a town as glamorous as Prague.

The darkest, most magical place was in the Mariatzka, the Church of St. Mary in the Market Place ...a chance to view a carved crucifixion by Veit Stoss, a Nuremberg carver who came to work in Krakow for a while. Poles claimed him as Polish, the Germans said he was German. I was troubled by these arguments...but the dark blue ceiling covered with stars and chandeliers heavy with holy dust helped one to feel uplifted and moved beyond all such pettiness.

Outside: the Cloth-market, the Flea-market, the Flower-market, life overflowing, activity in every direction. Every hour, on the hour, a trumpeter played a few bars high up on the church tower...he came to an abrupt stop...a reminder of an arrow from some Tartar Invasion, hundreds of years ago. Having heard this event several times a day we decided it must be a tape, rather like the muezzins in Egypt these days, the trumpeter's top A always too sharp...yet strangely moving.

We also studied life as it is: a wedding party across the road with a Gypsy band, swarthily following the car, leaning right into the open car doors... horse-drawn coaches, making a racket on the cobbles and later a trip to the Wawel, the Old Castle, bringing home to one what Mozart must have endured in his day, when *all* roads were cobbled.

***

After the first months in this strange country it began to dawn on me that 'representational' life in Poland was even more fulfilling than in other places because of the writers, artists, musicians, film-makers, and journalists we were meeting.

However, a key-person for me was a tiny, shrivelled old lady, Sofia Kaczkowska, to whom I had been sent with a gift from....oh, such a tangled story, I can't be bothered to tell the tale. I *found* the address I had been given: it was one of those forbidding high-rise communist-era-concrete blocks, just by side of the former Jewish Ghetto. There were three or four blocks; stepping warily into one of them, (strange unpleasant smells of an indefinable disinfectant, soapy substance everywhere)... and eventually locating her flat on the sixth floor, a short, emaciated lady opened the door...and so began our three year relationship, entirely in Polish.

A geologist, now retired and in her eighties; she had lived in this 'shoe-box' flat for twenty years: one miniscule bed-sit with a corridor containing a hidden stove, counter, storage, plus a washroom. As I struggled in faltering Polish she revealed a smattering of German, a few words of English... but only when communication occasionally became quite impossible. It was hard work. She had no family, knew Austria as a child; her husband was killed in the War. She'd seen better days. In a curious way she felt, after a few more visits from me, (she pressed me to come again and again) I needed 'mothering' and help with speaking Polish.

We began reading a Polish translation of Le Petit Prince, we drank cups of 'herbata' (tea) and devoured together the little luxuries I had brought . I told her about my mother, now becoming wretched in Cape Town.

Each time I called on Sofia we managed somehow to create a deeper bond. She 'mothered' me, I looked after her, admired her modesty, wisdom and resilience. She told me about her life (refusing to talk about her husband, something terrible must have happened to him) as we became a 'support-group of two', getting together every three weeks. Even Charles was dragged along to see her, as was my visiting aunt Dagi, from Vienna. Poor Sophia Kaczkowska, so tiny, so brave and resilient! *She helped me to come to terms.*

'Thanks to her my Polish improved immeasurably, while I managed to bring into *her* life a little of the outside world, with stories of my family and my music. This relationship, so far removed from my otherwise glamorous life, made me experience a slice of truly Polish fate. It was exhausting, trying to speak sensibly in such a difficult language. Eventually, when Charles and I were about to leave Poland, she gave me what was probably her most precious possession: a salt-cellar in the shape of a jointed silver fish: if you hold it up its tail jiggles too and fro. I cherish it. We corresponded for a while, but it was too difficult to keep up. She is surely dead now.

Life settled into a pleasing routine: a few pupils, all children of foreign diplomats, a newly formed piano trio with two fine Polish professionals, occasional concerts with players from the Warsaw Philharmonic, conducted by an American, (who was on to a 'good thing' since he got away with paying his players ten dollars a concert.) I was the 'token' female, one of six firsts, playing with a fervour you just don't get in English or Canadian groups.

I couldn't believe my luck; this was the kind of playing I loved.

And dollars, they were a good thing! They were still the only way forward in Poland; dollars changed into zloty's could buy many wondrous Polish things.

***

In Poland there is no such thing as 'amateur' music-making. If you play a musical instrument it is because you have been chosen, trained and supported financially by the State to become a working musician and you will become part of whatever group needs your skills. Poland has special music-schools where children go to learn their 'trade' while also receiving a normal education. The standards are high. If you have a job in the music world there is no desire to fool around playing quartets or trios for fun, as one does in the West…but when it comes to actual rehearsal with Poles the music-making is on a remarkable level of passionate commitment.

My 'big' recital at the Academy went well. One violinist from the Warsaw Philharmonic said he thought I owned the best-sounding violin in Poland. Other friends also said kind things.

But nothing exciting came of it….after all that build-up there was the inevitable deflating let-down feeling afterwards.

Why does one 'do' such things?

The Berlin Wall has 'fallen.'
A moment of history, not to be missed: I take my chances during one of my husband's trips to London and book myself on a FIRST CLASS SLEEPER WARSAW / BERLIN RETURN, an adventure, all on my own. Once ensconced in a 'wagon sypialny' (sleeping car), sharing with a Polish diplomat's wife, there is little choice but go to bed, with space at a premium. Fitful sleep on an uncomfortably narrow bed, listening to assorted snorers and other noises next door, I swear: never again!

At 9 am. the train pulled into Berlin's Haupt-Bahnhof. Having stood in line for a cab for thirty minutes I eventually woke up to the fact that this dreary place was *East* Berlin. What an idiot: I must retrace my steps, find a different train to get to Friedrichs-strasse...and only then I stood in a massive throng attempting to squeeze through Checkpoint Charlie, that famous crossing point which had been opened on Nov. 9th. I was one of thousands of Poles and East Germans, patiently lined up as far as the eye could see while good-natured border guards hurried us along with: 'was wollt ihr denn da drüben?' ('what do you want to go there for?) And yet, with the German equivalent of 'get a move on' each and every face, each and every passport was examined, slowing us all down to a steady trickle...but, there I was: one had arrived: the West, lights, cabs, noise, shops bursting with Christmas treats.

19th December. 'Great! I'm booked into a 'Pension' just around the corner from the Kurfürstendamm, Berlin's 5th Avenue. 80% of the centre was destroyed during the War.... but this elegantly proportioned pre-war building with elaborately carved stairs and the highest ceilings ever is just around the corner from those preserved ruins of the Gedächtnis-Kirche...around its base a real old-fashioned Christmas-fair selling crafts, delicious smells wafting; feelings of nostalgia for my childhood memories of Swinemünde and Eutin come flooding back: I suddenly feel desperately forlorn and sorry for myself, to be here all alone....'

'If my parents could see me now,' crosses my mind. Pulling myself together, I listened to the familiar sounds of Polish being spoken around me: Poles were flocking to Berlin and making themselves unpopular by emptying the stores. Where did they find the money? Some shops had queues forming outside and only ten customers were allowed in at a time because of the crowds of people from the 'East'.

A two-hour coach-tour of West Berlin: only traces of the War; but there were still pock-marked walls, nowhere near as many as in Warsaw, though. The pre-war Berlin I had studied in a glossy anthology in my hotel had vanished; the four Allied Powers still had their districts.... with no noticeable mark apart from their be-flagged headquarters. Here is the dreary Rathaus where Kennedy proclaimed he was a 'Berliner' and over there the Brandenburg Gate with a huge Christmas tree hoisted into position. They're already blasting away the Wall so pedestrians can move freely between East and West...The bus stops. I get off and buy a piece of 'wall'. On to the monumental Reichstag, sinister ...behind it more Wall with crosses marking spots where people, trying to escape, were shot.

Despite all that it seemed to be a pleasant, modern city,... parks, lakes and canals; on every corner fragrant Wurstbuden (sausage-stalls) where one picked up a steaming bowl of pea-soup or a baguette covering one of the hundreds of varieties of sausages. I ate at street-stalls for three days, apart from breakfast at the hotel. Outside one of the supermarkets, joining the accumulated Poles, I waited my turn to push a trolley around for Stollen, Marzipan and other delectable foods... the Poles grumbling loudly about the prices, but buying anyway. I visited galleries, museums, arcades and cinemas (Dustin Hoffman 'speaking' German in 'The Rain-man' was one of my treats)... and oh, those wondrous shops!

In my alone-ness I spoke to no-one. Only on the third day I decided it best to get to the station an hour earlier to be sure I caught the correct train to Poland....'your train will be leaving from East Berlin' I was informed, 'just get on *any* train you can, we're adding new ones all the time to cope with the traffic.' On the platform I saw a heaving mass of Poles plus mountains of boxes and packages containing VCR's, TV's and other large objects. In the old days it would have been chickens and geese.

What *have* I done...? The first train pulls in.... festooned with bodies. 'How can I possibly squeeze into that, with my case and two plastic bags?'...My heart sank.

'Can I help you,' a spotty German youth asked politely and I nodded, grateful for his assistance. He grabbed my case and like a crazed torpedo forced his way into the nearest carriage. I squeezed into the space he'd created. Jammed in I then decided to squeeze out again. The whole thing was patently absurd, impossible...

This was only the first of many mistakes: had I persevered I might have reached my booked first class sleeping compartment leaving from East Berlin. Instead, I again sat on a station bench to wait for a less crowded train. Here was my spotty young friend, settling down next to me with a confident smile: 'I'm here to look after things, I'm an *official*, you know!' He pulled back his lapel to reveal a pistol. He's only a teenager... my thoughts go into 'over-drive'...while my mouth uttered, 'oh good,' trying to keep on the right side of him. I wished to become invisible. Crossing my mind was the possibility of handing him my remaining Deutschmarks, so he'd refrained from shooting some-one, even me...

'The bullets are in my pocket,' he informed, 'I use the pistol only to frighten people.' I cleared my throat: 'Do you do that very often?'

'Oh, hardly ever'...he mumbled, surveying the crowds milling about, 'don't worry.' He's taken a shine to me: 'I'll get you on the next train....' He bustled about, returned, smiled at me in a proprietary manly manner.

Twenty minutes passed before the next train appeared. I'd lost sight of the teenage 'official'. I boxed my way past one overflowing carriage to the next. There, right at the front, a first-class carriage with hardly anyone in it... what a relief, what luck and why so empty? This carriage was for Leningrad and was 'coming off' at East Berlin...

When the train stopped, ten minutes later, the carriage wasn't even by a platform...we had to jump from our Fool's Paradise onto rough stones *way down there*,.in the dark. I stumbled, fell gracefully on my Christmas cakes...someone handed down my suitcase, then we groped our way past the hissing train, back towards the modest lights of the platform.

There: a uniformed man! He was fighting off at least fifty travellers, all with tickets to Poland. By now a ruthless and desperate liar, I waved my first-class ticket at him and 'explained' I was a British diplomat carrying important documents which had to be in Warsaw by early morning....

'The situation is hopeless, gnädige Frau, you have missed your train, all trains are full, hotels are full, there are no planes, it is better you return to West Berlin.' I looked at him helplessly. I blew my nose, gazed anxiously at my watch, shook my head from side to side. 'No, no, impossible.'

'I can't promise anything' he shrugged, pityingly, as I stood, stared and noted it was already ten pm. I had visions of sitting on this platform all night. It was freezing. Thirty minutes later another carriage was added to an incoming train. I was escorted on first, hiding behind dark glasses from the stares of other desperados on the platform. Soon everyone else was on too, every available inch inhabited by bodies, boxes, backpacks. I saw no women, only Polish men of every age-group. My five sweaty fellow passengers, youngish, all with annoyingly long legs, carefully arranged these, as we settled down for the next eleven hours or so.

Communication was in German and Polish. At three a.m., becoming dehydrated, we shared a can of warm coke, and took turns to stand up and stretch during dispiriting stops at sidings and a total of four passport and customs controls, unimaginably prolonged with all these imported 'western' goods in boxes. Any hopes of a visit down the corridor were shattered by putting ones head round the door: travellers and boxes as far as the eye can see. However, there came a time when such hurdles *had* to be overcome. One friendly, powerful Pole lifted me bodily over his precious new waist-high TV set. God knows what damage I did to other equipment along the way. Even in the WC there was a sleepy traveller, but he vacated the premises with reasonable grace. After Poznan matters improved, the corridor became passable, and the blackness outside turned to grey with heavy rain. I'd not slept at all and thought about these five good-natured men with whom I'd spent the night, instead of which I could have been at the Embassy ball, dancing to a live band.

Warsaw: 11 am. A very long queue. No cabs. And a heavy downpour.

I dragged myself to the other side of the station where the known-to-be bribe-able taxis were, counting their hard currency. Hair stuck to my skull and rain dripped down my specs while I tore open a car door to ask 'how many dollars to Mokotow...?' in Polish, of course.

***

Family matters were becoming an increasing headache. Every three months I flew to Cape Town to be with my mother in her posh Whitehall Court flat; it appears mixing with new persons had become an impossible task: she only wanted her 'old' friends, or her sister, or me. Her mind and body were letting her down.

***

And then...my daughters...

A mother's day greeting arrived from them on the 27th March,1990.

'First time ever,' it said in my diary 'quite amazing!'

Our 'connection' had been limited to their occasional requests for money and the usual Christmas felicities. Was it *all* my fault? The fact remained, I could not find it in me to approve of their vagabonding lifestyle; I saw them as 'rebels' to society....giving birth to children without having proper fathers to provide, give them names...making use of the benefit system in the UK,... thank goodness my father did not have to pass comment on such things. My mother gets varnished versions of the truth...she would have been horrified to see the way they were, what they did, the company they kept. I was 55 years old and felt despair about the way life had turned out, the endless rows I was having with my husband, my children, but also the loneliness of my day to day existence.

'If my mother were dead' I wrote in my diary, 'I might just consider living alone.' I don't stipulate where. I felt no great pull to London, nor

248

to Canada, nor CapeTown. It was depressing to be me, not knowing who Iwas , what Iwas , where I'd like to be. Was I even 'British' now? I so *preferred* the *Goethe Institute* events to the cheap and nasty attention-seeking over-the-top hyper-modern offerings of Theatre and Art sent out by Headquarters to Poland. It was all tat, and I hated it. Maybe I was German after all.

My daughters were 31 and 29. Jim, the once so shocking 'bovver-boots' partner of Luci was now the partner of Gabrielle. I despaired. It seemed Jim was here to stay, when I'd so hoped he'd soon be 'history'. I responded to this switch-over without any attempt to hide my true feelings, and received, in return the following letter from Gabi:

August 17th, 1990.

Dear Mum,   your idea of love stinks. If you can't love me for who I am then forget it. You are asking me to understand you without giving a toss who I really am. It's always been like this with you and Dad. Your love, your support is always conditional on me being who you think I should be, not who I am. You misunderstand me and it disgusts me that you judge and condemn Jim for nothing. He came to your flat in friendliness and you are a hypocrite to pretend all this time to tolerate him when you were seething with judgmental anger all along....She continues angrily, and I am cutting a very long letter: Charles made a decision -years ago, to withdraw from us because he thinks we are only after money etc. Even if that is the total truth ask yourselves WHY. The only thing you really offer is material things. Emotionally and spiritually it's always been put-downs, criticisms and sneers. You are nice to me when I give first-and it makes me feel really hurt.......... I know you'll make some dismissive judgment of me, on reading this letter.....I'm tired and weary of your disapproval. I feel so uncomfortable with you both. Why should I inform you about my babies' birth when all I know I'll get back is disapproval and patronizing criticism.....here she brings in her sister who has moved on to a new relationship,...then: I am manipulated by you....approval and love dependant on appearing to be the right kind of daughter. Your priority is always to appear normal..."do they go to school?".(her children...she was teaching them at home) I went to school- and it fucked me up. I've been unreal for years and so has Luci, ask her.... I think what I've been doing these

249

last seven years is courageous and valuable...to undo my knotted-up personality, to allow my creativity to breathe again. It doesn't matter to you, or Dad. What ever I do I deserve your love unconditionally JUST because you are my parents. I'm supposed to accept any crud you guys deal out, but you can criticise me freely. The money isn't the issue, it's your attitude behind it...if you were unconditional you'd want to see me and give to me regardless whether you like my life, boyfriend, face, whatever..............

It is valid to attempt to find your own happiness EVEN IF OTHER PEOPLE SEE YOU AS MISTAKEN . There are thousands of tribes in this world who don't live as we do in the West. ARE THEY WRONG? Anyway, you are no model of happiness either. You may have material security, but does your heart sing ? Do you really feel love, are you scared of death, disappointed by lack of real intimacy and fulfilment? Hate me if you want, or more satisfyingly, feel 'sorry' for me because I'm so immature or whatever.... I cannot change you and probably never will. So if you cannot accept me say so and consider yourself as having only ONE DAUGHTER ... and a son.

During three weeks on leave in London I drive to Wales to make contact with both daughters, but especially with Gabi, to patch up our terrible floundering relationship. But, after a bad row with her on the phone, she was 'not there', so I spend a day with Luci and her enchanting new born son. Gabi's angry letter I put in a folder by now full of letters asking for money, accounts of how much and when we'd sent to everyone ...just a general file. The thread between mother and eldest daughter is stretched beyond endurance. We could not put things right... a draining experience, even now, just writing about it.

I know of no other such set-to in earlier generations. I felt I was 5 billion years old. It overcomes one, that feeling of being prey to entropy. Is it true to say that the youngest-looking 50 year old has molecules the same age as the oldest-looking 50 year old...because their chronological age is, in both cases 5 billion years (the age of their component molecules)? Is this a consoling thought?

I throw a big dinner-party to 'celebrate' 25 years of marriage. I beg my man to write a poem, which duly appears, 'totally incomprehensible', even to his mother. I dash one off in return, a sad thing, on the back-cover of my diary. I never showed him.

So here we were, Charles and Evelyn-Ingeborg, dining with princes (Prince Edward, Prince Czatoreski,) film-makers (Wajda, Ken Russell, Zanussi), authors, (Applebaum, Kapucinski).... composers (Pendereczki, Lutosławski, Panufnik) and all the while, behind the scenes, our own bleak relationship, makeshift, not conforming to the pattern it is supposed to follow.

The world is changing: we are privileged to witness, each day, the end of Communism, the emerging New Poland. Sitting next to Prince Czatoreski, just an ordinary guy who enjoys boar-hunting and grows flowers for 'business,' he informs me: 'everyone at this table is tainted,' (by Communism), looking about the glamorous assembly of ministers and artists during an embassy dinner, 'everyone, without exception......' We are overheard. There is a momentary silence, a few embarrassed smiles...then mute nodding and a quick change of topic, in true diplomatic fashion.

What does the man mean?

Mute nodding, I suppose, is about all I managed with Gabi. How unfair of me to expect *her* to understand my impatient disappointment with her lifestyle of political rebellion and social upheaval at that time, how I was governed by my own staid background, customs, and expectations of the people surrounding me. Mute nodding: yes, yes, how right you are: one is not a 'good' mother.

The new Poland under our very eyes is a remarkable thing. Spring sets in motion a big clean-up, mostly by elderly street-sweepers with twig-brooms, but also by brand new street-washing trucks, a gift from Nordic countries. Householders dig patches of earth on the edge of pavements and plant grass-seed, much appreciated by the Warsaw pigeons.

There are spring flowers everywhere. Nowhere else in the world have I seen so many flower-vendors.

Poland was becoming more and then, *even* more expensive. Since private enterprise and 'market forces' had been unleashed there was constant wheeling and dealing: one could find, within 15 yards, spread out on the pavement, Belgian coffee, Polish butter, tropical fruits like Kiwi, Cape grapes, pineapples, bananas, cigarettes from Albania, soap from Istanbul, dictionaries, toilet-seats, jeans and gym shoes. All is fair in the price-war, stalls were set up in front of shops selling similar goods. Now that the West had come there were adverts on trams and walls, you could buy a coke to wash down your Zapiekanki (hot bread with cheese and spicy sauce) or your Hamburgeri or Hotdogi, you could contemplate buying electronic equipment or flying to New York, even to gamble in luxury hotels, if you had the cash. But petrol cost ten times as much as last year, nobody could afford it...so how much new happiness and hope was there? A friend said she'd witnessed two separate scenes in our neighbourhood...bodies covered with blankets, police and onlookers pointing to the windows above. I'd heard people wishing the Communist days were back, when everyone *had the same* and *knew where they stood.*

And so the longed- for re-birth began: a growing crime-wave, sprouting satellite dishes, cut-throat capitalism, bringing 'riches' and 'fulfilment'...The British Council was doing its bit to make riches flow into Poland, so were the Germans with their Goethe Institute, as was the Alliance Française.

My own *tiny* contribution came about unexpectedly: a school on the next block advertised 'English Lessons' in large letters on the gates, and at once there was that little voice: 'find out more, perhaps they'd like another teacher'...not that I had any idea how to teach English. 'Still, I did know how to teach violin, and it would be fun to pass the time more usefully'... After a sharp intake of breath I walked in, found the Head, who spoke passable English and looked extremely pleased to see me.

'British Council!' he exclaimed ecstatically. I knew instantly I'd got the job. Twice weekly I was in charge, for two hours, of a dozen adult Poles, mostly men, who for one reason or another needed to advance their language skills. The Council Library kitted me out with the latest teaching books. My students were keen and quick and eager. I became as devoted to them as they were to me.

There was one last Big Adventure before our time in Europe came to an end: I simply *had* get to the Baltic to visit my father's beloved home town, Swinemünde. Persuading Charles we needed this long drive north from Warsaw was not too difficult ...first, to see the Masurian Lakes, and on the way taking in the equally famous 'Wolfsschlucht,' also the ancient towns of Torun and Olsztyn. Copernicus, born in Torun in 1473, was the first man to displace the earth from the centre of the universe, his calculations a landmark in modern science. He had also lived in Olsztyn, both towns with gorgeous mediaeval centres, were now sorely in need of restoration. Driving through this region of forests and lakes, we eventually rented a tiny plane for thirty minutes, to get an overview of the vast area, seemingly deserted.....I was expecting yachts and hotels and holiday-makers, but it all looked blissfully peaceful.

More driving...my husband complained of chest pains...and arm pains, and now shoulder pains. I was more worried about this than he was. Was he tensed up because we were together all day long? He'd better get used to that, with retirement looming. Actually, we were getting along just fine, caught up in the imagining of so much history and now this interesting place: Hitler's military camp-hideout, the secret spot in former East Prussia, where he and his generals plotted and planned the course of the war. It was hard to find in the dense forest...all that remained were huge moss-covered concrete blocks and remnants of buildings, dark and silent, a spooky place, evil, by association... we were keen to move on. Charles continued to have chest pains. We shared the driving and ended up in Sopot, just outside Gdansk: in the Sopot Grand Hotel, where Erika and Reini had stayed sixty years earlier.

Swinemünde was now really near: only half a days' drive away. Acting on advice from friends we'd booked to spend two nights in a resplendently white place called Hotel Amber, just opened in Miedzydroje ... our base for 'the great visit' to my grandparents' home.

I took a deep breath and walk right into the Baltic, which looked green and felt toe-curlingly chilly. I did it again the next morning, before breakfast. Then on to a ferry which took our car across the river.

Steeled for an emotional day we motored into Swinemünde to the first landmark: my father's Lutheran church, still with the same model sailing-ship hanging from the domed roof above the aisle, even though it was now Catholic. Soon we found the 'Bollwerk', and the air-raid shelter...the one in which my life had been saved, looking half the size I remembered; now perhaps useful for storage or perhaps just too solid to knock down. But there was no house... just a bare plot of rubble and weeds. Why had no-one built on it? Perhaps Polish authorities thought it still belonged to those German Ihlenfeldts?

*****

I braved another early swim on the following morning. No-one else around, I gazed across the ocean, waded in three times, unable to say goodbye: it was *my* Baltic now, and, just like my father, I felt distress to be leaving.

We drove back to Warsaw, non-stop until dusk; we were peaceful with each other. Charles talked about 'early retirement'.

I would have been delighted to stay another six months, my Polish was terrific, my music had consolidated with the help of superb Polish musicians, I had a niche and dreaded going back. Charles, who travelled back and forth to London 'on business', could not wait to return to England. Why, I wondered.

At this time I was offered one glowing 'farewell–to-Poland' treat: the honour of presenting a program in Warsaw's Royal Palace. This could not have been more glamorous: a 'salute of honour' on arrival by the armed guards of the palace...and in the presence of two of Warsaw's most high-powered violinists, assorted diplomats, colleagues, friends and pupils, I had one last moment of happy elation: performing Schubert, Stravinsky, Richard Strauss, with a fantastic pianist, in these surroundings of immense beauty and prestige.

A dear friend, Poland's senior figure in the world of the violin, was also very keen on Astrology. While saying good-bye he felt I needed this warning: 'don't go back, Evelyn,' he pleaded, 'I will find you work here, a future in England is not what is right for you.' Not an 'old fool'.... he had held an important teaching post at Indiana University, even in Communist times..., he had studied my 'stars', he'd seen me together with Charles, and guessed, perhaps, what was becoming inevitable.... more clearly than I did.

In January 1992 I returned to London to get the 'home-fires burning'. Charles followed, by car, right across Europe. He had been awarded a CBE. We were going to see the Queen.

Buckingham Palace, although mostly an intimidating place, also had its charms. While my son and I sat on small gilt chairs, listening to a band playing 'out of tune' popular classics, I watched my best friend of over twenty-seven years, noted his stoop, his drawn pale face, (was he nervous?) and how thin he'd become in Poland. My heart contracted with the wish to protect him from sadness and disappointment. I had experienced so much in these years with him; he had taught me a great deal. I was no longer afraid of anyone. I felt free. But I was also conscious that *he* needed freedom even more than I did. Trevor McDonald, the Trinidadian newsreader, stood near us after the ceremony, proudly displaying *his* OBE to the photographers. How British was *he*? He and I had used up approximately the same amount of time, fossicking about, 'becoming British', shall I say thirty years?

It was a very British Day. I really *did* think, on *that* day, I'd made it.

****

The 'last chapter' begins with renewed classes, portraiture, this time, at the Hampstead School of Art. This was more than just pleasing...I showed some promise.

At that time, after much pleading for a bigger home, to end our lives in some comfort... builders were engaged to join our very small flat to the adjacent basement...to form a splendid space, now with a double garden (overlooked by at least a dozen other families peering at us from all those five-story Victorian houses).

I was still occasionally involved with former colleagues, now in the English Sinfonia, which meant getting out and about. Charles occupied himself with becoming a governor at a local school and by going abroad to supervise elections in foreign countries. There was the continuing pain of never-ending rejection slips for his novel and renewed attempts at re-writing and smartening it up. How many publishers had turned it down by now, some ridiculous number! In so many ways Charles seemed a crushed man, despite success in his British Council career.

So we 'rubbed' along, as they say, it all looked normal....a distant, lonesome 'normal'...his feelings were elsewhere all the time, if not with his writing, it must surely have been with other women.

This was the rawest of topics. One day, dusting the mantle-piece, I found a receipt for one dozen roses sent to Nicola, the pianist. I was devastated. Eleven years had gone by since we left for Canada, and *still* he was in touch with her. I made a scene. That evening, while attending a party given by the famous Anne Applebaum, squashed body to body with journalists and literary Poles in her tiny London flat I observed Charles making a complete ass of himself, flirting with her in a discomfiting way. Was she the proverbial 'red herring'? The next morning I said: 'I don't feel right'.... and passed out. Taken by ambulance to the Royal Free, I was tested and released a day later, still living. 'Not a heart-attack,' they told me, 'but we'll keep an eye on you.'

There were additional tensions: my daughters were on the telephone often enough asking for money. I went to Charles, questions were asked, accusations made and there was a very uncomfortable feeling about things all the time. James, the son and heir was set up without question in a house in Cardiff, but the girls....'well, they have a father of their own, why doesn't *he* sort them out?'

An understandable reaction of course; but the requests kept coming. Cheques were sent. Accounts were kept. What little we heard of their lives left us incredulous....where had it all gone so wrong? Grandchildren appeared in all directions; who were the fathers? What was the set-up? At least Luci was studying now...

Epilogue.1992, back in London. I drove to Wales, made various attempts to put matters right with my daughters, performed concerts with several amateur pianists.......one of them, a physicist just retiring from the Open University, was seen in our basement flat quite frequently; he had an obsession with Walton and I set out to learn the violin sonata written by this composer specially to please the man. He was so thrilled by this work, it was touching to see. With a paunch and holes in his sweaters, he drove a battered old car and lived in a large neglected house, with a skeletal pedigree cat called Pushka. He told me he was an environmentalist, and a widower. The latter brought forth my protective instincts.

Charles encouraged me: did I like him? 'Well, yes' I said, 'although he talks too much'…The pianists I was used to got on with the job and collected their cheques before they rushed off to their next employment. This Walton addict had an awful lot to say, about everything, a true polymath. With his numerous lady friends, from singers to flute-players, chemists, atomic physicists, and potters, he travelled to exotic places like Moscow and the French Alps, another he took to Prague and Barcelona; alarming, just trying to keep track of them all…..This was a man who had his hands full.

'Plainly a bit of a Don Giovanni... why doesn't he make a pass at *me*,' I wondered. For someone so recently widowed he exuded a great deal of energy. He spent weeks at mysterious summer events called 'Music Camp'…he was music director of an opera company in Milton Keynes and he plied me with books on every conceivable topic…

He was, sadly, planning to sell his house and move to the country.

'I'd really value your help with getting my house in order…to be sold,' he said, surveying our newly refurbished Hampstead basement, the fine kitchen and splendid music room. 'Do come and rehearse in *my* music-room, I have a nice Bechstein,' he urged; I don't really care for your Blüthner….'

It was 1993. One morning a cheque arrived in the post from a magazine called 'The Strad', read by the great fraternity of violinists world-wide. A few months before leaving Poland I had posted an account to the editor, about the important business of preparations for international violin competitions, with some 'insider information' of what was going on in Poland in this respect. I had no idea it had been both accepted and printed. I had, unwittingly, got myself into a marvellous new occupation: the magazine managed to track me down in London after we left Poland. Calling on the editor, I casually mentioned my relationship with an ex-teacher, who was now 'Mr Big' at the Menuhin School, and was immediately invited to write another article about *him*: Mauricio Fuks, the man who was 'knocking the Menuhin School' in shape. He was in Paris at that time. I dropped everything to locate him, and got the story together in just a few days.

The rest is history: the beginning of a mini-career as journalist for The Strad magazine, with eight years of journeys, to France, Germany, Denmark and even Japan…. and whenever I returned Charles was only too delighted to type out my handwritten notes and assist in turning everything into immaculate English prose. What a learning curve!

My mother-in-law came out with: 'Poor Charles. I hope he's not too jealous *you* are the one who is getting published.' But there was no sign of anything but generosity of spirit and helpfulness, at last: something we could 'do' together…a belated bonus.

I flew to Cape Town often, to comfort my poor demented mother. Charles disappeared to supervise elections in other countries. He also took two cruises on his own and then, once more, we travelled together, this time to Uzbekistan. Interesting as this was it turned out to be a 'splitting-up' trip. Both of us were openly buying souvenirs for our new 'friends'… while keeping the peace and reaping the benefit of the stimulus of being together in such an exotic remote, strange place.

******

'East House', (the Walton addict's) home, was finally having a make-over, at his instigation, but using my 'expertise'. Frankly, I had never done such a thing in all my life. Paint a room…you must be joking? Practical by nature I did know how to find handymen. Room by room the entire place was reborn.

In the event, even Alan and I were up those ladders.

Painting, renovating…throwing things out, all a ritual cleansing of *his* past. I became inspired, re-created an awful brown wardrobe into something gorgeous decorated with colourful Spring flowers. I discovered I could do things other than scratch around on a violin.

Alan's secret, walled-in garden was another place where we bonded…. sweetly trying to impress the other with our 'closeness to nature'. To be honest, until then I had not really considered gardening: but soon, while he was performing dazzling feats with heavy rocks, I cut, moved, dug up or planted living things. On one sweltering day we pranced around under a garden sprinkler hidden behind a shrub, completely naked.

Innocence returned… but not for long.

When we were not painting a wall or planting a plant we were playing music together. Soon we bought a giant bed at IKEA, decorated the biggest available room in unusual colours, and turned it into our 'sacred space'. I went 'home' regularly to teach pupils and to help Charles cook a decent meal from time to time. He seemed perfectly content with all this, now that we were both totally free to pursue whatever we felt needed pursuing, getting on really well, like exceptionally good friends. Wandering about in Hampstead I could not help grinning happily: 'at last, at last... I've found someone who actually *wants* me. I am female again.' My feet hardly touched the ground.

Alan and I hardly noticed the passing of four whole years...time spent learning to live together and enough time to sever the ties of thirty-three years with Charles who got on perfectly well without me. I had no desire to inflict wounds...be vindictive, I had loved him too much for that. Alan once revealed how devastated he'd be if I left *him* and I remember having to check with Charles what it meant, to be 'devastated'...one of those many words I'd heard often enough but never analysed.

When Charles finally landed himself with another partner, *and* discovered they were going to have a child, he suggested we divorce. Easy: in March 1998 we were free. But one truly distasteful moment came from an unexpected source: the Catholic Church. I was required to swear on the Bible that I had *'never been married'* to Charles Chadwick. Well, of course I had not, in the *eyes of the church*. But I had to *say it,* hand on the *Bible* ...for the sake of the new wife, who, as a Catholic, wanted a 'proper' wedding. Well, so she should, I *tried* to tell myself.....

It 'pissed me off', though. Will I be forgiven *one* lapse into coarse language? As I age I feel almost no further desire or need to impress others, but was nevertheless relieved that my mother's dementia hid this shameful event from her. In 2003 she died.

I was to tip her ashes into the sea in CapeTown: this was *her* wish. Looking across Table Bay, my trousers rolled up and my feet in the icy waters by Blauwberg Beach, I looked up to see the famous outline of Cape Town's beloved mountain, also known as the 'Grey Father.'

My mother's ashes danced above the water, reluctant to mingle, only gradually vanishing from sight. From the memory of those terrible moments, looking up at the mountain, then down again to see the ashes bobbing about, dancing lightly on the waves, she now comes to my mind each time I see the mountain from that angle.

My Mum! It's what she wanted for me: those heart-breaking moments, seeing the last traces of her vanish over and over again. I have already asked my own elder daughter to strew my ashes down from the top of the 'Grey Father,' from Table Mountain. I trust there will be a good 'South Easter' blowing on the day. It will be the moment when my 'simple being-ness' finds its fluttering end. Is it unkind to ask her to do that?

Now time is running out. I admit, try to come to terms with, even accept, my many imperfections. Getting old is predictable and possibly even interesting. Alan and I read, discuss, perform concerts, enjoy the seasons in our garden.... and we travel. He is the most dynamic person to travel with, always so stimulating and interested. We've criss-crossed the globe, the furthest places being Africa and China.

While roaming, learning, I have found one more treasure: the way 'back' to my daughters.

It has been the toughest, the most unusual journey of all.

Evelyn with Gabi and Luci in London, 1964

Evelyn, after a concerto in Lubeck, Germany, 1979

Gabrielle, 2013

Gabrielle with Polly c 1990

Polly with Leela 2007

Polly 2008

Leela 2009 (in Welsh costume)

Gabrielle's story

(in her own words)

'Once there was a way, to get back home.......'   The Beatles.

My earliest memory is writing. Sitting at a typewriter, three or four years old maybe, writing something about oranges. Could I spell? Could I write? I've no idea. Yet the power of the moment is still there. Things welled up inside as I wrote whatever it was, feelings of sunshine and joy that danced through and permeated my father's little study in our house in Ndola. Other memories are fragments of feeling and impressions; of life as kind and full of well being, dazzling sunlight on the water of our swimming pool, bright pink bougainvillea on warm white walls, teeny lizard's eggs in keyholes, brown/black children with ragged clothes, crunchy stones round our house; always, in all of it, my constant 'other,' my sister Luci.

Childhood hints of what people call the divine, that indefinable something that can be experienced when there's no separation between the self and life. It's one of its sweet gifts, simple 'being-ness', untouched by life experience.

Then comes the complexity that 'learning' brings, the scarier memories, experiences harder to understand or integrate. I'm older, hanging about in the doorway looking at my Mummy, in bed after an accident. I'm uncertain, wondering what to do, unclear, caught up in some nameless dread. She's in the little room, her recovery space, next to my parent's big bedroom. She has bruises all over her body. The feeling is trouble and turmoil, things not being ok. There are more memories. My Mummy is on the phone, crying, our puppy is dying, our cat ate one of her kittens, Nana is sad …Where do you start when the memories flood in?

How to organize the fragments? The easiest place is where everyone starts: at the beginning…..*my* beginning.

My mother is German, my father Lebanese. He would now challenge this simple fact, seeing himself as Christian Maronite, a distinction he finds important. He has denied he is Lebanese, though the two seem interchangeable to everyone else.

Pierre Mansour fell in love, with a beautiful German girl, Ingeborg Evelyn. She had the right kind of looks, he had the hang-ups. He was self conscious about his curly black hair and hooked nose, having issues about race. (He has issues about many things. His children had issues about his issues! But that is some time away.) During the years that he was a student in South Africa - years of the unjust system of Apartheid, the political climate was ripe ground for his paranoia. He was then and remains to this day uncomfortable about looking too foreign. Evelyn's regular features were an antidote to some of his fears.

Perhaps the cause of his insecurity lay in his own background. His mother, Adèle, died in childbirth when he was only three. There's a striking photograph of her, young and healthy, dark haired, exotic, dressed in white lace. She died young, poisoned by a baby growing for ten months in her womb. On her deathbed she called for tiny Pierre, who remembers her lying dying on purple velvet. She urged her small child to take care of his younger twin sisters, a heartbreaking scene and huge burden for someone so young. His new stepmother Josephine (Nana) brought him up as if she were his mother. Knowing her generous nature, she was trying to help protect the boy from pain. But Pierre was always proud that he never 'forgot' the truth: he knew who his real mother was and it wasn't Josephine. The white lie she told was not a kindness to him, but an injustice. He was unwilling to forgive this 'sin.' It's a tendency he has, not to see another's point of view. Just to hold on, attack and make them wrong. He has this trait to this day. Whatever his psychology, Ingeborg-Evelyn's parents, were not sympathetic to this foreigner who wanted to marry their only daughter.

It was not a blessed start. Evelyn, (who gave up the 'Ingeborg') and Pierre were an attractive couple. Black and white photos from their courting days show a fresh-faced young woman, a well shaved (no moustache yet!) sensitive young man. Good looking, sweet, vulnerable, their youthfulness shining out. Later photos show emerging glamour and wealth, sunglasses, designer dresses and suits, a young pair finding their style as they began to inhabit their new life together. After a modest start in a flat, their luxury home was built. It had every modern feature, a food lift from kitchen to upstairs, the latest furniture, gardens with swimming pool, servants' quarters filled with poor black Africans to service the couple's dreams. Pierre got busy building his empire, Evelyn adapted to this new world.

She was straightforward, pleasing, accommodating, likeable. It was not the complete truth. In those days women were expected to be attractive, amenable and undemanding. Hollywood's ideal women were gorgeous, feminine, spirited... but not assertive. It was a hindrance to finding direction in life, something Evelyn had yet to do. Books such as 'The good girl syndrome' a couple of decades later were to challenge these attitudes.

At this time Pierre expressed many ambitions, wanting to prove himself.....in later life his goal was simply 'to be the best poet in the world.' He used to say 'one day you'll realize you were living with a genius.' He was happiest changing things, which didn't bode well for us future children. He applied the same critical attitude to people as he did to current reality, working constantly to 'improve' things in some way. This made him exciting, charismatic, interesting.... and infuriating. We all worked hard for his acceptance, invariably failing to attain his idiosyncratic standard, especially as we got older. That is, when we were born, which we weren't yet!

So there was Pierre in Zambia, at the end of the fifties, with his brand new wife, in love. She was already pregnant. They lived in that small flat, hot and cheerless with an unattractive view, until their designer home was ready. They had bad luck in that flat, with a series of cats dying. An omen of what was to come?

Their firstborn, Luke, died at six days old. After that things were not the same. Evelyn coped with this sad event without crying, just went back to her wife-life. It began, slowly, to feel unsatisfying, something was wrong. She continued to look good, stylish, like everything around her, but quietly, insidiously, creeping like rot, estrangement was growing. On the surface things continued as before. There was no animosity. The couple felt the influence of the oncoming sixties, with its throw-away prosperity and focus on freedom and fun.

Then, about two years later when Nana prayed for the couple's fertility in Lourdes, a miracle happened! Evelyn was pregnant again! It was me, growing there quietly in the safe rosy-pinkness of her womb. Many years later, unaware of Nana's pilgrimage, I would visit Lourdes in a double-decker bus and experience first-hand, that magical atmosphere; people chanting in the streets, healing rituals, candlelight and imminent miracles.

A few months before my birth in 1958, Pierre's father Antoine died in a tragic car accident. A driver had fallen asleep at the wheel of a vehicle coming the opposite way. Antoine (Tony) was hit, his ribcage shattered, his lungs punctured. He died in an oxygen tent.

Pierre inherited Border Motors, the car company his father had founded in 1928. He had to work hard to learn the business, doing this successfully though his real interests were elsewhere. He was upset about the loss, as he'd loved and admired his Dad. Pierre had designed and built an outdoor chess table especially for his Dad's visits. He envisaged afternoon chess tournaments on the upstairs balcony, with a view of the gardens and pool. They were never to happen, the chess table was never used. I used to think about this wild granddad we never met when I passed that table and have a silent special feeling about him. My middle name Toni is in remembrance of him. Sometimes I feel superstitious about it, wanting it changed, in case it attracts a stray car...

Gabrielle Toni (me!) was born into this setting on December 24th 1958. I've been told I cried all the time for about three months, gulping down different formulas to try and settle me down. Photographs of me show a long skinny thing, with a worried face. Not a rosy cheeked advert-baby at all. There's an atmosphere in these early pictures of subtle stress. Evelyn was overwhelmed by the little screaming rabbit she'd given birth to. She chose not to breastfeed after one week. If I'd had any say I'd have yelled: 'persevere please Mummy, it'll improve the bonding process between us. Plus it's much, much better for my health. Don't give up so soon I beg you! You'll get used to it!'

I sprang from the soil of an inexperienced mother, beginning to be bored with her role, unprepared for the demands I was about to make. Some mothers fall madly in love with their children. Others don't engage. Evelyn didn't take naturally to the little charge bawling its way into her life. No wonder I cried.

One of my later influences was Jean Liedloff's 'Continuum Concept,' 1975, which advocates physical closeness between mother and child. The book broke new ground in the seventies; arguing that infants should be carried and kept close to their mother's bodies as much as possible early in life, sleep with parents, breastfeed on demand as long as they want to be. Her observations were formed while living with the Yequena tribe in Venezuela. Their children, she noticed, are unusually self possessed, co-operative and secure. The child's self esteem is formed through the quality of interaction with its parents, not only mother, but the entire 'tribe' or extended family that should ideally be there for a child all its life. If a child has its real needs met, the outcome can be social harmony. Unmet needs create psychological problems that can result in mental and social dysfunction.

She argues that a bonded mother naturally, non-verbally, intuits her children's needs. It takes intention, commitment, as well as lots of honesty and practice. I chose to apply what rang true to me to my own children. It shocks some people to know that my eldest child Polly, now twenty-four, was breastfed until she was four years old. My youngest child Saba, was breastfed for six years, my son Pablo lasted only one year, stopping reluctantly because Saba came along. Liedloff argues that each child has a different rhythm and needs; mothers are encouraged to listen to and take their cues from each individual child, to trust them and themselves.

The simple truth is that children thrive on love, attention and focus, yet are often dragged rather than brought up, treated with shocking insensitivity without real understanding of their needs. We expect to create a society of healthy balanced individuals without knowing what we're doing. It's such an important subject. Often we're more sensitive to the needs of our plants than the humans we are supposed to cultivate and tend.

The urge for centrality is major in childhood. We all come in, feeling like the centre of the universe, born into other people's unfinished stories, in which each person is the centre. Like Russian dolls we spring from each other, entering a continuum that's never ending. To love is to make another as central as yourself. Like plants, we're reliant on the quality of our soil. But unlike plants, we're each defined by our relationships with others. All of us weave a complex and unique web of inter-connectedness. Plants grow best under optimal conditions and so do we, blossoming when we receive the right blend of emotional, social, physical nutrients. We can grow when some nutrients are lacking, but are more challenged to reach our best potential.

Luckily I was a pretty toddler. I'd have to be to win my mum over! By the time I was two I'd become the golden-headed advert child I'd failed to be at birth. Just when things were looking up for me, along came a threat: Evelyn was pregnant with her second child. She decided to go away for a couple of months leaving me with a family appropriately called the Cares. The father was Pierre's lawyer. Their daughter was my friend.

This is my memory: I am alone in a sandpit, holding some beads and becoming aware, slowly, concentrating on the beads in my hand, that my mummy is gone. Really gone, the kind of gone where she doesn't come back. Ever. Or so it seems to a small child, when time is long and two months a concept you can't grasp. I was only a toddler, strong in feelings, weak in the power to articulate. Children form identities, in part, by how another sees them. A child's identity can fracture or collapse when no one is there to mirror feelings, or support them in making sense of the world. Later, in my twenties, when I started Primal Therapy, this was the memory my body took me to, remembering something long ago forgotten, so clearly, felt to me as shocking as a car crash. My parents didn't like the sound of the therapy, it seemed suspect to them. However, the experiences I had doing Primal Therapy affected me profoundly, altering my life direction permanently. At first, just talking to my therapist about other things… then some skilful questioning and touch activated something I wasn't aware of. After that, the upset that came out of my body had to be experienced to be understood. As an adult I was taken over, sobbing with a long forgotten childlike rage and terror at my source of security disappearing. I felt an animal anger and distress, primitive and violent in its intensity. It was unimaginably life changing. For a couple of hours I physically relived what I may not have even expressed in the moment. This memory was somehow lodged in my body, connections I'd not made before lit up my being. I felt different. Some things made sense that hadn't before. I realized I was terrified of rejection and abandonment, feeling somehow I was so bad I deserved it: 'Mummy's gone. I'm all alone. She doesn't want me. I did something wrong. She doesn't love me. She wouldn't leave me if she loved me. It's my fault. I'm not loveable. Mummy's good, I must be bad if she doesn't want me. I'm bad and not loveable'. We are born narcissistic, interpreting everything in relation to ourselves. Yet our 'souls' are always awake even if our minds are not developed, our hearts and feelings are all there. Adult insensitivity to our needs really hurts. I was deeply hurt and confused by being left.

Young children are sensitive to change, needing preparation and support to feel safe. Some adults think because children are not verbally articulate they have no real consciousness. Pierre used to insist that children were not worth talking to until they're eight or older. We had arguments when I'd attend to my first baby crying. 'You aren't going to be THAT kind of Mother,' he'd say every time I went to her.

When my sister Lucienne Erika was born, she found herself better received. To my chagrin, she took my place on Mummy's lap. Photographs showed me growing fatter; standing slightly to one side while Luci took central position. Evelyn felt more drawn to this baby, who was less miserable and stressed than I'd been. It was a self-perpetuating circuit, Evelyn was more relaxed and so was her baby. I'd become clingy when Evelyn returned from her trip abroad, terrified that she might do a disappearing act again. I wouldn't even let her go to the toilet without hanging on to her legs at first. I badly needed special attention and reassurance to feel secure again. It was not the best moment to have a rival for the precarious affections of my mother.

Luci's reign of power didn't last too long. After a while we became cute together. We began to discover the joy of playing with each other. She gradually shifted from threat to ally. 'GabiLu' was born, an alliance that lasted until our forties.

Evelyn had secretly hoped Luci might be someone else's daughter. She'd had an affair with an architect and Pierre knew about it. It was part of the 'open' marriage they had developed. Pierre also did his own thing, sometimes, when travelling, even visiting prostitutes, coming back smelling of sweat and another woman's perfume. They did all this without animosity, but things were changing. Conditions were ripe for new passions to emerge and they did. For Evelyn, it was not the architect but Charles; a tall Englishman she met through playing music, who brought that change. Charles's height was a factor in her attraction to him. Though Pierre had great charisma and drive, he was also one of those shorter men who make up for lack of height with personality. Evelyn wished he were different. Taller. There were jokes about wanting to stretch him. He could also be opinionated and overpowering, alienating traits that put some people's backs up. Gradually passion and intimacy began to fade between the couple. Pierre was essentially an idealist; probably compensating for the inadequacy he carried deep within. To this day he is frustrated by unrealized potential and the gulf between his visions and reality. He was too busy bridging the gap to notice where his wife was bored and frustrated, or distant and isolated in their life. Charles appeared just in time and he was refreshingly different from Pierre. Evelyn was ready. She took the leap, into a new and hopefully more meaningful life.

'Daddy is outside next to the pink and purple bougainvillea, he's telling us we are going to live with Mummy in England. He says they are divorcing. I feel sorry for my Daddy, he'll be all alone. I'm scared. I'm thinking about how sad and lonely he'll be. I'm going to draw pictures and send them to him to cheer him up. The wall behind Daddy, it's white with brown circles on it. You can put your hands on it and it's always warm. I'm feeling strange... like the whole world is cold and falling down. Mummy and Daddy know what to do, but it feels as if Mummy knows and Daddy doesn't. I have to help my Daddy, my heart aches.'

ENGLAND My first impressions made me determined to hate it. First of all it was cold and grey. Everything was wrong. Traffic lights were a different colour. The birds didn't sing right. Where were the crickets, the swimming pools? Airport Officials were efficient and quiet. I missed the crazy black officials at Ndola airport, I wanted noise and chaos, dust, sweat and heat. That was home.

We lived in a flat in Muswell Hill. I tried to be good for Mummy. She had left me once before and now she's left poor Daddy. She might leave me again! I had a dim fear the divorce was somehow my fault. In London, we went to a nearby school, finding it difficult to settle, though there were compensations. Like the landlady Yvonne with her family upstairs, especially her son Kimon who became our great friend. We'd sit on the outside steps and sing the Beatles, 'She loves you yeah yeah yeah,' feeling expansive and free; happy to forget the oddness, newness of everything and how far we were from our Ndola. Kimon's family were Greek Cypriots. They ate 'weird' food, which we were reluctant to try. Despite our travels across the world, like many kids we were conventional about what we ate. Yvonne was surprised that such worldly children were so unadventurous. There were some things we had to hold on to, for our own sanity. Too much was changing too fast.

After Mummy left Ndola, and we went back to visit, our father would feed us fillet steak and fizzy drinks, chocolate galore, toasted cheese sandwiches whenever we liked, plenty of calorie rich rubbish prepared for us on demand by Andy our 'house boy.' Later, travelling alone on planes, (first class of course), we ordered burgers and chips like 'Jughead' in our Archie comics. Obliging air-hostesses scurried off to make them for us; just like the pictures. That was as adventurous as we got.

We missed Daddy. We had to get back to our old life. We missed 'Bewitched' on T.V, our black and white cat 'Top Cat.' We wanted our bedroom, our huge sunny garden. In London the houses were too close together, everything was small and squashed up. We came up with a plan. Stowaways on an aeroplane! It seemed so easy. We just had to get to the airport, sneak up the ladder to the plane and climb in through its underbelly where the luggage was stored. We had total faith we'd find it and succeed. After tying clothes into a piece of material for the trip, we sneaked off when mum was doing her violin practice. We got as far as the top of the road by the Laundrette and felt hungry. We had no money, hadn't thought to pack something to eat or drink. A feeling of smallness, of powerlessness came over me. It was time to go home. We decided to try again some other day....

One day the ceiling fell down where we usually sat watching T.V. Luckily we were somewhere else that moment. The dust and debris was an eerie reminder that things could change in an instant. Perhaps there were things stronger than Mummy; now Daddy was gone we weren't quite safe.

Lusaka, 1965. Back in Africa again, it all felt strange. It was odd to have a new bedroom and to live in a house with our stepfather Charles. We needed reassurance and contact, but our Mum became more distant, her attention taken up by her new marriage. By the time her third child, James, was born, she'd made a choice: to let go of GabiLu and focus on her new family. Inwardly and outwardly, she handed over responsibility for her two girls to Pierre. The trouble was he didn't know. She thought he'd do the job better than her. He assumed she was doing it. As a result we fell into a kind of psychological no-parents land.

For a while we lived with Charles and Mum and went to school in Lusaka. I don't remember much, except the name 'Dominican Convent.' Until we went to boarding school there seemed to have been many nuns in our education. Years later we both did our First Communion in London, earnestly confessing invented sins to God, mouthing 'Hail Mary's' and 'Our Father's,' as penance. I lived in subtle fear of God's judgement; afraid I'd do something to displease him. Throughout the day I discreetly made the sign of the cross, making prayers to appease him, as a precaution.

Part of Evelyn's problem embracing us was Charles. He disliked Pierre, seeing him as an arrogant opinionated man. We were therefore Pierre's spoilt little brats; Charles was irritated by some of our attitudes and opinions. He wanted his life with Evelyn, not the baggage of her past life. We had no idea until we were grown up that he saw us like this. No matter how we seemed, we were just little girls who wanted love and approval wherever we went. If we had mannerisms that grated, we required guidance and compassion. We couldn't help what we'd been born into. Criticism and rejection were the last things we needed.

Charles seemed a kind man who gave us some of the normal attentions we craved as children: Simple things like reading stories and drawing pictures of his imagined ' King Murgatroyd'. We assumed he liked us. We both liked him. It was a blow in adulthood to discover how uncomfortable and uneasy he was about the 'princesses' invading his life. He had areas of low self esteem that we had no understanding of as young children. He could also be (irrationally to others but perhaps not himself) insecure and depressed. So for a while we were shipped off to Dad. I don't remember being sent to live with him. All I remember is being on holiday at his house and him trying to teach me the time, which mystified me. I do know that he treated us more like adults than young children. We didn't know until adulthood that we minded that.

We admired him, even worshipped him, despite his being too busy to spend much time with us. Luci and I were often left alone together, to invent our own little world. After Evelyn had left, there in our sunlit paradise, endless Coca Colas, Fantas, Seven Ups were available to us all day from our drinks freezer. All we had to do was grab one, click off its corrugated metal top on the special bottle opener, built in. There were no restrictions, we could grab two or three if we chose to. I'd drink seven or eight in a day. We'd drink them instead of water, taking them ice cold down to the boomerang shaped pool in our garden. We had a walk-in pantry stocked like a mini shop, full of, amongst other things, chocolate for us to help ourselves to. The result: I was a hefty eight stone at the age of ten. Our African 'servants' would ask us to slip them soft drinks and so on, some small compensation in servicing our luxurious lifestyle while they lived in relative poverty just across the garden. As children we were blind to the injustice in the situation.

Dad took me to his stepmother, Nana, to be appraised. She was a Lebanese woman with long salt and pepper hair worn in a bun, solid, reliable and generous always, ever loyal to my Mum. I trusted Nana and was asked to parade up and down in front of her. It seemed as if everyone was seeing me for the first time. She agreed sorrowfully that I appeared to have trouble breathing. I sensed her concern. Still nothing changed. Dad had other more important preoccupations than his daughter's obesity! I didn't really care if no one else did, happy to eat the same appalling diet that we loved, consuming vast quantities of sugar. Luci stayed skinny, but perhaps I was more of a pig! I was quite oversensitive and seemed to have an unmet need for reassurance and comfort. Food was one way to fill the need.

Dad had little modelling of family life, having been away at boarding school himself from five to eighteen, so our main contact with him became intellectual and verbal. He was not particularly demonstrative or affectionate even when we threw ourselves at him passionately for our bedtime kiss. If we squeezed too hard, held on too long, he'd push us away, embarrassed.

He did teach us to be articulate and sophisticated though. His passion was for ideas and action, creative projects, the arts, current affairs, theatre, music. There he was animated and interested in everything. He liked to be up to date, receiving boxes of singles to keep in touch with music in the charts and magazines from England. He disapproved of our Archie comics, trying to persuade me to read Plato's Republic when I was eight. I was an avid reader and did eventually find it interesting. He loved anything avant-garde, new, challenging, shaming the normal and mundane and encouraged us to be the same. We were allowed to stay up late and got indignant with lady-friends who tried to put us to bed. Dad would arrive home and give his permission to our resistance. We'd get back out of bed triumphant, to the bewilderment of his visitors.

One day he took us to a house to see his secretary. She had big blonde hair, a small waist and a little cardigan, buttoned up. Her daughter was our friend. This lady had a new baby over her shoulder, being sick down her back. 'This is your sister,' Dad told us. We stared, unimpressed by the dribble and sour smell of sick, accepting the statement as children do. We remembered this event, but Dad never mentioned it again.

We knew all our lives that this sister might turn up one day. We used to talk about it, it became a myth. When she contacted us in our forties it was as unreal as a long ago dream come to life. We knew it might happen but didn't believe in it, like Father Christmas or the tooth fairy. Dad's denial and deceit about it, the way he'd lied to his new wife about it, the way he forgot he'd once told us the truth…troubled us the most. Who was this man? This girl attempted to contact Pierre, but he'd have nothing to do with her, denying his paternity. That remains the situation to this day. We do know for a fact that Dad bought his secretary a house and gave her a generous amount of money at the time. That day though, back in Ndola, after we'd seen our baby sister, we just went home. We continued our life, staying up late, watching Dad have parties or chess tournaments in the living room. We swam in our boomerang shaped pool, ate what we liked, had racing cars from Border Motors that really drove, bicycles, everything we wanted. He'd say, "Remember, you can have anything as long as it doesn't hurt anyone." He promised us baby elephants, a Go Kart he was going to build himself, the world. When he bought a farm he planned to make a house just for the kids with their own pool. Some of it materialised, some didn't. All of it created a dizzying world without limits, full of colour and possibilities.

Dad ran 'Theatre Workshops' in the Border Motor building, another of his passions. He took us along, letting us play 'offices' at the desks. He also had a darkroom for producing black and white photographs. We knew fragments of his plays off by heart, such as 'Humbeat's Circle,' which explored black oppression. I loved the name Humbeat, it sounded like African drums to me! He used black African farm workers in that play. Their energy was phenomenal. I was impressed, excited and moved by their vitality and physicality. He had a verse in the play, which GabiLu knew off by heart and used to chant in unison:

'Let's sing the song of a glutton
Who took a large slice of the mutton.
He tasted the juice, the meat and the mince.
He ate and ate till he burst his buttons…
His friends were killed on the first explosion,
From that day on he ate alone.
For no more friends he ever won.

We had no idea what it meant. We never understood anything he wrote. He didn't help us. If we got him talking about his work, we'd end up bored and confused. Still, some pieces of his writing live on in my mind: 'A man walking....Saw miles of teeth....Under feet, biting...His eyes paralysed his nerves...Decomposed...Left his teeth in the sand.'

They rattle around in me, together with unfriendly thoughts about his pretentiousness. I had many painful experiences trying to be part of his artistic world. For years he put me off 'creativity.' Yet I couldn't help it, it was in the blood!

Pierre was deeply interested in black liberation, talked to us with passion about apartheid and white oppression. I sensed the importance of the subject, trying to grasp, aged eight, what he was saying. It did leave an impression of scary injustice going on in the world, which shocked my young mind. He attended mysterious meetings at night where he was the only white man. He told us he was helping the Africans. He had some kind of connection with President Kaunda, in office from 1964-1991. The president came to our house and was received upstairs in the important room used on special occasions. My claim to fame is that the President of Zambia carried me up the stairs to that room. Once we visited a place of his in Lusaka, which had sweeping green lawns and beautiful peacocks. Dad had a meeting with Kaunda; we've no idea to this day what about. On that occasion we were presented with two white rats. We were thrilled with our rodents, Ruby and Vagabond. They had tiny pink noses, snow-white fur and seemed perfect. Sadly our red-eyed rats became 'the disappeared'.

Whatever else Dad got up to, it was his writing that was the most important to him. It began to become so obscure I couldn't relate to it.

Many years later when we were in our twenties he visited us in Rotterdam, Holland. He read his work to a group asking everyone for feedback and opinions. There was a silence. He was, could be, extremely difficult and confrontational if you volunteered a real opinion. Was it worth it? Everyone was weighing up the situation. My boyfriend broke the silence by denouncing Dad's poetry as 'crap!' Dad leapt up, picked up a chair and shouted, 'I put this chair between you and me!' There was another silence as we waited, the chair standing harmlessly and pointlessly between them. Dad seemed a cornered animal. It was fight or flight so he left the room, a 'Great Man' in a huff. As an afterthought he gathered anyone he thought supportive to him on the way out. My sister went with him, I stayed in the room with my boyfriend.

Dad had little sense of humour about himself. He was very Mediterranean in that way. He sometimes recognized that his pride was a problem.

For years we laughed about that moment, away from him. We were members of a 'Kunst collectif' (Dutch Art collective) and becoming more independent of his influence. He no longer seemed as powerful and impressive as he used to. He was, at that time, younger than I am now. His marriage to second wife J was floundering. We were growing up, wanting to know him better as a person. Impossible: his pride prevented him being vulnerable, equal to others, hidden behind the role of 'Great Man' for so long.

Luci worked harder than me to be pleasing. She would have fiery arguments but in an almost intimate way, skilfully managing his personality while striving to 'win,' yet maintain his approval. She acted as if she had a special inroad to his affections. I was more critical and cynical, feeling that being close to him was impossible. It was only after she left home and he'd treated her the same as everyone else she realized it had all been an illusion. She has never spoken to him or seen him since she understood that he favoured her no more than anyone else, she was as rejectable as the rest of us. Dad's rejection of all his children has affected all of us in different ways. I've had moments in life, like most people, where anger and/or despair about the past has been overwhelming. Caring for my own children has made me aware of the neglect in our childhood. At times I've been very angry and upset. The neglect was not physical, but emotional, which is harder to see, but not to feel. Luckily, life experience can, over time, have a softening effect. As understanding of people's limitations and background grows, forgiveness becomes more possible. Having children helps. It's easier to see how hard parenting can be when you've experienced the daily grind yourself. I've used therapy many times, as a kind of re-parenting, to help me get clear on things that were hard to accept. Life is too good, people too precious, to waste time hurting. There's still a lot to understand, some of it may never make sense.

'GabiLu' weren't the kind of kids who had a say in what happened to them. We were told and expected to comply. We learned to soothe feelings of lack of control by uniting with each other, creating an independent unit 'us'. We needed something to make us secure in the world, big and scary out there. Soon we got used to travelling halfway across the world on planes, taking whatever crisis, bad weather etc. that life threw at us. Once, stranded in Dar es Salaam on our way to Ndola, a kind couple took pity on us. We'd been forced to spend the night in the airport lounge, sleeping anywhere we could find. We didn't really know what to do. This couple bought us dinner and as we ate, told us they were impressed at how grown up we seemed. It was only partly true. Really, most of the time we bluffed our way through situations, acting older and more capable than we felt. We were losing touch with what we really were, just two little girls.

BOARDING SCHOOL 1969. We had known we were going to boarding school, but not what that really meant. The day we were dropped off was a day like no other. I was ten years old, Luci was eight. Days your life changes can creep up on you without warning, the implications of that change can reverberate forever. Our significant day began with an uneventful car journey. I'm not even sure which combination of our then four parents delivered us. Was it Dad and Jane? Or Mum and Charles? All I know is whoever it had been, was gone. The next day they were still gone. Then the one after that. So it went on, without ceasing, the relentless 'gone-ness.'

Across a field in *her* new house Luci is biting and kicking her fellow inmates. I know about that. Now, ten years old, at my new school I don't even wonder how she is, or exactly where she is, even though we've never been apart. I'm too overwhelmed by my own experience. When I feel ready to take stock, it seems I am in a small room with five other girls. There are two windows, looking out on a garden. The garden looks green and inviting. I want to be out there, running away. But I sit still, looking at the walls and door. My eyes are fixed on the door but I am rooted to the bed. I notice my locker, a shabby little cupboard next to my bed. The room is small, painted some shade of light green. It's hard to find a place for me, somewhere away from the annoying noisy children I'm suddenly with. I stare at the bed, there are blue and purple striped bedcovers, thin cotton weave, the kind of thing Mum might have at home. The bed covers are quite nice. I don't really know what to do except stay on my bed with the bed cover, next to my locker, in the bit of the room that's mine. I'm drowning in a kind of swirling panic but act as if I'm fine because I want to be and really don't know what else to do. There are children shouting and lots of people I don't know.

There's no one to turn to. I'm just one of this crowd. I daren't move an inch. I've been left, they just left me here and they are going home. I can't go home. I can't think about it, I might cry, I don't want to cry.

Everyone is saying things, shouting. I'm trying to be invisible, don't want anyone to see me but I can't hide, there's nowhere to go. I just have to stay here, if I move I might cry. Maybe I'll put something in my locker but for now it's safer to do nothing, just wait and see, try not to think. If I look at this bed cover long enough this might all go away and I'll be safe and back where I know things, not here any more, I don't want to be here….

They had those bed covers throughout the school, a positive memory. Somehow, to me, they were a link to home. Where that was I'm not sure, anywhere we had a parent I think! We were allowed to wear our own clothes at St Chris, as it was a 'progressive' school, a 'groovy' school. Luci and I had identical brown cord pinafore dresses, wool tights, pleated brown wool skirts. Combined with my pointed black-framed glasses, sensible haircut and overweight, whatever good looks I'd had as a golden haired toddler were more than obscured. This all went against me in the point scheme invented by merciless eleven and twelve year olds!

Luckily the situation contained its own solution. It was at St Chris I lost weight and ended up (at fifteen) a healthy eight stone.

Boy's rooms were the other side of our house 'Little Arundale.' Luci was a brisk walk away with her house parents at 'Arunbank,' different age groups housed in different 'homes.' Main school was a short walk for every boarder, there was plenty of fresh air and exercise. The school was vegetarian, much to our dismay. I craved sausages and bought tins of frankfurters to eat in the toilets, with my friends. Most of the time though, I had to eat what was there. It did me good in the end, even if at first I was oblivious to the health benefits of my new diet.

Already an uncertain little girl, boarding school plunged me into the unknown. I missed everything. The freedom I'd felt as a normal child was over. I was controlled by rules from morning to night. It didn't matter that it was progressive, co-educational and Quaker. It wasn't a family. All I wanted was some kind of real 'home.' We were forced to come up with survival strategies.

At school we immediately began disconnection from adults, identification with peer group. Adults were the betrayers. Many of us felt abandoned and rejected. Unless parents reassure you, it's hard to feel wanted when there is no real explanation or real communication with anyone. I pushed away normal childish longings for 'Mummy and Daddy', and distracted from the pain by comforting 'victims' around me; girls and boys who felt their parents didn't want them either. We were the lost ones, all together. That was comforting; to be in the same boat. As the relentless routine of the institution called school claimed us all, we began to build loyalties to each other. One day I stood up and announced a meeting 'for kids only,' at the back of the house. At least twenty accomplices turned up to plan a mutiny. We stole eggs from the kitchen and played catch with them, then refused to go to bed at night.

'If we refuse,' I said, 'there'll be nothing they can do, we'll be free!' It seemed a way out at the time. Disrupt and take back power! There was perhaps some of Dad's non-conformist influence behind my great plan. I felt old and wise at eleven, entitled to this authority, certain that with team work we could build a new world! Eggs were 'nicked' from the kitchens and 'bunged around' the school grounds. Bedtime arrived and mutiny began in a fitful way. There were some shouts; lights went off all over the building. After five minutes I was standing alone with the light on in the middle of the dorm.

'What are you doing?' asked a member of staff. Minor disruption throughout the building had been effortlessly quelled by a few commands and stern voices from those in power. 'Standing on the floor' I answered, trying to be cocky and savvy, determined to stay true to the spirit of rebellion. I was mildly amazed that everyone had gone down so quickly.

As ringleader I was made to stand outside the housemother's flat, supposedly thinking about what I'd done. I was cold. The house was quiet and peaceful, all dormitory lights out. I felt lonely, angry, determined and defiant. My housemother leaned into my face and explained I must see her as my second mother. If I had problems I must feel free to come to her. She had one fat arm and grey hairs on her chin. She was nothing like my mum! I was repelled, vowed I would never ever go to her for anything. She died some time later of the cancer that had caused her arm to swell, leaving a sad husband and two young daughters.

****

While I wanted my Mum, I didn't end up with many memories of closeness with her. One positive memory I have, was while holidaying in Mombasa. Charles was upset that day. He had his moods, which as teenagers, we tried to ignore. We decided to wade into the sea at low tide, to search for coral. Mum took off her bikini top, swinging it in one hand while we set off. With our bare breasted mother and the sun shining, we waded into the sea at low tide, a memorable mood of light-hearted intimacy opening up between the three of us. Charles, in a dark mood, had been left onshore, as we walked out to the dazzling brightness. Finding a live sea cucumber with its little dark green mouth just added to the hilarity and fun. We wanted life to be good and simple, full of affection and laughter, to forget our stepfather's confusing emotional swings and self-pity, leave adult complexity behind. For that moment all was right, we had our mother which was as it should be. It was a rare moment of belonging. Years later Luci and I both remember that walk.

We inevitably adapted to our situation, as children do. I discovered my rebellious streak. I had tried 'earning' love by being a good pupil, for a while going down that road. I'd do what I was told, then take my rebellion sideways, secretly angry at feeling powerless and unimportant. I was the good child first, keen to earn approval and positive strokes from those around me. But it was not enough; I was left feeling hollow and became an explorer of the forbidden. After the mutiny came kiss-chase, then cigarettes and alcohol. I was by now about thirteen. One day a group of us managed to get hold of sherry, wine and gin in the town, bought for us by an obliging someone the right age whom we'd asked in the street.

We drank our stash out on the fields behind the main school, mixing the alcohol indiscriminately. Gin was disgusting, like hot perfume, but I slugged it down without caution, my mind soon blotted out. I have a vague recollection of my clothes being too hot, wee-ing in the school bin, people cheering, walking back to my house, people laughing, falling asleep the minute I hit my bed.

Next day I had a terrible headache, combined with a sickening sense of creeping shame. I was naked. Some vague memories of ripping clothes off, leaving them back at main school somewhere near a urine filled bin in the library, swam around my aching brain. My friends had further cringe-making stories to share. Things kept emerging like fragments of a bad dream. It was announced in school assembly that someone had been sick under the school piano.

The experience at school and a few others put me off drink, but not off other things. I became interested in altered states of consciousness and trying all the fashionable drugs of the seventies. I turned on, tuned in, dropped out. In common with many of my generation, I felt let down by what the older generation had to offer. It felt hollow, empty and essentially meaningless. It seemed all they cared about was material things, not about how people felt, or who anyone was. I wasn't terrified of lack or insecurity like the previous war-traumatized generation. I'd had material comfort. What I'd had less of was emotional security or intimacy, nothing to depend on that made me feel safe inwardly, or significant to anyone. Like many of my friends at the time, I suppressed emerging upset at feeling displaced and without any consistent 'other'.... with 'pot,' then 'grass' or 'dope' to us, LSD, speed, barbiturates, Mogadon, Mandrax, uppers, downers, anything that was going around at the time. It was a way of belonging to a family, a family of 'flower children' who cared about each other (or so we hoped!).

P., one of our teachers, had several pieces of work published, and founded the Mandeville Press in 1974 in nearby Hitchin. He took a special interest in me, saying I could 'write well about a piece of dust if that was required.' Writing was just normal to me. It felt easy to turn out the assignments required. P. (we called our teachers by their Christian names) was a poet, a hunchback and a real character. He broke his wife's heart by having an affair with the drama teacher. He and his mistress took a flattering interest in my progress. My confidence boosted, I organized a speaker from Amnesty International to give a talk at the school, as well as one with the author Sally Trench, who wrote 'Bury me in my Boots' about the homeless in 1968. The book had a huge impact. I felt passionate for both these causes, realizing I liked to help people. This was to prove a potential sticky place for me in later life, when I took this urge 'to give' beyond my capacity. I liked to make a difference to someone, to feel warm, needed and significant.

I also organized and directed a couple of plays and choreographed dances. As younger kids, Luci and I had made up lots of different performances and events. Sadly, over time I became disconnected from these talents. Even though I was singled out for my flair at English and Drama at school, at Art, French and German, I became bored with academic accomplishment. I was looking for knowledge about relationships, psychology, intimacy. I had this inward looking streak, wanting to know more about being human, about real people's lives. I had too many questions, few real answers.

HIPPY TEENS. By this time Dad had been through two houses, one in Ingram Avenue (one of the two hundred most expensive streets in Britain,) the other a restored and supposedly haunted ex-pub in Chiswick. His third house in Canterbury slightly resembled his house in Ndola, having a similar 'upside down' roof. He was still with J, and they'd had four gorgeous children. It was J. who encouraged us to change our image. GabiLu began to transform from 'nice' girls to longhaired hippy teens and to become more distinct from each other. I wore denim and cheesecloth, Laura Ashley skirts that brushed the floor, velour-panelled garments, John Lennon specs and patched jeans with inserts at the bottom…Luci had distinctive blue boots that she tucked in to jeans.

Dad's income from his business in Zambia became difficult to get out of the country. He wanted us both to leave St Chris to save money. I panicked. School had become home to me. I was scared to return to

Dad. At St Chris I finally belonged, in a way. At least there I knew what to expect – structure, predictability, no nasty shocks that took me out of my depth. At home though, Luci had an advantage: she was bonding with Dad, J. and the kids. They put her into a drama school, where she did well enough to land a part in a Shredded Wheat advert. Dad paid the term's fees with her wages, and then told her she had to leave. He gave no explanation, perhaps he had run out of funds. Sadly, that was the end of her career in drama, no one mentioned it again. I wonder what might have happened if she'd stayed. She did show real flair. Dad never encouraged his kid's talents, just seemed uncomfortable when others made an impact... he had to be the centre of everything, finding it hard even to make J. feel special. He used to say 'I come first, then J, then you lot.' We took that as the nature of things. It took me years to even question that.... it was so ingrained. I lost interest in achieving and began to decline academically. I cried often and didn't know why. Part of me no longer cared. I identified with the anti-materialist, anti- establishment, pro-people values that were the emerging hippy ethic at the time. It was now the seventies.

Mum and Charles seemed occupied with their own concerns, their marriage subtly stressed. Charles wasn't happy, she wasn't happy. He was quietly critical and terse with Evelyn, uncomfortable and constricted in himself. He dealt with his discontent by descending into the basement to work on his manuscripts, sending out finished work.... only to be rejected again and again.

Yet, he could be very amusing, becoming animated and witty talking about literature. He was also generous and good to us. We did like him, but thought he often put Mum down. He treated her as a bit stupid as if she didn't 'get' things. We didn't agree. She may not have always been knowledgeable, but her mind was all there. Sadly, with vitality missing from the marriage, everything was compromised. Charles had emotional problems that contradicted his more generous and expansive sides. Like many inhibited Englishmen he could become cold and dismissive.

Mum and Charles were by now critical of 'GabiLu', living in a different world. Dad and J. understood a little more about youth culture at that time. Easiest of all to relate to were our many siblings, I loved them; though we saw little of our stepbrother on mum's side. We also loved our stepmother, who tried hard with us. I didn't always like the way Dad treated us all, he seemed like a bully, had erratic 'scenes'. He was no longer king of his empire, but an uptight family man beginning to fear that he may not achieve his ambition (one of them!) to be the

282

greatest poet in the world. He felt we didn't appreciate his genius but he would be validated after death.

I began to find him tyrannical and ludicrous. Instead of feeling valued, I was put down, humiliated, and shamed by this increasingly stressed father. Intellectually he was as interesting as ever, we had many lively unconventional and challenging discussions at home, about politics, art, theatre, literature etc. I discovered I had a flair for drama and English as a result of that stimulating background.

LEBANON.....LEAVING HOME.

I left school aged fifteen and a half, doing GCE's early, as I was a year ahead. For the next few months we lived in Lebanon, in the tiny village of Ghazir, with Dad, J. and their clutch of children, Fran, Pebs, Clare and Doudy. These tiny tots ran amuck in sixties fashion through the attractive Lebanese home. J. was a true sixties chick, fairly wild, impulsive and freedom loving. She was also generous and extravagant, sometimes rumbled by Dad's discovery of items stuffed at the back of cupboards she was afraid to own up to, or worse, the arrival of his credit card statements!

The house in Ghazir was perched on a hillside with an extensive view of terraced land and a spectacular (especially at night) vista of the Bay of Jounie. It had wide spacious rooms, balconies both upstairs and down and was decorated simply with blown glass chandeliers and huge floor standing vases.

Once, during an argument with Dad (perhaps the items at the back of the cupboards?) my stepmother threw herself at the chandelier, shattering its blue and green glass globes all over the floor, then hurled the large vases over the edge of the balcony. They smashed satisfyingly on the terraces below. She probably cut up some of her clothes afterwards, she generally did! A bee went up my floor length skirt soon after that, which I ripped off, screaming, adding to the general mayhem.

Soon after this hysteria, Dad hired a Lebanese peasant woman, Hadla, to take care of the children. J. was exhausted! Hadla washed our faces with a flannel, though Luci and I were thirteen and fifteen years old. It was an affront to our dignity to be pursued by this tiny fearsome old hag in black flapping dress. Whatever she was really like, her shrivelled leathery face and darting bird-like eyes filled us with revulsion and indignation. Shortly, after a fiery bout of our complaints, the poor woman was dismissed.

And then came our Lebanese admirers: Dad spent an evening humouring a local man who offered a dowry for my hand in marriage. Some fishermen on the beach wanted me to run away with them. Young bloods on motorbikes turned up to find out more about us.

Beneath the house lived a young Syrian labourer, Mahmoud, in a rented basement room. One day Luci developed mysterious blotches on her lip. After various alibis unravelled, it emerged they were love bites. I had been keeping watch at Mahmoud's door, but hadn't really understood what was developing in there.

Dad and J, amused and tolerant, welcomed Mahmoud into the family. The young Syrian assured Dad and J that he would never compromise Luci's 'honour;' to show his integrity he produced pills to 'suppress his desire.' When we returned to Britain he swept Luci into a Hollywood kiss, later he sent passionate love letters in Arabic that we had to have translated, but Luci never saw him again. We assumed he was called to enlist in the Syrian army as hostilities escalated in Lebanon.

Lebanon was becoming a dangerous place to stay, so the whole family, returned to the UK. Luci wanted to be left to attend the American school near Beirut, but Pierre refused. He was aware of the political situation and knew it was a matter of time before things got very bad. So the whole family went back to Kent. I was happy as my boyfriend from St Chris was back in Britain.

In Kent I got myself a job at the King's School in Canterbury, rather than continue with any more academic education. I wanted real experiences! I joined a bunch of much older women to clean dormitories, make boy's beds, set and serve the boy's tea. The plus of the job was the interest the King's School boys had in their new cleaner! The minus was the drudgery. Being one of the only young girls there, (apart from a pair who came in to help with cooking) I got plenty of attention. After too many visits to our house from more interested King's School boys Dad had had enough. He arranged an interview for me at the local college and I was signed up for A levels. These had to be done in a year: I dropped French to concentrate on Economic and Social history, plus English. A year on, after I'd left college, Dad rushed me into leaving home. He gave me a little talk one night, saying, 'Fly girl, Fly!' For some reason I felt so rejected and hurt that I 'flew' a few days later.

I had no plan, no idea what I was doing.

So I went camping with my boyfriend. At Stromness camp site on Orkney, a wild storm blew our loosely pegged tent into the sea. A chance meeting in the street with the writer George Mackay Brown led to us staying in his house as his only guests. This lovely man introduced us to other writers and artists, including the composer Peter Maxwell Davies.

Maxwell Davis (as people called him) spent six months every year on the deserted island of Hoy where he drew inspiration for his work. My boyfriend and I camped on the impressive brooding island, near a lake where the last two children of the community had tragically drowned. Remaining inhabitants of the island believed the place was cursed so they packed up and left the Valley forever. We stayed a few days, the only people on the island at the time, soaking up the eerie atmosphere of the place. After this, we ended up in St Albans where my boyfriend lived. He was soon off to University in Sheffield. I tried to find a place to rent; it seemed wise to get somewhere now I'd left home. I hadn't a clue what I was to do next. Perhaps it was no surprise that I was ripped off by a con man at the first (slightly) acceptable place I found, a shabby room in a house where a man with one arm lurked, leering on the stairs. Trains ran past the back of the garden at regular intervals rattling everything! The 'landlord' wasn't a landlord at all. He didn't even own the house, had just 'obtained' the key and was letting the room to two of us simultaneously, to get two months rent in advance and two deposits. He'd done this in several places and was finally caught and the police got us our money back. My boyfriend's mother felt sorry for me after she witnessed this abuse. She offered me a room in their stylish St Albans home rent-free for the next three years. It was an incredible offer for a student, so of course I took it. I applied for and received a full grant and never had to worry for money once in that time.

I was treated like one of the family and got close to my boyfriend's mother. She was a vivacious, Pre-Raphaelite-looking red head, a lecturer at the local art college. We had fun going to exhibitions and discussing art. I became a member of the Tate Gallery, travelling by train to London for private exhibitions and shows. Every night I was cooked healthy meals and really looked after, I felt lucky to be there. She encouraged me to sign up for a degree in Humanities at a nearby Polytechnic and I graduated three years later having specialized in English literature. The degree had five modules: philosophy, logic, linguistics, English and computer studies. I loved the course and was expected to get a first. My dissertation 'The idea of nature in Beckett' was considered so original that my lecturers urged me to sign up to an American University to continue doing research for a book. The idea terrified me. I saw the years ahead as a long grey road to a trap: academia. Even Dad and J., back in Canterbury, were doing degrees at the University: J. graduated with first class honours, Dad a 2:1. He hit the roof, saying only conformists and unoriginal people got first class degrees. After this I was struck by an overwhelming bout of resistance to doing research for my dissertation. With skimpy research I missed a first by three marks, to the lecturer's puzzlement and disappointment. I didn't care. I just felt overwhelming relief to escape Dad's wrath and the pressure to go to America. I was twenty years old and sad to say goodbye to my nurturing landlady. She was puzzled that my parents had never come to visit the whole three years, but I wasn't, we weren't that kind of family.

THE PUNK PERIOD. In 1979 there was another short spell in Canterbury. For a few months I worked, first in a pop, then a classical record shop in Canterbury. Luci had met a 'punk' fiddle player, who she was excited about. We met in the Pub, where he sat surrounded by people, a kind of buzz around him. Luci's 'sister from London' did her best to look at ease: everyone else seemed to know each other. He told me later I had looked cool and unimpressed with the Canterbury hicks! Jim wore a pink knitted tank top, a leather jacket covered in badges, big black Dr Martin boots (that later terrified my mum,) spiky peroxide hair and ripped jeans. He was friendly, charming and funny, the life and soul of the pub, I liked him. Dad and J. did too, finding him a character. It wasn't long before he was Luci's boyfriend and my friend.

One day the three of us spontaneously jumped on the coach to Sheffield. We had no plan, just to visit *my* boyfriend. Sheffield was a friendly city, the University easy to blend into and get cheap hot meals from! We decided to stay a while, renting a couple of rooms; mine a single, Luci and Jim's a double in a terraced house.

My sister and I made Dennis the Menace finger puppets and colourful objects to sell at the local market, Jim played his violin and made far more money than we did. It didn't matter! We spent most of our time laughing, becoming a kind of performance because of the way we looked. In Canterbury, tourists often photographed Jim. In Sheffield the attention continued. We were labelled the 'Pop kids.' Jim attracted such crowds in the town centre that he was taken to court for 'obstruction'. He wore an oversized suit given to him by a barman and washed the blue out of his hair to be more respectable. The end result was an unthreatening 'fluffy chick' look that made him seem more innocent. The judge called him 'our wandering minstrel' and clearly amused, fined Jim five pounds for blocking the route, as there were 'mitigating circumstances'... people could get by at the back and he had caused no actual harm.

Punk was about being outrageous, challenging authority and doing things your own way. It was also an outlet for anger. We were more into fun and humour, but there was also anger. Some people were scared of us, especially of Jim. His own mother said she'd walk on the other side of the street if she didn't know him. When Evelyn met him she turned white with shock. She felt it necessary to wipe the chair he'd just sat on. We didn't intend to be frightening, just wanted to feel free. Yet we did identify with the feeling behind punk, the rebellion against something you felt had let you down. As with all youth movements you have to live it to really understand. Peer group was a factor and having an identity different from ones parents. It was also a statement, an identity, a rejection of certain values, an attempt to connect with passion, an expression of rage and outrage, as well as a refreshing change from studying.

After three months of fun we were ready to move on. I went to London, to stay with Mum and Charles in Hampstead until I found a job, Luci and Jim went back to his home in Whitstable where Luci did a secretarial course.

My job was at Marshall Cavendish on Wardour Street. At night I practised meditation in mum's toilet to cope with the demands of London life and living at home again. It was difficult to adapt to living with parents again. Later I moved to a flat in Kentish town, then another flat with a friend in East Finchley. Marshall Cavendish was a publishing company that produced part works: the magazine, 'Stitch by Stitch,' my role: editor's assistant. The editor, a lady, liked whole bottles of gin. I was too busy trying to bluff my way through the typing I'd lied I could do (secretly learning from the 'teach yourself' book under my desk) to worry about her tipsiness. Somehow we all got away with it! I left five months later to go travelling, amazed that the magazine had made all its deadlines on time. At my goodbye party I was given a cowboy teapot with hat and spotted scarf round its neck, many compliments and assurances I'd be missed.

I left my job with relief. It seemed wise to have the prospect of rising up the career ladder, but it wasn't exciting enough for me. My passions were not engaged by typing, and petty, stressful office politics. Instead I caught the famous 'Magic Bus' (a company providing cheap overland travel to students etc. throughout the 60's and 70's) to Perpignan, the south of France and also to Athens. I was enchanted by the beautiful city with such incredible light.

After eventful roaming I settled in the easy-going liberal city of Rotterdam, where, after renting a while, I ended up living in a squat rent-free. By now I'd met my boyfriend, a musician friend of Jim's. We began to live together, continuing this period of unstructured creativity and living on the edge. We asked our mother for to pay for a knitting machine and Luci and I immediately formed 'God Creations' a

287

colourful clothing line making unusual knitwear. We'd also hand knit intricate jumpers or leggings on commission. I once made a couple of 'poetry' jumpers.

One client's poem was so long, I had to use the tiniest needles: the finished work was a work of art. I can see now, looking back, that we could have made a success of this, it was doing quite well, but we were casual about it. We then formed 'God Creations' and managed to get a buyer for our ear-ring range with a chain store. Unfortunately we'd used weak glue and were embarrassed by our earrings sliding off their backs. Too full of other ideas, with too much success selling on the street and to our friends, we didn't persist in this effort. That was for capitalist entrepreneurs, not free spirits! Our talent was for living in the moment. We shunned success, boycotting the uncaring 'fat-cat' mentality responsible for producing greedy corporations that polluted the planet. We didn't want to strive for some elusive future, we wanted happiness now. To Mum and Charles this seemed irresponsible, immature and even deluded. Dad and J. saw us from a more artistic perspective. Dad was working at Canterbury Art College with young people just like us, which helped.

We spent that period of time playing, dressed in anything and everything. Fairy dresses with lace up boots, colourful dresses over trousers, patched jeans, jumpers, covered in toys or knitted foetuses. We dyed our hair blue, purple, green, pink, half red and yellow. Jim wore a kilt, fluorescent knitted jumpers, patched jeans, things tied round his trouser legs, the odd plastic fried egg from his belt, badges everywhere, my boyfriend had headscarves, pyjama trousers, pyjama tops. We'd chop up something during a conversation and wear it. Or find something in a second hand shop, flowery acrylic housecoats, things that sparkled, glinted, things eclectic and kitsch. We were walking art, a circus, theatre, a spectacle. My boyfriend played the accordion, Jim the violin, both individually and together, singing and attracting huge crowds. Our lives became a kind of street theatre; we had fun, having significance because of our clothes and the music. We laughed a lot! Humour, spontaneous experience was a large part of each day. We decorated everything we owned and also ourselves. Once, when my hair seemed dull, I grabbed a paint pot and dabbed dollops into my hair. It took months for the blobs to fall out.

We acted like children, on impulse. Perhaps tribal people know something of this urge to paint, decorate and parade the self. I don't know. Life was serious enough, why not make it fun? Perhaps we were just showing off. Whatever it was, we were enjoying ourselves! We were privileged to have the safety and freedom to live like this in a culture that was stable and relatively permissive. There wasn't much money but survival was never an issue. Ours was a spirit of optimism seen in some of the spoof 60's films, like 'Austin Powers.' All that was colourful kitsch and carefree; this was the path we took for a while.

DEPORTATION AND CHILDBIRTH. By 1981 Luci and Jim were expecting their first child: things got more serious with the arrival of Kizzy in 1982. Kizzy was a home birth, quite normal in Holland and born so fast she beat the midwife to it. Jim had to 'busk' the delivery, using a book and common sense. Apart from mistaking the black of her hair for something sinister, as the head crowned there were no complications. A little red 'Winston Churchill,' this baby was soon to become beautiful. I stayed in their flat to help out, knitting Kizzy a tiny baby jumper as a welcome-to-the world gift with 'Do not expect a bright pink freshly shampooed baby!' on the front.

Tragically, Jim's mother had died of breast cancer a few months earlier: Luci had no involved mother figure to help. She had me and we did our best, but having a child is something no one is fully prepared for. We had to make it all up as we went along. Luci became stressed trying to respond to her baby's needs; maternal impulses weren't flowing easily. Gaps in her relationship with Jim began to reveal themselves, but none of us could articulate these personal issues with enough precision to get insight into the changes. We just tried to continue what had worked before. Only, it no longer worked.

Not long after Kizzy was born, we decided to form a busking trio, 'The Baby Cavemen.' We practised songs, worked out clothes for the act. Before we could try out our set on the streets, I woke to intense hammering on my bedroom door. My room was on the top floor of the squat 'Heemraadsingel', an empty house now filled with creative types. Walls and doors were covered with graffiti, there were improvised electrics, wires trailing up the stairs. We'd applied to the council for permission to pay rent on the house and this was their first response. Someone was shouting, urgently, 'Wake up, wake up Gabi, there's an M.E. van parked outside (special riot police unit, equipped with tear gas and truncheons) the police are here…..' It didn't take me long to realize I wasn't dreaming.

I opened the door. Whoever had warned me had gone: eight policemen and a policewoman entered my room. I stood there, foolish in my nightdress, trying to grasp the situation. A couple of them kicked a few bits of furniture around, while the policewoman photographed the result. The pictures were published in the papers as evidence of our 'living like pigs.' Though I was informed I had fifteen minutes to pack,

I barely had time to dress, grab a small bag and a book, before time was up.

I left the building handcuffed, accompanied by a policeman who showed me to a police car. Riot police sat by, on the alert, in their van. There was a large crowd outside, reporters taking pictures. I was to be front-page news.

I realized I was shouting which I do when scared. If no one's listening, turn up the volume! Confused, stressed, in hastily grabbed fairy dress with rumpled purple hair, handcuffed and photographed, I was pushed into the car and driven somewhere I didn't recognize. Having just been asleep and without breakfast, it seemed like a dream. The journey through the streets of Rotterdam seemed endless, a stony faced driver ignored most of my questions. I asked if I could have a cup of tea when we got somewhere "You aren't going to a hotel," came the curt reply.

We arrived at a police building, I didn't know where, with no passport or valid papers. I kept explaining I had a valid passport; it was at Luci's house. All I needed was to phone, I could get her to deliver it. But the police were unhelpful. They'd already decided to make an example of the 'Engelse punk.' I was thrown into a cell with a thin stringy-haired heroin addict and some incoherent women. The heroine addict, who spoke good English wasn't encouraging. She understood the police better than I did. They had their own idea of what they wanted for me, which didn't include letting me get hold of my passport. I was denied that phone call no matter how much I shouted and banged on the cell door. What else was there to do? They'd taken most of my possessions on entry; pens, eye pencils, nail scissors etc. in case I tried to gouge my eyes out, break down the door with them, kill others or myself. They let me keep the book I'd grabbed as I left the squat, ironically Jiddu Krishnamurti's 'The first and Last Freedom.' Perhaps I could bash the door down with it! I had plenty of time to contemplate the concept of freedom, as I waited for something to happen. I felt sick and dizzy, not having eaten that day. A plastic tray of grey meat and over-boiled red cabbage arrived, but suddenly I had no appetite. We were brought nightgowns and shown a room of identical grey beds with thin beige blankets folded on them. I tried to adjust to the horror of spending the night. Then a policeman came looking for me: he had a key! It was a miracle to walk through the door instead of screaming through it. I was led through a room full of police, one was the chief. He was a broad man in a lilac shirt and I made the mistake of looking at him. He ran at me, bashed me with his big body hissing 'Get out of our country you dirty punk!' I was amazed. I wasn't dirty, except for not washing that morning! The clothes I wore were just fun to me. To this man they were a symbol of something dangerous, offensive. He hated what he thought I stood for. But he didn't even know me. I felt indignant, defiant and angry. Injustice makes me courageous. I lose all uncertainty in uncomfortable situations. Only when I am safe do I allow other more vulnerable emotions to emerge. I was taken to an empty courtyard and told to wait. It was a bit ominous to see the darkening sky. I just stood there, alone. Ten minutes later a gaunt Moroccan guy with several gold teeth joined me. He showed me some forged money hidden in his sock.

Half an hour later we were in a police car, driven to the nearest port. We were being deported. I began to argue, the more world weary Moroccan telling me it was futile. They hadn't let me get my passport! My sense of injustice was roused. I couldn't stop speaking, trying to justify myself. But the Moroccan was right: it made no difference. Before long I was on a boat heading for Dover. The Moroccan had his wad of forged money so he bought me a meal and a cabin. I slept after vomiting up the meal; stress had got to me. I never got to thank him, arriving in Dover penniless and hungry. British Rail allowed me a ticket, to be paid for later. It's not everyday you're deported. I met up with Dad mid-morning at the local school where he was doing some supply teaching; he drove me home. (Dad never walked anywhere no matter how near it was.) It was a beautiful day, England looking green and golden, bathed in sunshine. I spent the whole day sharing my story with people, so over stimulated and pumped with adrenaline that I stayed up all night writing down the details: it was impossible to sleep.

Next day Dad made a film of me talking about the experience. I'd rather have had some sympathy and a hug, but he wasn't that kind of a Dad. That was behaviour for 'ordinary normal' people, taboo concepts in his world. The 'dramatic and interesting' event was a shocking trauma to me. I was naïve and sheltered about the way the world could work. One of the conditions of deportation was that I didn't return to Holland for six months. I returned within three weeks. Shortly after arrival I spotted a couple of the policemen involved, who waved cheerfully at me and carried on with their day. No further problems. Nothing much changed; only I chose to rent my next place to live!

Luci and Jim let me stay with them a while. They went off on a busking trip to Italy with baby Kizzy, I stayed behind taking care of friend's flats, watering plants etc, catching a tram around the city to get it all done. My boyfriend joined me. We lived at Jim and Luci's until they returned and then found our next place. Visitors arrived. Several crazy musicians who knew Jim and Luci called the 'We Don't Want

The Peanuts We Want The Plantation Dance Band,' stayed with us a while, saying we were just like Jim and Luci. That's how much of a group we'd become.

FIRST HOUSE AND FIRST-BORN_ My boyfriend and I moved to a damp flat and conceived Polly. The night of her conception I had a strange experience, hard to describe. I seemed to leave my body and was 'told' I was pregnant. My boyfriend had exactly the same experience. It was strange. Was it a double dream? We both felt our personalities 'lift' away and 'somebody' spoke to us. We called it the 'critter' experience for some reason.

I wanted to return to England to have the baby. My boyfriend's parents were kind but worried. They decided to help. His mum sorted out a room in their house for us to stay long as we liked. I spent hours sleeping, suddenly unsure I wanted to be with this guy. I was out of my depth, unable to imagine us living together with a child. My desire was to give birth at home, a normal thing in Holland but problematic in Britain. Unlike Holland, there's no functioning 'flying squad,' mobile units complete with birthing equipment, everything set up for hospital births. There was also the small problem of not having a home. My man's mother, ever practical, helped us sort that out. She and her husband would act as guarantors, enabling us to get a mortgage. It was a big risk to them and they had some sleepless nights. My child's future grandmother was determined we'd have a home for her unborn grandchild. My stepfather provided the deposit. We were thrilled!

This formidable and impressive future grandma came with us to look at houses, many of them awful. Then we found OUR house; a grade two listed building in Faversham, Kent. It was spacious, with four floors and a long, generous garden. Future grandma cooked us a casserole for our first night alone together and treated us to a week's worth of groceries! We were home-owners! My boyfriend was upset with his Mum though, feeling critical of her 'interference', but I knew we couldn't have done it without her and astonished that he could mind. I was so happy with her attentions, tireless energy, generosity and willingness to get involved with us. I developed a huge affection for both these parents. I had no maternity clothes at that time, just pinned a tablecloth a certain way and wore that with pyjama trousers. We had little money but were inventive and relaxed about it. It didn't seem the most important thing.

'At home' things were difficult. Dad and J. were beginning to show signs of trouble in their relationship. He became increasingly dogmatic, overpowering and arrogant, picking on us all. I stayed sometimes and got to experience a few of his dysfunctional moments, no one was immune from his attacks. Recently, J. said it was a shame he thought being frightening was a way to communicate. I felt more and more resistant to and questioning of his authority, all I really wanted was his love and approval. To this day I've never got it, but I'm not alone in that. He became more and more bizarre and abusive, causing unbearable scenes and bullying all his children increasingly as time went on. We struggled individually and together to make sense of him. His second marriage was going into crisis.

Once, pregnant and having dinner, I couldn't finish my meal. He got aggressive about this, J stuck up for me. I found it hard to judge portion sizes as the baby's head was squashing my stomach. Dad began to attack J. Something welled up in me, I'd had enough. I stood up and shouted at him, telling him he was a 'bully' and a 'tyrant' that he 'dominated everyone.' I told him to stop putting J. down, she didn't deserve it. I think I told him to 'fuck off.' He said I was a 'witch' and hoped I'd have a miscarriage. Then he left for Dover, 'forever.' The younger kids cried and turned on me, but I was unrepentant. Years later J. told me that was the night she'd decided to leave him. To the kids' relief he came back later, joking that he'd left fifty pence on his desk and didn't want anyone to have it. No more was said.

In August 1983, Baby Polly was born in Canterbury. Pierre let us use his house while he took his family to France on holiday. This was a compromise with the medical establishment as it was against their policy to allow a first birth outside the hospital environment. This was hard to accept after the laid back atmosphere of the Dutch. No one was willing to budge, so it was agreed: we had to be near Canterbury hospital. Pierre's house was five minutes away.

The birth went well. My waters broke first thing in the morning, giving off the sweet smell of amniotic fluid, like rosewater. It was a lovely summer's day, the sun shone brightly so I spent some of my labour in the garden. I had a great birth team consisting of Luci, Jim, my boyfriend, little Kizzy, plus the midwife. Everyone was efficient and cheerful, lunch (which I couldn't eat) was provided by Luci. Everything just happened. All I had to do was concentrate on breathing, going with the mighty energy gathering in my body. It would be easy to be scared, but I had a key: surrender. I told myself, don't fight, or tense against the natural process happening in your body, relax! I gave no energy to what might go wrong. The only hitch was the arrival of a chatty back-up midwife, who ignored me and got involved in conversation. Didn't she realize this was *my* day? My contractions stopped and we sent her off to wait in another room. She was not the first midwife we sent out over the years. Luci and I developed our own standard about our births. We were fussy and fierce, tolerating no fear or distraction that caused tension in the birth environment. I was out of bed the whole time, moving around until the last few minutes. Lying down, especially on your back, goes against gravity, it invites complications, making it harder for the baby to come down. Polly was born that night with a full head of black hair and an alert expression. Later Jim's auntie would call her 'the new Jesus', she seemed so aware and bright with her dark Chinese-looking eyes.

****

My man got himself into a musical circuit in Faversham, connecting with people and working at the nearby Arden theatre. He had unusual ways of dealing with life, getting surprisingly hung up and tense, making mountains out of molehills. He was extremely creative and perfectionist as well as an excellent musician and singer, but he wasn't handy with a screwdriver. Neither of us were. Nor were we domesticated, preferring late night discussions about the meaning of life to homemaking. We made an odd team. It became harder and harder to relate to each others' idiosyncrasies. Years later there was a suggestion he might have Asperger's Syndrome, a condition related to autism. This knowledge might have helped us make sense of some of our difficulties.

TENSIONS. Things were complicated for me after we moved into our new home. Dad and J. came every Sunday for a while, bringing bottles of wine. They admired Polly and were enthusiastic about the house, but I hated their visits. Dad terrified me with his irrationality. Looking back, it's touching that they came. I had no idea then how much upset I was carrying in myself after my rootless childhood. It was not the best foundation from which to build a home. My man and I didn't have the faintest idea how to be domesticated and settled. It seemed impossible just to sit in a house with one person and a demanding baby. We started to argue. During one of our exchanges he phoned his mother. I tried to stop him phoning, feeling his relationship with her was too dependent; after all I didn't need my mother! He pushed me away. In the scuffle I fell and tore a ligament. The result? Ten days of bed rest with time to think. A kind neighbour lent me a book about Atlantis, a primal therapy community on the island of Innisfree in Ireland.

I'd never heard of a place like it. As soon as I'd read the book I wanted to visit. It sounded exciting and radical, a whole new way of thinking about things. In many ways I'm typical of my generation, the so-called Baby Boomers. This era, from the mid 40's to the beginning of the sixties produced a generation whose thought processes were significantly different to the war generation before them. It is fascinating how kids are brought up differently from one generation to the next. As a loose generalization, the Baby Boomers had a distrust of systems, an interest in individualism, and in the 'real self' (vague as that may sound). There was a growing exploration of psychology, imagination, intuition, freedom, inner, rather than outer authority. Our generation had experienced more material stability than our parents and were now in reaction against *their* preoccupation with security. At this time emerged 'New Age' thinking, an explosion of ideas and alternative values drawn from a range of influences, spiritual, religious and scientific. The musical 'Hair,' on stage in 1967, was an example of the seeds of it's emergence into mainstream culture. Its opening song 'This is the dawning of the Age of Aquarius' expressed the current astrological understanding that a new era was beginning. The media now ridicule the more 'woolly' sides of this individualistic movement, with its crystal reading and other wacky pursuits. Yet to many at the time, these numerous ways of exploring consciousness answered some of the deeper questions about life. I found it fascinating. As a twenty-something year old I threw myself head first into everything going, finding therapies and workshops that interested me. Some of it I rejected, much of it changed me forever.

****

With the next cycle of babies to be born it would all swing again. Values would change beyond recognition. Nowadays our children are looking for security, nice homes, being fed up with the spontaneity and free living that their 60's and 70's influenced parents had inflicted on them. They are still too young to evaluate the good bits and in many ways as reactionary as we were, but the other way! So it goes on. It cannot be denied that the time and environment in which you grow up influences who and what you become.

Typical of the 'New Age' movement was to value 'caring' and 'relationship' more than material security. To us, back then in the 'Age of Aquarius,' achievement was less important than people's 'being.' We watched the Beatles change with us, becoming psychedelic and cosmic. There seemed to be a sensitive balance to attain between the inner and outer if people were not to be neurotic and therefore destructive. In those days people were afraid of a nuclear war that would wipe out the human race. CND (Campaign for Nuclear

Disarmament) was on the upsurge. The Vietnam War and subsequent bloodbaths had already horrified a generation. We wanted the bomb banned and everything put right! A culture that is fundamentally neurotic does not bode well for mankind, so we set out to heal ourselves and do whatever we could to change society for the better!

Sitting at home was not for me, I felt hungry for experience. There was so much going on out there, many things I'd never heard of. Fed up with bickering with my man, I decided I'd had enough domestication. Just six weeks after Polly was born, we were off! We left our house with a pram, a tent, a couple of rucksacks and sleeping bags. Neither of us could drive, so we took the train and headed for Hampshire, sometimes carrying Polly and putting all our stuff in the pram. The plan was to camp in beautiful grounds, where the Indian teacher Jiddu Krishnamurti was giving talks in a marquee. A speaker and writer on spiritual and philosophical subjects, he spoke on human relationships, positive change in society, meditation, peace, awareness and had himself been proclaimed an incarnation of Maitreya Buddha. It was believed he was the 'vehicle' for a new world teacher and an organization, 'Order of the Star,' was set up to support his path. After being groomed for this destiny, aged 34, he shocked his followers by dissolving the organization and rejecting his role as a spiritual leader, asserting that truth was a 'pathless land.'

I loved his writings; he became one of my influences at that time.

Camping was tricky with a baby. Our little girl had to lie on my stomach all night to fit us in our tiny tent! In spite of the discomfort, we were happier living outdoors, with lots of people to talk to and good vegetarian food cooked by someone else....

During one of his talks Krishnamurti suddenly paused, noticing Polly, who was the only baby in the audience. She was the example of something he was talking about, so she was passed around the room, her tiny head of black hair moving away from us! She was happy, smiling obligingly at the cooing strangers, giving a perfect baby performance, centre stage, a typical Leo at six weeks old! We did get her back, eventually.

Luci and Jim were abroad, having their own adventures; we kept in touch. They decided to join us and experience something of Krishnamurti. Luci was not impressed by this serious man droning on about reality, truth and consciousness, though Jim was more interested. Later we all returned to Holland, where Jim and Luci had found a flat. My boyfriend wanted to busk around Germany, but I couldn't face it. My adventurousness had turned to tiredness; it was hard work being a new mum! I wanted to stay with my sister. It was not that easy: she had her own burdens, being a new mum too. We were overwhelmed by our own responsibilities. Little Kizzy, interested in the 'sparkle' in Polly's eyes, wanted to poke her fingers in them all the time. Luci was stressed with so many people in her house. After my man had taken some time out to busk for three weeks.... we reluctantly returned to England.

Dad had bought a studio in Canterbury where he did some of his work. Kizzy named it 'The Stripey House' because of its striking beams. While working there, he noticed his wife's car parked across the road a lot and wondered why. He chose to investigate, discovering J. was having an affair with a woman he referred to ever after as 'the Reptile.' Fidelity in marriage was by then a condition for him, things had changed since his Ndola days! At the very least he wanted honesty if there was attraction to another. There was a confrontation. He made the *entire family* come with him to 'The Reptile's' home. There we met a thin, plain woman with short brown hair, who stood quietly, saying nothing, just observing the raging husband and six confused kids. No matter. Dad had more than enough words for both of them! He wanted to show her the family she'd ruined. He also wanted our indignation, for us to back him up in his distress. We did feel for him. We felt for everyone! But we were unwilling to take sides, wanting the adults to communicate and work things out themselves. Pierre, being upset, became less and less flexible. He shut his heart and threw J. out, unwilling to examine any of the deeper issues behind this triangle. It seems our stepmother had become lesbian, we were not allowed to ask about her. 'The Reptile' bowed out gracefully and all the kids were left with Dad. Our ex-step-mother felt undeserving and incapable of motherhood. Confused, hurt, guilty and relieved to be free, she was too traumatized, paralyzed to take action around her children. So she just disappeared from their lives for a while.

Dad fell apart behind a front of competence. He would sit at the kitchen table for hours, drinking wine, ranting to anyone willing to listen. Our hearts ached. His wife had an affair with another woman: it was a lot to deal with. Dad had no time for anyone's feelings but his own, hostile and vicious about J., encouraging his kids to turn against her. Then he began to accuse Jim of having flirted with his now ex-wife. He became convinced Jim had touched her inappropriately and banned him from visiting. He would listen to no one and began to worry his four kids there was truth in this story. It was only years later they realized stress had brought on this paranoia, which got worse.

This period, when Dad was alone with the kids, is full of terrible stories. Particularly the youngest experienced things that she cannot talk about even now. For a while it was she and another sister living with Dad, after the others left home: together they experienced serious neglect, the youngest cutting her own arm in desperation to get some real attention. Dad was too afraid to take her to hospital in case social services intervened. He doesn't really communicate with any of us any more. He has married a librarian, C., a strange, sour, hostile woman who pulls him away from people he meets in the street; she turns all of us away when we try to visit. They hardly ever answer or return phone calls, unless I do my 'technique,' leaving so many messages they have to call, just to stop me clogging up their machine!

Dad also changed his name. He has cut himself off from virtually everyone in his past, refusing recently even to see one of his twin sisters, who had come all the way from Beirut. She was very hurt. There is so much more: I got Social Services involved, after discovering Pierre had had a serious fall, perhaps a stroke. They investigated to see if C. had some kind of sinister intent towards a vulnerable man, but data protection does not allow intrusion. The doctor advises Dad is being adequately taken care of by this C.

ATLANTIS AND LUCI'S SECOND CHILD_ Before things had got to this point, my sister gave birth to Minna, in the 'Stripey house.' It was October 9th 1984. This time a homebirth was allowed; she was the second child and the house was near Canterbury hospital. Minna had the cord wrapped around her leg, causing mild distress, until the midwife had slipped it off. She used to fuss and agitate about her socks as a child and we'd wonder if there was a connection! My boyfriend, Polly and I arrived late, just after Minna had emerged safely. Second babies are easier to relate to, not such a shock as first time around! We read stories to and played with Polly and Kizzy, so Luci and Jim could bond with their newborn. Our girls soon became like sisters. The three of them see themselves that way, so much of their lives have been linked.

In 1985 my sister asked Evelyn and Charles to match the deposit for Gabi's house to buy themselves a home. They needed a travelling home to fit their lifestyle, so they bought a Leyland PD3/4 Southdown 'Queen Mary' Double Decker bus! Jim wanted to work as a musician and be a hands-on father. Luci and I expected the fathers of our children to be involved with their offspring. As 'committed' parents, we believed our children should have what we hadn't. We studied books on nutrition and childcare, sharing ideas and tips with each other, and created an extended family, spending lots of time together. In 1985 we all decided to take a trip to Ireland to explore Atlantis, the community I'd read about when I'd hurt my knee. My relationship with my boyfriend was getting more challenging: a therapy commune might do some good. So two couples with three kids boarded the bus! It had a kitchen sink, working Rayburn, toilet and beds. Jim and my man busked through England on violin and accordion, singing and performing together, but my boyfriend and I were getting on each other's nerves. An argument began, Luci took my side and that was it. He decided to run away, jumping off the bus. The kids were upset by this drama; Polly losing her voice for a few days from shock. He reappeared some days later and we continued our trek west to Atlantis. There we explored Psychometry, that is, holding an object and 'picking up' information from it, then speaking aloud or acting anything that came to mind. This evolved to 'psychic readings,' holding a piece of paper with a name written on it and expressing in the same way. Most of the time these spontaneous 'readings' were uncannily accurate, seemingly providing a portrait of that person's inner thoughts and feelings. After leaving Atlantis we developed a craze for readings, doing them over and over with family and friends. Our kids loved this 'game,' they never got tired of it!

Throughout my life I've proved to have a psychic streak. This connection seems quite open with Luci and also with Polly. We know when it's the other one on the phone; sense each other's thoughts, that kind of thing. In earlier years when Luci and I used to do Ouija sessions with Evelyn, I would feel some kind of 'force' that ended up scaring me. I was too young and immature to know what to do with it. We stayed at Atlantis for two wild weeks, experiencing a way of life unlike any we'd known before. We joined in all their activities and were challenged constantly by their habit of communicating everything inside them. They encouraged us to do the same. They liked us, inviting us to join the commune and journey with them on a wooden boat to South America where they intended to settle. We were tempted, but not quite ready for that level of commitment. The commune moved to Colombia where they've been ever since. On July 9th 2000 guerrillas murdered two of their 18 year-old boys, Tristan and Javier. We read the tragic news and could hardly believe it, moved by the courage and guts expressed by the remaining communards and wondered what we'd have been like if we'd joined them.

****

In 1986 Jim successfully auditioned for a job with an animal-free circus, 'Circus Burlesque,' in Frome, Somerset. Of course we visited them, spending fun summer days with our kids playing inside and outside the brightly coloured circus tent. At show times Jim warmed up the audiences by playing his violin, singing and playing the guitar. During the show he did the same again adding drums and playing his violin while riding a unicycle, to packed audiences! Luci sold healthy snacks during the intervals.

FIRE!

At this time none of us wanted to continue our lives in Kent. My boyfriend and I sold our house to do primal therapy, as championed by the Atlanteans, with a therapist in Brighton. Luci and Jim decided to go to Spain in their bus, to find a farm in the sun.

We got a good deal for our house and rented a flat on the fourth floor of a terraced house on Brighton seafront. Oddly it was the same date, mid March, as my deportation, that again I was to become front-page news in the local paper: First thing in the morning my boyfriend shook me awake saying the house was on fire. I thought he was joking until I looked out of the window: enormous orange flames were visible, licking outwards from the flats below us. A huge crowd had gathered outside to watch the drama. I had on a frayed white nightdress and nothing else, there was no time to dress. What I looked like vaguely crossed my mind but was erased by the consuming thought of getting us all out. We had to leave! The flat had a fire door which we opened cautiously to try going down the stairs. Billowing black smoke drove us back. Our fire escape was red hot so we couldn't get out that way. Promptly two fire engines arrived and we had a ladder to safety against our window! Polly was the first out, a tiny tot in a yellow 'teddy bear' sleep suit. She was totally obedient, sensing the urgency of the situation, going without fuss to the fireman. My boyfriend and I waited our turn to go down the ladder; worried the floor might give way under us. What a relief to go next!

I was embarrassed and relieved, going down the ladder in my nightdress with my protective fireman/hero behind me! I've loved firemen ever since. My boyfriend was the last to be rescued, each of us had to wait for a fireman to be with us in case we were disorientated and slipped or fell. Curiously, the night before I'd been doing an exercise from a book on free association. The idea was to write down all your thoughts for fifteen minutes. What came out sounded pretty crazy, I'd read the garbled result to my boyfriend: something about 'Nigel smoking' and a fire. Neither of us knew any Nigel, these fragments had seemed meaningless. We went to bed without giving it another thought.

When we reached the ground, during the fire, an ambulance was waiting. In it sat a dazed man with a soot-stained face. Introducing himself as Nigel... he explained with deep shame that he'd borrowed the downstairs flat for a couple of days on condition that he didn't smoke. He'd ignored the condition, had a cigarette in bed, fallen asleep and set fire to a pile of clothes left on the floor! We saw the second floor flat afterwards, black and eerie with melted phones like some nihilistic modern art piece.

Years later, when my fluffy long-haired cat Pickle disappeared, I felt her dying. In bed at the time, the feeling of her body convulsing in muddy water and leaves came to me. I felt a 'gold' light all around her and a very physical feeling that everything was ok. I was wide awake and said to Jim: "I know Pickle has died." The 'knowing' was strong. Some days later a friend found Pickle dead in a ditch, covered in mud and leaves.

Another time I woke having dreamt of a huge tree with an anguished face falling over and dying. I was telling the family about it and heard a massive crashing sound. We ran outside to investigate and found a large Ash tree, fallen over, for no apparent reason. There had been winds for some days, it might have had a disease, we never really knew why, nor did our neighbours.

*****

After eight months apart, Luci, Jim, kids, my boyfriend, and I, all decided to reunite. We'd kept in touch but our various journeys had absorbed us. My boyfriend and I had been through many changes. Our therapist was surprised we were still together; he didn't expect our relationship to last. I'd had my doubts almost the minute I'd got pregnant, yet clung to hope that things might improve. Strange how life and fears can distract you from doing what might have been better for you. A lot of our life was 'going with the flow' making spontaneous choices without much thought of consequences.

Luci and Jim had spent much of their time in Spain, in Orgiva. Luci, ill with pneumonia, was treated by a French healer en route. They travelled with their children, enjoying the sun, being together and getting to know the locals. When they'd had enough they came to Brighton, parking their bus where they could, near the Steiner School in Hollingbury. It seemed an attractive place under the trees, but turned out to be surprisingly rough. Vandals had fun breaking in by smashing a bus window, then trashing it upstairs and downstairs. Becoming public property was one of the hazards of a high profile mobile home. In another parking place a businessman got on, opened his newspaper and waited for 'service.' He ordered an egg butty, going through huge embarrassment when it dawned on him this wasn't a mobile café, he'd just gate-crashed someone's living room. We did offer to make him one anyway, but he couldn't leave fast enough!

Though we were still together, my man decided to move into a room of his own and despite all the hazards, I moved onto the bus. Our relationship was hanging by a thread. Polly spent time with each of us and we all still spent time together, but emotionally her parents were moving further and further apart.

THE NEW AGE In August we all left in our the bus (my boyfriend included) for Glastonbury, the 'heart chakra' of England, to be part of a New Age Spiritual event, 'The Harmonic convergence.' Groups were gathering worldwide at sacred sites and places of 'mystical' energy to experience a major 'energy shift' heralding a 'New Era of universal peace.' Actress Shirley Maclaine called the event a 'window of light' for the world. Whatever you thought of it, Glastonbury was a pleasant place to be. We sat at the top of Glastonbury Tor at the critical astrological moment, sunrise, with all our little children, waiting sleepily for golden light to emerge on the horizon. Warmed by the rising sun, we did feel moved and connected to everyone. Critics of the event called it 'the Moronic Convergence,' but we enjoyed being part of this peaceful, non-violent worldwide event.

Before we left Brighton, we decided to experiment with 'group visualization'. I'd always loved books and owned some on the theme of 'creating your own reality.' The 'New Age' hadn't yet become discredited as it has been now by the media – it was still fashionable to experiment and explore in many circles. We sat down together each night to affirm (say out loud) that we now had a beautiful house in the countryside. We'd agreed various details and stuck to this routine each evening. After we'd enjoyed the campsite in Glastonbury for a day or two, a couple of older campers decided they objected to our bus: we were asked to leave. Fed up, we drove down to the municipal car park, to park among rubbish bins swarming with summer wasps. There was a slight drizzle. A vivid rainbow appeared, arching from one full bin, across to another, cheering us up. At that moment another vehicle, a small van, drove in. Luci said, "This is it, our future..." We laughed about how right she'd been afterwards. Jim, ever friendly, rushed off to greet the newcomers. They turned out to be a couple who were looking for people to rent their house in Wales. It seemed our group visualization, conscious creation, had worked!

This couple, the G's offered us a change of location that has lasted over twenty years. We still live only miles from 'Panteg,' their home at the time. We arrived unaware how small and winding the roads would get, challenging in a double Decker bus! Trying to get into the G's driveway was a major operation: the first encounter with some of our neighbours was while blocking their route. After digging away some of the bank to widen the road, we got the bus into 'Panteg' driveway, where we stopped to wait for a month, as the couple prepared their live-in vehicle for a road trip to France.

Eventually the G's went and we were left to do our own thing. We grew vegetables, chopped wood, made candles, brought up our kids, had our 'feelings' and enjoyed socializing. There was a flow of people, experiences, trips and parenting that absorbed our time. Influences such as Atlantis and primal therapy had worked their way into our days, we were free and open about feelings – our own and other people's. There was an atmosphere of exploration and mutual sharing, young people having fun.

Of course, with my boyfriend and Jim around, there was also music. We did quite a lot with friends we'd met, going up to the nearby lake together, Luci and I taking the kids for trips out with them. One in particular, Paul, became someone we spent a lot of time with. No one noticed Luci was getting closer to him than the rest of us, not even his current girlfriend. One night Paul and Luci slept together.

Jim's world was rocked to the core. After that Luci moved into the bus in the garden. Jim, having to watch Paul visit her, was devastated, the children were confused.

Shortly before a friend had taught us 'Dynamic Meditation' as practised by Bhagwan Shree Rajneesh. It was a ritual that took an hour, involving breathing, catharsis (letting go and doing whatever you felt) chanting and meditating. We invited people to join us at 5.00am, before the kids woke up to do this everyday. When Luci left it was a lifeline, allowing Jim to cry, rage and explore all his intense emotions safely, within a structure. It was therapeutic for Jim to 'let it all out' and express his pain around others. We continued to do the dynamic meditation daily until October 1988. In this time both the couples that had moved into Panteg, had separated or were beginning this process.

CHANGES. For the first time in our lives Luci and I began to experience changes in our relationship. The emotional 'closeness' we'd taken for granted all our lives began to crumble. Luci stayed living outside the house, I lived with Jim and the kids inside. She and Paul had a different way of looking at things and it was not sympathetic to the 'house people.' Suddenly we found ourselves divided, into 'us' and 'them,' a mini war. One day Jim got so fed up he called the police. Of course this just increased bad feeling between us. We didn't really know where anything was going, we could only use our therapy techniques to deal with the emotions stirred up. Wales is said to have that effect on people, the elemental landscape and ancient hills stirring up primal energies in the psyche! We definitely felt raw and stripped of defences, as if our old skins were falling away.

*****

When the year was up I decided I'd had enough and travelled back to Brighton with Polly. My man had gone ahead for some civilization and culture! After the countryside Brighton seemed unsafe, dirty and noisy, with too many people too close together. I stayed a while but yearned for space and nature. I returned to Wales with Polly, to see how things were developing....

Jim had rented a room in a house up the road. A single man called S. lived there with his dog. For a while Luci was in the bus on her own. Then, moving into the same house as Jim she immediately became involved with S., a man not her type at all. Jim was not thrilled. It's interesting to look back and see how, no matter what dramas there were...we all kept coming back to each other. You might have thought we'd run a million miles away! Perhaps we would have, if there'd been no children.

Luci stayed with S. for five years and had a son, Llyr. At that time I began to feel I'd lost touch with her emotionally. She seemed distant, harder, less open. Sometimes the tensions between us became blazing arguments. Her relationship with S. confused me: she often said she didn't like him and didn't know why she was with him. Like a moth to a flame, I added to the crazy emotional hotpot by also moving into S.'s house. Eventually there were eleven people, three couples, Jim and four kids. This was the way things were then, relationships were formed and dissolved, in the spirit of the time. There was a large 'alternative' population drawn to our town, having in common this tendency to challenge social rules.

In the middle of this flux something significant fluttered between Jim and me. Living together in Panteg we'd developed a much deeper friendship. One cold night I'd 'borrowed' Jim's bedroom to sleep in, where I usually slept was icy-cold, Jim was out doing a gig, but it was cancelled. We ended up sharing a bed. To our surprise, an overwhelmingly sweet feeling opened up for both of us, like breathing honey through every part of our bodies, just from being near each other. It was not a sexual experience at the time. I was still (just about) with my boyfriend, so I told him. It was the way we were, communicating about everything. He wasn't pleased. Human nature being what it is, it blossomed into more. I had two 'boyfriends' for a while, a good experience for me!

Eventually my man had had enough. He told me to choose between them. It was obvious, our relationship on the rocks anyway, without hesitation I chose Jim, which plunged my man into jealousy. He roared, banged his head on the wall, verbally attacked and insulted Jim. We weren't surprised. After primal therapy, Atlantis and the dynamic meditation, we were used to intense behaviour, saw 'letting it out' as healthy. Sometimes things went too far. We believed in honesty and being 'real' but with children sensitivity was required. In the climate of opening everything up we all went way out of balance. It was a reactionary time. The effect of all this on our children took years to emerge...

FLUX AND ANOTHER BIRTH. After months of us all living together, Jim reclaimed his autonomy by moving into the woods in the bus. I would walk several miles to visit him, day or night. It was a pleasure walking through the dark woods, even at night.

Little did I know that beneath the freedom from fear I felt at this time was a 'shadow side,' fears and vulnerabilities, packed away inside me, which would one day catch up. For now, we carried on with our 'crazy' ways, Polly, Kizzy and Minna were bundled together in an imposed sisterhood. Though they adored each other and had many benefits from their interactions, it was difficult for each of them. Polly had to adapt from centre of attention as an only child, to being one of a group. Kizzy and Minna had to adapt to her being around a lot more, to a new half brother, Llyr, *and* a new man in their mother's life. Until Jim moved out they had Daddy and step Daddy in the same house, Mummy and sister, who was now with Daddy... Polly had Daddy and Mummy, but Mummy had switched to Jim. Yet, Jim was Kizzy and Minna's Daddy. This conflict-producing mish-mash, broke down normal boundaries.

The positive side was plenty of contact, with none of the loneliness of nuclear family units. Everything was mutable and in flux, the adults so busy experimenting, it didn't occur to us the kids might feel differently about the ultimate value of all this. We didn't even think about the positive aspects of security and stability. We assumed as long as we were there, our kids would be fine. We gave them what we would have wanted, taking it for granted that it was right for them. There *are* things I would do very differently now, with the benefit of hindsight.

I was pregnant again. Pablo was born in April 1990, also at home. We wanted a water birth, but hiring a tub was expensive. So we bought a large children's swimming pool to put in an annex adjacent to my bedroom. The birth went well, apart from having to exclude the midwife, a kind, muddled, short-sighted ex sheep farmer who was getting too old for midwifery, forever fumbling, mumbling and dropping things. When we found another medical syringe under the Welsh dresser we knew we needed to take charge. We'd all done background reading on the subject of birth so were informed, having a passion for medical encyclopedias and books on health. e took matters into our own hands, asking the midwife to leave the room during the birth unless there was an emergency. Luckily there wasn't. Luci took charge and nature took its course. Polly, Kizzy and Minna joined Jim and me in the birthing pool. We had floating candles, the girls got into a party mood, giggling and eating green grapes. The warm water and happy atmosphere did wonders for my contractions. The atmosphere was relaxed, informal yet focused and finally Pablo's head and chest emerge; I'd been in labour about eight hours. Our baby hung suspended in the water, half in and half out of his mother. In the candlelight, the blue of the pool on his yellow hair made it look green as it waved in the water. We were all quiet, watching him. One more push and he was out.

We moved back into the bus in the woods with a contented and relaxed baby boy who seemed to love the trees with their fascinating rustling leaves. We had a peaceful and nurturing time, close to nature and all together. Five months later we were on the road again.

My ex boyfriend had a new partner who later bore him twins and a second son. Wherever Polly went there was a newly established family, where she felt like an outsider, working to belong, an echo of GabiLu's background. I worked hard to understand and to help her feel more central, valued and important.

Luci and S., also holidaying in Spain, met up with us to deliver Kizzy and Minna for 'our turn'. We parked the bus on the edge of a scrubby hillside. The kids played out on the hot dry earth while goats trekked up and down, bells jingling round their necks. The three girls were so creative, they never ran out of ideas for new games, amusing themselves dressing Pablo as a girl and taking photos of their efforts.

One detail had been overlooked: we discovered later there was no film in the camera!

****

Many foreign hippies had settled in the area. A young couple, one German and an Israeli, had a communal bath with their kids in a nearby hippy house. We were thinking of doing the same thing.

They went first. No one realized something was wrong with the gas-fired water heater. There was a dangerous build up of gas, the family began to slide into unconsciousness. Luckily one of the adults summoned enough strength to crawl to the door, let air in and save everyone's lives. The whole event took place just meters from the bus and had eerie overtones - the German/Jewish connection and the gas. It added to a dark feeling around Orgiva. I couldn't wait to leave the place.

We headed for the coastal village of Nerja for a change of mood and scenery, swimming in the sea and playing some tunes. It was the end of the season, the sun was weaker, more watery, and less hot. Everything felt tired, especially me, with Pablo only six months old and still breastfeeding. I needed to recover from my whole life: I could have lain on the beach resting forever! Having been on the move so long I didn't recognize the need to stop. Driving back to Britain slowly, the trip took a couple of months. On arrival in Wales we delivered the girls on Christmas Eve, my birthday.

In summer 1991 we set off on a tour around England with young Pablo and a new child in my belly. Yes, I was pregnant again!

WALES AND SPAIN   In Wales we lived a while parked next to tranquil Llanfair Lake, waking up to swim in undisturbed waters in the morning, often retreating to our bus when the crowds turned up. For the birth we rented a holiday cottage 'Felin Gogoyan'. After six months Pablo had become attached to the house, but it was time to leave. He stood firm and rigid in the doorway, making his one and a half year old protest, blocking the landlady from entering and us from exiting. She was amused and patient, letting him be passionate about his tiny cause.

Saba was born in November 1991, again a home and water birth, only we had no time to get into the tub. Pablo had woken up in the night, sitting up and shouting 'Girl!' Soon afterwards Saba shot out like a rocket.... we managed to start filling the tub but she couldn't wait. There was no midwife, only Jim, my friend Irene and of course me, rocking, squatting, on all fours, waiting for the next contraction and out she came! I thought I was waiting to go into the water, but I was giving birth! Jim just managed to catch her. Luci turned up not long afterwards with the three girls, having missed the whole thing. Polly, by chance, was staying the night with her. Finally the midwife arrived. Our doctor turned up to administer stitches, while Jim bonded with his beautiful new daughter. The doctor pulled on her surgical gloves, ready to begin. Luci who'd just been on a midwifery course, had a quick look and asked, 'does she really need stitches?' The doctor looked puzzled. Then slowly, sheepishly, to her credit, she removed her surgical gloves. 'Not really,' she admitted. The GabiLu birth team had triumphed once again!

Apart from situations like these, my relationship with Luci was strained. We were outwardly normal with each other but something had changed. We had become critical of each other, less at ease. We were also busier with our growing families and complex relationships with current men and exes. I found it a challenge having two infants under three. 'Baby Factory,' was developed for simultaneous nappy changing, Jim doing one child and me the other. As Jim was still a musician, he had time to be a hands-on father. We suffered none of the estrangement that many couples complain of, spending most of each day together, sharing experiences. The love we felt for each other was the centre of our life. We were almost equally involved in childcare, whether it was our two, or my three, or our five. Those were the permutations. Sometimes my ex took Polly. Luci and S. cared for Kizzy and Minna. Pablo and Saba we had all the time. We were one big extended family, all interconnected. Even so, there were growing tensions.

At last, in 1992, we found a house, 'Esgair Las'. The liberal-minded landlord had let the place to lesbian tenants before us, who had lived rent free, then later to a couple who paid rent by doing home improvements. Our landlord was a conservationist, easy-going and flexible and didn't mind the bus, allowing us to park it in the garden where it made a good venue for children's birthday parties. People either loved or hated that bus: one crazed woman in Kent had called it 'an abortion,' perhaps she meant 'abomination.' She was furious it was parked in a residential street with people living in it. Others would run out to meet us smiling and give us gifts. The Spanish were especially generous, making a fuss of us in our unusual home. In late summer of 1992 there was another trip, this time with Pablo and Saba to Northern Spain. The busking was excellent until disaster struck: Pablo fell on Jim's fiddle, smashing it. The sympathetic Spanish public helped us find a violin repairman: the tragedy was undone.

We made good money that summer; everyday our table in the bus was heavy with so many coins that we opened a Spanish deposit account. The bank was amused when we hauled in our bags of cash and impressed when they saw what the fiddle player could make!

The kids and I always went out busking with Jim. I hated staying at home cleaning the house. I'd read them stories and take care of them out there in public, even breastfeeding Saba, I wasn't shy. Sometimes the crowds took more interest in the woman and the cute blonde babies than in Jim. Once he stopped playing to join *them* watching *us*; the crowd loved that! Jim could be an incredible comedian, each show a one-off. I never knew when the urge to play up to the crowd would hit him. It all depended on their reactions and what was happening around him. Drunks and oddballs could be material for his spontaneous shows. He attracted huge crowds and a party atmosphere developed, people came to gush about how much they envied our lifestyle, not knowing how hard it could sometimes be. You had to have all kinds of strategies to cope with the lifestyle, endless energy and alertness, you couldn't switch off for a second.

By this time all three of GabiLu's parents, Pierre, Evelyn and Charles, were united by a common disrespect for our lifestyle. J. our stepmother, was the least judgmental, but she was living with a woman, so had made a non-mainstream lifestyle choice herself.

After a prosperous summer we drove the bus back to Esgair Las, to spend autumn in Cellan, with its wonderful trees and peace. But soon we were back in Spain to earn money for Christmas.

This time we took the car and caravan, judging the bus too much work. It was slowly sinking into the mud in our garden and would be an effort to get out of the drive. The caravan would be easier to travel in,... but we were wrong, it was much too small! It required military precision with four kids, (Polly stayed in Brighton with her father) two under five, and two adults. We couldn't get any space from each other. I made the girls sit without their feet hanging over their beds so they wouldn't kick the younger ones in the head.

This trip made me irritable and tense. There was too much washing up and so many clothes to wash; we had babies in nappies, making messes everywhere. It was noisy with all that chatter *and* it was snowing, the caravan walls were cold to touch, like living in a fridge. We only had ourselves to blame for our choice, but being a couple we blamed each other!

Back in the city of Vigo, during a busking act, we made a cardboard sign asking if anyone had a house to rent. In half an hour we had a first floor flat. Our hosts welcomed us warmly with small gifts, an embroidered handkerchief, toys and food. They were lovely, baby-sitting our kids and coming round often to check if we needed anything. We were accepted as the busking family, becoming minor celebrities in the town centre where Jim played. Sometimes Jim was offered a gig in a shop, bar or restaurant.

We stayed in Spain for Christmas and the New Year, but oddly it was melancholy. We were sad that Polly wasn't there and that we didn't really know anyone. The Spanish did celebrations with extravagance and flair, the streets exploded with people and vibrancy at midnight on New Years Eve. We joined in, aware that we had no family or real friends out there, which made us feel isolated and gave us a subtle attack of the blues.

We set off to Spain again, in the Spring, with all the girls. This time we went to a campsite in Lekeitio, a beautiful village on the northern coast. Polly was with us. During that trip 'The Brilliant Girls,' a busking act devised by Jim, was a hit. Everyone was charmed by the family and Polly's performance in particular was commented on. But some of the trip was spoiled by my health: I was suffering abscesses and intense toothaches. That was just the beginning of a severe health challenge that became serious for years.

We returned to Wales in October 1994, our travelling life ended. From then, until March 2003 we stayed at 'Esgair Las'. It's the longest I've ever settled in one place.

ILLNESS By this time Luci and S. had separated acrimoniously. She'd had a fling with his best friend, so their relationship ended abruptly, almost overnight. S. turned to Jim and me to help him make sense of this abandonment; we had seen it coming, but couldn't warn him, he wouldn't have believed it. Besides, my own relationship with Luci was still difficult. But like all members of my family, including my parents, I could be upset by and love someone at the same time. I had many emotions, which seemed to be springing forth in conjunction with my illness. The energy I was giving to parenting also took its toll. I gave it my all, but missed a sense of family of origin support in the background. The buried pain in my own life was knocking, but I tried to ignore it. I began a strict healing regime, consulting various medical professionals the world over, to try and make sense of my health problems. I began to understand what dying might feel like. It was dramatic. Everything was going wrong in my body. My legs were weak. I couldn't walk down the slightest slope. I had boils, ulcers and abscesses, as well as an almost permanent intense headache combined with a kind of buzzing sound. Sometimes I'd find it hard to form a word or sentence, my brain felt scrambled. I had such intense ear aches I lost some hearing permanently in my right ear; I still have to turn the other ear more toward someone to really hear them. I felt nauseous all the time, dizzy and 'wonky' if I moved my head too suddenly. I had terrible chest pain, yellow fingers and keratin growths on my feet. There was unbelievable bone pain, as if someone was drilling through my jaw with a red-hot drill.

Six of my teeth crumbled away, leaving unattractive gaps that embarrass me to this day. My energy felt so low as if my batteries had run out. I was used to having plenty of vitality.

One theory offered by my dentist was sensitivity to mercury that contributed to my health breakdown. There were also other factors. There are four files of papers in the attic filled with research I did on my problem. I decided to follow the mercury theory. My doctor had written 'mercury poisoning' on my file, considering I had fillings, the most likely source. So I consulted a Dr Levenson in London and had a test for body burden of mercury. The result indicated a significant level of mercury. A German laboratory confirmed this.

A routine was developed to support my liver and clean my blood of toxins. I have to keep to it, eat certain foods, mostly vegetables and organic vegetable juices to keep symptom free. I still have subtle problems with energy levels, but have come a long way since then. At the time I became ill, Luci and her new man were hostile and challenging about my 'problems.' Their conclusions about me didn't fit my feelings at all: communication broke down more and more, the relationship with my sister felt bleak. She seemed to me capable of being a real bitch, not that we don't all have our moments. I began to dislike her. But I never stopped loving her. All I wanted was to love and be loved by my family. It could all be so simple, but it's not. That's the strange thing. Life is full of conundrums that we should be able to solve but can't at times. Sometimes I hated Luci. It is said that hate is 'blocked love.' There seems to be truth in that.

Life in Esgair Las, involved parenting and 'counselling;' at least that's what people said I was doing. Some part of me seemed to collect people in need of help and support. Luci's new man said I was 'empathetic to a fault.' I found I had a flair for saying or doing just the right thing that could help someone with a difficulty in their lives. People urged me to get professional training and set up some kind of practice.

I didn't have time! I had too many children to care for and people who needed help. My health issues made me insecure about setting up anything away from home. It was necessary to be near the foods and equipment I needed. So the years at Esgair Las were devoted to my children, my own health and giving to others. I stayed still for the first time ever. It was a major learning experience. I got my most troubling symptoms under control. There was tendency to retch and vomit if I didn't stick strictly to this program. On my hands, under my rings, my skin was bleeding and rotting. What bothered me was my huge weight gain: I ballooned to about 16 stone. To his credit, Jim adapted to all of this, staying loving and affirming no matter how I mutated! Luci seemed disgusted by me. We grew further apart. I felt abandoned by my family, finding it hard to explain my life to anyone or reach out for help. My childhood had taught me to be independent. But one person I *had* been allowed to lean on, and her on me, was Luci. Now she'd had enough of 'us'... she certainly didn't want any part of my sordid problems!

Apart from all this, life was idyllic for the kids. They could roam free in the countryside and had plenty of friends to be with. We had time to give them attention. At first the three girls were often there and we were a family of seven. The girls created complex imaginative games; we had no television, computer or phone then, not even a washing machine. We had a joke of a cooker brought in from the bus. When we upgraded to a second hand dishwasher we had to wedge it shut each night with an axe. But no one cared, we had each other! There were great trees to climb, water holes to swim in, places to create dens or 'horse's stables' and 'pig pens' using junk that could be left out for days. There were no neighbours to offend or disturb.

Polly liked to initiate games of 'orphans' and 'poor little match girls in Victorian times.' She'd play 'woodchucks' with the little ones, leading Pablo and Saba over hill and dale in search of natural objects to collect, bossing them about happily. Or they would sit and draw or write poems and stories. Polly initiated long, elaborate projects that could take days. She loved organizing plays and dances and boss the others around. Saba was once cast as a doll, sitting silent and still with rouged cheeks the whole performance. At Esgair Las, we'd have meals outside on sunny days, or take the kids up to nearby Llanfair Lake to swim. Pablo and Saba had an incredible bond, Saba's nature the perfect complement to his. She has always been loving, patient and accommodating, both are affectionate and at ease with each other. They seem very wise and 'real' to me. One by one the girls have left home; each time we'd sob over their empty rooms. Now there are Pablo, Saba and often Llyr, Luci's son; he comes to stay, our bond goes way back and he entertains us with his surrealist sense of humour.

Polly too has stayed nearby, doing an acting degree, with a chance to use her variety of talents. We have a close relationship, sharing many aspects of our lives. Already her tutors have spotted her outstanding potential. I've no doubt she has what it takes to do whatever she sets her mind on. All three girls show great inventiveness and resourcefulness in their now independent lives.

With all our children, we'd a policy of allowing them to choose whether or not to go to school. We read, among others, John Holt's books 'How Children Learn,' and 'How Children Fail.' He argues that children learn naturally and don't need regulation, interference or control. He sees home not as an alternative to school, but as the best place to be educated no matter how good the school. His writings formed the basis of the 'un-schooling' movement. We felt it important that our children, unless they wanted it otherwise, be allowed authority over their own lives. This freedom of choice has been subtly undermined through ridicule by the media: home schooling is presented as creating 'geeky' and socially maladapted children, a distortion that makes people more reluctant to differ from the mainstream. We had no T.V, computers, and read few newspapers at the time, we were immune to this conditioning.

We left our children free to choose. Kizzy did chose school, loving the structure and daily routine. Polly and Minna both preferred to have days off every week. The school was in those days, surprisingly relaxed about this, as they liked the girls who produced high quality work no matter their attendance. All the girls got good exam results. Kizzy received the £250 A level prize. Polly was so good at art she did her GCSE'S early and got an A,* the highest. Pablo and Saba both tried school intermittently. Pablo only really began properly at fourteen, then went everyday and passed his GCSE's with excellent results. Saba started at thirteen and showed the same flair.

In 1994 we began a business, offering a telecommunications service, which neither of us knew anything about. In August 1995 Jim bought his first business suit and in 1996 our first computer. Financial life became more complicated as our business grew, stress levels increased. But we learnt to overcome all kinds of challenges and making it through the first three years. After surviving the crucial first years we began to expand into electricity and gas. The business has become more interesting as we move into more 'green' and environmentally aware projects. Before that, one of the main companies we were doing business with was Enron. By late 2001 it was involved in a scandal that rocked the financial world. 'Something is rotten in the state of Enron', stated the New York Times. The company had manipulated accounting rules, hiding the extent of their indebtedness. Enron was forced to file for bankruptcy in 2001. We lost a significant amount of money which had an effect on our business for some time.

We carried on, hanging on in there, each year our strength increased as the business grew. Problems from the past were dealt with. Although we weren't prepared for some of the exasperating aspects of business slowly we understood more and more, some of it sobering; in the end we have the satisfaction of overcoming obstacles and becoming increasingly independent.

Meanwhile Evelyn, by now separated from Charles, had found a new man, Alan who, finally, gave something real to her life. It was inspiring to see how vitality began to return in her. There is nothing that helps a person blossom more than being loved. Alan challenges stereotypes of ageing, encouraging interaction with a wide variety of people and enthusiastically embracing new projects and adventures all over the world. Evelyn's concern nowadays is that they don't overdo it, as they tend to do more than the average twenty year old!

Charles has also found love, with a woman about my age, whom I've not met.

THE 12-STEP PROGRAM.
The thing that was out of control in my life was still my relationship with Luci. Life wants movement and growth, the alternative is stagnation. For a couple of years my sister and others were causing concern, so much so that Jim and I signed up for a twelve-step program twice, not because *we* had a drug problem, but because others in the family had. We were taught (at the twelve-step program), that if we felt affected by an issue, it was *our* problem. There was much to learn: about family dynamics, dysfunctional relationships, addiction, boundaries, anger, self care, games, manipulation, enabling, people pleasing, co-dependency, forgiveness, caring, giving, self deception, denial; many things that helped us make some sense of subtle chaos and darkness settling over what had seemed to be something mutually beneficial and reciprocal between us and my sister's side of the family. We'd assumed we'd had a healthy dynamic between us, it was a lie. We had not. Some things I cannot detail here as there are issues of privacy were spiralling seriously out of control. I began to feel very strange, hurting about my sister and her way of relating to members of her family. I couldn't reach her, she was like a stranger.

No matter how well someone can put on a front, our childhood continues to run on inside us all. We can deny, transcend, push away, overcome things, but always there's an effect. Our childhood issues were catching up and it was time to look, to face areas of low self-esteem and worthlessness.

Jim and I continued to reach out to the twelve-step family program for support. In matters of addiction, no matter how much a family member may wish it, no-one can force anyone to take part, it has to be a free choice. Our counsellors advised taking the focus off others, putting it on ourselves, stressing self-care. The concept felt difficult to me, it was hard to admit I needed some even though I was feeling physically and emotionally exhausted. Problematically, as my own

314

confusion increased I was getting better at offering support and care to others. I was good at this, using everything I learned in all the courses. Unfortunately, like any house built on unstable foundations, something had to give way. My strength was masking weakness, the two existing intertwined like snakes. My nurturing ability was a role, a compensation for my own lack and pain. I was giving what I'd not really had, but wished I'd had, attracting more and more people to care for, friends in addition to my children. Everyone seemed to need mothering or help, a world full of people in distress looking to me for support.

As the giving increased I was getting emptier and emptier. My background had taught me to just get on with it, losing touch more and more with what I needed. That twelve-step family program began to reveal truths about myself that I was reluctant to face.

It was complicated. I had become mystified and confused about my worth and identity doubting all my own perceptions as a way to try to end the feeling of nothing making sense. The twelve-step program helped me to validate my own perceptions, allowing me to reclaim my own truth. I learned to accept that I was powerless over others, there I had no control there. So began the harder job of coming to terms with myself and take control of my own life.

Demons. There are days in your life when you are required to face your demons, no matter how much you try to get out of it. Days when you run slap bang into something you don't want. You are thinking your day is about one thing, but really it's about something else. January 15th 2002, was my demon-facing day. I had a serious argument with my sister which had roots in the events which as I said, for privacy reasons cannot be detailed here. This argument changed our relationship permanently.

There'd been increased strain between us over Christmas. There was a coldness coming from her; contempt for who I am emerged during that argument which can still activate painful shame in me. I was subjected to a tirade of venom and cruelty from which I tried to defend myself, but couldn't. I was so vulnerable at that time that my strength left me, I had no assertiveness left. Tired and sad, all I had left was pain and exhaustion. But Luci was fuelled by some purpose and mission to reject me. I seemed to disgust her. She became completely cold. I'd never seen her like it. We'd argued before, sometimes ferociously, but there was no contact, this was new. There was no Mediterranean passion here, the kind of healthy 'air clearing' that makes everyone closer. I was floundering in a sea of toxic treacle. I was really

315

drowning. I could find no handle on what was happening, no ground to hold me up. Wanting compassion from someone ice cold and full of hate for me my mind was working hard to find an explanation. What did she need? I couldn't find any softness in her. Jim was also bewildered. Luci announced I was 'banished' from her life. It was over. For two weeks it was hard to look anyone in the eye, I felt like the 'unclean,' worthless, contaminated, despised and grieving. It was like an amputation. Though we'd had years of estrangement, we were still entwined at the root, like two parasites, sustained by the blood of each other. I felt as if a heartless axe-man had chopped us apart, without concern for the bleeding and physical pain.

There was no one left, I was alone. Though my intellect knew it was all rubbish, that such behaviour is its own call for help, Gabi had fallen. I had uncovered a vulnerable, hurt, worthless child in me, afraid, alone and in need. I sensed that behind Luci's bravado and show of disdain she might feel the same.

There is an African saying that translates something like this 'I am because you are, you are because we are.' For me it was more like 'I'm not because you're not, you're not because we aren't!' Our culture of independence hides some truth, that we affect each other, we're interdependent and we need each other. There are invisible strands of connection that we rupture at our peril. That year Luci and her man experienced a similar 'blood bath.' It was almost a relief to know she was off attacking somebody else. For me trust was gone and has never really returned.

Something was changed forever.

WOUNDS, HEALING AND MOVING ON. Now it was my turn to be derailed. Throughout life, when I've felt bored, tense, frightened, stressed, lonely, unloved, confused, unsure, isolated, rejected, I've turned to words. Words are my friends. They can entertain, relax, comfort, inform, reassure, enlighten, connect and make me feel I belong. They have been a security, giving form to the formless, making sense of the chaotic, helping me feel safer when the world gets too much. Words can be hunters, capturing truths, tracking down what escapes. Our attic bulges with books, journals and magazines by the stack. Yet for all their power to define, express, clarify, bridge, convey passion, energy, aliveness, words are not life. They are not people. No matter how much I root around in words, digging deep to examine something, its people I long to trust, reach out to, be with and love.

Words had finally failed me. They would not reach the place my sister had opened up in me. It was a psychological wound hurting like a physical wound. Words couldn't heel a place *that* raw. I felt knocked by another family rejection into hopelessness and despair. It was the same loss and grief I'd felt about Dad over the years.

I spent a couple of years on a creative writing course with the playwright Dic Edwards. Unendingly generous, with time and praise, he is supporting me writing a book, an agonizing process, I don't know why. My sister once said to me that writing is 'for lonely people.' It does make me feel alone, facing my own mind and myself. There's something weird about it, yet satisfying, when you manage to express something you didn't know you thought!

The children I've brought up, the partner I've talked to for nearly thirty years, these people love me unconditionally. With them I find relief from the fear and uncertainty inside: 'little Gabi' who sits in me, living on, despite the years passing. It's up to me now. I have to provide for myself love, patience, tenderness and time. I got a therapist and started to work with a new technique developed for trauma victims, EMDR.

Evelyn is the only parent figure still to make contact and I'm grateful for that. She really wants something new, after all the years of estrangement. Slowly we are getting to know each other and find out we are just flesh and blood. Pain, generational distress, patterns of abandonment, all the muck and mire of being human has led me, after all these years, to a simple truth: no matter how messed up we are, how much there is to learn, how wrong we can get it…we are all in this together. The teacher Louise Hay once said, 'It's not 'them' and 'us.' It's all 'us.'

I've decided not to turn away from my sister, even if she turned away from me. I'll take care of myself *around* my sister, do things differently, look out for myself and do the best I can 'a day at a time,' as the twelve-steppers say. Luci will do what she does. Sometimes we connect, then I feel she has mellowed and changed. Other times I back off, knowing when things are not moving in the direction that is right for me. I can only hope one day we understand each other better, if we don't, so be it.

On July 3rd 2002 Polly gave birth to Leela, my first grandchild. It was another successful home and water birth. This time Luci wasn't there, but Polly's partner Jack, along with Pablo, Saba, Jim and I, were. The birth went well, Polly made lots of noise that must have been heard across the tiny village of Rhydowen. Born easily, caught by her Daddy Jack, (now a loved member of our family), in the water, Leela soon lay peacefully at her mother's breast, in the tub. Daughter of my daughter!

Incredible. Twelve-year old Pablo said the birth was 'the most amazing thing' he'd ever seen.

This baby girl helped my emotional life, drew me out of the desolation I felt, her tiny life an affirmation that life, even mine, goes on. All the kids help too of course, but Leela's newness accelerated this change. Her birth was a reminder that life springs back fresh and full of hope, her raw need pulled me out of self-absorption. I made a leap in myself to fully embrace everything again.

*****

In 2004 Jim and I were on the way to a' twelve-step' meeting in Aberystwyth. We knew Luci had gone into labour, but we no longer spent time together. I sent her love and went off to the meeting. On the way, we received a text message from her. Things were not going well with her home birth; she might have to go into hospital. An ambulance was stationed outside, ready. She didn't ask me for help. I hadn't entered her house for two years, yet I knew I must go to her. Jim stopped the car in a lay by while I wrestled with my feelings. Should I go? Did she even want me there? Would she tell me to go away? Confused, I couldn't decide. That little voice we all have insisted, "go"! We turned the car round.

It was my first moment back in Luci's house since our row. Ignoring my memories of the past I put my focus on the child still inside my sister's body. Her partner didn't seem to know what to do, but as soon as I was in that house, I did. There was no doubt, only certainty. I knew she just needed to relax. The intensity of the situation made it easy to put our differences aside. I wanted and needed to give to her, touch her, reassure her, say the familiar things we'd said at all our shared births. GabiLu was resuscitated, just for now. I kept focusing on relaxation, touching and talking to her. I knew it would work and it did. Her contractions became normal. The ambulance man hovered to assess whether or not to take her to hospital, but all was well, her strength had come back, her power came through.

Baby Rocco entered the world. He looked at me with alert twinkling eyes and I was hooked. It was a special moment, as if all the denied love between Luci and me flowed from her tiny boy. Through this little baby there was warmth and connection…then it was time to let go. Jim and I left soon after he was born and that was that.

Luci did acknowledge my contribution to her birth and I felt our bond. But we quickly went back to our usual distance. This is the child of Luci's we've now seen the least of. Her other son often comes to stay the night most weekends and feels like part of the family. Still, this new child has brought his parents closer. Luci and her partner have so much love to give to their tousled haired three year old, it warms my heart to see their devotion. A beautiful flower grows from all the muck.

As for Luci and Gabi? We'll always love each other but our connection from the past is now the real link. In the present being together isn't yet easy. I find myself longing for a softer, more affectionate, warmer sister. Time and communication may one day repair the damage.

******

In 2006 Polly's mother-in-law, died of lung cancer caused by asbestos. She died in almost exactly the same spot that Leela was born. They had a ritual when this grandmother was dying, of pouring tea from a matching rainbow teapot and cup. The ailing woman was always fascinated by the precise careful way Leela poured the tea, spilling not a drop. It gave her pleasure to share this intimacy with her little granddaughter. Leela's childhood has been idyllic up to this point, secure and adored in her extended family. This death was the only bad thing so far. We prepared her for it.

By the time she threw a red rose on her grandmother's grave she knew roughly what to expect. After the funeral she was furiously angry with me though, my presence reminding her of her loss. For a while it was my fault I was her only remaining grandmother.

I've now learned to run a home and a business, how to have some routine and security. Jim and I grow vegetables on our allotment behind our house. I'm writing a book and continue healing my body and mind. We've never had such a normal life. Values have changed, youth movements have been absorbed into the culture and life has moved on. It all still feels like an adventure.

Throughout my lifetime I have had many different perspectives on the same situation, looking back each time through wiser eyes that allow wider vision. We 'share the same biology, regardless of ideology' as the songwriter Sting puts it. The human vulnerabilities, needs and drives that make us distinct, paradoxically unite us all.

'All you need is love,' said the Beatles and I think they've got something there. Love is the magic ingredient that provides resilience for all life's challenges. It comes naturally and thankfully it's free! The love of my life, partner Jim, has been the most constant I've ever known. He continually steps up for me, sharing everything and giving more. We've had the challenges most couples experience, but he is always willing to learn, grow and reach out to me. From this foundation extends the love I feel for my children, my children's children, my sister's children, my sister, my other sisters, my brothers, my Mum and my Dad.

The influence on Mum of *her* third partner, Alan, has helped bring out *her* softer side. She is more confident, less judgmental. I am grateful to her for attempting to create a connection with us, and to Alan for his tolerant personality. In the climate of twisted bitterness from the 'father figures' in our lives, Alan's acceptance of and interest in others is a breath of fresh air.

Passion and intimacy matter, they are the perfume of life. Self esteem matters. That's the conclusion of my story so far, a story within millions of stories that ends with a feeling of life's incredible richness. It's all worth it, for the experience of being alive.

As for the home, that place of belonging and unconditional love? I've discovered it's a feeling, it's where the heart is, it is anywhere where there is real love.

Which is all anyone wants.

To be continued when I have lived it…..

******

Polly's turn now…number six of the seven women: an 'actor', in search of an 'author'. Polly is the busy one, all of twenty-five years old…trying to catch up on her missed chances at an acting school, so the 'author' will have to be me, Ingeborg Evelyn, her grandmother. I've seen so little of her, it's almost strange to admit I *am* such a thing… a grand-mother.

How disappointed I was with her when I heard she was pregnant, seven years ago. Seeing history repeat itself…..Up to then her life was uncharted and she could have had every opportunity. A granny's scolding and nagging is not appreciated…..

Adorable little Leela, *my* first great-grand child had appeared soon enough; another one of those water babies we've read about. She is much loved, and one hopes her gorgeous mother will still be able to fulfil her own dreams and talents.

I wait patiently to receive Polly's views as I become increasingly wary and conscious of my own position: the rusty fulcrum of an old-fashioned scale: on one side my daughter, my daughter's daughter and my daughter's daughter's daughter….on the other: my mother, my mother's mother and my mother's mother's mother. Just look at us once again, all seven of us, so neatly we are balanced…

	Evelyn	
Erika	**M**	**Gabrielle**
Cölestine	**M**	**Polly**
Josephine	**M**	**Leela**

How to weigh up the lives and stamina of these mothers and daughters?

The predominant language on the left was German, on the right…completely English with a Welsh, partly post-hippy flavour, and my goodness, what complicated lives so far!

Ingeborg-Evelyn is the mixed-up one, with five workable languages and as many souls. Has this brought idyllic contentment? I don't think so.

Did some 'rot' set in when she broke free, refusing to throw her life exclusively onto the altar of holy matrimony, dedicated motherhood? Oh dear, *evil* Evelyn, living up to her name…greedily wanting more, wanting something other than being a wife, and all that mothering.

Here we are, falling endlessly into the same old trap…*again and again*!

Life was so much easier on the '*old*' side of the diagram: find a man, become his wife, bring up his children, take up knitting or good works… die content. You've obeyed the rules. Brava!

And yet: look at Josephine's successes running the business in Neumarktl: it may have ruined her health, but she did a fine job. Then *her* eldest, Cölestine, became the archetypal mother, one who never looked back. Even Erika, *Cölestine's* eldest, such a clever woman, so much unrealised potential, was not brave enough to break free, or perhaps just too lazy and somehow life was against her, with that second WW and a decade in the sand-dunes of Namibia. She was the last of the *completely* fluent German speakers, although her English was fluent enough.

'If only'…comes to mind: if only one had been born in a different world, a new society, where exciting goals are set from an earlier age. Might it not be beginning to happen now? Now, in the third Millennium?

Will the Gabrielle-Polly-Leela team show a better way?

Is there a better way?

Meanwhile I wait for Polly's contribution. She is up to her ears preparing homework for the next course at drama school… I fear the task of writing down thoughts about her life so far has no appeal.

First Polly and her family must have a holiday in France, to recover from that terrible draining Welsh greyness.

Now at last: *Polly* the perfect baby,..

..cooing at strangers as she is handed round during a talk given by Jiddu Krishnamurti in her mother's 'hippy' days....that is how she emerges in my mind. She was just as perfect when *I* first met her, chatting, trusting and adorable, only three and content to come to me, even leave her mother for a few hours while we two held hands and wandered about.

'This is Glastonbury, Blueberry and Sunshine' she proclaimed, when I gave her three small Care-bears, to break the ice...but there *was* none!

'Is this what breast-fed babies are like?' I asked myself later, noticing how she interacted with her mother, the intensity of their eyes looking, it seemed, right inside each other. I had never seen such closeness before and felt a stab of jealousy contemplating such intimacy.

In her earliest years she too became a victim, finding herself pulled around as a 'visitor' between two families: her father in Brighton with his new dependants and her mother's new growing family. Not only once did Polly experience splitting-up parents, but even a second time there was the continuing theme of blending and re-blending families...when her father moved on. Such 'dysfunctional' patterns leave traces that may have to be worked on.... in order to 'let them go...'

According to Gabi, who knows only too well about such things: 'Polly felt she wasn't *central*...this only emerged with time, but she also felt she had to look after her father, and she still does. She is upset by him, but loves him.'

Crowding into Polly's being is the threatened loss of a young step-sister recently diagnosed with the rare disease of pulmonary arterial hypertension, apparently incurable. It stands to reason that happiness, under these circumstances, may, for a while, be hard to achieve.

Knowing which way to turn, when one is young and multi-talented, can become obstructed with all the twists of tempting choices. Polly has always shown a strong leaning to 'artiness', studying A-level Art, winning Eisteddfods in Wales and even trying her hand at 'making' beautiful objects...cards, jewellery. The first gift I ever had from *any* grandchild, were two handmade buttons, made of clay, painted with charming detail and stitched onto a card signed by Polly. She was probably about six or seven at the time and I've treasured them for almost two decades, not quite knowing what to sew them on.

The next time Polly came into my ken she was 13 years old; spending a few days with us she brought her cousin Minna with her. They came to London by train, I picked them up feeling vaguely apprehensive.

Polly, from the very start, appeared to be on a different level of existence, with an apparently sympathetic, yet 'keeping-her distance' approach, perfectly poised and polite, accepting and mildly amused by everything that was going on. I was in awe of her perfection, not just physically, but of what felt like such a strong core. What would become of this creature, *seemingly* so self assured? All three of us were undergoing a craze for painting. I showed them the Library on Stanmore Hill, where there happened to be my own first exhibition of pictures, all paintings of children in mysteriously frightening situations... later we spent time painting together and also visited the South Bank to see the sights, museums and galleries.

A decade later Gabi's maternal assessment was that 'Polly can be scary: she comes over with great authority, she speaks beautifully, very sure of her opinions, though often it's a bluff and she is uncertain underneath'. It now appears she is extraordinarily talented as an actress, and her acting school has high hopes: 'there has been no-one like her for twenty-five years' the management says. Well, who was *that* talented creature and what became of *her/ him*? Our budding actress however, wishes she were at a more prestigious drama school....

But, as I write, there appears to be a crisis. Polly, the goddess, has cracked: what has completely unhinged her is nothing other than a taste of holiday-life in the summer sunshine of France... the feeling of being fully alive and unstressed without deadlines; of good food, lounging on the beach, playing with her little girl, and to hell with running a home, becoming an actress and looking out onto that grey Welsh sky every day. Anyone of her age on a gruelling schedule such as hers would feel the same.

Speaking as someone who, at a similar age, had *everything* Polly has just now *so* enjoyed (sunshine, swimming, leisure,) I would just love to point out that opening up a career for oneself (as she will be in a position to do) is infinitely more rewarding in the long run...'something to die for' as the young say nowadays....that learning new skills is a real investment for the future, (huge, overwhelming amount of time stretching ahead into infinity....) which, seen from being *only* a quarter of a century old, can take place over decades and decades in a sunnier place than Wales, very soon…. after another two years have gone by. Two years is a blinking of an eyelid, when there is a quest for that elusive 'pot of gold'. And she might say: 'I don't care, I no longer want to live in dank, dark Wales, I will go abroad, take my chance.' Arguments would then centre on 'what's it all about' but, alas, no-one can instil any sense in some-one else's brain… we all have to make choices, we don't like to be told. She may decide to change course altogether.

Our wondrous Polly sits on a volcano, and I watch, helplessly, from a distance.

'Life is long, Polly, get that career going…*then* move out into the world', is surely everyone's advice. 'A famous British film director might pick you out of the crowd, bring your talents to the world…do you really want to chuck it all up and instead cultivate an early crop of wrinkles in the hot sun, or produce more babies, who will speak other languages better than you?'

Polly feels family is the most important thing in life. She wants to do something in the world AND be a good mother… That is hard.

We must wait. We will look out into the night-sky, at the moon…remembering the current space mission cavorting out there, Russians, Americans, learning on our behalf…soon even women will be opening up space for us all. What do we women, mothers, daughters really want these days? We move to the seventh and last name on our scale of mothers…to little Leela who also seems to fly through the air on a photograph I have just received.

Leela's (very tiny) Story

E-mails from Gabi were my daily fare, where would one be without them:

27th April 2008, 'Here are Leela's own words...I'll keep going each time we meet. I managed to interview her, here is the result so far, word for word (she loves the idea of being 'in a book' and is v. co-operative)........'

I was born on July the 3rd in 2002. My mother is Polly, my dad is Jack William. (Gabi must have started her off ...I don't see a six-year old doing that.)

I've lived in:

(1)	*The Willows*	*(Wales)*
(2)	*Rhyd Fechan*	"
(3)	*Gabi's house*	"
(4)	*Mandy's house*	*(Brighton)*
(5)	*Temple Terrace*	*(Wales)*

The one I like best is The Willows because it has bigger rooms than my last house. That one gave me illness, chickenpox, because I was breathing all the badness in... I got a really bad cough. What I liked about Rhyd Fechan was I had loads of kittens. They had to live under the stairs. Their bowl was bigger than the kittens! They had Whiskers pouches for food. Tabby was my friend. She used to come out and say hello to me. The sad thing was that Tabby had to leave... they all had to leave, Bawdry, Ginger and Tabby. There were more but I have forgotten their names-there were hundreds and hundreds.

Egg and Fizzy Water were their mum and dad. I also lived in Mandy's house in Brighton.

 Egg and Fizzy Water went to her house and changed their names to Pumpkin and Pippin, so I still lived with them but not with the kittens.

 Luckily now I've got a kitten called Mish-Mish. I'll tell you what colour she is: she is orange, black and white. She's beautiful and she's got a monkey face and she's really fluffy. She likes killing mice and she killed a blue-tit once and I felt sorry because I love blue tits. Guess what ! Mish Mish actually pulled a gut out of a dead slug and there was a dead mouse in there all mixed up together. And I've got a cat called Oscar. He's tabby-coloured and he's got a pink nose. He likes killing mice too, because they are all very hungry.

What I remember about my other grandmother is that she died and, well, I got very sad and we had to put her in a box and then Cameron (cousin) went to MacDonald's after the funeral and we went home. We had to throw flowers everywhere and then we came over to Gabi and Jim's house.

I think Gabi can be my best grandmother now because Mimi *used* to be my best grandmother...she had grey hair which she put up in a bun. I want Gabi to dye her hair grey because she looks too much like a mother. She's all young and that's not right for grandmothers because Mimi had wrinkled skin.....'

Gabi, and her grand-daughter were silent, for a while. Then, on another day:

'This is for the book, Gabi. It's about my violin. My violin has a special thing that has to go on the bottom of it, I can't remember what it's called...it's not the chin rest it's at the bottom of the chinrest, it's green, oh yes it's called the shoulder rest...and my violin has a special stick called a bow, and some soapy stuff called resin that you have to put on the bow, then you have to remember to put the resin back in the violin box. Every time I play it I'm so into it that it hurts my arm and neck but I'm so into it that I can't actually let go of it, and anyway it won't let go because I'm going to play it at Glastonbury.

You have to put lots of care into it to be really good. Also to be really good you have to rub the bow on the strings and that's how you make the music...that's how I do it so good- I just concentrate for ages and ages and try and practise and practise.

My violin just glues me to it- it's really funny. It won't let me go.

My violin has this red spot on it where you put your finger. The best thing about it is that it makes you strong and better at music...at first when you start your arms are all floppy and limp but it makes you get strong. My violin is brown and the strings are made of horse fur, no, horse hair.... the hair that goes down the manes and tails.... I like the sound of my violin, the sound it makes, because it is delicate and gentle. I like music. It can be fiery but mine is sort of gentle like when you are at a pond with dancing swans. Playing it makes me space off into a different world....it's got a special arm that's glue-ing me to it. I just love it! When I'm older I'm going to play at Glastonbury.'   (Gabi was the scribe).

***

The smallest person, the seventh daughter, and one day, mother number seven, is in 'seventh heaven' when playing a violin. God forbid she has the gene, the one that drives you to spend half your life getting the tiniest detail to perfection, in order to pierce the hearts of others. Unless she has exceptional talent, please God, do let this chalice pass! I am entitled to this view. (Evelyn is the scribe). *According to the latest scientific research it takes 10,000 hours to develop a talent to the point of excellence.* What good fortune Polly has such a patient mother, who baby-sits each day, while Polly does her course. Leela could not be in better hands... and the spin-off is: I get delicious accounts about kittens and violin lessons across the ether. Leela has just come second in the 'creative writing' competition in her class, beaten by one 'Theo', her arch enemy. Now she is allowed to sit on a golden throne, wearing a white cloth lace cap and a red cloak. They believe in that sort of thing in Wales, the home of Dylan Thomas. As for Leela's Mum: she is doubly blessed.... her husband does both, shopping *and* cooking. What more can a woman ask? There seems little reason to emigrate from 'potato-ey Wales'. Just think: Wales is about the same size as Slovenia, where our book began, it has a character of its own, and a language, and you may not realize it yet, but you are fond of it, and you will miss it one day, when and if you flee to another place. Mark my words.

Now Gabi and Jim confess to feeling like 'church-wardens', trying to help Polly make the 'right 'decisions, not just for herself but also for all three generations...Gabi, Polly *and* Leela...while I confess to a mild attack of 'Schadenfreude', that they too may be experiencing the frustrations of parenthood now, in *their* middle-years.

*****

The prospective 'prima-donna', our lovely Polly,(I must be careful not to make myself too unpopular).... how can she become one, I wonder, her growing-up period was everything but straight-forward... such a sensitive small person, how she will have suffered witnessing her Dad running away, dumped off the hippy bus. She *did* promptly lose her voice from this shock. More dramatic events followed:...being handed to a fire-man in Brighton, when the family was rescued from the 4th floor of a Brighton house; well, it's all in Gabi's story, the shuttling to and fro between separated parents, observing grown-ups trying out 'primal therapy' and other bizarre practices...what happened to her immature mind then? Polly, I beg you to continue this account in half a century from now. By then you will have had to come to terms with many ugly threats: overpopulation, Aids, Global warming, melting icecaps, acid rain and terrorism, financial meltdown...you may try, be able, to live according to different precepts with new, more *beautiful* theories, to allow our world, the world we are so 'using up'.... to recover.

Perhaps *your* daughter will find these jottings one day, just as Josephine did in Neumarktl in 1894, when sorting out *her* mothers' belongings...and should this be so I wish you well, great-grand-daughter; I pray I live long enough to see you become a grown-up. You *did* notice, Leela, the lace cap worn by your ancestor in Slovenia over 200 years ago... how it resembled the Welsh cap *you* were wearing when you won *your* essay Prize? One day, when you too are a granny, even better, a great-granny, please study what *your* daughters and granddaughters have been up to: will they still believe in marriage, will they have careers? Will our overcrowded world impose limits on the number of children they have (each day there are 150,000 more people in the world) and on the food available; and will everyone be munching scorpion lollipops and Cockroach à la King, or sweet and sour slippery silkworms? So, write down all you know about their lives, discover if *their* challenges resemble those in this book of ours. Will they be speaking English? Will the image of 'Germans,' which even today is out of date in this country, still be perpetuated by the English? This really hurts, you know. But then you can't possibly know. Just admire that eternal chain of mother-daughter-mother-daughter and how it continues in its unstoppable way. You will be the next mother in the chain. And so: mothers and daughters, on and on they go, for ever, unlike that 'Perpetuum Mobile' your unhappy great-great-great-great-great-great Uncle Sepp tried so hard to invent...)

There! I've made an attempt to enter your lives...and now, as the cold dust of time settles on my life, no, on *all* our lives... gives no reprieve to anyone, try to remember me, your 'Pomeranian Peasant', like it or not, 'discrete', (a new word in my vocabulary), now well advanced in years and *almost* British, except when getting through a British Christmas or even more painfully, when listening to German Lieder. I probe the wounds...and allow tears to stream, helplessly. For some it's alright now. And that happiness, where is it? Leela, Polly, and Gabi: believe me, it *is* there, but in secret places.

So now, farewell, for '*what we call the beginning is often the end. And to make an end is to make a beginning. The end is where we start from.   T.S. Eliot. 'Gerontion.*'

Leela leaping into the next century

Why and how this book began:

Years ago my grandmother, Cölestine, suggested I go, see her birthplace, her home until she was eighteen years old. She herself had returned just once; but by then, half a century later, the place had become part of Yugoslavia and 'unbearably changed' she claimed,...aggrieved, many old memories seemingly shattered.

There it was, at last, that small town nestling against green hillsides; her beloved craggy mountains, those grey protective sentinels, looming all around. Clutching a folder of family history collected by my grandfather, I emerged mole-like into blinding sunlight, found myself ambling up a narrow road, probably the main road of Neumarktl as my grandmother knew it. Now the place was called Tržič. This word means 'new market', but the tricky one is Slovene.

What a setting! I marvelled at houses, stylish, neglected, hundreds of years old. One of the bigger ones may well have been the family hotel owned by my great- and great-great grandparents. This was Austrian then, governed by the Habsburgs from early 1300, but at all times a melting pot of languages, Slovenian, German, Italian and Serbian tongues.

'If only they were still here, these ancestors!' Frustrated by the passing years and fragile ties I asked myself how I could possibly get inside their personalities, quirks and dreams; so many memories already slipping away, like mists and fogs, or fading photographs.

There appeared to be only three main roads. At the top of the hill, where buildings came to an end, a narrow stream sparkled opposite the modest 'Town Museum'. Inside I managed a self-conscious 'dober dan' (good morning) while my driver explained I was a guest from London related to... then followed a string of family names: Klander, Hofbauer, Malli, Pollak, Wuk, Kotnik, all ghosts from my grandfather's papers.

The curator, grinning with delight, explained with a torrent of words, all alas Slovenian. Our driver translated: '*Your* relative Magdalena Klander, she married at the age of thirteen and had twenty-five children'. Well, how's that, for starters!

One imagines Neumarktl a dull village with little to do after dark in those distant days.

The elderly curator shuffled off to bring the *official history* full of familiar names: Klanders have been here since 1600. I knew that already, nevertheless, awed, flattered, I bought the book. The language was Slovenian....what did I expect?

*****

A large painting of St. Florian, patron saint of Austria, with that great Fire below him, can be seen in a church in Tržič to this day.

Below St. Florian's feet are numerous small figures, arms held high, running downhill, fearing for homes and lives, followed by greedy flames and billowing smoke…among them no doubt all the ancestors.

Franz Mathias Klander, owner of the iron foundry situated near the top-end of the village was grandfather of that determined business-woman <u>Josephine</u>: the first of those 'seven maids'.

*****

www.ingramcontent.com/pod-product-compliance
Lightning Source LLC
Chambersburg PA
CBHW020148090426
42734CB00008B/745